*The Recovery of Philosophy in America*

Frontispiece: John E. Smith, Clark Prof. Emeritus of Philosophy, Yale University, New Haven, CT. Photo credit: Michael Marsland, Yale University, Office of Public Affairs.

# *The Recovery of Philosophy in America*

## Essays in Honor of John Edwin Smith

*Edited by Thomas P. Kasulis*
*and*
*Robert Cummings Neville*

STATE UNIVERSITY OF NEW YORK PRESS

Published by
State University of New York Press, Albany



Printed in the United States of America



For information, address State University of New York Press,
State University Plaza, Albany, N.Y., 12246

Production by Marilyn P. Semerad
Marketing by Dana E. Yanulavich

**Library of Congress Cataloging-in-Publication Data**

The recovery of philosophy in America : essays in honor of John Edwin
Smith / edited by Thomas P. Kasulis and Robert Cummings Neville.
p. cm.
Includes bibliographical references and index.
ISBN 0–7914–3355–2 (alk. paper). — ISBN 0–7914–3356–0 (pbk. :
alk. paper)
1. Philosophy, American. 2. Philosophy, American—20th century.
3. Philosophy. 4. Smith, John Edwin. I. Kasulis, Thomas P., 1948–
II. Neville, Robert C. III. Smith, John Edwin.
B936.R43 1997
191—dc21 96–53656
CIP

10 9 8 7 6 5 4 3 2 1

*Dedicated to*

John Edwin Smith:

*Thinker, Teacher, Statesman,*

*Complete Philosopher*

# *Contents*

# *Preface*

The friends of John E. Smith represented in these pages take great pleasure in dedicating this book to him in honor of his seventy-fifth birthday. We speak for a great many more thinkers who also would do him honor. At the meeting of the Metaphysical Society of America on March 16, 1996, in New York City, the Society conferred upon John Smith its Founder's Medal. The citation read at that conferring, which is also published in the May 1996 volume of the *Review of Metaphysics*, is as follows:

> John Edwin Smith has served the cause of philosophy in America, especially in its speculative and metaphysical practice, as a thinker, a teacher, and a statesman. In each of these roles he has surpassed nearly all others, and in uniting them he has been a model for us all of the integrity of the academic philosophic life in a time of adversity.
>
> The heart of his thinking, the central idea, has been his interpretation of the concept of experience as developed in American philosophy, and its ramifications in social theory, ethics, metaphysics, and philosophy of religion. Much of his work has involved the interpretation of the European tradition of philosophy, especially Kant, Hegel, and the British empiricists, from the standpoint of the American approach to experience. His very first book, *Royce's Social Infinite*, conjured with the impact of Peirce's theory of interpretation on Royce's European idealistic roots; that book with its approach to community is as relevant to the communitarian-liberal debates of today as to the situation when it was published in 1950. His second book, *Reason and God*, set American philosophy in the context of European philosophy and introduced the major

metaphysical theme of existence, on which he has written ever since. Among his many writings are the books *Experience and God, The Spirit of American Philosophy, Themes in American Philosophy, Religion and Empiricism, Purpose and Thought: The Meaning of Pragmatism, America's Philosophical Vision, Jonathan Edwards: Puritan, Preacher, Philosopher,* and *Quasi-Religions*. He has also been the General Editor of the Yale Edition of the *Works of Jonathan Edwards*. Never taking a back seat to the scholars who study, analyze, and classify American philosophy, John Smith in contrast to most has *interpreted* American philosophy, that is, made its power available to shape the present philosophical situation. Perhaps nowhere is this more surprisingly the case than in his approach to Chinese philosophy during the last twenty years, which he has brought into the world-philosophical discussion with the interpretive tools of pragmatism.

As a teacher John Smith has been the master to many in the Metaphysical Society of America, as well as to those who flourish in the Society for the Advancement of American Philosophy, the Society for Phenomenology and Existential Philosophy, and the International Society for Chinese Philosophy. He began his teaching career at Barnard and went to Yale in the early 1950s. His introductory course probably turned more undergraduates to the study of philosophy at Yale than all the other philosophy courses put together. His courses in philosophy of religion and American philosophy defined those fields for many years. His undergraduate senior seminars on Dewey and Royce were as powerful as his books for those privileged to take them. As a graduate teacher he centered the modern tradition for his students with seminars on Kant and Hegel; his course on the *1st Critique* was probably the only one in the country to get to the Canon of Pure Reason, although his course on Hegel's *Lesser Logic* never got beyond Essence. Many members of this Society became such philosophers as we are through the classroom and personal teaching of John Smith, who understands the role of friendship in teaching. Or is it the role of teaching in friendship?

As a philosophical statesman, John Smith early recognized that the mainline structures of American academic philosophy were not supportive of philosophy in the grand tradition, to which American philosophy had so much to contribute. He was therefore active in this Society and in promoting *The Review of Metaphysics* from the earliest days. He struggled to keep the Yale Philosophy Department a fertile ground for cultivating many different philosophic traditions, often with little help besides his own presence. For many years he was a leading member of the Saturday Group, which met in New York City to plan ways to practice philosophy besides the analytic. He was the standard bearer of the Pluralist movement in the American Philosophical Association and was the first person to be elected president of its Eastern Division under that standard. He was the founder of the Society of Philosophers in America and remains its president. Perhaps most important of all, he has educated a younger generation in the importance of the public life of philosophy and in how to practice philosophy publically. It used to be that this Society was important to protect metaphysics as a marginalized philosophic practice, spurned by the centers of academic power. But now the deconstructionists have taught us that centers are bad and margins are good and, besides, this Society has been around nearly half a century, not bad for life on the margin. Much of our staying power, and the vitality of the current resurgence of original metaphysical speculation, owe to the lifetime of philosophical statesmanship of John E. Smith.

Your friends and colleagues, students and readers, admirers and followers, take great pride in presenting you the Founder's Medal of the Metaphysical Society of America. We thank you for your service, pay tribute to your accomplishments, honor you for the way your work has honored our profession, and hope you will not stop.

The essays in this volume spell out many of these points in greater detail. Some give personal meaning to these fairly abstract claims. John Smith's students especially, but also many other colleagues over a long career, have private stories about how he has shaped our lives to be more adventuresome, engaged, serious, and self-reflective in humor. Therefore we offer this book as a testimony to an excellence that far exceeds the fit subjects of an academic book.

That broad personal gratitude notwithstanding, the subjects in this book coalesce tightly around the title theme of the recovery of philosophy in America. The authors here exhibit a wide variety of philosophical interests and practices. Yet all show the influence of John E. Smith in their reflections back to the theme of the recovery of philosophy in a troubled time. That theme is double-barreled, as John would say. As a recovery it is retrospective and reconstructive. But because recovery is for the sake of being a resource for philosophy engaged in the present, our theme is mainly future oriented. This book aims to shine lights down new paths for philosophy, many of them opened by John E. Smith.

The editors are grateful to the Hocking-Cabot Fund for Systematic Philosophy for support for this volume. "All Philosophy is *Religiousphilosophie*" first appeared in *The Spirit of Hegel* by Errol E. Harris ©

1993, Humanities Press International, Inc.; Atlantic Highlands, NJ 07716; reprinted with permission. We are also grateful to William Eastman, Lois Patton, Carola Sautter, and Marilyn Semerad of the State University of New York Press for bringing this volume to public light.

TPK
RCN

# *Editorial Introduction*

Thomas P. Kasulis

When Robert Neville and I first discussed the prospect of editing a collection of essays honoring John E. Smith, we immediately discounted the idea of putting together a festschrift in the traditional style. As the term indicates, the festschrift is a Germanic idea that works best if the honoree is either a scholar of technical expertise or a philosophical system builder who has written an architectonic body of work that can be measured, tested for soundness, and, where need be, remodeled. Our concern was not that Smith was not a scholar. His editorial work with the writings of Jonathan Edwards alone (not to mention his commentaries on a variety of other American philosophers and German idealists) would qualify him as that. Nor were we concerned that Smith had not developed a sustained philosophical view. Only the most superficial reading of Smith's corpus of philosophical writings could miss his constant attention to the analysis of experience throughout his career. No, the problem for us was that neither of these pictures of Smith does justice to the man and his work. In fact, they may even assume a vision of the philosopher that Smith's own activities in the profession and his own writings have sometimes sought to undermine.

According to Smith, philosophy should be a communal, not a merely individualistic, enterprise. Long before it became fashionable in a postmodernist sense, Smith reminded us that philosophy is not the disembodied march of abstract ideas through history, but the reflection of flesh-and-blood human beings who try to understand their experience and address the problems of their time and place. This is one reason why Smith has always maintained the philosophical importance of understanding the history of philosophy. Historians of philosophy recognize that the ideas they analyze can only be understood and appreciated in their larger social and historical context. Those who deny that the history of philosophy is itself a philosophical project only show their ignorance of their own social and historical conditions. That philosophy can be studied independently of history is in fact an idea we can date, that is, philosophical ahistoricism is itself best understood as a development in the history of philosophy.

As we discussed the possible contents of this book, Neville and I realized that a distinctive contribution of Smith's life as a philosopher was his contribution to rebuilding a communal sense of philosophy in America when it often seemed intellectual community was under attack on many fronts. There were those ahistoricists who liked to think philosophy had been reborn and that the past was only the record of philosophical sins, unworthy of careful attention. There were those Gnostics influenced by the European continent who marginalized themselves by developing a jargon unintelligible to all but the initiate. There were those Anglo-based neoscholastic analysts who would cite no one (except each other) and who tried to bring under reign the messiness of life by refusing to discuss anything but the most desiccated version of human experience. The community of philosophers in America was about to dissolve. In the following introductory essay, Robert Neville explains some of Smith's role in reestablishing philosophical pluralism in America during that time. It helps explain why we think of Smith when we think of the "recovery of philosophy in America."

Against this background, we called on a diverse group of people to contribute to this volume. It includes both colleagues and students of John E. Smith, and the chapters address various topics in the history of philosophy—American philosophy, German idealism, process philosophy, the philosophy of religion, and comparative philosophy. These fields have all been addressed by Smith in his varied writings, and the individual essays often discuss directly some aspect of Smith's thought. However, the unifying theme is not a direct discussion of Smith's individual ideas themselves, but rather the communication of a clear sense of the type of American community of philosophers Smith has helped create and nurture. Some chapters discuss directly the recovery of philosophy that is underway and that has been inspired by Smith's leadership as a scholar, a member of the academic community, and a philosopher. Other chapters simply address the kinds of issues that find a place within that recovery. All the essays share a sense of philosophy as the enterprise that takes seriously the richness and complexity of human experience as its starting point.

In the next chapter, "Philosophy's Recovery of Its History," George Lucas traces more fully one key aspect of the recovery of philosophy, the renewed interest in the history of philosophy as a form of doing philosophy. In this far-ranging essay that covers a trend in metaphilosophical thinking from Kant to Reichenbach, Lucas shows an acute awareness of philosophy as an enterprise increasingly located within, and responsive to, the needs of the modern academy.

The next two chapters, my own essay "Intimations of Religious Experience and Interreligious Truth" and Kuang-ming Wu's "The Spirit of Pragmatism and the Pragmatic Spirit," remind us that philosophy in America today is not limited to the ideas of Western Europe and North America. Asian traditions of thought have become part of the dialogue in our pluralistic philosophical discourse. My discussion deals with the impact of Buddhist-Christian dialogue on my thinking as a philosopher of religion. Because of my experience with that dialogue, I have found it necessary to reevaluate some basic presuppositions both of the philosophy of language and of epistemology as they have usually been applied to the understanding of religion. Wu's essay engages a topic that Smith himself initiated: the discussion of common ground in certain traditions of Chinese philosophy and American pragmatism. As a student of Smith and one sensitive to the role of culture and history in the development of philosophy, Wu explores the similarities and differences between Chinese and American humanism as they apply to their respective pragmatic orientations.

The Asian thought discussed by Wu and myself is part of the pluralistic context of education in America today. Increasingly, Americans wonder whether it is not only permissible but even essential that we expand the "canon" in our schools to include the voices of what had been marginalized, Orientalized, or ignored in our traditional syllabi. This is a sticky issue in our society today, but in his essay "Modernism, Postmodernism, and the Pragmatic Recovery of an Educational Canon," George Allan addresses the problem head on using William James as an inspiration to show the merits and limitations of both sides of the debate.

Douglas Anderson's essay, "John E. Smith and the Heart of Experience," also draws on the tradition of American pragmatism, especially Dewey, in analyzing poignantly Smith's view of experience and the nature of self. In his balanced analysis of the problems involved, Anderson shows ways in which Smith's use of pragmatism can addresses issues related to self that the so-called neopragmatists cannot.

In his "Whitehead's Distinctive Features," Lewis S. Ford begins his clear and perceptive account of the major features in Whitehead's thought by arguing that Whitehead should be included as an *American* philosopher. In doing so, he agrees with the position taken by Smith. However, Ford notes, that although Whitehead's thought has been embraced by many philosophical theologians in the United States, philosophers have typically ignored him. Ford sees this as a common lack of understanding about the nature of Whitehead's metaphysics, the ineluctably important problems it addresses, and the significance of its approach. Ford then outlines the key features of that metaphysical vision, showing its radical reconception of subjectivity, the theory of relations, and the importance of novelty.

Richard Hocking's essay, "Emergence and Embodiment: A Dialectic within Process," complements Ford's discussion by exploring more fully the nature of process philosophy in terms of two kinds of process: that of nature and that of history. Hocking initially explains why these two processes are often considered exclusive and separate, but then constructs a powerful argument for why they should be understood as complementary and interdependent. He does this through a provocative analysis of the two processes in terms of what he calls "emergence" and "embodiment."

As the sequence of the last three essays has shown, in thinking about Smith and the recovery of philosophy in America, it is possible to go either in the direction of John Dewey or in that of Alfred North Whitehead. Both philosophers have been important to Smith in different ways. This is a point of departure for Donald W. Sherburne in his essay, "The Goldilocks Syndrome. " He suggests that, like most philosophers today, Smith is pulled in at least two directions as to defining the limits and capabilities of our "philosophical aspirations." In a metaphilosophical discussion rich with metaphor and insight, Sherburne challenges philosophers like Smith to articulate where they stand on this important issue and develops a justification for his own, basically Whiteheadian, point of view.

Merold Westphal takes us further into metaphilosophical questions in his essay, "Philosophy as Critique and as Vision." In his reflection on what the recovery of philosophy can and should mean, he draws provocatively on the two images of philosophy as critique (identified with Socrates) and philosophy as vision (identified with Plato). In the dialectic between these two as represented in the Platonic *Dialogues*, Westphal argues, philosophy can recover its original mission of where the practical and the contemplative, the political and the metaphysical can meet. In the conclusion of this chapter, he suggests that the dialectic between these poles is exemplified in the lifework of Smith.

In analyzing the nature of philosophy, the issue also arises as to the relationship between philosophy and religion. For exploring this relationship, the position of Hegel is an almost inevitable starting point. Errol Harris's essay, "All Philosophy as *Religionsphilosophie*," gives a thorough and well-documented interpretation of Hegel's position, showing that Hegel believed that philosophy depends on religion and cannot be separated from it. By articulating carefully and incisively the relations among philosophy, philosophy of religion, and religion in Hegel's thought, Harris shows that philosophy aspires to the knowledge of God as expressed in the Christian Trinity.

Of course, Hegel was not (despite what he himself might have thought) the first Christian philosopher to reflect on the nature of religion. Of the ancients, probably no Christian philosopher was as perceptive in analyzing his own religious experience as was Augustine. Carl Vaught's "Theft and Conversion" adds a new layer of insight to Augustine's own reflections on the relationship between the individual and the community. Vaught's interpretation shows beautifully the way the stealing pears episode led Augustine from community to a negative association of isolated individuals, whereas his religious conversion took him from individuating personal experiences to religious community. One lesson of Vaught's analysis that confirms a fundamental premise of Smith's own approach is that religion is best understood from the standpoint of religious experience, and that experience must be studied in its full richness and complexity. Augustine's autobiographical reflections and Vaught's own attention to detail and connectedness combine to give us just the kind of deep description needed to help us better understand the fundamental character of religion.

In his essay, "American Philosophy's Way around Modernism (and Postmodernism)," Robert Cummings Neville performs a major recovery of the American tradition of philosophy. Building on formulations first worked out by Smith in relation to the American pragmatists, Neville identifies a distinctively American philosophical tradition that includes key thinkers as far back as Jonathan Edwards and as far forward as today. What is more important, Neville articulates how this tradition contributes its own perspective that eludes several of the key shortcomings both of modernism and of postmodernism. In so doing, he sets an agenda for the recovery of philosophy in America.

The culmination of this volume is, of course, John Smith's own "Philosophy in America." As we have seen, the various contributions to the book span a broad range of interests and special concerns. Yet Smith engages each one individually, showing both his philosophical virtuosity and his ability to engage in a variety of conversations. At the same time, he sprinkles into this commentary the discussion of formative experiences in his philosophical thinking, demonstrating yet again that philosophy is most vigorous insofar as it engages the world of experience. By sharing our reflection on experience, we build a reflective philosophical community. That has been the goal of his teaching and writing throughout his career, and it is appropriate that in this concluding essay we see him doing what he does best and what he (and all of us who have contributed to this volume) value most.

In conclusion, I too will reflect on a formative experience in my own philosophical career. I was in my second year of graduate school at Yale, and I had a chance meeting with an old friend from undergraduate days who was also attending graduate school, but in a different department. In an almost rhetorical manner I asked him how he was doing in his degree program. He had always been an excellent scholar and had graduated from Yale *summa cum laude*. I was shocked, therefore, when I learned that he was failing his courses and was going to drop out. When I asked what happened, he replied, "I started to look carefully at my professors as people, not just scholars, and I asked myself whether I wanted to be like them. I decided there wasn't a single one I would want to be like. "Stunned by his comment, I turned the inquiry to my own situation. After a moment's reflection, I said, "If I could become someone like

John Smith, that would not be a bad thing." That was almost a quarter of a century ago, but I stand by the analysis.

Robert Cummings Neville

# Reflections on Philosophic Recovery

The "recovery of philosophy in America" refers to at least two things in this volume. First, it refers to philosophy's recovery of health as a profession in North America, both in its strictly academic employment and more broadly in its cultural manifestations. Second, it refers to the development and reconstruction of the classic tradition of American philosophy, juxtaposed to British and Continental philosophies, and to the return of that developed classic tradition to the center of the discussion. Both senses of recovery, although not yet fully actual, seem to be well underway. John E. Smith has been a major force in the recovery of philosophy in America in both of these senses, and our celebration of the recovery is at once a celebration of his distinguished career.

## THE RECOVERY OF PHILOSOPHY AS A PROFESSION

Smith published his first book, *Royce's Social Infinite,* in 1950. That was a time of philosophic alienation and of important endings and beginnings.

During the previous two decades the German-speaking countries of Europe had lost many of their best philosophers as refugees to North America, and these thinkers brought exciting projects, new to our scene. But as the projects of logical positivism and continental phenomenology had communicated little with each other in Europe, they became even more isolated from one another and from every other philosophic movement as they established their ghettos in America. The positivists tended to congregate in state universities, and the continental phenomenologists in small private institutions such as the New School for Social Research, Duquesne, Marquette, and other Roman Catholic colleges. Those of us who remember the 1950s recall the scorn with which these two philosophic projects regarded the other when they bothered to address one another at all. The inner dynamic of each project was influenced not at all by the other.

Immediately after World War II there was an intense and vigorous interchange of visiting philosophers between Britain and America, and British analytic philosophy, both in its focus on formal language and in the development of ordinary language, gained prominence in American philosophy departments, mainly at the elite universities and colleges. The interest in formal language had a natural affinity with German positivism, and A. J. Ayer's *Language, Truth, and Logic* had consummated a marriage of the two. Ordinary language philosophy was in its most creative phase during the 1940s and 1950s. Linked to positivism through formal language analysis, it defined the project(s) of "analytic philosophy" that came to dominate the profession by virtue of controlling most of the elite graduate schools that trained the next generation of philosophers in America. The domination consisted in holding the major offices in the American Philosophical Association, and in defining for granting agencies and the media what was supposed to count as real philosophy. Instead of presenting analytic philosophy as a family of projects among a much wider field, that movement presented itself as legitimate philosophy, and the others as not legitimate, or not "philosophical."

Meanwhile, the family of American philosophies that had dominated the scene during the first four decades of the twentieth century—pragmatism, idealism, realism, and process philosophy—found itself pushed to the periphery, increasingly ignored and suppressed where possible. Whitehead had died in 1947, but had been ignored by his colleagues at Harvard for far longer than that. Dewey died in 1952. Wilfrid Sellars, brilliant son of the important American realist Roy Wood Sellars, carried on the main drift of his father's philosophy but in a form wholly adapted to the analytic mode so as to offer no support or continuity for the earlier American discussion. Not until the late 1970s did the heirs of that earlier American discussion carefully address the projects of continental philosophy, positivism, and ordinary language philosophy, and there was virtually no reciprocity.

In that situation of warring ghettos, the philosophy department at Yale University was a wondrous island of philosophic engagement. When Smith joined it in 1952, its chairman, Charles Hendel, enforced the policy that each philosophic project should be seen as part of the tapestry of philosophic history, even if the project were antihistorical. Theodore Greene was senior in philosophy of religion. Arthur Pap succeeded Charles Stevenson during the early 1950s, and Wilfrid Sellars, Alan Anderson, and David Braybrooke during the later years manifested the best in analytic philosophy. Henry Margenau, whose main appointment was in physics, was vitally interested in the philosophical implications of certain ideas and had a profound impact on philosophy students. F. S. C. Northrop too taught philosophy of science, in touch with the actual practice of science and interested in the place of science in culture. Northrop was the author of what might turn out to be the most symbolic and prescient book of that period, *The Meeting of East and West* (1946), because the students of the 1950s, 1960s, and 1970s, led by Smith, mainly have been instrumental in bringing Chinese and Indian philosophies into the mainstream of discussion in America. Northrop's other great senior colleague of the 1950s was Brand Blanshard, the idealist of the grand tradition who not only enlivened the American tradition of Royce but brought to the department the erudition and capacious intelligence of cosmopolitan British thinking. Careful as any analytic philosopher, Blanshard's books on reason and analysis with respect both to knowledge and to goodness provided an alternate way to think about those subjects, and he epitomized philosophy as a central genre of humane letters. Also during the 1950s Errol Harris came to Yale as the Terry Lecturer, bringing yet another representation of the idealist tradition, more sympathetic to its German origins than Blanshard.

During that decade at Yale, Paul Weiss, student of Whitehead and co-editor of the *Collected Papers of Charles Sanders Peirce*, wrote *Modes of Being* (1958), the first major speculative system in the American tradition since Whitehead's. He began then the series of books on philosophic topics such as ethics, art, politics, and religion that makes his philosophy the most comprehensive, technically precise system of the century. Sophisticated study of philosophy of religion was encouraged in the department by the powerful presence in the Yale Divinity School of Robert Calhoun and H. Richard Niebuhr. Rulon Wells, originally a Sanskritist in the linguistics department, joined the philosophy department to teach linguistics and history of philosophy, focusing on Aristotle as a complement to Robert S. Brumbaugh's exciting studies of Plato. When George Schrader and Louis Mackay came as young professors to teach continental philosophy, Smith joined a department that from the most senior to the junior ranks provided ripe companionship for his project of rethinking the American tradition. Among his teaching assistants in the 1950s were Fred Oscanyon, Richard Rorty, and Donald Sherburne, and Richard Bernstein was one of his dissertation students. From that Yale department of the 1950s has come much of the recovery of philosophy in America.

With the professional delegitimation of other philosophic projects by analytic philosophy, those other projects had to find support at the profession's margins. Around 1950 Paul Weiss founded the Metaphysical Society of America and *The Review of Metaphysics*. In 1952 came the Charles S. Peirce Society, and by the end of the decade The Society for Phenomenology and Existential Philosophy had been established. The Society for the Advancement of American Philosophy began in 1976. The American Catholic Philosophical Association rose to the challenge of providing refuge for those who were not Roman Catholic but who were interested in philosophic topics in continuity with the Catholic tradition; indeed, Ernan McMullin came to Yale for two years in the early 1960s and then moved to Notre Dame where he introduced a new spirit of bringing non-Catholics into Catholic departments, a spirit that took hold in several Roman Catholic universities and colleges. Shortly the Hegel Society, the Society for Studies of Process Philosophies, *Process Studies* edited by Lewis S. Ford, The Center for Process Studies, The International Society for Metaphysics, the International Society for Chinese Philosophy with its *Journal of Chinese Philosophy* edited by Cheng Chung-ying, and many other centers of nonanalytic philosophic work were established.

By the end of the 1970s representatives of these various centers, as well as of universities other than Yale that were not dominated by analytic philosophy—such as Fordham, Vanderbilt, Emory, Pennsylvania State University, Stony Brook, New York University, Queens College, Hunter College, and City College in CUNY, and Boston University—recognized that they had a common interest and formed the Pluralist movement. An informal political movement within the American Philosophical Association, particularly the Eastern Division, this group forced open the nomination process for officers in the APA, secured the election of Smith as president of the Eastern Division (the first nonanalytic philosopher in decades), and raised the consciousness of analytic philosophers about parochialism. A large part of the recovery of philosophy as an academic profession consists in the increasing representation of nonanalytic philosophic interests in the program and various committees of the APA. In 1991 the Pluralist movement declared itself to be finished with its work and discontinued its political mailings and meetings, having spawned a thoroughly establishment, nonrevolutionary, organization, the Society of Philosophers in America (SOPHIA), to carry on the explicit interchange of philosophic ideas across diverse projects and definitions of the discipline. Smith not only has been the leader of the Pluralist group, but he also remains the president of SOPHIA. Although most of the elite graduate departments of philosophy in America, now including that at Yale, remain dominated by second-, third-, and fourth-generation analytic philosophers, attention has been called to the viability of other projects. Now that French philosophers have declared that margins are good and centers are bad, we can respect the work that takes place outside of the elite institutions and identify a plurality of focal projects that can learn from one another. As a profession, philosophy has recovered its sense of tolerance and engagement of many approaches, each of which is an "other" for the others, a source of learning and a critic.

## THE RECOVERY OF THE TRADITION OF CLASSIC AMERICAN PHILOSOPHY

At no time has philosophy in America ever been parochial or unresponsive to philosophic currents elsewhere; to talk about the "classic American tradition" is thus always something of a chauvinist enterprise. Yet there is a tradition of genius that runs from Jonathan Edwards to Ralph Waldo Emerson and Henry David Thoreau to Charles S. Peirce,

William James, Josiah Royce, John Dewey, George Herbert Mead, and Alfred North Whitehead. Perhaps the golden era of American philosophy began in the 1880s when Peirce, James, and Royce were coming into their own and ended in the 1930s when Dewey and Whitehead finished their best work. Surely to be included within the conversation constituting the golden age, even if not represented by an outstanding genius, are the "New Realists," Ralph Barton Perry, William P. Montague, E. G. Spaulding, and others, the "Critical Realists," George Santayana, Arthur O. Lovejoy, Roy Wood Sellars, and others, and the "Boston Personalists," Borden Parker Bowne, Edgar Sheffield Brightman, Albert C. Knudson, and Peter Bertocci. Sometimes stimulated to carry on some of the golden age positions, other times stimulated to provide alternatives, the first half or two thirds of the twentieth century witnessed many other outstanding American philosophers who deserve to be read again after the polemical dust has settled. One thinks of William Ernest Hocking, John Elof Boodin, Wilbur Marshall Urban, Dewitt H. Parker, Elijah Jordan, Walter G. Muelder, Morris R. Cohen, Sidney Hook, Ernest Nagel, and Paul Tillich. Tillich, like Whitehead, was born abroad and had some significant portion of his career there before coming to America. Both Tillich and Whitehead found the American situation to be congenial to their work in ways their homelands were not, however, and for this reason they should be included among those whose work takes life in the American tradition.

In 1950, none of the philosophers mentioned just now would have been considered a serious thinker by the analytic mainstream, save perhaps Nagel and Hook because of their love of science; none would have been taken seriously by the continental philosophers, except perhaps Tillich who would have been thought to be just a theologian. In 1997 there has been a recovery of interest in at least some of these thinkers. Moreover, the contemporary scene outside analytic and continental philosophies is remarkably like that of the first third of this century: filled with interesting and original positions, each reinterpreting the history of philosophy so as to provide a context for itself, each construing itself as a development of at least some part of the American tradition, each in serious dialogue with at least some of the other positions, and yet each thinking of itself more as an independent position than as part of a larger project.

Three points can be made here in an introductory way about the change from 1950 to the present. First, despite the fact that both continental philosophy and analytic philosophy said that metaphysics is dead and incapable of rebirth, there have been three splendid metaphysical systems developed in this period, each unique but in its way a flowering of the speculative impulse in the classic American tradition. The one common theme in that tradition, from Jonathan Edwards through the transcendentalists, pragmatists, process philosophers, realists, and personalists, is a speculative flair for developing conceptual devices for articulating the whole of things, and doing so with a penchant for aesthetic categories. Contrary to Richard Rorty and Richard Bernstein, who dismiss the metaphysics of process philosophy, read the metaphysics out of pragmatism in favor of epistemological and praxis orientations, and ignore the rest, speculative philosophy has been the genre that has flourished in America while stumbling elsewhere.

Whereas Charles Peirce was a polymath who studied things and developed brilliant nets of categories to integrate them, without ever working out the details of a system, Paul Weiss has performed "the labor of the notion," to use Hegel's phrase. As mentioned earlier, he has written not only central metaphysical works but also investigations by means of these metaphysical ideas into all main topic areas of philosophy. Actually, there are three periods in Weiss's thought. The earliest, exemplified in *Reality* (1939), is a kind of Peircean anti-Whiteheadian position. The middle period, as in *Modes of Being*, develops a categorial classification of the whole of things based on the balancing of interdefined ideas, like Peirce's firstness, secondness, and thirdness, yet in Weiss's case with a fourth category. The later period, beginning with *Beyond All Appearances* (1974), presses the project of understanding the world as a function of the interaction of ultimates, again a Peircean theme. Although deeply interested by Whitehead and by the New York naturalists, Weiss has fulfilled the impulse to speculative philosophy in a Peircean way.

By contrast, Charles Hartshorne has developed an extraordinary metaphysical system by refining and rectifying Whitehead's process philosophy. Although influenced by Peirce, whose papers he co-edited with Paul Weiss, and also by Josiah Royce, Hartshorne has articulated and held to a system of unusual consistency ever since his remarkable *Divine Relativity* (1948). More than Weiss, he has contributed an extensive commentary on the history of philosophy as read from his process perspective. One of the most important points to note about process philosophy, beginning with Whitehead, is its helpfulness in understanding religion. Theology has always been in need of metaphysical categories, and Whitehead's have been peculiarly fruitful. The first generation to develop Whitehead's categories was typified by Henry Nelson Weiman and the Chicago school of empirical theology. Hartshorne came next with a degree of technical precision that hitherto had been lacking in Whitehead and his interpreters. Hartshorne's students, such as John B. Cobb, Jr., and Schubert Ogden, along with others such as Daniel Day Williams, have developed process theology to play the orienting role for philosophical theology that Thomism and idealism played earlier. The speculative facility of philosophical theology in America created by the development of process theology is a powerful contributor to the current dialogue that is recovering the contributions of Paul Tillich.

Whereas Weiss developed the spirit of Peirce, and Hartshorne that of Whitehead, Justus Buchler has developed a gem of a system from the orientation of John Dewey. A close reader of Peirce and Whitehead, Buchler has fastened on the idea of naturalism and its antipathy to transcendence and hierarchy. Dewey wrote too much, and nearly all of it was of an occasional nature. The diffuseness of his work makes it understandable if not excusable for his pragmatism to be read as nonmetaphysical; indeed, long before Rorty, Dewey was read as a scientistic epistemologist by many of his own Columbia University colleagues. However, Buchler got the point and with great originality articulated an extraordinarily elegant system, expressed perhaps best in *The Metaphysics of Natural Complexes* (1966).

What Weiss, Hartshorne, and Buchler have proved, in addition to the intrinsic merits of their own systems, is that the speculative genius of the American tradition in its variety has contemporary viability. Many if not most of the people currently flourishing in the recovery of American philosophy's own tradition are students of one or more of these three speculative philosophers.

The second point to be made about this recovery of American philosophy's classical tradition is that it has opened itself and the Western tradition in general to engagement with Eastern traditions of philosophy. For those in the classical American tradition now, "our tradition" includes Chinese and Indian classical thought, or at least the dialogue with representatives of that classical thought. Thus an open philosophy of culture underlies the revival of American philosophy. In contrast to this, formal language philosophers have tended to be acultural in their philosophy, ordinary language philosophers have been preoccupied with English because that philosophy draws a blank where they cannot speak the language, and continental philosophers of nearly all stripes are preoccupied with identifying and excoriating the Western tradition.

The dialogue with Indian and Chinese philosophies has arisen from many sources, only a few of which are associated with the classic American tradition. These sources include the scholarship that has now produced a critical mass of translations of Eastern texts and also the training in America of creative Chinese philosophers, such as Cheng Chung-ying, Antonio Cua, and Tu Wei-ming; others such as Julia Ching have focused the main part of their career in America. The openness of the American tradition to the dialogue arises from its own interpretation of experience and the readiness to learn from cultural enterprises that can call one's own categories into question. Perhaps the date that symbolizes the transformation of Western philosophy into global philosophy is 1964, when the University of Hawaii sponsored the East-West Conference in Honolulu. Smith attended that meeting and led the opening of dialogue—not comparison but rather a joint grappling with common issues. He has been the chief American spokesperson at many conferences since then and, although he makes no pretense at being a scholar of Eastern materials, is respected as a philosopher who is ready with the riches of the Western traditions to engage those of the East. Some of Smith's students, such as Kasulis and Wu, have gone on to become true scholars of Eastern traditions, and others, such as Hall and Neville, have become comparativist philosophers of culture, to name only those represented in this volume.

The third factor in the recovery of America's tradition of philosophy, now expanded to include dialogue with Chinese and Indian philosophies, has been Smith's clear discrimination of the classic American tradition's sense of experience from the empiricisms of European philosophy, including analytic and continental philosophies. Thoroughly analyzed in his writings, this discrimination is the chief lesson that he has passed on to four decades' worth of students. Because the point is discussed at length in several of the papers in this volume, especially Anderson's and Neville's, it need not be dwelt upon here. The distinction is that, for the American tradition, experience is not perception, nor the act of description, nor like the interpretation of texts, but rather is an engagement with things such that one learns better about them. Experience is activity that corrects and teaches, that changes habits so as to be less parochial or mistaken. From Edwards' "consenting" through Peirce's "inquiry" to Buchler's "query," American philosophy has treated experience as a learning activity, not as a window, a filter, or a translator. No wonder, then, that Smith can approach Chinese philosophers, for instance, as partners in philosophical study rather than as representatives of a tradition to be translated.

The optimistic way to look at the recovery of philosophy in America is to see beyond both the return to professional authenticity and the continued development of the classic American tradition to an opportunity for world-philosophy. There is no such thing as philosophy without local historical roots, and there are many such historical traditions. However, there have been times when the encounter of different traditions has produced a new philosophy with a language of its own emerging from the encounter and an excellence resulting from new angles of criticism. One thinks of the axial fifth century B.C.E. in China, Greece, and India, or of the thirteenth century C.E. in Europe. Both because of the particular character of its classic historical tradition and because of its professional academic commitment to openness, America may be ready to host the next creative situation in world-philosophy. To be sure, genuine intellectual creativity cannot be invoked by readiness. But it can be snuffed by unreadiness. If America is a ready host, it is largely because John E. Smith has prevailed against professional parochialism and historical forgetfulness.

George R. Lucas, Jr.

# Philosophy's Recovery of Its History: A Tribute to John E. Smith

## PROLOGUE

Philosophy in America during the past decade or more can be characterized chiefly by the return to prominence and respectability of the study and interpretation of its *history*.

Historians of philosophy, Continental hermeneuts, and specialists in one or another historical figure might complain about this characterization, arguing that *they* had never forsaken such interests, nor ceased to "do philosophy historically" in the first place. Still, it is remarkable how prominent philosophers from Richard Rorty, Charles Taylor, and Arthur Danto, to Hilary Putnam, Ian Hacking, and most recently Keith Lehrer—none of whom would have been classified in the historical camp twenty years ago—have come forward during the past ten years or so[1] to declare a renewed interest in the historical figures and traditions of Western philosophical thought. Willard V. A. Quine's derogatory distinction between those who pursue philosophy "proper," and those who merely engage in the history of philosophy, apparently is no longer taken seriously.[2]

Thus, no matter how central historical and cultural traditions may have been within *non*-Anglo-American philosophies, it is now undeniably the case that, during recent years, we have witnessed a decisive new tendency among a number of America's leading philosophers toward renewing a kind of "living dialogue" with the principal figures and with the classical literary and philosophical texts of Western culture. Even further, we have witnessed attempts by at least a few of these philosophers to bring these Western traditions, in turn, into an extended dialogue with the major works and figures of *non*-Western philosophy. And, as the reference to Quine's earlier view suggests, this recent "historical turn" in American philosophy apparently marks the end of a lengthy hiatus, during which such approaches to historical studies and cultural traditions were relegated to a barely respectable, and decidedly second-class, status within the discipline of philosophy—concurrent (one should also observe) with the increased relegation of that discipline itself to a decidedly second-class stature within the larger culture of disciplines comprising the modern university.

Not the least among the many ironies exhibited in this recent historical turn in American philosophy is that this movement offers a sweeping vindication of the life, teachings, and philosophical career of John E. Smith, whom Robert Neville once aptly characterized as "the Jeremiah of American philosophy." For it was precisely the importance of "doing philosophy historically" and of working out native philosophical traditions that John Smith both advocated and practiced, precisely during the period in which such views were most out of favor among the other leaders of philosophy in America.

Smith's original and constructive interpretations of the thought of Jonathan Edwards and John Dewey, as well as of William James and of C. S. Peirce, were informed by a larger conviction that American philosophy issued from a unique and important cultural tradition. Smith often remarked that, while a German would not think of philosophizing apart from an obligatory encounter with Leibniz, Kant, and Hegel—and while British philosophy tended to proceed (even if unconsciously) against a cultural backdrop shaped by Locke, Hume, and J. S. Mill—that twentieth-century *American* philosophy and philosophers, by contrast, deliberately ignored their own history and traditions and intentionally cut themselves off from their philosophical roots. The clear implication of Smith's "Lamentation" was that this century's

American philosophers provided a uniquely destructive example of philosophy gone astray, cut loose from its moorings, and therefore bound to issue in sterile and infecund insights.

Now, at the close of the century, as we witness the "rediscovery" of John Dewey, the intensive scholarly attention to the works of Jonathan Edwards, and the almost-maniacal international obsession with the brilliant but elusive genius of Charles S. Peirce—all concatenated in turn by the decisive collapse and the self-evident intellectual bankruptcy of earlier, nonhistorical philosophical agendas—Smith's longstanding observations seem profoundly prophetic.

This chapter provides a brief documentary account and philosophical analysis of philosophy's recovery of history and an evaluation of the future of philosophy in America in light of this recovery of history.

## PHILOSOPHY, HISTORY, AND THE RISE OF A "CULTURE OF DISCIPLINES"

From a time dating back at least to the first appearance of Diogenes Laertius' classic *The Lives and Opinions of Eminent Philosophers*,[3] the history of philosophy has served as a useful pedagogical and heuristic introduction to the *discipline* or *practice* of philosophy. In the modern academy, in addition, the history of philosophy customarily serves dutifully alongside courses in Western history, art history, and the history of literature to provide students with a general introduction to the broad intellectual heritage of Western civilization.

Increasingly during the early decades of the twentieth century, however, the history of philosophy came to be portrayed as a bloodless procession of quaint, outmoded ideas and arcane disputes offering little in the way of insight, guidance, value, or significance for the practice of *contemporary* philosophy. Often without realizing it, philosophy teachers and textbooks portrayed the history of philosophy as a "captain's log" of the difficult and perplexing voyage to present privileged, and finally settled, perspectives on significant philosophic issues.[4] Once the student "passengers" on this voyage had arrived at their desired destination and the proper contemporary philosophical perspectives had been fully appreciated, then the historical "voyage" itself—like the pedogogical ladder of Ludwig Wittgenstein or the mythical raft of Mahayana

Buddhism—served no further useful purpose. Indeed, on some accounts, the history of philosophy is depicted as a bleak and infertile landscape, littered with the failed attempts of "false philosophies" and with what Bertrand Russell described as the decaying lumber of antiquated metaphysical systems.[5]

The majority of academic philosophers, of course, do not overtly disparage the value or efficacy of introducing students to philosophy as a discipline, nor do they object to the custom of defining for such students the intellectual heritage of Western civilization, by means of historical illustrations and accounts describing what past philosophers had thought and done. Nonetheless, it has seemed increasingly plausible throughout the twentieth century, until quite recently in fact, to regard the history of philosophy as in some sense optional for the essential understanding of what philosophy is, and at least as philosophers have come to practice it today.

The history of philosophy has been increasingly regarded as comparable to the history of mathematics or of physics, in this sense: the history of philosophy is no more essential to the understanding of philosophy as currently practiced than is the history of physics or of mathematics regarded as essential to an understanding of the practices of mathematics or of the physical sciences at present. Thus, just as it seemed feasible to function as a fully competent and proficient physicist or mathematician without knowing more than the barest rudiments of the history of science, so—admittedly to a lesser degree—it has become acceptable to embark on the analysis of questions in applied medical ethics or linguistics, or to construct models of memory and mental representation or of psychological concept formation in the newly labeled "cognitive sciences," without necessarily making reference to prior developments in ethics, metaphysics, and epistemology.

This internal disciplinary perspective on the history of philosophy would strike scholars from other disciplines as strange indeed. The widespread conventional or popular image of philosophy, after all, is invariably framed in terms of anecdotes drawn from its history: the peripatetic teacher, Socrates; the pious and scholarly proponents of faith and reason, Maimonides and St. Thomas Aquinas; the despised and forsaken lens grinder and solitary apostle of Stoic wisdom, Spinoza; the brilliant but eccentric Renaissance genius, Vico; or the obscure, abstruse, unintelligible "professional" academic philosophers on the

Germanic model, such as Kant and Hegel. Colleagues in literature, classics, or history might wonder how philosophers ever came to abandon these familiar images of their lives and vocations as humanists and sages.

As R. G. Collingwood complains,[6] the impulse to jettison the familiar historical image of the philosopher as sage came chiefly in this century from philosophers such as G. E. Moore and Bertrand Russell in England, as well as from leading members of the "Vienna Circle" at around the same period in Europe, including Rudolf Carnap, Moritz Schlick, and Hans Reichenbach. These philosophers rejected the historically grounded view of philosophy in favor of a new vision for their profession, grounded more centrally in the newly emerging "culture of disciplines" within the modern university. This new vision of philosophy, moreover, was strongly influenced by awareness of the special prestige accorded to the natural sciences and technological fields within what Alasdair MacIntyre terms "this peculiar academic division of labor" within the university,[7] as symbolized by the culture of disciplines.

This academic division of labor within which we currently dwell is itself a comparatively recent historical phenomenon. It constitutes, in fact, the legacy of Alexander von Humboldt's vision in the mid nineteenth century of a modern "scientific" university concentrated upon graduate study and research, comprising specialized schools, academic departments, and increased intellectual specialization. Von Humboldt's educational vision, in turn, was transparently derived from Adam Smith's analysis of the vast increases in efficiency and productivity brought about precisely by the same division of labor within the economic and industrial sphere.

Philosophy subsists, at best, very uncomfortably in the midst of the resultant culture of disciplines that von Humboldt's vision of the modern research university ultimately brought about. That discomfort only increased, moreover, as the earlier "nondiscipline" or parent discipline of philosophy witnessed, time and again, essential parts of itself "slough off" and reconstitute themselves as separate and independent disciplines, only to turn upon the original parent discipline and declare it of no further usefulness, or of only "historical" interest. Not just physics and biology and mathematics were "lost" to philosophy in this manner, but even more essentially the ill-titled "social sciences"—political science, sociology, economics, and psychology, each so profoundly and inherently philosophical both in methodological orientation and in cultural justification—went on to achieve this disciplinary independence.

While they thus unwittingly robbed themselves of their essential philosophical heritage, these new disciplines tended more tangibly to present the newly conceived "discipline" of philosophy with a kind of existential crisis by appearing to leave it without a unique subject matter or methodology of its own and hence devoid of justification either of place or of stature within the modern university. As a result, during the two centuries from the first publication by Immanuel Kant of his *Critique of Pure Reason* in 1781, to the appearance of Hans Reichenbach's highly influential book *The Rise of Scientific Philosophy* in 1951, one can trace the steady development of a strong impulse toward purging philosophy once and for all of speculative and historical concerns. We can now appreciate that this familiar agenda was not independently motivated by selfless normative notions of what philosophy ought to be, but rather was driven by the desperate and powerful desire to establish philosophy itself as a pure, well-defined, and thoroughly respectable discipline within the larger, emerging "culture of disciplines" in higher education generally.

In order to achieve this radical disciplinary transformation, moreover, it proved necessary to engage in a special kind of apologetics: in effect, to establish and maintain that philosophy *itself* was in possession of a clearly delineated (though hitherto poorly understood) subject matter and a shared methodology, both of which were now properly to be seen as the domain of technical specialists (analytic philosophers), rather than speculative dilettantes and avocational dabblers.

The course of this disciplinary transformation required that what had already transpired in physics and chemistry must now occur in philosophy as well. Chiefly, the history of the discipline (philosophers now argued) will come to be viewed as largely irrelevant to philosophy's new content, focus, and methodological consensus. At best, the history of philosophy, like the history of physics or mathematics, proves to be relevant only in Reichenbach's *negative* sense of showing the irremedial defects of historically prior views of the proper philosophic vocation, and of providing simultaneously a background chronicle of the slow course of progress by early "scientifically minded" philosophical pioneers, trudging dauntlessly under the banner of Galileo and Descartes toward ultimately true, definable, and verifiable perspectives on legitimately philosophical (rather than pseudo-philosophical) problems.

Scholars who became overly infatuated with the narrative of this journey itself—scholars such as Collingwood, Foucault, Gadamer, Smith, or MacIntyre—would hereafter be politely relegated to a secondary status as mere historians of the discipline, rather than being classified as philosophers proper (as Willard V. A. Quine graciously observed). That, at least, was better than the fate envisioned for Vico, St. Thomas, Hegel, Bergson, Schelling, Whitehead, Dewey, William James, and C. Lloyd Morgan—not to mention a whole host of other individual philosopher-sages such as Boethius, Confucius, or Lao-Tzu—let alone even others whose modest but essential contributions to their culture enjoy a degree of footnote immortality, or whose names have altogether slipped beneath the turbulent seas of world history. In the popular view, such lesser and even unknown figures had always constituted a harmless cottage industry in philosophy. The new official disciplinary record, however, could no longer tolerate their presence. Richard Rorty rather shockingly endorses Reichenbach's earlier attempt to consign the works of all of these historical figures to the flames for having *failed* to perceive "the philosophic discoveries immanent in the science of their time," and accordingly for having "developed, under the name of philosophy, systems of naive generalizations and analogies."[8]

The atmosphere of urgency stemmed from an underlying concern that philosophy would receive respect and stature as an academic and professional discipline only by achieving success in the delineation of problems that would fall solely within its professional or disciplinary purview, in a manner in which the older "perennial" philosophical questions regarding the best form of political order, the highest good for a human life, the conflict between duty and desire, the foundations of logic, and the significance of individual mortality apparently did not. Moreover, achieving the status of a discipline in the university required that professionals in the discipline engage in the effective analysis and solution of these new problems solely within the boundaries of a clearly determined subject matter that did not significantly overlap the "territories" of rival disciplines such as physics, biology, history, or psychology—areas of study with which philosophy had been so thoroughly intertwined at least through the late Renaissance.

In fairness, the proponents of the new philosophy faced an array of political and intellectual pressures building in the academy at this time, not wholly of their own making—political pressures that are still much with us, of a sort that critics such as Collingwood perhaps did not fully recognize. These growing academic constraints on the pursuit of teaching and research in higher education were certainly less "Fascist" (as Collingwood characterized them in his *Autobiography*) than they were insidiously bureaucratic in stressing efficiency, progress, and quantitative productivity in the most mundane sense imaginable. For what we would today term "assessment" in the university—the specific enumeration, the attainment, and ultimately the quantitative evaluation of, such precise and measurable disciplinary goals and objectives—had become the *raison d'être* of a rapidly expanding managerial, administrative class overseeing the organization and operation of the modern university.

The new conception of philosophy as a distinct, methodologically precise discipline offered certain definite advantages in coping with these pressures when compared to its predecessor "historical" model. The disciplinary claims of contemporary philosophers—whether in symbolic logic, in language analysis, or in conceptual elucidation and the dissolving of puzzles and paradoxes encountered in other fields—seemed at once more precise and less pretentious than the objectives sought by the earlier systematic, synoptic, and historical purveyors of what Edmund Husserl (yet another proponent of philosophy as a scientific discipline) disparaged as merely *weltanschauung*: a matrix of beliefs and intellectual commitments attained through a vague, diffuse, and illusive search for wisdom and truth. The new philosophy, like the new technological model of the sciences, offered its overseers the chimera of measurable progress and realistically attainable results. Results, in turn, justified risk, growth, retention, and the kind of expenditures of funds (not to mention the justification for acquisition of further funds) requisite to the continued maintenance and operation of the sort of organization a "university" had increasingly become in the technological society.

My account relies on broad allusions to the newly emerging organizational and political features within educational institutions.[9] Readers will also readily discern a resemblance between this specific, self-conscious attempt at transformation within philosophy, and the now-familiar account of the revolutionary transformation from a "preparadigm state" to a "normal science" in Thomas Kuhn's *The Structure of Scientific Revolutions*.[10]

We might now plausibly say, with the benefit of hindsight as well as of Kuhn's sociological and historical categories, that the "new philosophers" early in this century desired nothing less than that philosophy itself should achieve in this century and in this culture the status of a "normal science" in Kuhn's sense, and hence emerge at last from the chaotic immaturity inherent in preparidigm, "prescientific" fields. The history of the discipline would gradually lose its prior normative significance. The well-defined journal article would replace the book as the medium of research and scholarly communication, while classroom textbooks would reflect the emerging methodological consensus to be imparted to novices in the discipline. Each of these historical innovations (now associated by Kuhn with the usual development of a disciplinary *science*) was stridently urged and repeatedly defended over a period of decades by proponents of the new philosophy in conscious analogy with demonstrable developments in their sister disciplines in the natural sciences, long before Kuhn's illuminating analysis had itself entered the historical picture.

## PHILOSOPHY AND THE RECOVERY OF HISTORY

Ironically, it would seem that precisely the opposite results issued from these attempts. Whether these intentions of earlier generations of philosophers in this century are portrayed as nobly misguided or (following Collingwood) as nefarious and destructive, it remains undeniably the case that philosophy, at the close of the twentieth century, resembles more than ever what Kuhn himself describes as a *pre*paradigm science. There is no agreed upon method, subject matter, or set of definable problems in the field. Adherents of different philosophic methods and traditions often cannot even communicate across the boundaries of the various resulting subdisciplinary communities now grouped within philosophy proper. Journals have proliferated in response to the fragmenting of the earlier fragile philosophic consensus; no one journal nor group of journals can any longer claim legitimacy in the profession as a whole. One result is that the book has once again replaced the scholarly research article as the preferred means of communication. And, most important, the fact that they share a history is now the *only* thing that the rival camps have in common.

Beyond these massive failures, there were often more immediate and irritating deficiencies noticeable even to the triumphalist visionaries themselves. For example, the decidedly hostile antihistorical attitudes of early realists, positivists, and analytic philosophers often tended to produce superficial, unflattering, and historically inauthentic caricatures of earlier philosophical viewpoints. If we require in ethics, for example, that every historically prior approach to moral theory be classified as either teleological or deontological, we inadvertently suppress or downplay approaches to morality that stress the cultivation of virtues within a moral community—richly informative and complex elements of morality clearly evident in Aristotle, Hume, Kant, and even in J. S. Mill, but conspicuously absent from "the attenuated and improverished discipline that modern philosophical ethics has become at the hands of most of its modern practitioners," as Alasdair MacIntyre complains.[11] In metaphysics and epistemology, Berkeley's idealism is liable to be indistinguishable from Hegel's, and both confused with something either completely different or decidedly less sophisticated, such as the Advaita Vedanta nondualism of F. H. Bradley or the Christian idealism of A. E. Taylor, respectively.[12] In textual analysis, obscure or neglected passages of Aristotle's corpus are combed meticulously in a search for "publishable" logical or linguistic infelicities. Indeed, in the approaches to the history of philosophy that have been prevalent until quite recently, it is common (as Arthur Danto complains) to find a treatment of Plato written as though "he to whom the whole of subsequent philosophy since is said to be so many footnotes, were in effect a footnote to himself, and being coached to get a paper accepted by *The Philosophical Review*."[13]

The most dramatic development to occur in academic philosophy in the Anglo-American tradition during the past two decades has been the decisive collapse of this earlier consensus regarding philosophic method and subject content characteristic of positivism and subsequent logical and linguistic (or "analytic") philosophy. This collapse or demise occurred gradually and was slow to be recognized by professional academic philosophers. Again with the benefit of hindsight, we can now locate the beginnings of the unravelling of this methodological antihistoricism and the undoing of the analytic consensus with the publication in the field of logic of Quine's own skeptical essay "Two Dogmas of Empiricism," disparaging the analytic-synthetic distinction, and in epistemology with the publication of Thomas Kuhn's aforementioned monograph on *The Structure of Scientific Revolutions*, and perhaps also in the corresponding rise to prominence of studies in the "sociology of knowledge" signaled in Berger and Luckmann's *The Social Construction of Reality*.

However, the recognition of a kind of "crisis in confidence" in professional philosophy burst full on the scene with the appearance of Richard Rorty's brilliant and controversial *Philosophy and the Mirror of Nature* in 1979. Almost simultaneously followed a decisive refutation of the ahistorical and antiliterary analytic consensus in moral philosophy by Alasdair MacIntyre in *After Virtue* (1981). Rorty's work has stimulated renewed interest in pragmatism and its relationship to hermeneutics in European thought. More generally, Rorty's characterization of philosophy as "edifying conversation" has prompted a vigorous renewed interest in the history of philosophy, and especially in the re-interpretation of classical texts and figures in the Western tradition.

MacIntyre's work effected a dramatic sea-change in the customary modes of thought of two generations of self-styled "professional experts" in so-called applied and theoretical ethics by exposing the impoverished and truncated intellectual foundations of rationalistic, calculative "decision theory" advocated by economic utilitarian theorists and deontological, legalistic "rights" theorists in moral philosophy. His work has likewise spawned a renewed interest in the teaching of historical figures in ethics (Aristotle, Hume, Aquinas, Marx, and Nietzsche), as well as of literary-moral traditions ranging from Sophocles, Dante, and Cervantes to Jane Austen. These developments, in turn, have prompted a renewed and vigorous inquiry into the role played by culturally and historically conditioned narratives in the natural and social sciences, as well as in literature and art.

Collectively, such revolutionary developments have made an impact on the profession of philosophy, as well as on the customary teaching of philosophy, in a number of ways. Once again under the aegis of John E. Smith, canons of membership and inclusion in the profession have been transformed by the rise of a "pluralistic" movement in the American Philosophical Association, stressing the importance of European philosophy, non-Western traditions, indigenous American philosophy, and a return to the importance of the history of philosophy. Kant, Locke, and Hume have been joined of late by previously neglected or disparaged philosophers such as Hegel, Vico, Husserl,

Heidegger, Kierkegaard, Dewey, and Whitehead in philosophy curricula from Harvard, MIT, and Chicago to Berkeley, Stanford, and UCLA. A kind of Hegelian hysteria of *ungluckliche bewusstsein* has taken hold of philosophers, who, at virtually every professional gathering, now engage with depressing regularity in obligatory acts of ritual self-flagellation in seminars announcing "The Death of Philosophy" and featuring the work of Rorty, MacIntyre, Foucault, Lyotard, and Derrida, set against the brooding Nordic background of a philosophical *gotterdammerung* suggested by Nietzsche and Heidegger. Critics and proponents of such changes alike have come to refer to this collection of diverse directions and postmodern currents in philosophy as "postanalytic philosophy."[14]

## PHILOSOPHY, HISTORY, AND OTHER DISCIPLINES

What seems transparently obvious, in light of the recent developments just chronicled, is that philosophers, as members of a discipline in the academy, seem deeply troubled and decidedly ill at ease with their relationship to their history. It is as if the disease that Nietzsche complained of in Germany—the obsession with history, the bad historical conscience that constituted one of the *disadvantages* of history for life—has come to consume philosophers everywhere. Philosophers seem concerned about being ahistorical, or antiquarian, or anachronistic, or classified by their peers *merely* as intellectual historians, and the like. In itself, this phenomenon of historical consternation in philosophy is not likely to prove interesting to those who are not themselves members of this particular academic discipline.

But suppose that the very consternation and conflict over history itself is somehow symptomatic of a deeper malaise. I have suggested that the conflict over the understanding and the role of its history in the recently defined "discipline" of philosophy is itself a function of philosophy and philosophers having first come to see themselves, and indeed, wanting to see themselves, as one among many disciplines in the modern university. Toward what sort of understanding of the present state and the future of philosophy might this historical-sociological observation then lead us? And how ought philosophy in the future relate to the other disciplines in the modern university?

In her elegant historical reconstruction of the conflict between late Renaissance humanism and the rise of the modern notion of a purely quantitative, mathematical, and ahistorical conception of the natural sciences, Lynn Joy provides an important insight into our present dilemma. Late Renaissance philosophers such as Gassendi (on whom Joy primarily focuses) disagreed sharply with Galileo, Descartes, and other proponents of modernism, not only in distrusting their confident application of mathematical principles to events in the physical world, but also by opposing "the views that philosophy, science, and history are autonomous academic disciplines." Gassendi, Joy informs us, rejected in particular "the Cartesian assumption that the central problems of science and philosophy can be articulated independently of a historical understanding of the places they occupy within their respective scientific or philosophical traditions."[15]

Gassendi, as we know, lost that argument. Joy portrays the ironic difficulty that modern scholars now face in knowing how to classify Gassendi—is he, for example, a philosopher, a historian, a scientist, a mathematician? Yet somehow, we sense, these questions are not rightly put. History is not a problem for Gassendi on Joy's account; rather, history is seen by this Renaissance scholar as the prior normative background for the studies we now classify as "disciplines" in the natural sciences.

What does this example of Gassendi's losing struggle against antihistoricism in the late Renaissance, however, teach us in the late twentieth century?

History becomes a problem, I suggest, only when one accepts the academic division of labor proposed at the dawn of modern science and modern philosophy by Galileo and Descartes. In this division of labor, history itself becomes one discipline among many, or else is perceived as integral to some of the new disciplines and irrelevant to the others. The *disciplinary division itself* forces the question: which disciplines are primarily narrative and historical, and which are, by contrast, quantitative, mathematical, and nonnarrative?

This question, in turn, does more than engage us in idle taxonomy. Precisely in the course of modern history, it has become more and more a badge of honor, a mark of prestige, to be ranked in the latter—the quantitative, "scientific"—classification. It is here, ever since the triumph of Galileo and Descartes, that knowledge is seen as certain and growing, that progress is being made, that problems are being solved, that work is being done. While there is seemingly no end to the stories one might tell, or the historical tales one might weave, the scientific disciplines offer the realizable goal of knowledge, of genuine discovery, and of progress. It follows that, where possible, the practitioners of each resulting discipline will want, in due course, to declare independence from their history in behalf of science, to effect the famous modern divorce between *questio juris* and *questio facti*, between subjective value judgments and objective facts, between uncertain interpretive narrative historical accounts and the certitudes of nomological explanation.

We have been examining, in the special case of philosophy, the consternation that will arise within *any* discipline when—despite strong desires and vigorous programmatic attempts by adherents of the discipline—this divorce proves impossible to effect. If the historical analysis of this situation that I have offered is correct, it further implies that some of the other academic disciplines will share with philosophy this consternation over the role of history in their profession, while others (in which such a divorce from historical narrative and tradition would not seem the least desirable) would not appear to share in this consternation.

In order to test this implication, let us, on the one hand, consider the academic departments and disciplines in the modern university which encompass literature, languages, and the fine arts. There is so far as I know not the same degree of consternation among artists, art critics, or art historians—or *mutatis mutandis*, musicians, music critics, and music historians—regarding the histories of their respective enterprises, as one finds among philosophers about theirs. Histories of literature and of fine arts are understood as significant, as fascinating in themselves, as worthy of study for their own sake by scholars in these fields and as worthy of being presented, taught, and interpreted to students in these fields. Histories of art, music, or literature chronicle evolutionary developments and record radical discontinuities, breakthroughs, periods of stagnation and creativity, all of which offer a narrative, a saga, which collectively purports to answer questions such as: what is art, or music, or literature, or poetry; what does it mean to be an artist, a musician, or a composer, or a writer or poet; and what roles do art, music, literature, and poetry play within the larger scheme of human cultures? So far, so good.

It would be fatuous to suggest that there are no controversies here: surely there are. Which artists or periods, for example, ought to receive emphasis in the canon or doxography of art history? Johnson, the traditionalist, thinks that literature declined after Milton and Shakespeare, while Jones, the modernist, believes that the literary enterprise only flourishes in the work of Austen and Woolf. Jones, in addition, holds (*contra* Johnson) that only bourgeois pedants and young, upwardly mobile professionals listen to Pachelbel or Bach, while Wagner—or perhaps Schoenberg, or Shostakovich—denote the transition to genuine sophistication in taste.

But these controversies over individual aesthetic preference are generally taken as merely that: the historian of art, music, or literature does not seem to be haunted by these aesthetic disputes over historical preferences in anything remotely resembling the sense philosophers are. These controversies mask a kind of underlying peaceful consensus regarding the sacred canon tradition, and the histories of these activities and interests are seldom portrayed by any save the most tendentious, opionated bigot as establishing a record of "progress" in the field from ignorance and quaintness to sophisticated, deeper, and richer understandings in the present.

In art history, for example, one notes the development of techniques for expressing perspective and dimensionality on a two-dimension canvas early in the Renaissance by Alberti, without necessarily denigrating medieval iconography as having somehow rested upon a mistake or as having been thereby "repudiated." The transition from Baroque to classical styles of composition and performance in the work of Mozart, or from classical, in turn to romantic in the later work of Beethoven, is not taken to "repudiate" or "refute" all that has gone before, nor does it imply that predecessors were quaint, ignorant, or incompetent idiots. Rather, such histories record both gradual evolution and radical discontinuities, innovations, and resulting transformations of outlook and practice, none of which repudiate their predecessors except perhaps in Hegel's famous sense in which the flower refutes or "repudiates" the bud, or the fruit the flower: that is, by replacing or succeeding, by absorbing and transforming.

To borrow a phrase of Collingwood: what a lunatic idea of history it would seem were we solemnly admonished that, after Mozart, we could never again listen to Bach or Vivaldi with a straight face, or that, after Rembrandt, we must come to realize that the brothers Jan and Hubert van Eyck were little more than primitive exponents of "pre-artistic" form.[16]

My point is that such historical claims, which would seem prejudiced, idiosyncratic, or even nonsensical in the fine arts, are coin of the realm in the academic discipline of philosophy, as the earlier citations from Reichenbach and Rorty bear witness.

But perhaps these comparisons merely demonstrate that there is no real or meaningful comparison to be made between philosophy and art, music, or literature, at least so far as all these take their place in the modern university's disciplinary culture. Let us then consider the opposite side of the disciplinary field as conventionally understood: the natural sciences themselves. History does not constitute a "problem" in the natural sciences either, but for quite different reasons. According to Ian Hacking (who cites the views of contemporary scientists in this dispute), it is still the case that the history of science is perceived as a respectable scholarly amusement that plays no integral part in contemporary practices.[17] To ring a change on Whitehead: Physicists have remained as blandly indifferent to their historical refutation by Thomas Kuhn as they have to their philosophical refutation by Hume, despite the convincing arguments of scholars such as Kuhn, Collingwood, MacIntyre, and Lynn Joy that history is, after all, normative for these disciplines as well. Biology and chemistry customarily are not taught, and need not be taught, or practiced, historically. The courses might be more interesting, the practitioners more enlightened and appreciative of their role as technically expert citizens in the polis, were such subjects approached in this manner. But hard-core cynics would still insist that this cultural improvement would not affect the technical ability of those who (in Hacking's phrase) get their "license from the world" to develop a biodegradable pesticide, decode DNA strings, or formulate the correct version of unified field theory.

It is in the social or "human" sciences, interestingly enough, that one finds the greatest parallels with the crisis of history in philosophy. Economics is a discipline that (in the words of American humorist James Thurber) "amuses with its pretentions" yet is utterly lacking in the kind of methodological consensus characteristic of normal science on Kuhn's account. Today's Nobel laureate is likely, tomorrow, to be vilified as the antichrist. Despite a clear desire within the discipline to model itself after mathematical physics, economics as a discipline is still much more closely allied with philosophy, as some of its most astute quantitative practitioners, such as Amartya Sen, have acknowledged. Similar stories can be told regarding the ambiguous role assigned to historical studies in psychology, in sociology, and in political science. Those disciplines are deeply divided between scholars who see the history as integral to the discipline, and those who see the histories as "prehistoric," prescientific tales of decidedly secondary import to the discipline. Political science is often portrayed as divided between those described by their critics as "quantitative number crunchers," and the political philosophers and historians, described by *their* critics as armchair scientists or medievalists.

Hacking suggests that Kuhn's analysis has had far more impact on social scientists than upon natural scientists. MacIntyre confirmed this diagnosis a decade ago in describing "the ritual obeisance towards Kuhn . . . required in presidential addresses to the American Political Science Association—to license the theoretical failures of social science."[18] This is so for several reasons.

First, most of those fields are beset from within by a host of methodological and conceptual controversies—but then, so are literature and the arts. Unlike the case with literature and the arts, however, there is an implicit *telos* in these fields—a yearning, or perhaps a dogmatic lust for power which Dilthey's tepid distinctions fail to capture, but to which Kuhn's conceptual analysis speaks with almost messianic forcefulness.

Kuhn's *Structure*, in effect, offers an eschatological vision of disciplinary history in which the vagaries of history will be overcome and history itself may be transcended. The controversies to which I alluded above seem to be precisely (as they seemed also in philosophy) characteristic of the preparadigm state *of a science*. These very controversies with which philosophy and the human sciences are beset by their very existence seem to entail the promise, at least, of a "normal" scientific state of the discipline, one *unbeset* by such controversies. This condition lies beyond some historical parousia (or perhaps apocalypse) yet to come, in which the discipline will rid itself once and for all of "those idiots" who still have not caught onto the proper methodology (whatever it may be), just as Descartes and Galileo finally rid themselves of Gassendi and his supporters.

Now, contrast that fervent eschatology with the "normal" state of methodological controversy found within fine arts and literature. I know of not a single member of the Modern Language Association who envisions a day when he or she will not be at war with his or her colleagues over style and methodology. Such warfare is the lifeblood of literary scholars, who seem to have preserved the ancient wisdom of Heraclitus: that an end of strife would mean the end of their world.

Tragically, for philosophers and social scientists, by contrast, the eschatology of consensus promises a "New Jerusalem," a stage of benign progress, achievement, and the final attainment of self-respect for practicioners of the discipline. Philosophers, in particular, cast themselves as the "new Evangelicals" of the present academic situation. The promise of the kingdom clearly motivated the iconoclastic and often ruthlessly arrogant and single-minded intellectual and academic agendas of the positivism of Mach, Carnap, and Schlick in the Vienna Circle, as well as of Collingwood's "realist" colleagues at Oxford. Through Reichenbach, Carnap, and others, this evangelical movement made its way into the academic institutions of this country during the present century and set about transforming those structures into their own image in the name of excellence and rigor, in a precise emulation of one of Kuhn's "scientific revolutions."

However, the effects upon teaching and research, and upon the role of philosophy and the regard for philosophers in the wider culture have been quite different than expected. They have unleashed a divisive and destructive force of remarkable power, but of no lasting creativity or achievement, of the sort that Stanley Rosen identifies as the essential form of nihilism.[19] These dismal effects and this disappointing outcome have been quietly repudiated by the prominent apostates from philosophy's own ranks, such as Rorty.

## THE FUTURE OF PHILOSOPHY AND THE HISTORY OF PHILOSOPHY

In the conclusion of *Philosophy and the Mirror of Nature*, Rorty himself wonders whether "a new form of systematic philosophy will be found which has nothing whatever to do with epistemology but which nevertheless makes normal philosophical inquiry possible."

The term *systematic philosophy* is utilized here as an acceptable euphemism for metaphysics or synoptic philosophy. Bearing this in mind, Rorty's interesting speculation has indeed come to pass in the recent development of a variety of new forms of systematic metaphysical inquiry, in a manner that few save Collingwood himself would have imagined possible, let alone acceptable, as recently as a decade ago. In many cases, this new systematic, synoptic, and "nonepistemological" metaphysical inquiry is espoused and practiced by philosophers who had previously held such modes of inquiry to be infeasible or superfluous.[20] This resurgent interest has, in turn, fostered renewed attention to the "classical" metaphysical tradition symbolized by Aristotle, Aquinas, Spinoza, Leibniz, Hegel, Whitehead, and Collingwood himself—figures who collectively emphasize the importance of and illustrate the potential achievements to be won from greater attention to philosophy's synoptic, systematic, and integrative task within historical cultures.

Most characteristically, however, the decisive end of the hegemony of what has been termed here "the analytic consensus" in philosophy is evidenced by the growing list of distinguished thinkers educated and sanctioned within that consensus—including Rorty, Putnam, Taylor, Hacking, Danto, and others mentioned at the outset of this chapter—each having lately come forward with almost evangelical fervor to call for a renewed dialogue with what Martin Heidegger liked to call "the tradition." For Heidegger believed—in common with Hegel, Collingwood, Smith, and MacIntyre—that philosophy *is* its history. Indeed, as we have now reluctantly and painfully come to understand, the history of philosophy is nothing more nor less than (in the words of Hans-Georg Gadamer) "that conversation which we are."

A host of competing options is available for the use and interpretation of history. These options have already begun to generate their own controversies and subdisciplinary divisions. Richard Rorty's generally tolerant and eclectic view would brand only the thoughtless doxography—what is earlier termed the "bloodless procession of ideas and figures"—as a genuine abuse of historical traditions.[21] Charles Taylor joins MacIntyre and Collingwood in calling for a kind of contextualism regarding truth, and he advocates a post-Hegelian "historicism," according to which our grasping the truth of an idea is wholly dependent upon our ability to recover and to understand its historical genesis and evolutionary development. In order to understand why the Cartesian foundationalism in epistemology that we are currently engaged in rejecting ever "caught on" in the first place, we must engage in the difficult activity of (in Taylor's words) articulating the unsayable, or, as the idea-archaeologist Michel Foucault puts it: we must "show that things 'weren't as necessary as all that.' . . . [We must learn to] breach . . . those self evidences on which our knowledges, acquiescences, and practices rest."[22]

At first glance, it might seem possible for the historicist, perhaps surprisingly, to forge an alliance with a deconstructionist such as Derrida, who intends to burrow beneath the appearances of unity and continuity in a given historical text, and thereby to overturn the veneer of arbitrarily superimposed conceptual orderings in philosophical or literary systems. The purpose of this project is at least in part to bring to light the kinds of tensions and discontinuities, the suppressed contradictions and paradoxes, that every author and philosopher faces and must overcome in the eventual transformation of his or her living thought from the chaos of irrational and disordered *mythos* into the tidy conceptual categories of the written *logos*. Indeed, Derrida argues that his project embodies precisely the sort of complaint that one finds Socrates leveling against the newly emerging art of writing in Plato's *Phaedrus*.[23]

However, both such approaches to history stand in sharp contrast to the views of students and disciples of Leo Strauss, such as Stanley Rosen, for whom both Hegelian historicism and literary-textual deconstructionism constitute abusive, conceptually flawed, and inappropriately relativistic uses of historical traditions. From this perspective, there is no more advantage to be gained from Derrida or Collingwood than from the analytic philosopher's attempts either to ignore or to anachronistically co-opt history.[24] Indeed, Taylor's frequent admonitions to "go back to genetic sources" sounds suspiciously like the attitudes of young Phaedrus himself, whom Socrates gently lampoons for his obsession with sources and details rather than truth.[25]

A way around the apparent impasse between historicism and the Straussian adultation of the timeless and transhistorical features of culture and tradition might be found within a broad and less dogmatic and mysterious understanding of the techniques of hermeneutics. However, such an understanding would need to move us beyond the seemingly endless and utterly fruitless technical discussions of the fine structure of distinctions (from Dilthey through Gadamer and Habermas) between *erklaerung* and *verstehen*—that is, between the role of nomological or causal descriptive explanations in the natural sciences and the role of "understanding" or historical narrative accounts in the *Geisteswissens-*

*chaften* or "human sciences."[26] The obsession with such issues has tended to elicit and even encourage an unflattering portrayal of hermeneutics by analytic critics such as Adolph Grunbaum,[27] who see in such preoccupations merely the dogmatically self-justifying attempt to put the results of hermeneutical studies beyond the pale of evaluation and criticism. What is even more important, however, in light of the most recent interpretation of the essential role of historical narratives in the sciences as well as the humanities offered by Alasdair MacIntyre, is that the belaboring of these dogmatic distinctions might prove to be utterly irrelevant.[28]

The deeper and more fruitful avenue of approach to hermeneutics lies in exploring the possible implications of Gadamer's suggestive comparisons between the role of interpretation in historically grounded philosophy and the sort of interpretation necessary in aesthetics, or, in a different sense, in law and in theology.[29] Gadamer's instructive comparison of philosophy with legal reasoning and with theology in particular, seems close to but not precisely on target in defining the philosopher's task in the wake of this new historical turn. Law, grounded in precedent, honors tradition but is not itself sufficiently reflective; reflection on the ground of law constitutes, instead, "philosophy" of law. Christian theology, which Gadamer has in mind (as opposed to Islamic or Hindu theology) often either is mired in dogmatism and unreflective traditionalism or else celebrates the avant-garde and freedom from tradition. Neither practice, I would argue, precisely captures through analogy the point that Gadamer intends to make.

An even more instructive and appropriate analogy is, I believe, suggested by the orientation and activity of the rabbinical scholar. The philosopher, like the rabbi, inherits and indeed is called to display a special degree of custodial or stewardly reverence for a long and richly self-reflective tradition. But the philosopher is likewise called upon simultaneously to apply, extend, extrapolate, and so contribute to that tradition—and in so doing, ultimately transform it—in the process of bringing the tradition to bear upon new and novel problems, and in order to obtain the fresh insights without which the tradition and the culture whose conversation it is must necessarily wither and die.

Philosophy, if it is anything at all, is precisely this sort of thing—that is, the quest for *sophia* involves the tenuous and ongoing dialectical tension and interplay between *arche* and *telos*, between "first principles" and provisional "final ends" that Aristotle prescribed for the so-called incomplete sciences in the *Posterior Analytics*. And it is precisely this sort of intellectual struggle between foundational principles and goals that one finds motivating the quest for Torah or Law in the rabbinical tradition. As with the tentative formulations of rabbinical law, philosophy and philosophical reflection likewise begin in the crucible of issues bequeathed by accumulated historical wisdom; yet, almost paradoxically, it is wisdom, *sophia*, which serves as the end or goal of philosophical reflection. Philosophy, that is to say, is not a scientific pursuit of random novel insights or discoveries; it is, rather, a living tradition: reflective, discursive, and dialogical. Properly understood, philosophy *is* that historical melieu (what Whitehead meant by the accumulated stream of causal efficacy) within which we stand, not merely to view the world, but also of necessity to engage it.

## CONCLUSION

Philosophy's problem with its history is a kind shared precisely with the "social sciences" to which it gave birth. The practitioners of each desire to be seen, and perhaps more important, to see themselves as custodians of certain knowledge and some particular type of expertise, as keepers of some eternal flame, or perhaps as priestly "stewards of the mysteries of God"—and hence as deserving of special priestly status in modern culture.

The tragedy of this sad adventure in this century—this narrative of priestly *hybris*—is that it represents the triumph of an inversion of values and priorities more to be feared (according both to Plato and to Aristotle) than any other: namely, the elevation of *episteme* and unreflective *techne*—merely encyclopedic and instrumental forms of knowing—to a status in our culture that renders them more to be sought after than good judgment, practical sensibility, and wisdom for its own sake—*sophrosune, phronesis*, and most of all, *sophia*.

The reemergence of history after its forceable suppression and denigration in philosophy provides an important object lesson: that this "discipline" of philosophy is no discipline and that the professionalized, eschatological or ideological model of its activity is unworkable—that, indeed, such a conception forsakes the deepest values and the most cherished historical traditions of philosophy itself.

The neglect of this insight at the beginning of this century led to an extraordinarily barren and unproductive career for philosophy—a record of largely unintelligible solutions to problems of interest to virtually no one. Precisely the dissatisfaction with the arid and barren "results" of philosophic pursuit in this century led to a recovery of history by philosophy at the close of this same century. Surely this episode will itself now serve as one of the most instructive ironies encompassed with that living historical tradition which philosophy inescapably, ineluctably, and irreducibly is.

## NOTES

1. The dating of this issue is hardly precise. The trend "back" to the history of philosophy by prominent American philosophers is usually taken to begin with Rorty"s publication of *Philosophy and the Mirror of Nature* (Princeton: Princeton University Press) in 1979, followed by the work cited below. Others would point to the influence of Alasdair MacIntyre's *After Virtue* (Notre Dame: Notre Dame University Press), in 1981. But Charles Taylor had already signaled this emerging trend on the part of analytic philosophers with his publication of *Hegel* (Cambridge: Cambridge University Press) in 1975. Ian Hacking dates his "conversion" from "the commonplaces of a perfectly conventional training in analytic philosophy" to what he terms a "historico-linguistic point of view" informed by Michel Foucault as occurring sometime after 1974 (cf. "Five Parables," in *Philosophy in History*, ed. Richard Rorty, J. B. Schneewind, and Quentin Skinner [Cambridge: Cambridge University Press, 1984], esp. 109–113). Putnam was by this time deeply embroiled in the question of whether Aristotle was "right or wrong" about real essences, and henceforth has seemed bent (as Edward Pols remarks) on "transforming himself before retirement into the Complete Continental Philosopher" (*Review of Metaphysics* 43, no. 4 [June, 1990], 733). Danto's reformation is symbolized in the contrasting treatments of philosophy of history and historically minded philosophers in *The Analytic Philosophy of History* (Cambridge: Cambridge University Press, 1965) and the considerably revised and expanded version of that work, *Narration and Knowledge* (New York: Columbia University Press, 1985), as well as in the contrast between the treatment of Hegel in 1965, and the subsequent use of Hegel to forge Danto's own revolutionary views on the "End of Art" in *The Philosophical Disenfranchisement of Art* (New York: Columbia University Press, 1986). Keith Lehrer's recent work on the Scottish enlightenment philosopher, *Thomas Reid* (New York:

Routledge, 1989) and the current widespread interest in Martha Nussbaum's *The Fragility of Goodness* (New York: Cambridge University Press 1986) constitute some of the more recent episodes in this historical trend.

2. Quine's remark is cited by Richard Rorty in *The Consequences of Pragmatism* (Minneapolis, MN: University of Minnesota Press, 1982), 211.

3. There are certainly earlier histories or "doxographies" of philosophy than that of Diogenes, including Hermippus of Smyrna's *Lives* (third century B.C.), and Favorinus' *Memorabilia.* The beautifully preserved "Philosophers' Mosaic" dating from the beginning of the Common Era (displayed in the Koln Rheinische-Germanische Museum) testifies, even before Diogenes, to a widespread public acknowledgment of a kind of "pantheon" of great thinkers, in which Plato, Aristotle, and Socrates figured prominently. Perhaps one would date this concept of "teaching" philosophy through biography and history to Aristotle's historical accounts, e.g., in book *Alpha* of the *Metaphysics*, or Xenophanes' *Memorabilia.* I focus on Diogenes simply because of its strategic historical significance, evident in the widespread influence his work had on the teaching and transmission of philosophy in our culture, and also because his work appears to signify an important transition from purely biographical accounts of great individuals, on the one hand, and partial and tendentious summaries of opponent's doctrines (as by Aristotle) on the other, to a genre in which both biography and an attempt at faithful doctrinal summary were combined for pedagogic, rather than for apologetic or polemical, purposes.

4. Witness, for example, Richard Rorty's claims about Aristotle and "real essences," Leibniz and belief in God, or the "correct" contemporary view that "the mind is just the central nervous system under an alternative description." Cf. "The Historiography of Philosophy: Four Genres," in ed. *Philosophy in History* Rorty, Schneewind, and Skinner (Cambridge: Cambridge University Press, 1984), 49.

5. Compare Rorty's conclusion to *The Consequences of Pragmatism* 213–14, with Russell's attitude, evident throughout his *History of Western Philosophy* (London: George Allan & Unwin, 1946).

6. Cf. his *Autobiography* (Oxford: The Clarendon Press, 1939), 27–31.

7. Alasdair MacIntyre, "The Relationship of Philosophy to Its Past," in *Philosophy in History*, ed. Rorty, Schneewind, and Skinner, 31.

8. The quotations are from Hans Reichenbach, *The Rise of Scientific Philosophy* (Berkeley: University of California Press, 1951), 121; the endorsement by Rorty of at least the more radical of Reichenbach's negative historical assessments is found in *Consequences of Pragmatism*, 214.

9. Bruce Wilshire comments at length on such developments in *The Moral Collapse of the University* (Albany, NY: The State University of New York Press, 1989).

10. Thomas Kuhn, *The Structure of Scientific Revolutions* (1960; rev. ed., Chicago: University of Chicago Press, 1972).

11. "The Relationship of Philosophy to Its Past," 32.

12. As, for example, in G. E. Moore's famous "refutation" of idealism in *Principia Ethica* (Cambridge: Cambridge University Press, 1903), in which the quotations cited are from A. E. Taylor, *Elements of Metaphysics* (London: Methuen, 1903), and the position refuted is at best marginally related to Berkeley's idealism, and not at all relevant of the mystical monism of Bradley or to the "objective" or "Absolute" idealism of Hegel, with which Moore had no direct acquaintance.

13. Arthur Danto, *The Philosophical Disenfranchisement of Art* (New York: Columbia University Press, 1986), 140.

14. Cf. the essays in *Post Analytic Philosophy*, ed. John Rajchman and Cornel West (New York: Columbia University Press, 1985). For a more intercontinental treatment of these issues, see *After Philosophy: End or Transformation?* ed. Baynes, Bohman, and McCarthy (Cambridge, MA: MIT Press, 1987).

15. Cf. Lynn Sumida Joy, *Gassendi the Atomist: Advocate of History in an Age of Science* (London: Cambridge University Press, 1987), part 2 ch. 5, esp. 103–5 for a summary of Gassendi's concerns both over linguistic and over ontological incoherence inherent in the use by Galileo, Kepler, and others of mathematical demonstrations to model quite distinct physical processes. The quotations on Gassendi's opposition to disciplinary distinctions are found at 19.

16. Such arguments regarding the history of art were made during the pre-Raphaelite movement; but I maintain that this polemical treatment of the history of art did not ever constitute the norm for understanding art history, as it did for the history of philosophy.

17. "Five Parables," 114–19.

18. Cf. Hacking, "Five Parables," 117–19, and Alasdair MacIntyre, "Epistemological Crises, Dramatic Narrative, and the Philosophy of Science," *The Monist* 60, no. 4 (October, 1977): 464. MacIntyre updates this Kuhnian diagnosis of the social sciences in their debates of Kuhn and the "end of ideology" in their fields in his recent Aquinas Lecture. Cf. *First Principles, Final Ends, and Contemporary Philosophical Issues* (Milwaukee, WI: Marquette University Press, 1990), 21.

19. "Nihilism is fundamentally an attempt to overcome or to repudiate the past on behalf of an unknown and unknowable yet hoped-for future. The danger implicit in this attempt is that it seems necessarily to entail a negation of the present, or to remove the ground upon which man must stand in order to carry out or even merely to witness the process of historical transformation. . . . The nihilist invokes us to destroy the past on behalf of a wish which he cannot articulate, let alone guarantee fulfillment" (Stanley Rosen, *Nihilism* [New Haven, CT: Yale University Press, 1969], 140).

20. These developments were both chronicled and characterized by the contributors to Robert C. Neville's recent anthology, *New Essays in Metaphysics* (Albany: The State University of New York Press, 1987). Collectively, the concept of metaphysics advocated in these essays follows closely the model first set forth by Collingwood in his *Essay on Metaphysics* (Oxford: Oxford University Press, 1940), part 2, chs. 6 and 7.

21. "The Historiography of Philosophy: 4 genres," 65–67.

22. Foucault, "Questions of Method," in *After Philosophy*, 104.

23. Cf. Jacques Derrida, *Margins of Philosophy* (Chicago: University of Chicago Press, 1982).

24. Such claims are found throughout the essays in Stanley Rosen, *The Ancients and the Moderns* (New Haven, CT: Yale University Press, 1990), as well as in Rosen, *Hermeneutics as Politics* (London: Oxford University Press, 1987).

25. "The authorities of the temple of Zeus at Dodona, my friend, said that the first prophetic utterances came from an oak tree. In fact the people of those days, lacking the wisdom of you young people, were content in their simplicity to listen to trees or rocks, provided these told the truth. For you [Phaedrus], apparently it makes a difference who the speaker is, and what country he comes from" (*Phaedrus* 275 b–c; trans. R. Hackforth, in *Plato: the Collected Dialogues*, ed. Edith Hamilton and

Huntington Cairns [Princeton, NJ: Princeton University Press, 1961], 520.

This passage occurs in the midst of Socrates' denunciation of writing, upon which Derrida is commenting. The passage itself, in dialogical context, also has (by implication) something rather interesting to say about the contemporary practice of "celebrity philosophy." I am grateful to Patricia Cook for several very pointed and helpful exchanges of views regarding this passage.

26. I tend toward Paul Ricoeur's view that the relationship between "understanding" and "explanation" should not be viewed simply as one of opposition; rather "understanding precedes, accompanies, closes, and thus *envelops* explanation. In return, explanation *develops* understanding analytically." Cf. *The Philosophy of Paul Ricoeur: An Anthology of His Work*, ed. C. Reagan and D. Stewart (Boston: Beacon Press, 1978), 165.

27. See *The Foundations of Psychoanalysis: A Philosophical Critique* (Berkeley, CA: University of California Press, 1984).

28. I offer a succinct account of MacIntyre's neo-Aristotelian formulation of totalizing narratives and their role in scientific revolutions in "Refutation, Narrative, and Engagement: Three Conceptions of the History of Philosophy," in *Philosophical Imagination and Cultural Memory*, ed. Patricia J. Cook (Durham, NC: Duke University Press, 1993).

29. See, for example, "Hermeneutics as Practical Philosophy," in *Reason in the Age of Science*, trans. Frederick G. Lawrence (Cambridge, MA: MIT Press, 1981), 94–97.

Thomas P. Kasulis

# Intimations of Religious Experience and Interreligious Truth

As a student of John E. Smith, I try to keep three points in mind when I consider an issue in the philosophy of religion. First, I try to remember that I should bring my analysis to the religious experience in all its richness and complexity. I try not to let the categories of analysis impoverish the nature of the experience. If the experience does not fit my epistemological categories, I try to rethink my epistemology before I let the theory convince me there is something "wrong" or "philosophically suspicious" with the experience. This does not mean that I never conclude a religious person, doctrine, or action is wrong, but I do check my tools of analysis for distortion before I jump to a hasty conclusion.

Second, I try to remember that religion, like most other cultural phenomena, has an intrinsically social or communal dimension. I am continually shocked, for example, at how often philosophers of religion try to analyze a particular religious utterance without first asking who the audience of that utterance is and what practices and assumptions the audience and speaker might share. For too many philosophers of religion, religious belief, religious statements, and religious practices are treated as if they were totally individual affairs, rather than things that both derive from and constitute communal existence.

Third, from early in my graduate school career, Smith convinced me of the inescapability of pluralism in our society and our world today. Whether we like it or not, people experience life through different world views and as philosophers we need to understand and account for those differences. Even more important, however, Smith showed me that pluralism is not only unavoidable, but also useful to philosophical reflection. If constructively engaged, the plurality of voices, contexts, and perspectives leads us all to reexamine our most fundamental assumptions. This is especially provocative philosophically when those assumptions have been so deeply embedded in our ways of thinking that if it were not for the other perspectives, we might not even notice them, not to mention question them.

So, about twenty-five years ago John Smith pushed me out of the warm nest of the cozy issues that so often define philosophy of religion textbooks: the study of arguments about theodicy or the existence of God, for example. Many of these issues are secularized versions of what have been, and still often are, the grist of theology courses in seminaries. Once he saw my natural inclinations, Smith encouraged me to go off to Hawaii and Japan to learn Japanese and to get closer to the experience of religious people from traditions such as Buddhism for whom the existence of God is not even an issue, not to mention an argument.

One of Smith's most endearing qualities as a teacher is that he does not try to fit his students into his own mold. He does not try to establish a "school" of philosophy in which his students should or must enroll. Like the pragmatists he admires, he realizes that thought, if it is not to become vacuous or overly professionalized, must address the "problematic." Smith has a gift for helping students find that problematic within themselves and then encourages them to address it. If this means that his students go off in many directions (and, as in my case, to many corners of the world), so be it. It adds to the pluralism, and, just as important, because we address the problems we find in our own experiences, we continually revitalize our own thought. We become a philosophical community that continues to engage ourselves and the world.

Because of the philosophical adventure Smith encouraged me to take, I find myself in communities of discourse that barely existed a quarter century ago. One of these is the community of "Buddhist-

Christian dialogue." When I bring my philosophical reflection to my experience of that dialogue, many questions arise. A problematic emerges.

Sometimes I find people saying what I have heard them say to each other in their own traditional communities, but also sometimes I find they say something new. What happens to religious discourse when it enters into this cross-traditional dialogue? The term *truth* is a good example of a key term that seems to shift its coloration depending on whether it is being used to address one's fellow believers or a community consisting of nonbelievers (or believers who believe in something else). As a philosopher, this situation intrigues me, and I discovered early on that some of the common philosophical theories of language and truth did not quite fit the situation in a way that helped me address what is actually going on. As suggested by the first principle I learned from Smith, that caused me to rethink my theories of language and knowledge. I found I had to generate an analysis of what I call "intimation" as a mode of discourse and of "expert" or "intimate" knowledge as a mode of cognition.

At the same time, I have found the second principle concerning community and audience pertinent. To whom are people in this dialogue speaking when they speak as they do? What kinds of communities were involved, and how did the statements address those different communities' concerns?

Finally, the very existence of this kind of dialogue attests to the pluralism Smith taught me to respect. It is an inevitable encounter: even in the world of business Christians find themselves interacting increasingly with Buddhists, Hindus, and Muslims, as well as Catholics, Protestants, and Jews. As much as it might be more comfortable if these differences among us human beings might simply go away, they will not. The daily news reports continually remind us of the importance of recognizing these differences and coming to grips with them. Even in the United States, there are now more Muslims than Jews.

At the same time, the recognition of the pluralism occasions new opportunities for interreligious contact and dialogue. But what are the ground rules for such dialogue? I have found that if misunderstandings are to be avoided, the participants need to be more critical and self-reflective. Using my revamped notions of intimation and communal audience, I hope I can shed some light on how that critical self-reflection might begin. With these preliminary points in mind, let us enter into this experience of interreligious dialogue and try to reflect on its nature, its promise, and its obstacles.

In the religious pluralistic world in which we live, we are generally learning to accept and live with our differences, to make tolerance rather than persecution the norm, to engage in dialogue rather than confrontation. This openness to traditions other than our own is laudable. Interreligious understanding is at its highest level in history. We have made such progress because we could temporarily suspend our own religious beliefs to see the other view without prejudice.

At some point, however, particularly for those of us with a philosophical bent, we must face the issue of truth. Are the statements we hear from the other religion justified? Have they been, or can they be, verified? Can that religion and my religion both be right? These are nasty questions, the makings of heated argument. These are the kinds of religious issues that, along with politics, nice people do not bring up at a party. But when the music is over, and we go out into the dark night to return home, *quo vadis*? which path do you follow?

For the past several years, I have been an observer of, and sometime participant in, Buddhist-Christian dialogue. I have seen politeness occasionally take over the discussion so that individuals talked about soul and *anātman* with as much detachment as discussing the differences between beef stew and sukiyaki. The terminology of the census taker notwithstanding, however, religion is not a preference. It is a commitment. And few of us would consciously commit ourselves to a position we know to be false. So we cannot take it lightly when another person comes along who is equally committed to a view which, if true, entails the falseness of our own religious beliefs.

In looking for truth across boundaries, we should avoid two oversimplifications. The first error would be to think that all significant religious statements have embedded within them propositions asserting universal truth. According to that mistaken approach, what is true in religion must be objective and publicly verifiable. This is merely a case of trying to submit religious statements to the same criteria used in evaluating empirical statements.

The other erroneous approach, one often arising as a foil to the previous view, considers religious discourse to be no more than the expression or report of an inclination, feeling, or sentiment. In other words, religious language is subjective and personal, or at least communally restricted. From this perspective, to say "Jesus Christ is Lord" is not much different in form from saying "Chocolate tastes good," which itself can be further analyzed into "We like chocolate" or "We eat chocolate whenever we can" or even "Chocolate—yummy!" According to such an analysis, nothing universal about chocolate or Jesus Christ is being asserted; the statement only expresses something about my attitude or behavior toward an object. In short, from this mistaken vantage point, religious language is no more than the report of subjective states of mind or will.

Faced with the dilemma of choosing between these two simplistic views of truth in religious language, it is tempting to avoid both extremes by claiming that religious language is *sui generis*, intrinsically unlike any other form of discourse. This approach has the unfortunate consequence of hermetically, and hermeneutically, sealing off religious discourse from all other speech acts and their analyses. In so doing, we run the risk of also isolating religion from everyday experience. Therefore, it would be better to find another way of dealing with the dilemma.

The dilemma is actually a false one. There is another alternative, one more in tune with our experience of how religious language works. Unfortunately, we often overlook this alternative because of a weakness in our dominant epistemological theories. Specifically, our theories tend to assume that knowledge is either objective and public or subjective and private. Because of that epistemological premise, we can inadvertently distort our experience of religious language in order to make it fit our premise. Of course, it should be the other way around: we should adjust our theory to fit the reality of the experience. In fact, there does exist a common form of knowledge that is objective but nonpublic, and it is a form of knowing experienced commonly in everyday life. Because our epistemologies slight its importance, we tend to ignore an important dimension of religious knowledge and the language it uses.

To develop an analysis of religious discourse that adequately describes the experience of speaking religiously, we must, therefore, first enrich our common epistemological assumptions. In particular, what kind of knowledge is objective, but nonpublic? Consider the case of a judge in a gymnastic, diving, surfing, or figure skating competition. The judge's score has two components: a degree-of-difficulty rating and a style or form rating. The grounds for the first are generally objective and public, and certain maneuvers are, without exception, rated at a given level of difficulty. It is the other part of the judgment, however, that concerns us here.

On one hand, the judge's rating for style is objective. The different evaluators are expected to quantify the performance with nearly identical scores (on the championship level, scores seldom vary more than 5 percent). Indeed, if the variation is too large, coaches will often accuse the judges of political bias. In other words, the accusation is dishonesty. Yet, dishonesty only has significance when a claim to objective truth can be made. The judges are doing more than signifying how much they subjectively *liked* the performance; they are objectively evaluating the performance. Where there is objectivity we expect fundamental agreement.

On the other hand, the judge's evaluation for style is *not* publicly verifiable like the degree-of-difficulty score. If a diver does a backward dive with two somersaults, that aspect of the performance could be seen by anyone. The rule book dictates how many points for difficulty such a dive is awarded. Similarly, the gymnastics judge uses a publicly verifiable form of judgment in declaring a performer to have illegally stepped outside the designated area for performing a free-style exercise. In such a case, a properly placed television camera may decisively show whether the judge's call was correct or not. For the style rating, however, the videotape replay can never establish whether the assigned score is correct. The judge's expert knowledge, although considered objective, is not based on publicly verifiable evidence.

How does one achieve such an objective, but not publicly verifiable, knowledge? The judge's expert or intimate knowledge of gymnastics is not taught through a discursive, book-learning process. Rather, the judge learns about excellence in style through years of praxis within the sport. In effect, the knowledge is achieved through apprenticeship. The individual learns by practicing gymnastics oneself, by observing masters, by coaching, by being judged, and by judging; in short, by being a practicing member of the gymnastics community.

We may note that much cultural learning occurs in a similar way. The members of one culture will generally share, for example, a sense of which musical tones, colors, or tastes coordinate well with each other. Similarly, certain behaviors will be considered appropriate and others impolite. Across cultures there may be disagreements, but when one knows of no other culture, one's own tradition will be taken to be objective and universal.

The relevance to religious knowledge can now be stated. Religious knowledge is primarily expert knowledge of an objective, but nonpublic, form. It is learned through praxis in a specific community, and it is not primarily communicated through ordinary discursive linguistic techniques. It derives from an acquired sensitivity rather than from step-by-step, explicit instruction. Religious knowledge is closer to the way a loving parent intuitively knows a child than the way a scientist knows a natural phenomenon; it is closer to the way a connoisseur evaluates a wine than the way a person selects a color for a new automobile. The truth of religious knowledge most often requires a particular form of communication, namely, intimation.

The word *intimation* derives from the Latin root *intimāre*, "to make known." In its earlier English usage, an intimation was a formal notice or announcement such as a constitution's "intimation of rights." In its modern use, of course, it is a suggestion or hint as in "he gave no intimation he would soon be leaving us." In both cases, the term preserves its etymological sense of conveying or revealing information.

For our purposes, it is useful to think of intimation in conjunction with intimacy. The word *intimacy* derives from the Latin *intimus* which means, interestingly enough, either "innermost" or "close friend." An intimation is, after all, a hint of one's inner feelings revealed to one's intimates. An intimation is not public in the sense that its message is for everyone. Rather, it is an encoded language that conveys information to an insider while not revealing its inner meaning to an outsider.

The more profound the intimacy, the more goes unsaid: the need to be explicit, the effort to explain, and the urge to fill in the silence all become secondary to ever deeper levels of intimation. To one's inner circle, a tremble of the eyelid, a pucker at the side of the mouth, a subtle gesture, or a barely audible sigh expresses all that is necessary. Among those who have shared their innermost selves for years, such intimations communicate more than hours of chatter about one's personal concerns. An intimate is someone to whom we feel free to say anything, but ironically, do not have to speak at all to be understood.

Intimation is clearly an appropriate mode of religious discourse. First, religious language is primarily meant for those within the community. In today's context of interreligious dialogue, it is easy to forget that most religious language was developed within a given religious community for the members of that community. It was intended for insiders, not outsiders. Whenever we intellectually eavesdrop on the speech of people from a foreign spiritual tradition, we may totally misconstrue the context, mood, and purpose of a given utterance. The language is encoded with special terms, intonations, and even gestures that may have great significance to a member of the group, but be obscure or even imperceptible to someone else.

In this regard, it is useful to think of humorous intimations as a parallel. An insider joke is funny only to those people with a common set of experiences and values. We have all at some time tried to explain an in-joke to an outsider and, even though we may have succeeded in communicating the content of the joke, the outsider still did not find it humorous. At such times we often mutter, "Well, you had to *be* there." Where is there? Within the intimate circle of the group. It is not simply a matter of being present when the joke was told. An insider to the group may have been absent when the joke was originally told, but will find the retelling funny nonetheless. However, an outsider to the intimate circle may be present when the joke is first told, but still not find it humorous, even though everyone else is laughing.

Similarly, when an outsider to a religious tradition hears the religious statement, the observer may or may not get it. Like some jokes, much religious discourse is aimed at a specific intimate community having a set of common experiences, practices, and values. If we take a joke out of its context and analyze it, the words may not change, but it will not do the same thing as it did in its original context. In the same way, a religious statement should not be analyzed outside its original context.

The consideration of religious context leads us to the second dimension of religious language as the intimation of an objective, nonpublic form of knowledge. When the religious speaker makes an intimation to an audience who, it is assumed, will "get it," the speaker assumes a shared spiritual praxis. Through that praxis, the individual is impressed by the symbol system of the tradition until the individual spontaneously expresses those symbols in one's own action. The purpose of the praxis is to develop the person's sensitivity to what the particular religious community finds objective, but nonpublic. We can draw a parallel with music appreciation.

Suppose a couple, not wishing to be authoritarian, tried to be completely undirective in the development of their children's tastes, including their taste in music. There are many varieties of music, ranging from classical to rock to folk to jazz, and different people obviously prefer different genres. Afraid they might inadvertently influence their children's taste in music by exposing them more to one variety than another, the parents had a special device implanted in their children's ears so they would be incapable of hearing musical tones at all. Then, on reaching adulthood, the device would be removed and they would hear music for the first time. As freely choosing adults, they could then decide which music they liked best.

Such a plan could be a disaster. Suddenly hearing all the forms of music for the first time, the young adults might be disoriented and alienated, possibly enough to request the device be reimplanted. On a more limited level, we often have the same sense of disorientation, for example, when we first hear the music of an alien culture, especially if its rhythmic and tonal qualities are unlike those to which we are accustomed. The more we hear different kinds of music, however, the more readily we can overcome the sense of disorientation. This suggests that the best way to develop taste in music is by exposing the children to it as much as possible, letting the children have the personal experience of playing an instrument, singing, learning to read music, and studying the works of masters in different genres. As the children mature, their sensitivity, nurtured by the expert knowledge inherited from one's cultural tradition, will develop naturally. In other words, by participating in the praxis of musical appreciation, the child comes to appreciate music.

The development of the religious person is much the same. A sensitivity to religious language develops within the praxis of a religious tradition. The outsider to the praxis may, therefore, be as insensitive to the character of the language as a person who had heard of music without ever having heard music. In fact, in dealing with intimate, nondiscursive forms of knowledge, the discourse is often more about the praxis behind the knowledge than about the knowledge itself. Let us consider another analogous example.

How often have we witnessed the following conversation in a postgame television interview?

Interviewer: "Great game, Buck. With less than thirty seconds left, you broke loose for the winning touchdown. Tell the fans at

> home—how did you know when to cut against the grain like that?"
>
> Buck: "Well, we started with a quick-opener on the right side. When I made my cut, there was no hole. But then I saw daylight on the other side, so I just took it."

Buck's answer is genuinely disappointing. By watching the game on television, we already knew as much. The interviewer asked why Buck knew what to do, and Buck simply told us what he did. Obviously, Buck did not know how he knew what to do.

Now let us imagine Buck, abashed by his initial lack of articulation, gave the matter some deeper reflection. The next time he is asked about the big play, he responds as follows.

> Buck: "Do you mean how did I know where to look for the daylight? Well, first of all, we practice that play maybe ten times a day, so our defense can read it pretty well and react quickly to it. In practice, then, the hole is often not there, and I guess I've just formed the habit of always checking the opposite side. Actually I probably made virtually the same move maybe a hundred times in practice. It was just a matter of seeing it and doing it during the game."

At first glance, this description is more satisfying. On reflection, though, we realize that Buck has still not answered the interviewer's question. In fact, with a few minor word changes, Buck's description would be true of virtually any play, not just the game-winner. What Buck has done is shift from describing the play to describing the praxis of football training. Although the reporter has asked about the uniqueness of the play, the answer is only an explanation of constants in all plays.

The question we must consider is whether any adequate reply could be offered. In an important sense, the answer is no. Buck can explain how he became a football star, but not the special knowledge learned through training. How does a baseball pitcher know when to throw a change-up? How does a prosecuting attorney know when to press a witness further and when to back away? How does a teacher know which example will help the student? How does a parent know when a child is worried? One cannot exactly say. The best one can do, as Buck did in his more reflective mood, is explain the practical experience, perhaps the praxis guided by an expert or master, that brought one to that intimate, expert knowledge. Indeed, if a completely satisfactory explanation of the intimate knowledge were given, that would prove the praxis bogus. There was no point in Buck's spending hundreds of hours practicing on the field, if what he knew could have been explained via a blackboard diagram.

Religious knowledge is similar. It emerges in the context of a religious praxis and is not communicated directly to outsiders. When an outsider asks about the nature of that knowledge, the religious speaker is often, like Buck, at a loss, tending either to describe a significant event or to explain the praxis resulting in the knowledge. Religious language, as a facet of religious praxis aimed at people within the tradition, primarily attempts to sensitize the person to an objective reality not publicly observable. The religious adept, like the coach or accomplished player, is sensitive to nuances invisible to the nonexpert, yet objectively there for the sensitized insiders. For the person who knows a truth in a religious way, the basis and character of the knowledge itself cannot be related directly. The knowledge is typically only intimated in language and gestures significant to people within the tradition, but not fully intelligible to those outside it.

Does this mean that interreligious communication is impossible? Does this imply that religious truth is not open to discussion across boundaries? Not necessarily. But we must be alert to the differences between religious truth within a tradition versus religious truth about a tradition. One uses the language of intimation; the other the language of discursive explication. One last parallel with yet another example of expert knowledge will help us here.

Consider the role played by the critic in some field of specialization. Music critics, for example, do not speak as musicians or even as voice coaches, but neither are they outsiders to musical circles. Critics stand in the boundary area and interpret what is within the circle for those outside it. The actors in a play, for example, try to suggest truths about the human condition. The director tries to find those truths in the script and to sensitize the actors to it through coaching. The critics, on the other hand, explain and evaluate that truth for a larger audience. In short, the critic tries to explicate discursively what is only intimated in the performance. Let us apply this now to the situation of talking about and in religious discourse.

Religious discourse occurs, therefore, in at least three dimensions. Within the circle of intimacy established by religious praxis, we find mostly intimation. Such suggestive expression sensitizes the adept to objective realities not ordinarily available to outsiders. Insofar as this language is by and for insiders and its truths knowable only to those trained in the praxis, truth claims on this level cannot be evaluated by outsiders. However, we must remember that this level of religious discourse is not reducible to mere performatives having no truth value, nor is the truth reduced to the personal and subjective. The truth on this level is the truth of objective, but nonpublic, expert knowledge. Profound disagreement among insiders about the truth of various claims is what leads to accusations of heresy and schisms, for example, just as such disagreements among gymnastic judges lead to accusations of dishonesty and political favoritism.

On the second level, we find the discourse of critics, including most of the scholars of religion, particularly those in the history, phenomenology, and sometimes philosophy, of religion. These critics interpret the intimations of the inner circle to those outside it. They cannot express the truths known within the circle; the outsiders cannot be discursively taught what only an expert can know through years of praxis. Yet, the outsiders can be taught about the training, the praxis of the expert. They can be sensitized to the presence of intimations and made to recognize that, as outsiders, they cannot evaluate the truth of what they have not been trained to notice. Within this dimension, religious discourse is somewhat more public. If one critic says Buddhists do *x* and another says they do not, we expect the argument to be settled on publicly available grounds. If, on the other hand, one critic says a particular Buddhist intimation can be interpreted discursively as meaning *x* and another critic disagrees, only other critics (or insiders who can stand enough outside their own tradition to critique it) can adjudicate the matter. A complete outsider obviously has no grounds for deciding whose interpretation is correct.

The third level of criticism is most distant from the inner circle and, consequently, most public in its truth claims. This is the level of what we might call "metacriticism" or "comparative criticism." Critics involved in this enterprise, whether technically philosophers, historians, social scientists, or whatever, address the nature of religion itself across traditions. There is, for example, a difference between someone writing a general philosophy of art and someone who is a newspaper art critic. In effect, the metacritic builds on the observations of critics to formulate a general theory. This chapter is itself an example of metacriticism. To determine whether my claims about religious discourse are true, one can evaluate my theory in light of generally accepted observations by critics of various religious traditions. However, we should note that the metacritical perspective makes no religious truth claims itself. It does not adjudicate religious truth, but rather tries to explain what truth means in a religious context.

If this general characterization of religious discourse and its truth is correct, how should we approach the issue of truth across religious boundaries? I will conclude with a few general remarks. For the sake of concreteness, I will use the example of Buddhist-Christian dialogue about truth, but the principles here would apply, with some modification, to any dialogue between significantly different traditions.

First, we may quickly handle the area of metacritical truth. Since metacritical truth claims are not themselves religious but claims about religion, they do not really have much bearing on the question at hand. We must note one precaution, however. Since metacritical theories use critical interpretations as their foundation, if the methodology of the critical interpretations is faulty, the metacritical theory will crumble. In particular, if critics of religion confuse intimations within a religious tradition with discursive explanations for persons outside the tradition, the metacritic may be grossly misled.

In this regard many metacritical theories have treated religion as intrinsically irrational, nonobjective, and nontruth-claiming. These accounts developed out of the confusion caused by critics who tried to explain a religious perspective by simply repeating intimations found in the praxis of that religion. Some grossly inaccurate metacritical interpretations of the religious character of Zen Buddhism, for example, can be traced to D. T. Suzuki's unclarity about whether he was describing how nothingness is discussed intimately in Zen practice or whether he was attempting to explain to non-Zen Buddhists what nothingness means. The Kyoto School philosopher, Nishitani Keiji, for example, would better exemplify a critical standpoint at the boundary of Zen in his book *Religion and Nothingness.* Based on Nishitani's discussions instead of Suzuki's, one would be unlikely to say baldly that Zen is an irrational religion rejecting all concepts and theories.

Second, for evaluating questions of truth, there is little to be gained from the direct dialogue between, say, a Buddhist speaking religiously as a Buddhist and a Christian as a Christian. On the face of the matter, this seems an odd conclusion. After all, it is the Buddhist who has the strongest conviction about the truths of Buddhism and the Christian of Christianity.

Yet, as we have seen, Buddhist discourse is primarily designed as intimations for fellow Buddhists and Christian discourse for fellow Christians. If the Buddhist and the Christian are to understand each other, they must develop a mode of discourse specifically designed for speaking with each other. This implies that certain phraseology central to the religious praxis may be abandoned for the sake of dialogue and radically new terminology developed. It is as counterproductive for a Buddhist and Christian to share their traditions' intimations as it is to keep telling inside jokes to an outsider. At some point, you must stop telling inside jokes, or try to explain the context, or find a way of bringing the outsider inside.

It is not that dialogue between Buddhists as Buddhists and Christians as Christians is totally worthless. It is only worthless for evaluating claims to truth. Such dialogue does serve the important goal of tolerance and appreciation of each other as human beings. It is comparable to, say, the spontaneous sharing of folk songs that often occurs when an international group gets together around a campfire or at a party. No one understands the other person's songs, but the activity contributes to goodwill. I assume, correctly it is hoped, that such goodwill already exists between Buddhists and Christians, at least among those who would even entertain the idea of interreligious conversation.

Third, if the points innermost and outermost to the religious tradition are not the grounds for the discussion of interreligious truth, the burden must rest primarily on the level of religious criticism. The complexity of the task must not be taken lightly. What must be primarily compared and evaluated is not, for example, Buddhist discourse and Christian discourse. Such discourse is too heavily laden with intimations appropriate only for those within the religious praxis. Admittedly, some religious discourse is analyzable straightforwardly outside the tradition. For example, when a Christian claims Jesus was born in Bethlehem, that statement is either true or false, and its verification has nothing whatsoever to do with one's being in the Christian community or not. Yet, almost all the important statements such as "Jesus Christ is the incarnation of the second person of trinity" is a statement of Christian belief before fellow Christians. Unless we are in the in-group of that religion, we run the risk of not "getting" the statement in the way we might not "get" an insider joke.

Again, we must not fall into the trap of saying the truth of such a statement is merely subjective or tradition bound. The claim is about an objective, albeit nonpublic, truth. If one wants to verify that statement, the Christian might say, one must first become expert in the sensitizing process of Christian praxis. Then one can judge the reality for oneself. Just as we are not qualified to make expert judgments about the style of gymnastics performances unless we are involved in the praxis of gymnastics, we are not qualified to make judgments about religious performance (linguistic or otherwise) unless we are part of that praxis.

Historically, in propagating their religions across the world, Buddhists and Christians have, therefore, often emphasized the "try it, you'll see" approach to religious truth, rather than a "we'll submit public evidence to prove" tactic. That is, religious truth was found within religious praxis. Consequently, most religions have not tried very often to articulate their views for public scrutiny and verification, at least in any open sense of dialogue rather than dogmatic debate. Scrutiny has been restricted mostly to insiders. Since most crucial truth claims of a religious tradition are intimations rather than public explanations, the scholarly critics of religion must interpret those intimations for the larger public. These interpretations will become the basis for interreligious dialogue with regard to truth.

At least in passing, we should note a problem that can occur in religious proselytizing. A praxis-embedded principle can be inappropriately universalized by religious adherents. For example, the claim that something is necessary to achieving expert knowledge of *x* can incorrectly be exaggerated into a claim that it is simply necessary to achieve "truth." This confuses the objectivity of nonpublic expert knowledge with the objectivity of universal, public knowledge. For instance, as a gymnast, there are some practices one must do if one is to be good. That does not mean that all good people must do those practices. If one does not follow the principles of gymnastic praxis, one may never be able to make true judgments about the style of a gymnastic performance. One will not be sensitized to see what is objectively, but nonpublicly, there. Yet, one is certainly entitled as an individual not to be concerned about the objective truth of gymnastic judgments.

Perhaps the parallel holds for at least some kinds of religious claims to truth. There may be an objective (nonpublic) truth that is discernible only through years of involvement in Aztec praxis, for example. It is then correct to say that "unless I adopt the way of the Aztec, I will never know the truth" if "truth" here refers specifically to that objective truth known through the expert knowledge achieved in Aztec practice. Of course, that same Aztec may not be able to see the objective truth in a judgment about gymnastics. We can only exert our energies into so many praxes in one lifetime.

Certainly, this issue of universalization is compounded by the fact that many religions seem to make "metaphysical" claims and, therefore, create problems of incompatibility with the claims of other religions (or of science, for that matter). The problem is not as profound, however, if we remember the audience of the apparent metaphysical statements. The religious discourse was originally developed for those within the religious community of shared praxis. Hence, they may be intimations for insiders that have been incorrectly taken as statements of public truth. To shift again to sport analogies, our football player might well talk to fellow sports enthusiasts about the "momentum" of the game or how the quarterback was "hot" in the third quarter. Yet, if an unwitting physics student tried to measure that momentum or heat, it would not be there. Is there a true opposition here between the metaphysics of football and the metaphysics of physics? Certainly not. Is one sense of "momentum" subjective and the other objective? Certainly not. To every one of the fans watching the game, the momentum was as objectively there as the momentum one feels in a speeding car trying to make a sudden stop. The difference is that the momentum at the game was not *publicly* objective. A person who knows nothing about sports and who watches the game on television would probably not sense it at all, yet *anyone* who was conscious in that speeding automobile would sense the physical momentum. Perhaps, and this hypothesis would demand a great deal of study, many statements in religious traditions that are taken to be claims about objective public reality are really claims about objective nonpublic reality truly experienced by people in the appropriate praxis. If so, the claims of religion about truth may not be as universally applicable (and therefore inconsistent across traditions) as many people think. Yet, that does not mean the truths of religion are not objective.

In short, those who stand on the boundaries between the religious insiders and the outsiders—those whom I call the "critics"—will have to say things for Christians that Christians may never have said before. The same will be true for the critics' role in restating Buddhism. In other words, rather than trying to explain what atonement, say, means for a Christian or satori for a Zen Buddhist, the critics will, in effect, have to say what atonement means for a non-Christian, satori for a non-Buddhist. Only then can at least a semipublic evaluation of religious truth claims be undertaken.

This development, of course, augurs a new development in religious consciousness, a new way of understanding a world religion. Up to now, we have tended to think of a world religion as a tradition that embraces within itself the world, in a sense, welcoming into its intimate circle anyone willing to undertake its praxis. Now, however, in the context of interreligious dialogue, we can see a different sense as well. A world religion can be understood as a tradition that presents itself to the world, gives an account of its truth to outsiders. Obviously, such a development will be difficult and time-consuming. The members of the tradition must be in constant dialogue with its critics, its interpreters to the outside. Of course, some of the critics will also be recognized authorities within the tradition as well, although I suspect this will be rather rare. After all, to be a good Zen Buddhist, to be a good master for Zen Buddhists, is quite different from being able to explain Zen Buddhism to outsiders. How many great artists are also great art critics?

Fourth, another kind of interreligious dialogue about truth is possible, but it can be so intimate, it is difficult to analyze in general terms. Namely, the Buddhist may become a Buddhist-Christian, the Christian a Christian-Buddhist. This involves much more than studying the other religion and having fireside chats with some of its members. It involves a commitment to the religious praxis of the other tradition. One must become enough a part of the other community that one is profoundly impressed by its symbols and can express oneself fully through them. One must become, as it were, a native speaker of that tradition's intimations. The spiritual problematic in that formerly foreign tradition must become one's own problematic.

For this model, authentic Buddhist-Christian dialogue is primarily a discussion within oneself, the member of both communities. The quest is not for truth as public verification, but rather for truth as self-understanding, truth as the litmus test of internal consistency. Now a Buddhist as well as a Christian, the person speaks to Buddhists as a Buddhist and to Christians as a Christian. Each community recognizes the speaker as one of its own, appreciates her or his intimations, yet also recognizes in the person's interpretations a freshness of nuance and emphasis.

In seeking truth, the individual involved in this process attempts a self-consistency by giving traditional discourse an interpretation consistent with the whole fabric of one's own beliefs and simultaneously acceptable as an interpretation to the religious communities involved. This resembles a coherence rather than correspondence theory of truth. One's own position is both internally consistent and consistent with each of the two traditions involved.

We must not take the terms *coherence* and *consistency* in too narrow a logical sense, however. The coherence spoken of here is not, for example, relationally transitive. In other words, this view does not require that Christianity as a whole be consistent with Buddhism as a whole, only that the particular individual's Buddhism (recognized as Buddhism by the Buddhist community) be consistent with that individual's Christianity (recognized as Christianity by the Christian community). If I am fully bilingual in, say, English and Japanese, I can express my humor effectively in either language. I tell jokes in Japanese that Japanese find funny and jokes in English that English speakers find funny. Both groups find me humorous, "one of the guys," a member of the in-group. However, it does not follow, that my Japanese jokes would be funny to English speakers or my English jokes to Japanese. Nor does it follow that I have two senses of humor just because I can be funny in either Japanese or English. Rather, I have one sense of humor that can be expressed in two different modes, one English and one Japanese.

Obviously, the presence of such bitraditional religious people will also be transformative. Accompanying the external dialogue between the members of the religious community and its critical interpreters to the world mentioned in the third point, there will also be an internal dialogue between the traditional and the new kind of member, between those who have always lived in one tradition and those who are living in two. These new external and internal dialogues will gradually clarify what is coincidental and contingent in cultural and historical trappings and what is essential to the core of praxis, intimation, and public articulation.

This is a startling and exciting development, but it is not completely new. We have been there before, for example, when Christianity went from the Aramaic and Judaic context to the Greco-Roman world community, when Chinese Taoists-turned-Buddhists translated the sutras from Sanskrit into Chinese. The major difference is that with two thousand years of experience under our belts, we are methodologically more self-conscious, or at least we should be. That is our debt to history.

Kuang-ming Wu

# The Spirit of Pragmatism and the Pragmatic Spirit[1]

Professor John Edwin Smith[2] is indisputably a major reference point in American pragmatic philosophy, which "reconstructs" Western philosophy by grounding thinking in the experiential matrix.[3] Such a pragmatism often is equated with the pragmatic thrust of Chinese philosophy. Moreover, as a philosopher in open pluralistic[4] America, Professor Smith is an ardent champion of communication across boundaries, both philosophical and cultural. His frequent lectures in conferences on Chinese philosophy benefit all participants, Chinese and non-Chinese alike.

This chapter picks up "pragmatism" in a broad sense[5] and follows what Smith began: interpreting pragmatism across cultural boundaries between American and Chinese thinking. Both share something pragmatic, yet they are somewhat different and they do well to communicate mutually. For, as Smith said, American pragmatists were all "devoted to the need for philosophical conversation cutting across party lines."[6] For Smith, communication involves comparative interpretation in three areas: inquiries into (1) same problems with same answers, (2) same problems with different answers, and (3) different problems with different answers.[7] This chapter adds one more area: (4)

seeing that even the same answers are produced in different contexts (philosophical, cultural), all the above amount to investigations of differences, which can only benefit all parties compared—complementing each other and deepening respective self-understandings.[8] Hence, comparative communication manifests "differences" so as to comprise a symbiotic community of differences.[9]

Thus the following pages concern four points: (1) Classical American philosophy and classical Chinese philosophy share humanism of a pragmatic sort. (2) However, family resemblance bespeaks family difference. American pragmatic humanism is scientific, instrumental, aggressive, problem-oriented, critical, and philosophizes about philosophizing. Chinese pragmatic humanism is harmonious, natural, cosmic, and concrete. (3) These differences come from different styles of reasoning. The Western spirit of pragmatism is a theoretical movement that coheres fragmentary experiences; the Chinese pragmatic spirit is a metaphorical story-telling that goes from a typical situation to situational universals. (4) These two styles of reasoning should come together to form a humanistic community of differences.

## I

Both classical American philosophy and classical Chinese philosophy are broadly humanistic and pragmatic. According to M. R. Konvitz and Gail Kennedy, "the word 'pragmatism' is a misnomer—because it is a noun. The pragmatists . . . are not adherents to a doctrine but proponents of a method."[10] One must go further. "Pragmatism" is not just method but a temper, a "sentiment of rationality" (James). Such a sentiment is a "spirit" that uses the method in a certain existential manner. Smith characterized the spirit as "a style, a stance" "deeply rooted in . . . people," an "unwritten philosophy," the "muscle" within our "formulated beliefs."[11]

Smith defines the spirit of American philosophy as having "a basically humanistic outlook."[12] Wing-tsit Chan characterized Chinese philosophy "with one word . . . humanism."[13] This humanism is deeply pragmatic, for American philosophy is as much dipped in experience as Chinese philosophy is full of reverence for nature (human and cosmic).

That pragmatic thinking both in America and in China is *humanistic* is important. For our life activity can run idle and become false to life.

As Smith said, when we do epistemology we tend to forget that "we do not know with epistemology."[14] Living that is disengaged from life becomes false. Only an engaged life is true, and only true life is worth living. An engaged life makes a difference to thought and action. Engaged thinking is part of, and indeed part and parcel of, true life, pragmatism broadly so called; here thinking is doing, praxis with a tangible difference to actual life and actual world. This was true even of Royce;[15] in his later years, Royce called his Absolute Idealism "Absolute Pragmatism."

Smith enables us to see how crucial it is to engage in *pragmatic* thinking and how central such thinking is *both* in American and in Chinese philosophies. He said, "I could not help but be struck by the parallels" between them. In a felicitous style reminiscent of the pragmatists themselves (both American and Chinese), Smith summarized the common undercurrent of pragmatic humanism both in American and in Chinese thinking when he compared Wang Yang-ming with American pragmatists on three counts.

First, there is a connection between purpose and thought; all activity is teleological (biological, evolutionary), all thought is activity, and so all thought is teleological. Knowledge leads and guides us in our inquiry toward becoming truly human; purpose directs and gives meaning to conduct.

Second, ideas have a transformatory power; to know kindness is to act kindly; thinking changes us and the world. To think is to adjust means to ends so as to change reality and harmonize feelings with reality, with our situation; otherwise thinking is not true thinking.

Third, action leads to knowledge, and to believe in something is to act it out truthfully, thereby confirming the person and his or her sincerity. And so, belief is tested in its being carried out in life; belief in equality should issue in equal treatment of other people.[16]

The common pragmatic *manner* of the flowing of this undercurrent—within both American and Chinese arenas—can be conveniently dubbed a family "spirit" that is pragmatism.

## II

This sharing of the humanistic outlook of pragmatism is a familylike sharing, with family resemblances as described above. But family resemblance entails family differences, that is, the common undercurrent of pragmatism flows one way among American philosophers and another way among the Chinese. Mencius is not quite a Chinese Dewey any more than James is an American Wang Yang-ming. This essay claims that the American spirit of pragmatism differs from the Chinese pragmatic spirit.

The American spirit of pragmatism insists, for Smith,[17] that thinking is an activity of solving problems; ideas must make a difference to human life; the earth can be civilized through scientific technology. Chan described the pragmatic spirit of Chinese humanism as "not the humanism that denies or slights a Supreme Power, but one that professes the unity of man and Heaven."[18] We see at once three aspects of difference between them.

First, in American humanism all human activities aim at changing a situation. As Peirce puts it, the quality of a thing, the idea of that object, is obtained as follows: "Consider what effects, which might conceivably have practical bearings, we conceive the object of our conception to have. Then, our conception of these effects is the whole of our conception of the object."[19] An idea's conceivable *effects* are its meaning. Similarly, for James, ideas reveal their meaning when we know the conduct to which they lead.[20] An idea is what makes practical difference to us through our acting on it, to let it guide our actions.[21] This is an intervening "aggressive enterprise" (Santayana).[22] Man is an external objective sovereign over the empire of instrumental intelligence (Dewey) that handles practical problems with scientific experimental method,[23] so as to deliberately transform real dissonances into real harmonies.

A shift of the wind is felt in Chinese humanism. Here all human endeavors are dipped in regardful harmony with nature, vernerated as "Heaven"; Chinese allusions to natural phenomena are often references to human affairs. In response to Confucius's sighing, "Filial and fraternal [love]—are they not [the] roots of human[e]ness?"[24] Mencius mused,

> Originative spring [keeps] bubbling, bubbling [forth], not stopping day [or] night, filling-up [every] crevasse and then flow-forward, going-all-the-way into the Four Seas. Whatever has origin-and-root [is] like this. . . . If [it is] without origin . . . its drying-up [we] can stand and wait [to see]. Therefore, [having one's] reputation exceed [true] conditions—[the] gentleman [is] ashamed [of] it.[25]
>
> Whoever has four buds [of human nature] in "myself" [and] knows [how to] expand all [of them] and fulfill them, is like [having the] fire starting to burn, [the] spring starting to reach-out.[26]

Mencius's contemporary Chuang Tzu nonchalantly said, "People never mirror [themselves] in streaming water, but mirror in still[ed] water."[27] Although opposed in sentiment (water welling up, water stopping still), all these references to nature refer to the self. Chinese people love to appeal to authority to make a point; they appeal to natural phenomena to make a point in human affairs. Chinese reverence of nature is unmistakable.

Second, American classical philosophers are serious about how to tackle problems, serious about means. By solving the questions of means, those of ends solve themselves. Science and technology are highly prized.[28] Dewey said that "means and ends are two names for the same reality."[29] The spirit of pragmatism is thus technical, future-oriented, and always in the process of accomplishing something to actively shape the future now.[30]

In contrast, echoing Chan, Smith said, "Chinese spirituality is . . . a Humanism . . . not of a reductive sort, that sees no place for a Supreme Power, but rather [one in] which human nature and Heaven are in essential unity. This harmony is both the Ideal and measure of knowledge and action."[31] In China a human act has cosmic significance.[32] Praxis is part of Nature, pervaded by the Breath of vitality.[33] Thus in Mo Tzu's pragmatism, *Jen*-human[e]ness is the will of Heaven, and religious asceticism is combined with political utilitarianism. Han Fei Tzu's totalitarian statecraft is an explication and application of Lao Tzu's cosmo-political nondoing; the law should be applied—in the manner of "nondoing"—according to the situation and its natural tendencies.

Third, American pragmatism often practices a critical philosophizing about philosophy. It warns that we do not see with geometry nor do we know with epistemology;[34] it lays down the theory of truth (and the conditions of recovery of philosophy) as experiential, as a critical weighing of alternative *means*, in short, as pragmatic. Thus to *claim* that philosophy is not mere thinking, but acting is itself to think *about* thinking. It is not surprising that Peirce the pragmaticist has a theory of signs and interpretation, and Whitehead the organicist has a grand process metaphysics. They are possible only in a reflective objective perspective.

In contrast, in China, to think *is* to meditate, to live, and to act; to teach is to reform the person and the society; to argue is both to persuade the rulers and ministers to create benevolent government and to exhort the people to cultivate themselves for an authentic life. Even in the seemingly abstruse controversies over original human nature, there lurks political factional strife.[35] And, as Lau said,

> One great difference between moral philosophers in the Chinese tradition and those in the Western tradition is that the latter do not look upon it as their concern to help people to become sages while the former assume that that is their main concern. Western philosophers deal only with the problem of what morality is.[36]

In other words, the Chinese pragmatic spirit—distinct from pragmatism as an ism—not only stresses the means (as in Western pragmatism). The means should not only be appropriate to the ends, but also appropriately used; how the means should be used is as important as what means should be used.

In sum, we have noted some differences between American pragmatism and Chinese pragmatic philosophy—acting on things versus living in/with nature revered as Heaven, problem-solving versus praxis as cosmic, philosophizing about philosophy versus thinking as itself being engaged in living.

## III

The above differences ultimately stem from their different styles of argumentation. And the different styles are due to different *spirits*—the Western spirit of pragmatism versus the Chinese pragmatic spirit. Their differences are as follows.

First, perhaps except for James, all classical American philosophers (Peirce, Royce, Dewey, Whitehead, Santayana) wrote about logic. Royce agonized over the relation between the immediately practical and the timelessly eternal,[37] and over how to join concrete particulars with rational universals. Whitehead saw how the many enter into a one; an actual entity is a concrescence of prehensions. In contrast, Chinese philosophy sees a concrete particular situation as significant for many other concrete occasions. Each actual situation radiates concrete implications for our generic concern; it is up to us to discern them by undergoing the situation. Each concrete particular is (pregnant with) a focused fecund generality.

Smith observed that Dewey's stress on specific questions led modern philosophy to fall within the scope of special sciences.[38] Since a specific question bespeaks a specific universal as does a specific science a group of concrete particulars, Smith's observation indicates the Western trend of thinking that goes from the abstract universal to concrete particulars. In China a reverse trend holds; particulars beam with an aura of generality, so much so that an empirical pursuit tends toward cosmological significance. The *I Ching* correlates our daily activities with cosmic movements. Medicine, martial arts, government, poetry, and culinary arts are full of metaphysical significance, the *li*, the "vein of similarities" that runs through everything.

Second, the above contrast makes sense if we see how different the style of reasoning in the West is from that in China.

Let us first look into American pragmatists. Despite the moving earthy style, concrete exposition, and vivid examples, their treatises on logic[39] are abstruse in tone and conceptual in content, bespeaking their stance of external observation. Dewey stands off to watch "how we think."[40]

Despite claiming for experience the entirety of our living and undergoing,[41] experiential qualities flowing into and succeeding each other in various purposeful patterns,[42] we must still imaginatively reconstruct our experience (James)[43] so as to organize, criticize, and regulate it logically in our inquiry (Dewey). Experience *itself* has no critical cognitive function.[44]

Then the dualism (or dualism as "problem") between thought and experience is denied, and their continuity is called "inquiry."[45] And it is here that the purposeful human *treatment* of experiential materials is apparent. Dewey's inquiry becomes our deliberate control of change toward desired outcomes—building a better mousetrap, developing a vaccine—that would not occur without human intervention. This is thinking or inquiry which is art, craft, skill, *techne*. Inquiry is the synthesis of theory and practice, a logic of practice or practical logic. Logic is the method of inquiry—not timeless truths—invented by the human subject to process the experiential given. This is a far cry from a Chinese responsive mirroring that follows and reflects what is the case.

In Western pragmatism, thinking is "a movement [inductively] *to* and [deductively] *from* a meaning"[46] because the situational data are brute meaning-less (though meaning-amenable) facts, which are "isolated, fragmentary, and discrepant," "partial and confused." Their "lack of coherence perplexes and stimulates to reflection."[47] They await "an idea [i.e., "principle, universal"[48]] . . . to connect these with one another."[49] Such is the task of thinking that is the "double movement" of induction and deduction. This double movement fits perfectly with Whitehead's characterization of thinking as "the flight of an aeroplane:" "It starts from the ground of particular observation; it makes a flight in the thin air of imaginative generalization; and it again lands for renewed observation rendered acute by rational interpretation."[50] This aeroplane-like movement is later identified by Dewey as "inquiry."[51] All this is allegedly derived from Peirce's logical insights; Dewey's logic owes much to Peirce.[52] Peirce, Royce, and Whitehead are also formal logicians.[53]

Even for Dewey there is a distinctness in abstract logical derivation that is set apart from derivation by "suggestion . . . from existential material."[54] Dewey quoted Peirce, saying, "No determination of things, no fact [producing only "buzzing, booming sensations" (James)] can result in the validity of . . . argument," and only "application of the [logical] *method* must correct the error," for "material . . . [is] ordered by methods."[53]

The word *application* above, is crucial. The American spirit of pragmatism applies autonomous logical methods *to* the demands (for order and meaning) of the meaning-less situation.[56]

The Chinese pragmatic spirit, in contrast, argues from one specific (typical) situation to many other (common) situations; here the very logical move itself is situational and pragmatic. For there is a vein of similarities ("universals," if you will) in actuality. To find this "vein" (*li*) and to co-respond with it—following it—is to argue rationally.

Such a concrete argumentation is usually dubbed (somewhat condescendingly) "analogical." This is an innocent flow of concrete metaphorical thinking. There is no room for the sort of paradox of American pragmatism perceived by Smith, saying,

> On the one hand stands the reluctance of pragmatists to engage in theorizing about the relation between perception and the external world and their hesitancy in specifying any general relation between thought and reality at large, and on the other hand . . . there is elaborated a theory concerning the nature and status of logical forms and their relation to the world of nature.[57]

In China there is no consciousness of the instrumentality of intelligence (Dewey), no theoretical elaboration of empiricism as an ism, radical (James) or absolute (Royce), no thoughtful stress on experience, sensory or inclusive. The child does not harp on childhood; he *is*. Pragmatism (as an ism) is not *being* pragmatic; only the sick person eagerly talks about fitness, in terms of which he is sick. Chuang Tzu's words recur:

> Forgetting [the] foot is [the] fit of [the] shoe; forgetting [the] waist is [the] fit of [the] belt. [Similarly,] knowing [how to] forget right [and] wrong is [the] fit[ness] of mindheart. No inside change, no outside compliance—is [the] fit of events meeting. Starting at [the] fit and never without [the] fit—is [the] fit[ness] of forgetting [the] fit.[58]

This self-forgetful "fit" is where the pragmatic *spirit* operates. In American pragmatism, one thinks to solve problems. When things mutually adapt and fit well together, there is no problem, and so no thinking arises. But obviously it makes sense to discern the structure of such a situational fit, which is to engage in "logic" in a pragmatic sense.[59]

In Chinese philosophy logic is more than a middle stage ("middle term"[60])—in Whitehead's high "thin air"—in our progress from initial data (and problem) to its solution, that is, the organization of brute data into a logically coherent whole. For the factual data are more than non logical; this move from a problematic situation to its solution is possible only if the situation is amenable to our logical maneuver. The situation itself must somehow be rational. To adapt Pascal, the percept has a reason of whose kinship theoretical reason may not be aware. This is prudence (Aristotle) or "informal logic."[61] It is the visceral reason uncanny in its quick aptness. It is the reason of life (Ortega) that cannot be mocked but can only be sung: "Day after day utters speech, and night after night shows knowledge ."[63]

This is the un-*tao*-able Tao, the vein-of-actuality (*li*), as natural and rhythmical as the Breathing of cosmic Life (*ch'i*) that pervades the human self. Here is a logic that is not imposed *on* but discernible *in* the way we talk (language),[64] stringing together whatever connections are sensed in things and events. The speech thus strung together tells a story. This story-logic moves from concrete specifics to concrete universals.

Thus in the story of a sudden unbearable surge of alarm, completely uncalculated, at seeing a baby about to crawl into a well, Mencius sees a primal budding forth (*tuan*) of human[e]ness (*jen*).[65] This surge of unbearable mindheart (*hsin*) of human[e]ness is as irresistible as the unstoppable wellspring. The force of felt moral sentiment is as natural and inevitable as the force of nature, which is the basis, explanation, and justification of morality. The story of Ox Mount[66]—as the originally lush Mount was denuded by man's daily choppings of trees, so the original human goodness is now denatured by man's daily deprivings of nourishment—intimates, in a compelling parsimony, that morality is as naturally ecological as ecological concerns are intrinsically moral. This sort of "argument" from the concrete specific to the concrete universal often packs itself into single terms, which are however routinely mistaken to be mere theoretical concepts.

In order to understand how different the two spirits in pragmatism are, we must see how Chinese reasoning goes. Let us consider, then, (1) the Chinese affirmative notions, then (2) the Chinese negative notions, and then (3) the Chinese argumentation that is built on them.

First, as to the Chinese *affirmative* notions. A Chinese "concept" is a scene, a compressed story; for all "theoretical concepts" in China are generalized concretes. "*Tao* is the road walked out"[67] by things, by us; *li* is the vein[68] of things's similarity, the grain of the wood of things; *ch'i* is the breathing[69] of life of things and of us; *te* (virtue) is what is obtained (*te*)[70] by nature; *jen* is what is (truly) human(e);[71] *hsing* (nature) is what we are born with;[72] *shen* (divine, spirit) is what spreads[73] dynamically in the world; *wu* (things) is the oxen[74] of things (as precious and powerful as the ox); *tzu-jan* (naturalness, Nature) is the self-so[75] of things.

Often a four-character phrase sums up a short story that makes a point. The phrase then comes to be a "concept" to circulate. Two examples will suffice. "Cite one, infer three" (*chu i, fan san*) comes from Confucius's description of his manner of teaching: "No resolution, no revelation; no vexation, no evocation. Having raised one corner, [ if ] three [other] corners [were] not returned, then [ I do ] no more."[76] Thus "cite one, infer three" came to represent the concept of "education. "

Again, "clothes off, legs apart" (*chieh i pan po*) sums up "nonchalant naturalness" in Chuang Tzu ' s pungent story:

> Duke Yuan of Sung was-about-to [have some] picture painted. Crowds [of ] artists all came. Receiving orders and standing, [they] licked brushes and [mixed ink, [while] half [of] them stayed outside. There-was one artist who came late; leisurely, leisurely, [he did] not rush. Receiving orders [he did] not stand [but] went straight to [the assigned] studio. Duke sent [a] man [to] observe him, who [was found] clothes off, legs apart, naked. Duke said, "Good. This is [a] true painter."[77]

Thus, instead of the abstract notion of "nonchalance, "China has "clothes off, legs apart."

We see now how compressed phrases—often of four characters—are equivalents of affirmative notions telling of concrete specifics logically (analogically, metaphorically) spread to concrete universals.

The affirmation of notions (names) takes on an existential significance in the famous "rectification of names (*cheng ming*)," righting of the wronged names back to what they ought to mean. That this has a far-reaching political significance is vividly put by Confucius, when he said,

> Names [being] not right, then words [would] not accord [with actuality]; words not [in] accord [with actuality], then affairs [would] not accomplish; affairs not accomplished, then rites, music, [would] not flourish; rites, music, not flourish, then punishments [would] not hit-right [the crimes]; punishments not hit-right, then people have nowhere to put [their] hands, feet. *Analects*, 13:3[78]

This dynamic affirmation ("rectification," *cheng*) of names is what "government" (*cheng*) is all about, says Confucius.[79] Hsun Tzu expanded this theme into a full-fledged moral epistemology (chapter 22); *The Great Learning* and *The Doctrine of the Mean* expanded the theme into a political cosmology; the book of *Mencius* can be taken as an elaboration of this theme on two fronts: becoming human[e]—which we are—in all aspects of life,[80] on one hand, and ruling human[e]ly always,[81] which it *means*, on the other.

All this comes down to becoming human as we are, and humanity (*jen*) means humaneness (*jen*). This dynamic attainment of humaneness is what the name of humanity *means*; to affirm and mean a notion is to achieve it in life.[82] In general, to understand an affirmative notion is to explore its meaning, as coherent as a picture, to affirm it in life. To affirm a notion means to confirm its self-identity (*a* is *a*) throughout life, "[letting the] father [be a] father, son, son, etc."[83] Affirmative notion is a performative, accomplishing its meaning contents in life.

How about Chinese *negatives*? Friedrich Waismann, after the manner of Wittgenstein, sensitively enumerated experiential variations of connotations in a simple negation: graded "more or less," "not quite"; directional "not yet," "no longer"; hollow and empty phrases ringing false; "not only . . . but also" against the completeness of a statement;

weakened negation in "hardly"; or even vagueness and indeterminate impressions in "roughly like that," and so on.[84] These are all varied shades of experiential meaning of "negation."

Chinese thinking includes all the above and more. Chinese negations affirm, even emphasize affirmation; Chinese argumentative thinking (especially Taoism) takes full advantage of these positive connotations in negative propositions. In Chinese philosophy negative statements have at least four features.

First, negation indicates meticulous total coverage, such as the careful maintenance of an engagement in "day [and] night without slackening" (*ssu yeh fei hsieh*).[85] Second, negation directs our attention to *all* areas other than the one negated. "Without worries" (*wu lu*), "without limit" (*wu ch'iung, wu hsien*), and "regardless" (*wu lun*), readily come to mind. "*Wu shang*" or "*wu fang*" means "no harm," and so "quite all right,"[86] "*wu t'a*" (no other) is "nothing else," and "*wu ti*" (no enemy) is "matchless."[87]

Third, because of positive affirmative thrust in negation, double negatives have an emphatic concentration of affirmation. "*Wu pu*" (nothing not) is "without exception."[88] Confucius cited "people not know [you] and [you] not hurt"[89] (transcending over what is denied) as a sign of the gentleman. Mencius used "*pu . . . wei*" for example, "It is impossible for their prince not to be a true king"[90]—as a powerful conclusion after a long persuasive series of arguments from metaphor. Chuang Tzu's "what [I] see is nothing but (*wu fei*) oxen"[91] is much stronger than "all oxen."

Fourth, we see a subtle play on distinct nuances of negation in Chinese philosophical exposition. That famous "*wu wei*" (nondoing), different from "*pu wei*" (not doing), has enamored Confucian[92] and Taoists[93] alike.[94] "Forgetting" (*wang*)[95] and "losing" (*sang*)[96] are Chuang Tzu's constant favorites. The mindheart that cannot bear to see others suffer (*pu jen jen chih hsin*) is the heart of morality.[97] In Taoism, "*wu ch'ing*" (feeling-less, beyond feeling) is not unfeeling; "*wu yen*" (wordless) is not blank silence; "*pu jen*" (ruth-less[98]) is not "ruthless"; "*wu chih*" (ignorant, without knowledge) is not stupidity; "*wu yu*" (desireless)[99] is not desiring nothing; "*wu yung*" (use-less)[100] is not "useless."[101] One of the most complex and subtle Chinese notions is "*wu chi*" (self-less) that is not "no self." There is Chuang Tzu's "*sang wo*" (self-losing)[102] (different from "*sang chi* [losing oneself][103]) and "*wang chi*,"[104] "*wang shen*,"[105] "*wang wo*"[106] (self-forgetting). In mind-fasting (*hsin chai*) oneself away, in this active self-losing, the true self manifests itself.[107]

These examples show that in China thinking is not formal abstract theorizing, but a sensitive discernment of the many-layered meanings of a concrete experience—of affirmation, of negation. Such a sensitive discernment of experiential meanings differs from Dewey's definition of logic as a formulated rule—or principle of habit, way, manner—of action that has been successful in inferential inquiry,[108] or a recognition of relations of interdependence between considerations previously disconnected, this recognition being brought about by discovery of new facts.[109] In contrast, all the above examples of Chinese concrete thinking come from our ordinary experience of the commonly human in daily living; Chinese logic is no formulated rule but experiential understanding.

How does such concrete thinking proceeds? How does Chinese concrete thinking *argue*? We have seen how negation directs, spreads, concentrates, transcends, and affirms, and how affirmation leads us through a concrete understanding to affirming things according to their nature. We discern concepts in the compressed stories of experience, being led to notions through the "argument" of storytelling, and catapulted into an expansive novelty through subtle negations.

All this amounts to an extending of our familiar framework of understanding to reach a new hitherto unknown actuality; and then we change our old framework to accommodate that novelty. How? By discerning a new vein of similarity between the familiar and the novel, reaching to the novel as a new familiar. Thus the familiar is our metaphor toward the novel; the novel *is* now the new familiar though it is *not* the familiar. It is thus that we live by metaphor.[110] Metaphor says the *that* is both what the *this* is and is not,[111] moving us from the familiar to the novel, because movement is what is and is not. This going is—through metaphor—from the typical concrete to the novel concrete. Learning is a movement of understanding that goes from the known *this* to (expand to) the unknown *that*.

We formulate—formalize—this going as "proof." Proof is a transition (movement) within a calculus (Waismann,[112] Dewey[113]) that is decided by our practical purposes. This transition is a bisociation[114] to produce recombinant ideas.[115] Judgment is our decision at the end of this transition—move, story, proof—to settle on a specific understanding, a conclusion. Thus the sudden alarm on seeing a baby crawling into a well brings us toward (transition) an understanding of "our true human(e)ness" (Mencius). This transition toward experiential understanding constitutes what Waismann calls "natural logic."[116]

Let us follow the reasoning—situational, metaphorical—in the dialogues of *Mencius*, 1A7,[117] a typical example of how Mencius—and all Chinese thinkers—"argue." We see four points in Mencius's argument here.

Point 1: King Hsuan of Ch'i asked about two despotic dukes, Huan and Wen. The King was obviously interested only in brutal statecraft (*pa*). Mencius gently proposed to talk about our royal legacy, princely rulership.[118] Thus this polite exchange correctly identified an urgent topic the king ought to pursue.

Point 2: Mencius mentioned a recent court incident. King Liang Hui could not bear to see an ox shrinking with frightened innocence—being led to blood-consecration of a new bell—and ordered that it be let go. Asked if the consecration should cease, the king ordered exchanging the ox with a lamb. This incident indicates to Mencius not that the king is grudging an ox but that he is a princely gentleman. Seeing an animal alive, he cannot bear its death fright, and so keeps his distance from the slaughterhouse and the kitchen. This mindheart (*hsin*) of human(e)ness is enough to enable his princely rule. Here the king's princely capability in his spontaneous feeling ("unbearing heartmind") was *discerned*, again in a concrete dialogue.

Point 2a: It is impossible to be indifferent (without visceral reaction) to people's suffering while being unable to bear an animal's suffering. Yet the king's gracious solicitude reaches animals, while his people are not benefiting from his grace. This curious fact is due to the king's refusal to act on his visceral humaneness, not to his inability. To deny his ability in this case is as incredible as denying the ability to lift a feather while being capable of lifting 100 *chin* (about 7 kilograms), or denying the sight of a cartload of wood while capable of seeing the fine tip of an autumnal feather. This negative point reinforces point 2 above.

Point 3: Then Mencius urged the king to apply (*chia*) and extend (*t'ui*) this spontaneous practice of the root feeling (the inability to bear other's suffering) from one's immediate family to other families. To properly 'treat one's own aged folks as aged (literally, "to 'age' one's aged"), thereby to extend (such a treatment) to others ' aged folks and, similarly, to properly treat one's own young ("to ' young' one's young") thereby to extend (such a treatment) to others' young—this is a spontaneous inevitable *application* of our natural practice, an extension of our root sensitivity. This is a pragmatic expression of our original nature.

Point 3a: Extending such a princely favor-bounty, the king shall be able freely to turn in his palm *all* under heaven (as the turn of fate), as he cares for and protects all. Merely striving after universal rulership, without extending his root empathy, is worse than climbing a tree for a fish; the King shall have nothing with which to protect even his own family. Once discarded, the natural spontaneity of root (in its defective mode) entails the inevitability of disasters. This point negatively reinforces point 3 above.

Point 4: To extend the ruler's root feeling in practice is tantamount to—means—leaving his people with enough secure resources so as to secure their constant heartmind to serve their parents properly and to provide for their families. Such a benevolent rule is an expression of the king's return to his own human root—inevitable, necessary—if he is human at all. This concludes Mencius's argument.

We see here a three-stage argument: a situational problem (point 1), a metaphorical movement (points 2, 3), and a judgment (point 4).

First, we see that a concrete situation provides a problem. The king inquires about statecraft, asking for a clever scheme to further his autocratic ambition. Mencius tactfully steers him into the basic problem of how best to rule spontaneously from the depths of his humanity. The discussion is all too concrete, all too human and urgent, yet involves deep reflections on the fundamentals of things.

Then, we see a two-staged argumentative move: metaphorical discernment, metaphorical extension. A casual spontaneous incident of the king's empathy for the trembling ox clues Mencius—and the king—into the discernment of our deep human(e) feeling, a discovery of our heartmind unable to bear others' suffering. Mencius identifies this feeling for others as the king's root of being human . This is a metaphorical move from a concrete incident toward discovering the concrete principle of human(e)ness. And then the king is urged to put this "root" principle in practice, extending it to all people. This is a metaphorical move from a concrete principle to its pragmatic application.

Let us look into one phrase to observe such a concrete argumentative move: "[We had better] age our [own] aged [folks], with [which to] extend-to aged [folks] of [other] people (*lau wu lau, i chi jen chih lau*)." We see here three metaphorical extensions.

(1) In "our [own] aged [folks]," "aged" as an adjective is extended to become "aged *folks* worthy of respect as such," a noun. (2) In "to 'age' our aged [folks]," "age" is extended into a deserved *treatment* (verb) of such persons as such. This is the Golden Rule—"Do to others as you would have others do to you"—turned "Do-as-others to others" or even "'Other' others." In the duplication of the same word—extended into different parts of speech—we see a powerful metaphorical parsimony in an affirmation of "*A* is *A*." (3) In "extend to aged [folks] of [other] people," we reach out—in our practice of root humanness—metaphorically, appropriately, toward others; as we do to our own aged folks, so we do to others's aged folks.

Finally, there is a conclusive metaphorical *judgment*; this is the royal road, the fool-proof Way, to princely—and universal—rulership. As we "age" our aged folks and thereby "age" people's aged folks, princely rulership in universal concord shall obtain all by itself. Mencius' rhetorical negative statement clinches all. "The aged wear silk, eat meat, and the common people are not hungry, not cold, yet without (*pu*) princely [rule]—[we have] yet (*wei*) [to] have such."[119] Mencius elsewhere said succinctly, "The Way lies here, and then seek-to-apply-to the far. Person [to] person, [each] 'parents' [the] parents, 'elderly' [the] elderly, and [all] under Heaven [are at] peace."[120] The judgment enlightens the situation, and we say, "Aha! There we have it."

And so, as with 1A7 above, so with the entire Book of *Mencius*, a dynamic montage of arguments by metaphor,[121] "extending (pushing, *t'ui*) what we practice."[122] Besides, those vibrant stories tossed out in the conversation were later compressed into pungent four-charactered phrases, vivid and unforgettable—"trace tree [to] seek fish (*yuan mu ch'iu yü*)," "heartmind of un-bearable [feeling for others] (*jen chih hsin*)," and so on. They are habitually used later—as "technical notions"—in further extended arguments.

In sum, Chinese thinking is not *applied* to concrete situations; it is itself concretely situated and situationally (metaphorically) extended. Chinese argumentation shifts our paradigm of reality to change our pattern of behavior. The argumentation is the movement *of* the situation itself, to move us into a new discernment, to create a new situation. Our everyday language is used to give us new insights, a felt change of reality, and a change of life itself. Chinese pragmatic argumentation renews *us*.

The renewal of ourselves is accomplished by argument by metaphorical extension. To cite the ox incident is to point to the heart-mind of empathy of unbearable intensity which is to point to the humane government. The ox, the heartmind, and the government are different, yet they become systematically connected by being pointed at serially, metaphorically—in a story, a conversation—thereby pointing at us to renew us. Thus "[things within] Heaven [and] earth are one finger-pointer," and "myriads of things are one horse-marker."[123] For " 'ox' illustrates . . . an object . . . while 'horse' is the typical class name."[124]

To cite and point to is to call. "Tao [we] walk (*hsing*) it and [it is] formed; thing [we] call them and [they are so."[125] To call is to walk which is to form the way things go as they do. Things, names, they are ways of walking forth the formation of the world. Naming is a way of thinking which is a way of life. As Graham noted, in Chinese philosophy to apply a name to an object is to use it for all similar objects, and such usage establishes a road we "walk" or "proceed" (*hsing*) to all objects to form a configuration, called "of the same kind" (*lei*). All this proceeds by "metaphor."[126] And all this is to impress on us that we and the sage are "of the same kind." Strive after sagehood.[127] Arguing for a point urges us to act on it.

Here Chinese philosophers see eye to eye with American pragmatists who take the "meaning" of a thing to be the possible consequences of acting on it; to call a thing "hard" is to say that it would not be scratched. As we cited earlier, Peirce told us to "consider what effects [and] practical bearings we conceive the object of our conception to have. Then our conception of these effects is the whole of our conception of the objects." To conceive a thing *is* to conceive its effects, and vice versa.

However, this is a far cry from Peirce's later metaphysical debates over the meanings of quality, fact, and law,[128] leading him to formulate cosmological systems in his pragmaticism, such as an "elaborate categorial scheme for expressing the generic structure of reality."[129] The same could be said of Whitehead's organic processive cosmology, Royce's "social infinite," Dewey's naturalistic metaphysics, James's pluralistic universe, and so on. All of these are foreign to Chinese philosophy.

## IV

Logic is usually taken as a formal calculus system, having little to do with actual living. But as its etymology shows, "logic" (logos) originally meant collecting, gleaning, or gathering, which later came to mean counting, on the one hand, and accounting and taking into account, on the other.[130] "Counting" came to dominate the meaning of logic in the West—logic is now primarily a formal calculus system. "Taking account of" something, however, is no less rational—a gathering in of something hitherto unfamiliar, leading us from the "ground" (another meaning of "logos") of what is familiar toward what is not. And language is a vehicle of gathering in.[131]

All above makes it sensible for Waismann to say that our logic is molded on the structure of language, which reflects experience.[132] It would not be surprising if an exotic language reveals another variety of logical structure.[133] "The structure of logic reflects . . . characteristic attitudes of our life" and "social substructure,"[134] which is our culture. To decide in favor of one system of logic is to achieve a definite style of thinking and pattern of life; different cultures (types of behavior and language) make for different types of logic.[135]

In light of this general observation we see here at least two kinds of thinking. One unfolds formally in an argumentation of a coercive logic.[136] The other enfolds the subject who is in a situation where points are arranged and interfused in configurative self-referential circles, be they concentric, co-implicative, epicyclic, or otherwise. What is an enfolding thinking?

When one is soaked in a warm bath, or when one is rapt in music, the whole person is sensibly fit, enfolded—as the baby in the womb—and one is dipped in "Of course, I am here." It is this "of course" that makes sense. And this making of sense is the rational aspect of the situation. This rationality is less coercive than inevitable, less deductive than concrete.

And so we have two sorts of rationality. The first rationality is describable by an external logic and the second one by an inner "logic." Existence comprises an inside and an outside; a complete rationality of existence is a unity of an objective, schematic, unfolding logic with an intimate, situational, enfolding logic. This all-round reason of existence fulfills humanity. Dewey's words recur:

> We have discriminated logic in its wider sense—concerned with the sequence of characteristic functions and attitudes in experience—from logic in its stricter meaning, concerned with the function of reflective thought. We must avoid yielding to the temptation of identifying logic with either of these to the exclusion of the other; or of supposing that it is possible to isolate one finally from the other. The more detailed treatment of the organs and methods of reflection cannot be carried on with security save as we have a correct idea of the position of reflection amid the typical functions of experience. Yet it is impossible to determine this larger placing, save as we have a defined and analytic, as distinct from a merely vague and gross, view of what we mean by reflection—what is its actual constitution. It is necessary to work back and forth between the larger and the narrower fields, transforming every increment upon one side into a method of work upon the other, and thereby testing it. (*EEL*, 103)

With these two sorts of logic, Dewey here describes well the composition of the community of the spirit of pragmatism and the pragmatic spirit, the community of spirited pragmatism. We yearn for the dawning of such a community of differences, where we understand the outside through the inside and become genuine, thereby understanding the inside through the outside, and become all of a piece, experientially wise; we need here both the spirit of pragmatism *and* the pragmatic spirit.

Already we see germs of such a coming together. Both for James and for Dewey, thinking is dipped in desire and emotion, and truth is what satisfies in the long run and on the whole.[137] What constitutes a situation, what makes it distinct from other situations, is its unique pervasive quality: unease, joy, foreboding, and so on. All thinking, however abstract, is guided by the situation's distinctive pervasive quality, which provides the connective tissue for all elements of thought; logic as the study of connectives is based on situational quality. All this strikes a sympathetic cord with Chinese concrete thinking by metaphor, by situational similarities.

Smith in his presidential address at the American Philosophical Association (Eastern Division) in 1981 proclaimed that American pragmatists were "above all" "devoted to the need for philosophical conversation cutting across party lines."[138] This philosophical duty should be extended and implemented across *cultural* lines as well, as Smith himself did.[139] This chapter has followed his lead. It is important to see the why and the how of our doing so.

We have two ways of thinking. The first is theoretical. When applied, it becomes experimental reasoning. It is visual, objective, analytical, controlling, and tends to be formal, if not strictly deductive. The second style of thinking is experiential. It is auditory, echoing actuality, co-responding with the mighty undercurrent of the situation. It is responsive, visceral, metaphorical, configurative, situational, if not straight story-telling. The former thinking is a tool of the spirit of pragmatism; the latter is the pragmatic spirit in action. The two need to communicate with each other. For a mere application of theoretical reasoning risks becoming sterile; experiential sensibility alone tends to get lost in concrete particulars. Both need each other to become a lived pragmatism.

First of all, how does the pragmatic spirit get lost without the spirit of pragmatism? We have seen Mencius advancing his argument by metaphor *from* our heartmind that cannot bear a sight of a sacrificial ox in jitters, *to* "aging" one's aged folks, then extending to "aging" others' aged folks, and finally to a universal rule of human(e)ness. Now, it is symmetrical to argue—also by metaphor—from our natural propensity to "fight [for] drinks [and] foods"[140] to the necessity of training-shaping (*wei*)[141] oneself in the reverence for decency (*li*), and further on to the rulership of universal imposition of such a compulsory character education. This is what Hsun Tzu in fact did.

Here we note three points. First, such a Chinese debate between Mencius and Hsun Tzu is couched in the *same* pattern of concrete argumentation by metaphor.[142] Second, to adjudicate between them the Chinese thinker can only resort to another concrete argument by metaphor, to find another concrete incident perhaps inclusive of the initial ones cited both by Mencius and by Hsun Tzu, and metaphorically push to a new conclusion, either for or against either one.[143] This is in fact what happened among the later Neo-Confucians.[144] Third, in concrete argumentation the conclusive solution to this problem is impossible. The most one could do is to observe how the *history* of debates on this issue (whether human nature is originally good or bad) somehow rallies itself on Mencius.[145] Why Hsun Tzu came to be neglected is unclear. This is an example of losing one's way in the thicket of *concrete* particulars.[146] Besides, such metaphorical application, extension, and explication of a notion (or an argument) render it elusive, requiring some special discernment on *what* it should mean in each specific context. This makes it difficult to understand, much less discuss, all matters concerned.

In short, to be concretely situational in understanding is the business of the pragmatic spirit. To survey and analyze concrete reasoning can help spot its dangers, and analysis and survey are performed by the spirit of pragmatism. The Chinese pragmatic spirit does well to embrace the American spirit of pragmatism.

We must be careful here, however; and this brings us to the other danger—of the spirit of pragmatism—to turn sterile. "Pragmatism is that life experience from which, for which, and in which our reasoning moves and has its being," *says* the spirit of pragmatism. And it is this "saying" that is the source of the problem. Let me explain.

To begin with, the spirit of pragmatism rightly says that thinking that is not pragmatism-that-we-*are* at work, but merely thinking about how thinking ought to be pragmatic, is as crippled the other extreme, sheer animal vitality not conscious of it being alive. The former is a pretension to disembodied rationality in thin Platonic air; the latter is brute intelligence merely instinctual, nonverbal. The former can deteriorate worse than the latter, however, for animal vitality can bud forth human intelligence (as Darwin observed), while a mere formal scrutiny gets trapped in its own pedantic satisfaction ("Look how beautifully self-coherent and universal our reasoning is!"), running idle, referring to nothing.

And yet, this correct warning breeds a problem for the spirit of pragmatism. The pragmatic spirit may discern that this very *concern* with pragmatism is as odd as is a paradox noted by Smith in Dewey's handling of logic. Having denied any general relation between thought and reality at large, Dewey went ahead to elaborate a theory about the general nature of logic and its general relation to nature.[147]

There walked—in Kierkegaard's wry irony—a man with a sandwich board, saying, "I am normal." He is abnormal; to be normal is to be silently natural. "Don't say; show it." One's experience breathes off its expression as a flower breathes forth its fragrance. Nothing is odd about our being normal; saying that we are is. What the American pragmatists said may well be what is the case; *that* they claimed so makes them Kierkegaard's sandwich man. Not surprisingly, Gabriel Marcel feared that Martin Buber's very *explication* of our nature as "I-Thou" may have denatured the Thou into an It.[148]

Fortunately, the sandwich man has a cure. He *can* be a therapeutic Diogenes with a lit candle—the sandwich board—roaming in broad daylight. Such a therapeutic sandwich man requires a sense of Diogenes, however. That sense can be given by the forthrightness of the pragmatic spirit of Chinese philosophy.

For the absurdity of the sandwich man (with or without an ulterior motive) is due to violation of a simple truth that what nature has joined, man (for only "man" splits) should not—and cannot—put asunder. The exhibitionism of the sandwich man splits that unity of spontaneity. Thus a mere spirit of pragmatism is as odd as a pragmatic spirit alone. We need to *combine* the two spirits to do justice to the real situation—the concrete unity—of our thinking in living, and our living in thinking. We must follow the two spirits as they are, the two sides of our integral original nature, and appreciate the mystery of their communal unity which we are. We must be unconcernedly concerned with pragmatic thinking, in order to let our concern breathe forth a lived pragmatism.

But how? We must realize that "Diogenes the sandwich man" requires three stages to produce: (1) the sandwich man unknowingly displaying his abnormality by announcing his "normality"; (2) the Diogenes knowingly displaying his therapeutic abnormality by playing the sandwich man; (3) our awareness that the complex structure of this Diogenes displays therapeutic sanity by displaying insanity by displaying "sanity." To understand this complex composition of Diogenes the sandwich man, and to play it spontaneously, is true pragmatism.

Chinese philosophy has two delightful counterparts to Diogenes the sandwich man, one negative, one positive. Both are stories circulating in four-charactered phrases—"pulling seedlings, helping [them] grow" (*yah miao chu chang*[149]), and "clothes off, legs apart" (*chieh i pan po*[150]). The second story has been mentioned above. The first one goes as follows: "There-was a-man of-Sung who worried [that] his seedlings did-not grow, and pulled them. He came-back tired [with a] tired [look], telling his folks [at home], '[I] am-tired today! I [have] helped seedlings grow!' His son rushed and went to-observe them, and seedlings [were all] wilted."

We have three points of comparison between Diogenes the sandwich man and his Chinese counterparts. First, they are all dramatic rehearsals (Dewey) of concrete situations, compressed stories laden with significance. Second, Diogenes the sandwich man is my new coinage, a clumsy unnatural one. The Chinese counterparts are not, and have long been circulating as common notions. Third, in all these cases, cultural activities (candle, sandwich board, agriculture, painting, clothes) are so naturalized as to be unnoticeable. They are all our *natural* activities.

All these examples—in the West, in China—can be said to be various ways of *tao*ing the un*tao*able Tao (Lao Tzu), in the elemental breathing of life (Mencius) that bloweth where it listeth. Genuine pragmatism is the piping of heaven—of nature—which we overhear and (in) which we pipe.[151] What is a human piping in relation to the heavenly one?

The piping of Nature is *presented* in music and in poetry in all its glories—that is, with all its primal rustles and silence, without a human whisper—yet through human artistry. Natural vitality steadily appears as contrivance disappears; the zenith of rational effort lies in its disappearance into the muscle of actuality.[152] Pragmatism should be so pragmatic that it perfects its self-oblivion within historical situations.

We understand an action by watching how its agent's intention interacts with and within his situation. This "logic" of existential *how*—the logic of the *situation*—can be understood by its history. The rationality of action is natural, historical, and narrative oriented.[153] To argue is to tell stories, "pulling seedlings, helping [them] grow," "clothes off, legs apart."[154] This is in the pragmatic spirit. But we must *argue* for such a peculiar argumentation, in the way of Diogenes the sandwich man. This is in the spirit of pragmatism. All this—combined—is the true philosophy of "experience," pragmatic philosophy truly so called. This is the symbiotic community of family differences where the American spirit of pragmatism lives in the Chinese pragmatic spirit, and the latter spirit in the former.[155]

## Abbreviations of Works Cited
(Works Cited Without Abbreviations Are Not Listed Here)


*BC* Wu, Kuang-ming, *The Butterfly as Companion: Meditations of the First Three Chapters of the Chuang Tzu*, Albany, NY: State University of New York Press, 1990.

*CAP* Smith, John E., ed. *Contemporary American Philosophy: Second Series*. London: George Allen & Unwin, 1970.

*EEL* Dewey, John. *Essays In Experimental Logic*. Chicago: The University of Chicago Press, 1916.

*HISP* Waismann, F. *How I See Philosophy*, ed. R. Harre, London: Macmillan, 1968.

*HWT* Dewey, John. *How We Think*. Boston: D. C. Heath & Co., 1910.

*LMLES* Graham, A. C. *Later Mohist Logic. Ethics and Science*. Hong Kong: The Chinese University Press & London: University of London, 1978.

*LTI* Dewey, John. *Logic: The Theory of Inquiry*. NY: Henry Holt and Company, 1938.

*M* Lau, D. C., tr.: *Mencius*. Two volumes. Hong Kong: The Chinese University Press, 1984.

*PM* Huang, Chun-chieh. *Praxis and Metaphysics: A History of Mencius Scholarship*, in preparation.

*PR* Whitehead, Alfred North, *Process and Reality*, NY: Macmillan, 1929, The Free Press, 1978.

*PT* Smith, John E. *Purpose and Thought: The Meaning of Pragmatism*, New Haven, CT: Yale University Press, 1978.

*RE* Smith, John E. *Religion and Empiricism*. Milwaukee: Marquette University Press, 1967.

*SAP* Smith, John E. *The Spirit of American Philosophy*. Revised Edition. Albany, NY: State University of New York Press, 1983.

*SBCP* Chan, Wing-tsit. *A Source Book in Chinese Philosophy*. Princeton: Princeton University Press, 1963.

*TAP* Smith, John E. *Themes in American Philosophy: Purpose Experience and Community*. NY: Harper Torchbooks, 1970.

*UCM* Allinson, Robert E., *Understanding the Chinese Mind*. Hong Kong: Oxford University Press, 1989.

## NOTES

1. I acknowledge a meticulous critique and assistance of Professors John R. Burr, Marshall Missner, and Garrett Thomson, who thereby saved me from many a blunder, although I alone am responsible for the remaining defects in the following pages.

2. Among my many professors since the sixties, Mr. Smith remains my paradigm of wit and wisdom, my fortress of parental grace. Whatever is said in these pages is a mere extension of his pedagogical Socratism. However, all my blunders belong to my failure to implement his advice and instruction.

3. *PT*, 8–9. For a list of abbreviations of cited works see the end of this chapter.

4. For the importance of openness and otherness (which implies plurality) for truth (in pragmatic, coherence, and correspondence conceptions), see Carl G. Vaught in ed. Robert C. Neville *New Essays in Metaphysics*, (Albany, NY: State University of New York Press, 1987), 217–26. He also approximates (in essays 226–35) the thesis advanced here on metaphor, with the following caveat.

Vaught's "philosophical reconstruction" is strangely unmetaphorical, i.e., literalistic and analytical, in all this "complex interplay" and "metaphorical and analogical nexus." "The purity of heart is to will one thing," said Kierkegaard. A system of thought is to be so pure as to exhibit and inspire life's natural integrity and organic simplicity; here exhibition and inspiration are themselves a metaphoric resonance between thinking and things, and thinking and thinking. Between Vaught's "metaphorical thinking" and "metaphorical object," there is a mutuality of metaphoring which has a *natural inevitability*, sadly bypassed if not smothered by his contrived (almost scholastic) analysis, which, however systematized, kills a natural one. Pragmatism is (or should be) another clarion call back to things themselves. This chapter explores two types of such a spirit.

5. I said "in a broad sense" advisedly. "Pragmatism" as it is usually and condescendingly, interpreted is perhaps as Smith described (in *PT*, 8), i.e., all thoughts are for action in response to situational change (no autonomy for thought), that propositions become true by passional willing (no dispassionate objectivity). Not surprisingly, "many American thinkers [Peirce, Royce, Whitehead] who have talked about the function of reason in human life or the intimate connection between logic and the human will have at the same time refused to accept a place in the ranks of the pragmatists" (*SAP*, 191). Smith insists that "pragmatism" (as usually so interpreted) is "one form only of the general thesis," that "thinking is an activity performed by man, that it is a means of answering questions and of solving problems" (*SAP*, 190). Thus the classical American philosophers practiced the broad pragmatism, the spirit that "forget[s] preliminaries [such as theory of knowledge, of language], do[es] to direct treatment of problems of the culture" (*SAP*, 226–27), in Peirce's pragmaticism, James's radical empiricism, Royce's absolute pragmatism, Dewey's instrumentalism, and Whitehead's

process as itself reality (*SAP*, 5, 40, 55, 66ff. 85–90, 123–24, 134, 176–78). Pragmatism in this chapter is this broad "general thesis," also called "pragmatism" by Smith in *SAP*, x, 40–66, 85–90, 198, 200, 206, 224, *TAP*, 132. In sum, classical American philosophy can be characterized broadly as "American pragmatism" (*SAP*, 226).

6. *SAP*, 225. Recently Smith devoted an entire chapter to "Interpreting Across [cultural] Boundaries." This chapter begins *UCM*.

7. *UCM*, 30.

8. Cf. *UCM*, 35, 38, 41, 45.

9. Cf. *SAP*, 84ff., 224. 242.

10. Foreword to *The American Pragmatists*, ed. Milton R. Konvitz and Gail Kennedy (NY: Meridian Books, 1960).

11. *SAP*, 187 *EEL*, 303.

12. *SAP*, 188.

13. *SBCP*, 3. This statement begins the book.

14. *SAP*, 230, 232–33.

15. Ibid. 85–86.

16. *UCM*, 30–33.

17. *SAP*, 188; *CAP*, 13–14.

18. *SBCP*, 3.

19. *Collected Papers of Charles Sanders Peirce*, ed. Charles Hartshorne, and Paul Weiss, (Harvard University Press, 1931–35), vol. 5, paragraph 402. Cf. EEL, 309–10.

20. *SAP*, 194.

21. Ibid., 189.

22. Ibid., 195.

23. *SAP*, 193, 195, 196; *TAP*, 130–31.

24. *The Analects* 1.2. Unless otherwise noted, all English translations of Chinese quotations are mine.

25. *M*, 4B18; cf. 7A24.

26. 2A6.

27. *Chuang Tzu* 5.9–10.

28. *SAP*, 143.

29. Quoted in ibid., 130.

30. *SAP*, 66.

31. *UCM*, 35.

32. As stressed in the *I Ching* and the Yin-Yang school.

33. *M*, 2A2.

34. *SAP*, 230.

35. On the political factional implications of metaphysical debates in China, see *PM*.

36. *M*, xxii.

37. *SAP*, 83.

38. Ibid., 199.

39. Even Dewey's.

40. Remember Dewey wrote *HWT*.

41. *RE*, 50.

42. Ibid., 48.

43. Ibid., 49.

44. *TAP*, 51. Conversely, knowing is only one kind of experiencing among other kinds.

45. *TAP*, 131.

46. *HWT*, 80.

47. Ibid., 79.

48. Ibid., 80.

49. Ibid., 79.

50. *PR*, 7 [1929], 5 [1978].

51. *LTI*, 8, 11ff.

52. Ibid., 9n., 13–14, 14n.

53. *SAP*, 189–90.

54. *LTI*, 468.

55. Ibid., 469, 470; cf. *PT*, 33.

56. *PT*, 102–03, 116–17, 128–29.

57. *TAP*, 130–31.

58. *Chuang Tzu*, 19. 62–64.

59. *EEL*, 177, 178.

60. *HWT*, 79.

61. Gilbert Ryle, *Dilemmas* (Cambridge University Press, 1964), 115–29.

62. Max Black acknowledged it as "basic reason using" although, sadly, he termed it "primitive," "minimal," and only "quasi-rational." See his *Prevalence of Humbug and Other Essays* (Ithaca, NY: Cornell University Press, 1983), 33–36. See my comments in *BC*, 269–72.

63. Psalm 19:2.

64. *HISP*, 80; cf. *EEL*, 174–76.

65. *M*, 2A6, 6A6.

66. Ibid., 6A8.

67. *Chuang Tzu*, 2.33. See my *BC*, 244–46, 284, et passim.

68. See my *BC*, 293.

69. See ibid., 426–27; cf. 472, et passim.

70. In Chinese, "to obtain" and "virtue" are pronounced the same, though they are written differently. See my *BC*, 162, 165.

71. In Chinese, "human" and "humane" ( or "benevolent") are two meanings packed into the same character.

72. In Chinese, part of the character, "nature," is "birth" (or being born). This compares instructively with the Western "nature" and "nascence."

73. In Chinese, part of the character "spirit" means "to spread" (or "extend"). See my *BC*, 319–20.

74. In Chinese, the character "thing" is made up of "ox" and "knife." This symbolizes how things appear as precious oxen and such, "cut" out of nonseparated Con-fusion, the primal Chaos. See my *BC*, 170.

75. This is a literal translation of two Chinese characters meaning "nature" or "naturalness." See my *BC*, 184.

76. *The Analects* 7.8.

77. *Chuang Tzu*, 21.45–47.

78. The modern significance of rectification of names is felt in the feminist movement. The feminist insists on treating the woman as the *person* she is. Actually, we ought to go further and insist on treating the woman as *she* is. However, the problem, is that "womanhood" is so twisted as to mean something else than what it *is* basically, a person. We must investigate what it means to be a woman before we can right the wronged name of womanhood, not just personhood. Again, the wrong of Saddam Hussein lies in his wronging of names, such as claiming to be "his" what does not belong to him (i.e., Kuwait), claiming to "save Palestine" by invading Kuwait, claiming to love his people by exploiting them. One only hopes that the Gulf War will be shown to have been fought to right those wronged names by the future behavior of the Coalition Nations.

79. *Analects*, 12.11, 17, 19. cf. 16.2, 3, 18.5.20.2. In Chinese, "rectification" and "government" are mutually homophonous.

80. Cf. 1A7.

81. Cf. 1B8, 4B3.

82. This is why the reverse is also true. For Mencius, to "chih yen" (2A2)—"understand words" (Legge) or "have insights into words" (Lau)—is to understand what a person is by the way he talks. Human[e]ness is the home that nestles a person (2A7). And human[e]ness is intimately linked to the unbearing mindheart (to see others suffer) (2A6; this is a negative expression of roomy accommodation to others), on the one hand, and with the Flooding Elan of Life-Breath (2A2, 6A8), on the other. Affirmative words are a link connecting our inner recesses—secret inclination, intention, attitude—and the vast nature both within and around us.

83. *Analects*, 12.11.

84. *HISP*, 78–82.

85. *Shih Ching* 260.4, 261.1. This phrase is so famous as to be adopted in the national anthem of the Republic of China.

86. *M*, 1A7, 7B19.

87. Ibid., 1A5, 2A5, 4A8, 7B3.

88. *The Analects* 1.8, 4.14, 7.24, 10.5, 11.4, 12.7, 17.13, 20.3; 7A4; *Tao Te Ching*, 3; *Chuang Tzu*, 5.26, 6.42.

89. *The Analects*, 1.1. This phrase is one of those that begin *The Analects*.

90. *M*, lA7; D. C. Lau's translation, M 23. Will be examined later.

91. *Chuang Tzu*, 3.5.

92. *The Analectes*, 15.5.

93. *Tao Te Ching*, 2, 43, 48; *Chuang Tzu* 6.29, and so forth.

94. Roger T. Ames has a whole chapter on *wu wei* in his *The Art of Rulership: A Study in Ancient Chinese Political Thought*, (Honolulu: The University of Hawaii Press, 1983, 28–64). On a philosophical exposition of *wu* and *wu wei* in Chuang Tzu, see aria 1, aria 2 in my *Chuang Tzu: World Philosopher at Play* (NY: The Crossroad Publishing Company & Chico, CA: Scholars Press, 1982), 61–114.

95. *Chuang Tzu*, 2.92, and so forth.

96. Ibid., 1.35, etc.

97. *M*, 1A7, 2A6, 4A1, 7B31. As we saw before, this phrase is a compression of the story of our unbearably empathic alarm at seeing a baby about to crawl into a well.

98. *Tao Te Ching*, 5.

99. Ibid., 3, 34.

100. *Chuang Tzu*, 4.73, 9.2.

101. One is reminded of Adam and Eve's shameless (*wu k'uei*) innocence (Genesis 2:25) falling into Cain's shameless (*wu ch'ih*) fratricide (Genesis 4:9).

102. *Chuang Tzu*, 2.3.

103. Ibid., 16.21.

104. Ibid., 12.45.

105. Ibid., 4.43.

106. Ibid., 14.10.

107. On self-losing see the index under "self," and "loss of self" in my *BC*.

108. *LTI*, 13–14.

109. *HWT*, 81.

110. George Lakoff, & Mark Johnson, *Metaphors We Live By* (University of Chicago Press, 1980), elaborates on this theme. On metaphor in general, see Mark Johnson, ed., *Philosophical Perspectives on Metaphor* (Minneapolis: University of Minnesota Press, 1981). On argument by metaphor in China, see my *History, Thinking, and Literature in Chinese Philosophy*, esp. chapter 6, "Mencius's Concrete Thinking" (Taipei, Taiwan: Academia Sinica, 1991).

111. As Ricoeur and McFague insisted. See Paul Ricoeur, *The Rule of Metaphor*, trans. Robert Czerny, et al. (London: Routledge & Kegan Paul, 1978), 224, 248–49, and Sallie McFague, *Metaphorical Theology* (Philadelphia: Fortress Press, 1982), pp. 13, 19.

112. *HISP*, 69–70.

113. *HWT*, 80.

114. The phrase is Arthur Koestler's in his *The Act of Creation* (NY: The Macmillan Company, 1964), 35, et seq.

115. The phrase is Douglas R. Hofstadter's, somewhere in his *Meta- magical Themas: Questing for the Essence of Mind and Pattern*, (NY: Basic Books, Inc., 1985). Also cf. Howard Margolis, *Patterns, Thinking and Cognition: Theory of Judgment* (The University of Chicago Press, 1987).

116. *HISP*, 68.

117. The perceptive reader, comparing my phraseology here and D. C. Lau's excellent translation in *M*, may note my occasional departures from him.

118. In China, princely rulership (*wang*) of humane (*jen*) government is customarily contrasted with Machievellian autocracy (*pa*).

119. Lau rendered the final phrase as "It is impossible for their prince not to be a true King" (*M*, 23), as above.

120. *M*, 4A11.

121. This exposition hopefully puts coherence into D. C. Lau's excellent though fragmentary essay, "On Mencius' Use of Analogy in Argument" in M, 334–56. Cf. also "Mencius' Concrete Thinking" (co-authored with a Mencius scholar, Professor Huang Chun-chieh) in my *History, Thinking. and Literature in Chinese Philosophy* (Taipei, Taiwan: Academia Sinica, 1991).

122. *M*, 1A7.

123. *Chuang Tzu*, 2.33.

124. Graham, *LMLES*, 217–18. "Finger-pointer (*chih*)" and "horse-marker (*ma*)" are coupled in Chuang Tzu's reflections on things (2.32). "Horse" is used to argue for things in general in the last section of chapter 25 (from 25.60 on).

125. *Chuang Tzu*, 2.33.

126. *LMLES*, 227–28.

127. *M*, 2A2, 6A7.

128. *PT*, 130–31.

129. Ibid., 140.

130. On the origin of the word *logos* see A. Debrunner and H Klienknecht's articles in Gerhard Kittel, ed., *Theological Dictionary of the New Testament*, 4: 71–91, (Grand Rapids, MI: Wm. E. Eerdmans Publishing Co., 1967).

131. This is the well-known theme that occupied later Heidegger.

132. *HISP*, 68.

133. Ibid.

134. Ibid., 89–90.

135. Ibid., 90.

136. On the "coercive" nature of usual "philosophy," see Robert Nozick, *Philosophical Explanations* (Harvard University Press, 1981), 4–8.

137. See James's famous essay, "The Sentiment of Rationality" and what he has to say about reasoning in *The Principles of Psychology*, (NY: Henry Holt & Co., 1890, 2 volumes. What he says about "association by similarity" in 2: 345–48 is particularly germane to reasoning by metaphor. Also Dewey's (especially "Qualitative Thought and Affective Thought" in) *Philosophy and Civilization* (NY: Minton, Balch & Co., 1931), supplements what he has to say about situations in LTI. Furthermore, a

work of art is just as much a product of intelligent thought as a scientific theory. Dewey's aesthetic experience (in his *Art as Experience* [NY: Minton, Balch & Co., 1934]) is a consummatory one, fusing inner and outer, feeling and thought, subjective and objective; toward this consummatory fusion instrumentalism as a method pushes our experience.

However, they pointed out these situational features of thinking, whereas Chinese philosophers mutely *practiced* it in their thinking. The significance of this *pragmatic* difference is discussed in the following pages.

138. *SAP*, 225.

139. In the first essay of *UCM*.

140. *Hsun Tzu*, 4.17, 23.18.

141. Ibid., 23.25.

142. Another notorious example may well be the debates—reciprocal pilings up of nonsequiturs against each other—between Mencius and Kao Tzu on whether or not human nature is innately good, as reported in *M*, 6Al–5.

143. Mencius's argument from the story of Ox Mount (in 6A8) is presumably designed to explain man's behavior that seems to run counter to his theory of the "original goodness of human nature."

144. See *PM*.

145. Ibid.

146. This is similar to what Thomas Kuhn noted as "scientific revolution" by a paradigm shift; revolution in science happens, all too concretely, when extrapolations from an initial concrete model get unwieldy (see his *The Structure of Scientific Revolution*, (The University of Chicago Press, 1962), and "Metaphor in Science," ed. A. Ortony [Cambridge University Press, 1979], 409–19). But in China not even such an explanation by the principle of simplicity has been forthcoming.

147. *TAP*, 130–31.

148. Gabriel Marcel's incisive comments appear in Paul A. Schilpp and Maurice Friedman, eds., *The Philosophy of Martin Buber* (La Salle, IL: Open Court, 1967, 44. Buber's answer is equally instructive: "I do not see that this is so. If one uses the expression '*the* Thou,' which is alien to natural speech, one does not at all mean the real man to whom I say Thou, but the word which is used in saying it; it is not otherwise when one uses the expression 'the I.' But if I really say 'Thou,' then I as

little mean by it a thing as when I say 'I' to myself" (Schlipp and Friedman, 706). In other words, *how* we speak about the situation in which we are becomes decisive.

149. *M*, 2A2.

150. *Chuang Tzu*, 21.45–47.

151. *Chuang Tzu*, 2.3–9. See my *BC*, 503, under "pipings."

152. This is another expression of nondoing (*wu wei*).

153. This is what Alasdair MacIntyre tried in his *After Virtue* (University of Notre Dame Press, 1981).

154. As well as all examples of Chinese "arguments" in stories and metaphors cited so far.

155. For instance, to say *of* a story that showing differs from saying, as American pragmatism and Western analytic philosophy do, is one thing; to show it by telling a story, as Chinese philosophy tends to do, is quite another. The former says; the latter shows. But can we have both? Can we have that idyllic kindergartners' moment of "show and tell"—showing by telling, telling by showing—in philosophy? It would be a lived pragmatism that embraces analysis and sensibility. This chapter totteringly attempts it. Cf. note 4, this chapter, my comments on Carl Vaught's insights.

George Allan

# Modernism, Postmodernism, and the Pragmatic Recovery of an Educational Canon

## EDUCATION IN AMERICA

Americans believe in education. It provides them with the skills and contacts by means of which they hope to succeed in life, to do better than their parents and to become the envy of their siblings and neighbors. It provides them with the information they need in order to avoid being duped by politicians, in order to protect their interests against raids on local, state, and federal treasuries by fat cats and welfare queens. Or, as Thomas Jefferson would have put it, an educated citizenry is the bulwark of democracy.

John Smith, echoing Dewey's earlier unheeded plea, has been calling of late for a recovery of philosophy in America "in the form of a concerted attack upon problems arising from our efforts to define and sustain a life that is human." He contrasts this with philosophy become irrelevant through a practice that is little more than "a war between philosophers largely bent on scoring points in an academic intelligence test."[1] If we take Smith seriously, if we agree that the task of American philosophy today is to help in the resolution of problems that

Americans consider vital to the survival and well-being of themselves and their communities, then the contemporary scene in American education is certainly one area well worth philosophic attention.

The current state of education in the United States is viewed with alarm from all quarters. Reports of special commissions bemoan the failure of students to learn, of their teachers to teach, of administrators to get things properly organized, of school boards and boards of trustees to provide adequate leadership, and of governments to provide requisite financial support. That a recent president of the United States should indicate that he wishes to be known as "the education president" bespeaks the perceived national importance of these issues, apart from whatever he and the other politicians in Washington might or might not be doing to address the problems that label spotlights.

In this chapter I shall discuss one issue from the roster of problems which comprise the nation's education agenda: that of the intellectual canon. The dispute is over whether there is one and what the ramifications are of this for curricular coherence and hence for pedagogical effectiveness. The dispute is loudest at the college and university levels, especially when focused on matters of general education. Unfortunately, the exchange of views is carried on with little attention to underlying assumptions and in a rhetorical mode that leaves no space for compromise. It is as though we were once again with William James's camping party in the mountains, red-faced from shouting down our friends, engaged in a new version of the wrangle regarding whether or not a man goes around the squirrel when he goes around the tree to which that ever-watchful creature clings, its face kept always toward him.

The American pragmatists thought of philosophy as a method designed for use on such occasions, evoked by such disputes as an instrument of reasonable common sense and creative imagination, one that would serve to fix what had broken down and to get things running smoothly once again. As James expected the camping party to get back to the useful business of chopping firewood and cooking supper once he had "assuaged the dispute" by his pragmatic observations, so the recovery of philosophy in reference to the canonical wars now ravaging American higher education should be the means by which faculty might be led back from their endless idle arguments to the real work of designing good courses and teaching them well.

Over the years Smith has been an active participant in the recurrent problems of academe, most notably in his sensible approach to the late and unlamented campfire dispute within the American Philosophical Association between "analysts" and "pluralists." Whatever his wisdom might be on the canonical dispute to which this text now turns, he would agree with me, I am sure, that William James should provide us with the measure of success or failure in this endeavor through his classic criterion for the resolution of metaphysical disagreement:

> There can *be* no difference anywhere that doesn't *make* a difference elsewhere—no difference in abstract truth that doesn't express itself in a difference in concrete fact and in conduct consequent upon that fact, imposed on somebody, somehow, somewhere, and somewhen. The whole function of philosophy ought to be to find out what definite difference it will make to you and me, at definite instants of our life, if this world-formula or that world-formula be the true one.[2]

## A CANON: FIGHT OR FLIGHT

A "canon" is the set of general rules and fundamental principles that govern a subject, that reveal systematically its structure of relationships. The fundamental principles are the essential or core features of the subject, those upon which the other features, the accidental or peripheral ones, depend. Thus an "educational canon" with respect to some subject is the set of rules for determining what materials—ideas, methods, heuristics, texts, data—are essential for someone to learn if he or she is to grasp adequately that subject. By an obvious process of metonymy, the educational canon is usually taken as referring to those materials themselves rather than to the rules for their determination, and the subject at issue is taken to be human knowledge in general. Hence within the context of the present dispute in American undergraduate education, the canon at issue is the set of texts that contain those ideas which it is essential for American young people to know in order for them to become responsible citizens. As William Bennett puts it, paraphrasing Matthew Arnold, the educational canon is "the best that has been said, thought, written, and otherwise expressed about the human experience."[3]

Advocates of canonical education view with dismay the decline over the last century in the "authority of tradition." They see an old consensus about what it is essential to know eroded by the acid rains of professional specialization. The explosion in information, the need for increasingly specialized skills to acquire or understand that information, and the resulting emergence of a professionalized faculty more interested in their narrow research programs than the general education of students: these have led, the canonicists argue, to a dangerous "dispersal of authority," to a "loss of integrity in the bachelor's degree."[4]

A curriculum without "integrity" (AAC) is one without "coherence" (Cheney), one in which "intellectual authority" is replaced by "intellectual relativism" (Bennett). The roster of evidence showing the failure of the American educational system to teach its young people what they need to know is said by the canonicists to be the result of this fragmentation, this collapse of any distinction between essential and unessential materials. The solution they advocate, therefore, can be said to be "modernist": it believes in essential structures and proposes that we recover the old and proper integrity of the undergraduate curriculum by reaffirming the centrality, and hence the authority, of these essential structures of understanding defined by the traditional educational canon.

"Some books are more important than others" (B, 10), says Bennett, and these should be studied with care. They bring students into "the company of great souls" (B, 11), confront them with "the questions that are central to human existence" (B, 29), and so by the universality of that encounter provide them with a common heritage that serves as "the glue that binds together our pluralistic nation" (B, 30). Bennett's list of the great books authored by such great souls, limited to the humanities which are his immediate concern, run from Homer to Nietzsche, and from the *Federalist Papers* to *Letter from the Birmingham Jail.*

Other reports focus on method rather than content. The AAC monograph, for instance, identifies nine "methods and processes, modes of access to understanding and judgment" (A, 15) that it thinks are essential to know: logical analysis, verbal literacy, numerical understanding, historical awareness, scientific method, informed and responsible moral choice, art appreciation and experience, international and multicultural experiences, and study of one field in depth. These it takes as the conditions for nurturing "qualities of mind and character" (A, 25) that have enabled and should again serve to enable "generations of men and women to grasp a vision of the good life, a life of responsible citizenship and human decency" (A, 6).

The critics of canonic learning do not simply direct their attack at these sometimes atavistic proposals for what counts as the essential content or methodology for undergraduate education. That would be like shooting fish in a barrel. Bennett, for instance, skips over the Middle Ages, omitting everyone from Augustine to Ockham; mentions Locke and Hobbes but not Hume, Kant, or Hegel; affirms Hawthorne and Melville but not Dickinson, Faulkner but not Hemingway; and completely ignores the American pragmatists. Such a line of criticism would be superficial, however. Bennett is quick to note that his list is by no means exhaustive. He also acknowledges that it would benefit from more attention to great souls who are neither Western nor culturally mainstream nor male. His point is not that education should be confined to reading what he has recommended, but that for Americans what is essential to their education can and must be learned from a traditional collection of works by North American and West European authors, along with certain of their Hebrew, Greek, and Roman predecessors. On this foundation one can then construct a fuller cultural edifice of other authors who are worth reading, a house of intellect that is wide, diverse, and generously pluralistic. But it would be a house built upon the sand, say Bennett and his colleagues, except that it reaches to bedrock by means of a canon such as the one they propose.

What upsets Bennett and the canonicists, therefore, is not that his critics object to the content of his canon nor to its scope, but that they object to its very nature. Because Western culture is essentially oppressive, these critics argue, the canon that marks that essence celebrates values which instead should be rejected. Those great Western souls, along with their great ideas, methods, and attitudes, are hegemonic, imperialistic, colonial, patriarchal, logocentric, exclusionary. They need to be repudiated in the name of other more humane, more encompassing values, values respectful of ethnic difference and cultural variety, values of liberation, equality, and free association. As black writer Henry Louis Gates puts it, "The return to 'the' canon, the high canon of Western masterpieces, represents the return of an order in which my people were the subjugated, the voiceless, the invisible, the unrepresented, and the unrepresentable. Who would return us to that medieval never-never land?"[5]

The problem is not that the traditional canon offers a roster of repugnant ideas but that the very notion of a canon is itself one of those repugnant ideas. For a canon is hierarchical and it is hierarchy, not this hierarchy or that but hierarchy as such, that is the enemy of the multicultural and democratic ideals which it should be the goal of American education to inculcate in the nation's youth. Hierarchical thinking and action, says Mary Louise Pratt, are "historically as well as morally distortive" because they divide everything into privileged and unprivileged groupings, condemning some ideas, texts, and persons to the margins of a culture while exalting others to positions of primacy. Because their attack is thus directed against the keystone presuppositions of modernism, noncanonicalists have often earned for themselves the deconstructive sobriquet of "postmodernist."

Jean Ferguson Carr proposes a noncanonical approach when she argues that literary studies should be renamed "cultural studies." The shift, she claims, "emphasizes the changed understanding of "literature" and its relationship to society. Cultural studies move away from "history of ideas" to a contested history of struggles for power and authority, to complicated relations between "center" and "margin," between dominant and minority positions."[6] Texts need to be seen within their cultural settings in order to be revealed as they truly are, as one of the ways by which persons pursue their individual and collective interests. The sorts of books, ideas, and authors that make it into a traditional canon do so because they are taken to have been influential expressions of such interests. But this role they play will be misunderstood, absolutized, unless they are "set against a panoply of other voices" from that same cultural milieu which exhibits the same or competing interests. A popular broadside, the private diary or letters of an ordinary person, bureaucratic memos, and subliterary or nonliterary artifacts are all "productions worthy of study" because they all in their different ways provide access to the culture and to the play of interests that define it.

Cultural studies, Carr insists, is "not a game to play or a code to keep people out, but (is) a method of refiguring how we have gotten to where we are and how we can effect some significant change" (C, 28). Canon making, she implies, is an exclusionary stratagem, a way to define an elite. Privileged authors imply privileged readers, those who are like them with respect to background, experience, and interests, and who as a consequence respond appreciatively to what they have to say. To stop studying those authors as exemplars and to inquire instead into how they came to be revered and how others came to be reviled or ignored is to find ourselves caught up in the moral and political question of why this should be so. Carr envisions cultural studies so practiced as to have an activist outcome because her students are ethnically diverse "ordinary readers," people whom the canon brands as having an unimportant past and a naive understanding of what they read. Students who discover that the supposed great souls are different than they are but not their betters, furthering their own interests rather than expressing universal truths, gain a new respect for their own heritage, for their own ideas and recommendations, and are emboldened to act within the culture accordingly. Thus for Carr cultural studies "tries to dispel the mystique surrounding authorized knowledge" and to empower marginalized people "to enter critical conversations at diverse levels and with the authority of their own experiences and knowledges" (C, 28).

John Searle chides the "cultural left," one of the *soi-disant* labels for postmodern noncanonicalists, for confusing epistemology with ontology. "All investigations are relative to investigators. But it does not follow, nor is it indeed true, that all the matters investigated are relative to investigators."[7] Metaphysical realism, contends Searle, is presumed in the sciences, indeed everywhere except in English, French, and cultural studies. It is the presupposition of linguistic communication and so even to argue against it is to exemplify it. He dismisses noncanonicalism as philosophically muddle-headed and its views on education, therefore, as not worthy of serious consideration.

But the arguments about the canon are not really between modernist metaphysical realists and postmodernist metaphysical relativists. The dispute is over two claims about reality, one contending that reality is ordered hierarchically into essential and accidental elements, one insisting that it is not. If there are essential ingredients in any aspect of the world, then the canonicalists are correct and the study of that aspect needs to give primary attention to those essential features. If there is no such distinction, however, if the ingredients of things are related interdependently rather than dependently, then the noncanonicalists have it right and the study of those things needs to take equal account of all of its various relata.

The canonicalists and the noncanonicalists fire cannonades of assertion and invective at one another, each outraged at the refusal of the other to acknowledge the obvious, each muttering about the dark reasons which must constitute their opponents' real motivation. Each side seems to ignore the fact that their differences are ontological. "Political correctness" is a donkey's tail of vilification recently pinned on the cultural left. But it belongs on the rump of the cultural right as well, for Robert Caserio has usefully defined "political correctness" to mean "a prefabricated sense of values, a predetermined set of assumptions about what is good for people and what is bad for them."[8] Both sides in the dispute over the reality of an educational canon argue in just this way, presupposing the truth of their predetermined views concerning the nature of reality and hence of how best to learn about it.

Two human temperaments committed to two ontologies. One rationalist in its insistence upon essential truth, one empiricist in its insistence upon the plurality of conflicting truths. One side is tenderly enraptured by the notion of a few, great sacred texts to be preserved against the ravage of time as a precious resource without which we shall surely perish as a people. One side is tough-mindedly open to the incredibly diverse and divergent ways of belief and practice comprising the human adventure through time, that very pluralism a precious resource surely without which we shall perish as a people.

The campfire talk grows heated. Enter a recovered pragmatism.

## THE PRAGMATIC BALANCE

The pragmatic critique of every "copy theory" of truth, in William James's way of putting it, is twofold. First, there is no apparent reason for wanting to create a mental copy of an antecedent physical reality. Like the Irishman, carried to a banquet in a bottomless sedan chair, who remarks that had it not been for the honor he might just as well have walked, whether or not you copy reality would seem to make no real difference (P, 105). The world remains the same either way, and so do you. Second, moreover, reality can never be simply copied anyway. "The trail of the human serpent is . . . over everything" (P, 33), elements of human perspective, concern, and interest inextricably mixed with the elements of reality. "Does a man walk with his right leg or with his left leg more essentially? Just as impossible may it be to separate the real from the human factors in the growth of our cognitive experience" (P, 113).

James readily meets the conditions for being a metaphysical realist by characterizing "reality" as composed both of what we experience, of what our sensations are of, and of what the abstract relations are that hold among ideas. The human factor has to do with fitting the two together, making judgments about which relations obtain among the sensations, subsuming facts under theories. But the fitting must conform to the necessities of what is given: the obdurancy of the sensations, the logical demands of coherence and consistency inherent in the patterns of relationship by which they are ordered. "Between the coercions of the sensible order and those of the ideal order, our mind is thus wedged tightly. Our ideas must agree with realities, be such realities concrete or abstract, be they facts or be they principles, under penalty of endless inconsistency and frustration." (P, 96). But no matter how tightly we may be wedged, there is still wiggle room. If it is misleading to say, as F. C. S. Schiller did, that reality is indeterminately "plastic" to whatever fittings of its elements we might choose to make, we nonetheless still make additions as best we can to suit our purposes, and reality "tolerates" the additions. Reality is like a client who has given his case to a lawyer and then must listen passively "to whatever account of his affairs, pleasant or unpleasant, the lawyer finds it most expedient to give" (P, 111). The lawyer's case is constrained by the need to be adequate to the facts, but the constraint is only partial; he still has his task of arguing the case cut out for him, and quite a bit rides on whether he does so effectively. "We receive . . . the block of marble, but we carve the statue ourselves" (P, 112).

James calls these fittings "perspectives" or "hypotheses," sometimes "frameworks" or "editions of the world." He complains that the copy theory of truth presupposes an absolutist perspective, an *édition de luxe* above and beyond all finite, fallible editions. It can do so only by neglecting the human factor, the presence of which necessarily relativizes all perspectives into working hypotheses, necessarily turns the claim about an absolute edition of the world into one among the many fallible claims about the world proposed by fallible human beings. Truth is always a framed work; all frameworks are temporary expedients.

Canons, taken in this Jamesian sense, are thus framing devices. In Erving Goffman's phraseology,[9] they are "schemata of interpretation" (G, 21), "principles of organization which govern events . . . and our subjective involvement in them" (G, 10). A "primary framework" is one "seen as rendering what would otherwise be a meaningless aspect of the scene into something that is meaningful" (G, 21), and the frame for all such primary frameworks, the understandings shared by a group regarding interpretive schemata, their interrelationships, and "the sum total of forces and agents that these (schemata) acknowledge to be loose in the world," constitute its "belief system" or "cosmology" (G, 27).

A natural canon, such as a scientific theory, frames the "unguided events" of inanimate nature, and the canon for such canons sets the boundary conditions for scientific inquiry in general, the conditions for what count as empirically verifiable facts or rationally intelligible concepts. A social canon differs from a natural one in that its framing also includes "guided doings," events that involve human agency. A social canon provides for the "serial management of consequentiality" by intentional agents (G, 22). An educational canon, even when it is about elements comprised by the natural canon, is a framework of this latter social sort. Its function is to make sense of human interactions, to advise us regarding how properly to act with respect to any situation framed by that canon and how by such a framing to understand properly our own and others' actions.

In saying that a knowledge of certain facts, concepts, or methods, of certain books and certain authors, is indispensable to an educated citizenry, advocates of an educational canon provide us with a guidebook for living effectively within the culture that defines what it means for us to be citizens. The canon teaches us what to feel, what to think, and what to do. It teaches us how; it teaches us why. It instructs us in what it means to be a human being dwelling, interacting, living, and dying within the horizons of time and space that encompass us. A culture's educational canon is an orientation program for membership in its community. Without it, we would be left to founder in a sea of confusion, feeling alienated, thinking confusedly, and acting strangely.

Plato is one of the great souls. At least one of his dialogues is typically high on the list of any canon for American undergraduates to ingest. *The Republic*, for instance, provides an aesthetic standard for us to emulate. It is a well-crafted work of art, well worth studying for the formalistic criteria it suggests regarding what should count as good dramatic structure, literary composition, conceptual coherence, and affective import. We learn from a close reading of the text about the formal conditions for aesthetic enjoyment and symbolic significance. *The Republic* also offers a moral standard. Its subject matter explores the question of justice as it relates to persons, communities, and the whole of the cosmos. It offers positive and negative role models for this virtue through its portraits of Socrates, Thrasymachus, and their friends, and in the action of the dialogue offers exemplary insight into how such virtue might be best acquired by an individual or by a state. By attending carefully to what Plato has to say, we learn about the conditions for right understanding, action, and sensibility. This dialogue also teaches a critical standard. It invites extrapolation of its exemplary ideas, agents, and procedures. It lures readers into applying its aesthetic and moral standards to other situations, to step out by metaphor, analogy, or generalization beyond its parochial limitations in order to bring its truths to bear upon matters of current relevance, and so perhaps to find that those matters are actually recurrent instances of timeless concerns.

James says that extrapolation of this sort is the way that cosmologies, cultural world views, arise. "Our fundamental ways of thinking about things are discoveries of exceedingly remote ancestors, which have been able to preserve themselves throughout the experience of all subsequent time" (P, 79). A certain way of framing a situation provided someone with useful guidance on some occasion long, long ago. That idea, or affective mood, or procedure was subsequently brought to bear upon another situation and here also led its utilizer prosperously. Continued use eventually made its presence canonical, a rule of thumb for dealing with certain kinds of situations, or a rule for determining the type of a given situation and hence for knowing the most appropriate way of dealing with it. Social canons of this sort eventuate in learned habits, in accustomed practices of such longstanding and unquestioned relevance that they seem natural rather than acquired. The cosmology of a people, its common sense, is thus foundational for it, the solid ground upon which its meanings, its presumptions about reality, and its sense of purpose, rest.

The purpose of a canon for education is that it be able to define what must be done in order for a culture to teach its rising generation the cosmology that frames it and makes it work. If the culture is functioning properly, commonsense beliefs will be taught in family and peer group interactions, imbibed in the language and attitudes of the people, in the taken-for-granted everyday assumptions of their social intercourse. Schooling serves to make common sense explicit where this is thought necessary, but also to correct common sense with respect to the technical beliefs and institutional practices that constitute the reigning science, criticism, and legal system of the culture. From cradle to grave, cultural guidance must be endlessly inculcated and reenforced if a society is to survive. For its principles of order, the foundations for its reality, are solely cultural.

But does the necessity for such a canon entail that its rules simply be copied, that the world it frames be mirrored accurately and fully in the world view of each citizen? This is precisely the absolutistic perspective against which James warns us. It is the reactionary claim that there is no human factor in what needs to be mirrored, or rather that the presence of such a factor distorts reality and so should as far as possible be transcended. There is a half-truth to this demand for slavish imitation, this insistence on the direct *mimesis* of cultural norms. Novices to a group are well advised to begin their acculturation by attempting to emulate its veteran practitioners, to learn its ways, its affective, effective, and cognitive dimensions, from the inside, in emic mode, by empathy.

This is what apprenticeship is all about, and in modern Western nations schooling is the way by which young people are apprenticed in the skills of citizenship required of adults. We learn to think well by thinking about an issue while utilizing the concepts a great thinker once fashioned when struggling with some similar issue. This is akin to learning how to make good cabinets by utilizing the techniques and tools a master craftsman has used, by copying one of the master's cabinets as exactly as possible.

But these are training wheels. When a cabinetmaker's apprentice is ready to be a master, she must demonstrate that she is by making her own master piece. She must cease replicating her teacher and make instead a cabinet of her own design and workmanship. Whatever the value of imitation, mature accomplishment means moving beyond our mentors, developing our own voice, a personal style, a distinctive mode of operation. The aim of education is to outgrow the need for training wheels, to gain the maturity needed to step out on our own. We yearn to write books and not just read them, to become leaders rather than memorizing tips on leadership, to actually love and work, and even suffer, rather than to do so only vicariously. Without the instructors to mimic faithfully and the prefashioned tools to utilize properly, we would never have been able to function on our own. But when that time comes, the old slavishness is put away and a new distinctive version of the old becomes at last a viable reality.

The wisdom of the modernists lies in realizing the heuristic necessity for interpretive frameworks and the prudential value in having canonical ones. A "great books" curriculum or core course requirement presumes the importance of selective valuation. It frames for students the need for frames, reminds them of the silliness in reinventing wheels and the further sight that will come to them if they learn to stand on another's shoulders. Our concern may be with axles instead of wheels, and our seeing may turn in another direction than was intended by those who invited us to use their shoulders for our vantage point. But without the wheel we would have never thought of linking them in pairs, and without our predecessors' invitation we would not have thought a further seeing possible, perhaps not even conceived of it. We outgrow the truths of our cultural heritage only by first growing into them. But we never outgrow the need for truths and hence for frameworks by which to make them.

However, no item in a canon was ever created to be a norm for others to emulate. The problems that particular idea was fashioned to address, the reasons that specific book was written, that experiment conducted, that policy approved were thoroughly situational. Therefore there is something too self-conscious, too mannered, too artificial in a work undertaken with one eye on its likely place in history. It has purposefully modulated its distinctive voice in order to blend in better with the voices of its heritage. Yet in doing so it has sacrificed its own mastery, settled for being a permanent apprentice of the cultural norms. Such a work has lost what it sought to gain by the very attempt to gain it.

Concretely, amid the rough and tumble of the real world, there are no canonical happenings, no higher truths or normative ideas, except those that are self-proclaimed. Genuinely canonical achievements thrive best in the murk of an ancestral past. Contemporary candidates for the canon are notoriously suspect when paraded in the bright light of peer criticism. No one can agree on whom the greatest thinkers or artists or leaders of the present generation are. No new idea strikes us as equal in stature to the great, world-shaking concepts of former times. The problem is not that we are too close to see; nor is it that familiarity breeds contempt. It is that up close, within the context of the immediate, the timeless truths and universal norms that compose the frame for our beliefs and practices have no root. We bring norms to the present; we do not find them there.

This is the wisdom of the postmodernists: that there is no natural hierarchy to things, that people, deeds, and ideas are all born equal. Each concrete thing is just what it is. What it is that it is, to be sure, is not something atomistic, self-enclosed. Anything is related to other things in complex, intertwining ways. But no thing is reducible to its relationships, nor defined by them: each is a distinctive integration of its relations and relata, a one-time-only this-not-those accomplishment. The equality of the things that are should be celebrated, each of them recognized for its uniqueness, its special voice adding a new melodic line to the ongoing and unending world chorale.

To see Plato through fourth-century Athenian eyes as just another young aristocrat, his dialogues a way to attract a following by which to further his own political agenda or feather his nest financially, is to strip away the later accretions of canonicity and to see him for what he was rather than for what the Western world has made of him. This Plato is best understood by studying other young Athenian aristocrats, by piecing together information about high-born women of that time, by investigating the character of slavery, the status of foreigners, the dynamics of commerce, war, and demographics. There is an egalitarian and pluralistic tropism to such inquiry because what makes a given voice distinctive is best shown through comparison with other voices, including those that share with it all but its most subtle aspects.

The value of this approach to pedagogy is obvious. Pull down the idols of the tribe, debunk the status of the proud and powerful, desanctify the saints, and desecrate the holy places: as the blinding sunlight of their glory fades, the gathering dusk reveals a hundred thousand points of lesser light, each with a glory of its own. Ideas, authors, methods, books that the canon has neglected or vilified come into their own this way. Each has its proper framing concepts to offer, its point of view, its cosmology. But these are no longer lunar frameworks, valued only as reflections, supplementary or distortive, of a greater light. They shine by their own glory now, in contrast or complement to other accomplishments. Hence Shakespeare's sister, writing in a world where gender did not debilitate, would have written plays the equal of her brother's plays.[10] The Harlequin romances are the equal of Faulkner's fiction as expressions of American culture. The critique by a young freshman in the back row of the class can hold its own against the views of Richard Rorty, for the one no less than the other provides a fresh reading of the text. America is a congeries of ethnicity, and each deserves its equal due in any educational curriculum devoted to transmitting the nation's heritage to a younger generation.

When the postmodernist argues that justice is a game we play, a set of rules two or more people agree upon as the frame within which to carry on their social intercourse,[11] the discussion shifts from a celebration of various uniquenesses to the difficult question of how they interact. If there are no natural frames, if each individual accomplishment is so by virtue of the willful framings it has created in order to integrate the elements of its experience, then the shift from "I" to "us" requires that some sort of encompassing frame be fashioned. There are none, objective and ready at hand, to rely upon. This fashioning can be done either by mutual consent or by one person imposing it through force of logic, rhetoric, or military armament. In Sartrean fashion, our self-creative acts involve canons of integration that present themselves, whether we like it or not, as principles of organization available for others to use for whatever self-creative or self-agrandizing purposes they might choose. Education in a postmodern mode must do more than celebrate difference; it must come to terms with its necessarily hegemonic implications.

James was always willing to agree with the tough-minded among his critics that "the world we live in exists diffused and distributed, in the form of an indefinitely numerous lot of *eaches*" (P, 118). But he also saw the unavoidable need and the utility of bringing those eaches together, both conceptually and physically, into larger unities. His name for the ideal of increasing the number and scope of such unities was *meliorism*, an ideal neither necessary nor impossible of implementation and hence inviting our commitment and courage on its behalf: "Our act, our turning-place, where we seem to ourselves to make ourselves and grow. . . . Why may they not be the actual turning-place and growing place which they seem to be, of the world—why not the workshop of being, where we catch fact in the making, so that nowhere may the world grow in any other kind of way than this?" (P, 129).

The postmodernist is correct to point out the ways in which hegemonic framing marginalizes a good many people, ideas, and practices at the expense of others. It is important for us to go back constantly to the basics, to the raw truth of things, and through a close reading of the original realities to recover or gain a genuine appreciation of those things in all their uniqueness. But it is naive to imagine that we can dwell forever in a world that is no more than a random pile of eaches. Maturity comes as we learn the hegemonic skills by which communities are built up, by which one and one become a pair, pairs become families, families are gathered into a gens, the gentes become a state, the states a united nations of the Earth, the worlds a galactic federation.

This need not be an imperial effort. Language games can be fashioned through mutual give and take rather than by fiat; metanarratives can be woven rather than imposed. Power can be an agent of empowerment, and self-interest need not be merely self-serving. An educational program aiming to nurture citizens who can function justly within the mosaic of American culture and within the world's multicultural pluralism should teach students the dynamics of various hegemonic orders, the reasons for their emergence, the conditions of their continuance, the factors that lead to their decline and fall. There is abundant learning here, ample for helping young people see both the value and the vice of social canons, their intertwined necessity and risk.

This way of framing the aims of education would provide students with access to the process by which particular perspectives, working hypotheses, and dumb guesses sometimes are prized for more than their momentary usefulness, how they come into general use, are embedded in habits and common sense, generalized into legal conventions and scientific theories, questioned for their inadequacies and then reformed or cast aside. A pragmatically justified appreciation of social canons can be taught through a pedagogical strategy that begins with their critique, that expunges them from the natural given furnishings of the immediately real in order to rediscover them as the inherited cultural accretions by which we transform the immediately real into a world of enduring meanings and human significance.

## CANON AND COMMUNITY

The attack on American society by the cultural left, its diatribe against American beliefs and practices as hierarchical, hegemonic, and exclusionary, presumes that it is possible for people to live without shared frameworks or that it is somehow possible to invent frameworks that do not order what they encompass into structures of importance, hierarchies of subordination and superordination, lattices of means and ends.

This presupposition is the radical equivalent to the reactionary's copy theory of cultural framing. The educational reactionary thinks there is a single natural canon for the regulation of a good and just society, and that it should be the core of any undergraduate curriculum. The educational radical thinks that since there is no natural canon the best society is an unregulated one, and that the design of an undergraduate curriculum should therefore be the responsibility of each individual student. The Kantian kingdom of ends, each member assigned by the state its proper place and fully consenting to the role defined by that place; the Marxian classless society, each member without benefit of state supervision making anew each day the place that best serves its needs and exercises its abilities. Between the rock and the whirlpool of these absolutes, pragmatism offers us an uncertain but navigable passage.

When James characterized "reality" as made up of eaches and suches, of concrete particular facts and abstract relational concepts, he added a third element: "the whole body of other truths already in our possession" (P, 96), the "ancient stock" of truths I have called our "social canon." "The most violent revolutions in an individual's beliefs leave most of his old order standing. . . . New truth is always a go-between, a smoother-over of transitions. It married old opinion to new fact so as ever to show a minimum of jolt, a maximum of continuity." (P, 31). The ancient stock, if absolutized, sets rules that eventually prove inadequate to the ever-changing eaches of the world. For that stock was canonized because of its relevance to worlds past, and even then its relevance was partial, its adequacy approximate, its flaws, its bugs, not fully appreciated. Things change, and old truths become uncouth because they are no longer able to frame the world. But new truths, if designed solely by reference to their immediate relevance, have all the limitations that result from inexperience, expedience, and the absence of thoughtful criticism. Designed to solve a particular problem, their usefulness may not be generalizable. In healing one wound, they may cause a hundred others. Absolutized, a frame tailored to the moment of its need is only a band-aid. Another frame is soon needed, and another, the disconnected orders of the days growing into a general incoherence of things. And so our world is no longer framed meaningfully.

Thus a community functions viably insofar as it can marry its traditional canons with the novelty of present experiences. Our work as citizens is to attempt to effect that marriage for our country. It is our duty as

Americans to know and appreciate the systems of belief—the mythic cosmologies, the scientific laws, the common sense attitudes—that in times past have served to give coherence and purpose to our life together. It is also our duty as Americans to be acquainted with and appreciate the motley of particulars—individuals whatever their kinds or styles or stations in life, ideas whatever their seeming worth, practices whatever their scope or legitimacy—that are encircled by the horizons of that coherence and purpose. And if this is so, our work as educators and as advocates of a well-functioning American educational system is to develop citizens who are at home in the canons that comprise the formal reality of their heritage, who are equally at home with the varied individual things that comprise the material reality of that heritage and of their present life, and who are able to devise constantly new frames that are adequate to both, that marry ancient canon and novel particular in a new canon which integrates as fully and complexly as possible all its participant elements.

This means that the social canons, and therefore the educational canon, ought always to be put in question. Like the ancient kings or like contemporary CEOs, they must defend themselves constantly against younger challengers. For such struggles there must be rules, just as much as there must be rules for the placid periods of uncontested authority. We require a canon of procedure every bit as much as we require a canon of achievement.

Even that most encrusted of modernists, the canon of the canonicists, Leo Strauss, notes the need for a continuing reinterpretation of the works of great minds: "Since the greatest minds contradict one another regarding the most important matters, they compel us to judge of their monologue; we cannot take on trust what any one of them say. On the other hand, we cannot but notice that we are not competent to be judges."[12] Strauss claims that it is the collapse of "authoritative traditions in which we could trust" that has forced us into an active but unjustified role as judges reconciling the divergent views of our great-souled mentors. But we have rejected his presumption of a lost, maybe-someday-to-be recovered absolute canon of great works, a conversation of ultimate voices speaking in timeless harmony. In its place, our pragmatic reading of the canon is that the great minds of the tradition are always in need of present-day judges. We may be incompetent insofar as we cannot claim to be ourselves great souled, but we alone can judge between the canonical voices and the new-sprung experiences. And in doing so, we create canons of process by virtue of which the canons of accomplishment are continually renewed.

One obvious way to make this dynamic explicit within a curriculum is for courses to "teach the conflicts,"[13] not only those among the canonical thinkers as Strauss would have us do but also those between canonical and noncanonical authors. To teach Milton's *Paradise Lost* alongside Mary Shelley's *Frankenstein* is a way to ask if the latter can be read as a reply to the former. The question is not which is greater in its use of language and its power of insight, but why Milton has been the more important for our culture and what we can learn about the limits both of canonical writings and of their challengers through this interesting juxtaposition. To read Shakespeare's *Tempest* in tandem with a contemporary black Caribbean writer's retelling of the play, framing both tellings in their respective contexts of self- and world-understanding, is to appreciate aspects of meaning available through Shakespeare's version that are easily overlooked and to hear resonances in the contemporary version otherwise drowned out by its overtly political agenda. The canonical texts are taught, but not as a set of isolated finalities. They are taught in conversation with other texts, other framings, some merely different, some once or presently contending with them for canonical relevance. The dynamics of the classroom thereby models that of the culture, teaching tomorrow's citizens the knowledge and appreciation of ancient authorities and fresh sassy pretenders to authority, and the skill in marrying them, which they will need if our nation is to long endure.

The marriage process, as it is carried on over time, thus results in a dynamic nicely caught in James's metaphor of grease spots. The intruding inappropriate glop of grease falls onto the cloth of tradition, spotting it. "The novelty soaks in; it stains the ancient mass; but it is also tinged by what absorbs it" (P, 78). The new fact stains the ancient truths, forcing them to adjust their framings in some small but irreversible way in order to take account of it. But the new fact is changed as well by the encompassing system of beliefs into which it is now set. Always ready with yet another metaphor, James shifts in midsentence to the notion of a stew: "It happens relatively seldom that the new fact is added *raw*. More usually it is embedded cooked, as one might say, or stewed down in the sauce of the old" (P, 78). The flavor and substance of the stew are altered because of the new ingredient; however, the ingredient is altered too, cooked down by the stewing until it becomes an integral aspect of the whole.

Metaphysical realism, pragmatically understood, requires this triple sense of objectivity: novel human doings in need of guidance, long-enduring systems of belief that provide the schemata of interpretation by which that guiding can be done, and opportunistic skill in sculpting act and theory, fact and canon, into a coherent, fruitful basis for intelligent action. An educational canon, pragmatically understood, marries modernists and postmodernists, shows their disputes to leave them trapped in an ideological isolation of partial truths, and invites them instead to exchange rings in celebration of a vow to share in the adventure toward a better American culture and a better world, an adventure that requires them both.

## CONCLUSION

I have tried in this chapter to practice what I preach. So I have framed the question of appropriate educational framings in a way that I think best does justice both to traditional views of what constitutes a proper undergraduate education and to the recent critique of those views. I have offered the thought of William James as a canonical paradigm for how to frame any such framing of the question of appropriate framings, and I have forced his ideas up against the challenge of fresh realities he would have thought neither desirable nor possible. I have supported the defense of canonicity through writers whose canonical authority is obvious by virtue of the national standing of the organizations they represent, and I have drawn from obscure and marginalized authors for my advocates of noncanonicity. I have invited all of these voices into a conversation, and legitimated the nature and scope of my undertaking by appeal to the wisdom of one of my own mentors in philosophy.

John Smith is no great soul, being too much a creative iconoclast amid his many self-canonizing colleagues to warrant such an honor. But let me give him the last word as I gave him the first, framing all these framings by reminding us of his insistence on how important it is for us to "regain the boldness and independence" of the philosophers comprising the classical American philosophical tradition not by "merely repeating their doctrines" but by developing "new basic ideas that can be used to control our interpretation of a wide range of experience."[14] May this chapter be read in such a spirit and for such a use.

## NOTES

1. John E. Smith, "The New Need for a Recovery of Philosophy," Presidential Address, American Philosophical Association, Eastern Division, 29 December 1981. Reprinted as chapter 7 of Smith, *The Spirit of American Philosophy* (revised edition, Albany: State University of New York Press, 1983). The quote is from p. 223.

2. William James, *Pragmatism*, lecture 2; 1907. The quote is from the Hacket Publishing Company edition, Indianapolis, 1981, 27. Henceforth P, followed by the page number cited.

3. William J. Bennett, *To Reclaim a Legacy: A Report on the Humanities In Higher Education* (Washington D.C.: National Endowment for the Humanities, 1984); 3. Henceforth B followed by the page number cited.

4. This is the argument of *Integrity in the College Curriculum*, published in 1985 by the Association of American Colleges, under the aegis of its Project on Redefining the Meaning and Purpose of Baccalaureate Degrees. Henceforth identified as A followed by the page number cited. The AAC report is echoed by Lynne V. Cheney in her 1990 NEH publication, *Tyrannical Machines: A Report on Educational Practices Gone Wrong and Our Best Hopes for Setting Them Right.*

5. Quoted by John Searle, "The Storm over the University," *New York Review of Books*, 6 December 1990, 34ff. Gates is one of the authors whose essays are included in a collection edited by Darryl L. Gless and Barbara Hernstein Smith, *The Politics of Liberal Education* (Durham: Duke University Press, 1990). Mary Louise Pratt, quoted next and again from Searle, is also represented in this collection of essays.

6. Jean Ferguson Carr, "Cultural Studies and Curricular Change," *Academe* (Nov.–Dec. 1990), 25. Henceforth C, followed by the page number cited.

7. Searle, section 3.

8. Caserio is quoted so in *The Chronicle for Higher Education* (21 November 1990): 1.

9. Erving Goffman, *Frame Analysis* (Boston: Northeastern University Press, 1986 [1974]). Henceforth G, followed by the page

number cited. See also Gregory Bateson, *Steps to an Ecology of Mind* (San Francisco: Chandler Publishing Co., 1972).

10. This is the point Virginia Woolf makes in *A Room of One's Own* (New York: Harcourt Brace Jovanovich, 1957 [1930]).

11. See, for instance, Jean-François Lyotard and Jean-Loup Thébaud, *Just Gaming* (Minneapolis: University of Minnesota Press, 1985 [1979]).

12. Leo Strauss, "What is Liberal Education?" in *Liberalism Ancient and Modern* (New York: Basic Books, 1968).

13. The phrase is Gerald Graff's, but this author does not know the when or why of it. The examples that follow are borrowed from the rationale for Dickinson College's recently approved new undergraduate English curriculum, which is a fine example of, and in part an inspiration for, the position developed in this chapter.

14. Smith, vi.

Douglas R. Anderson

# John E. Smith and the Heart of Experience

In his presidential address at the 1981 Eastern Division Meeting of the American Philosophical Association, John E. Smith outlined four points he believed to be involved in the recovery of philosophy in America. What I have to say here concerning Smith's own work in the recovery of philosophy has to do with the first of these: "There is *first*, the need for philosophy to root itself in the crude experience we all undergo or live through."[1] Following James, Peirce, and Dewey, Smith reconceived the notion of experience in such a way as to embrace the richness of experience as lived and to overcome the separation between "experience" and the world instituted by traditional empiricism. This chapter focuses on one aspect of Smith's reconception of experience—his attention to the self—and shows how it leads into the recovery as well as the reconception of several ideas important to the history of philosophy.

It is perhaps misleading to talk about "the heart" of experience in connection with Smith's work. It would be ironic to suggest the attribution of a sentimentalism to one who has devoted much of his life to marking out a space for the exercise of reason broadly conceived. I have, rather, two other reasons for using the term "heart." On the one hand, I want to attend to what Smith finds at the heart or locus of experience as a center of intention and interest: the self.[2] On the other hand, I want to suggest that the self is not only the locus of experience but is its *animus*, its heart.

There are two difficulties that need to be addressed at the outset. First, for those not familiar with the American philosophical tradition, it will sound strange to suggest that identifying the self as the heart of experience is anything novel. After all, traditional empiricisms and rationalisms identify experience with the self in a kind of subjective enclosure. Indeed, the self was understood not only as the heart of experience but *as* experience. The novelty, then, has to do with Smith's refocusing on the self in light of pragmatism's reconstructed notion of experience. Indeed, it was precisely the point of Dewey's conception of experience to overcome the identity of self and experience. As Smith puts it:

> For too long it has been supposed that experience is a mental affair and that we begin our relations with the world confined to an "inside" view so that the problem is that of finding ways to move to the world "outside." But if the dogma about experience as private, mental content is challenged as a nonempirical and erroneous view of experience, the problem is transformed.[3]

The reconception of experience in the hands of Dewey, however, had the effect of marginalizing concern for the individual self. In effect Dewey sometimes appeared to be throwing the baby out with the bath water. Smith is acutely aware of this tendency in Dewey's work:

> One might say that Dewey laid such stress on the objective and public nature of experience that there are grounds for questioning whether he did justice to its personal and individualized aspects. As I shall point out, he did not indeed omit this dimension of experience, but no reader of Dewey can entirely suppress the impulse to ask from time to time the question, "Whose experience?"[4]

Thus, as suggested, what is significant is that Smith refocuses attention on the self in light of the reconstructed notion of experience that Dewey provided. Smith's replacement of the self at the heart of experience generates a tension with the general trend in pragmatism to downplay the import of the individual. This tension is of some concern, for Smith clearly envisions his own work to be largely in concert with Dewey's thinking; he in fact confesses "a certain ambivalence" in criticizing Dewey (*RG*, 109). Given this concern, it is perhaps best to construe Smith's recovery of the self as a Roycean tempering of Dewey's conception of experience.

All of this, however, raises another issue. To many working in the American philosophical tradition today, it might seem at first glance that Smith is trying to rekindle interest in the kind of narrow individualism against which Peirce and Dewey constantly fought. This is not the case. Smith's recovery of the self, because it takes place in light of his reconceived notion of experience, does not recover the self as an isolated subject but as a center of interest and purpose living in and through experiential encounter.

Let me proceed, then, by turning to a brief sketch of some features of Smith's conception of the self in experience. I shall then consider how this conception allows Smith to recover and reconceive two perennial issues from the history of philosophy: the question of direct or "immediate" knowing and the notion of self-realization. These cases are exemplary not only of the importance of Smith's work but of the importance of pragmatism as a medium for the recovery of philosophy.

## THE SELF IN EXPERIENCE

In describing experience in terms of encounter, Smith, following Dewey, seeks to reject some well-established empiricist myths. The first is that experience is a veil or "tissue" of subjectivity that is over against an external world. As Smith often points out, what is experienced is the world, not experience. Experience is the encounter of an experiencer with what is experienced. The problem of "getting to" the world is therefore a problem manufactured by rationalist and empiricist separations of self and world. "Experience is, instead," Smith says, "a valid medium of disclosure through which we come to know what there is."[5] The rejection of mere subjectivity also entailed Dewey's well-known attack on a "spectator" theory of knowledge. Insofar as we are in encounter in experience, we are not simply perceiving (or conceiving) photographers passively gathering information. Rather, to know the world is also to transform it; knowing is an active engagement with the world. Finally, Smith and Dewey both reject the corollary to traditional empiricism's subjectivism that all experience is private. As Smith argues, "for Dewey, experience, in virtue of its being the meaningful and funded result of many interactions between the individual and the environment, attains a *public* character evidenced among other things by the fact that it can be communicated, shared and compared" (*RE*, 86).

In Smith's hands the new conception of experience displaced the self from its empiricist lodging, but it did not dismiss it. The self is not equivalent to experience, but it *is* a dimension of it. Moreover, the self, insofar as it is *in* experience, cannot be, as Smith and Dewey see it, merely mental—it is not only a mind. This is evident once we admit, as it would seem we have to, that experiencing is not reducible to knowing. For Smith, experience can be seen as the biography of an encounter of a self (or community of selves). In this biography the self finds itself as it responds to that which it encounters: "The experience of the 'mine' is, in short, the experience of *finding myself* in the contents of experience by way of response to them."[6] As the "I" finds the "me" in response to encounter, it finds also the multiplicity of dimensions of the experiencing self. Persons not only know, they fear, hate, enjoy, and so on. As Smith sees it, then, experience reveals that the self is "more than a mind; it is a dynamic, organic system of habits, feelings, desires, tendencies and thoughts, unified through plans and purposes framed and projected by what I call a centre of intention."[7]

The import of opening up the dimensions of experience and the experiencing self is that it fosters discussion of human problems and issues other than the problem of knowing in its narrow sense. It helps philosophy move beyond what Dewey called the "epistemology industry." Moreover, in Smith's case it provided the opportunity for recovering ideas and insights from the philosophical tradition, for the acknowledgement of experiential complexity introduced the need to make adjustments to well-established insights. This recovery takes place through the lens of his reconceived notion of experience and therefore establishes an important dialogue between pragmatism and its predecessors. Let us turn, then, to the two cases at hand.

## SELF AND DIRECT EXPERIENCE

Throughout the history of Western thinking, abstract, reflective knowing has been opposed to immediate knowing in a variety of guises such as intuition, instinct, and revelation. Both Dewey and Peirce considered the issue at length and stood adamantly on the side of mediated, reflective knowing. To be sure, their motive was primarily a negative one; given the spread of experience, it was difficult to see how any judgment could be unmediated; as Peirce argued, the sign system is perfusive. Moreover, since both made criticism central to the improvement or growth of knowledge and culture, they feared any claims to immediate knowing that might close the door on inquiry. Therefore, both developed accounts of knowing as inferential and, in Dewey's case, experimental. In working this point into his account of experience, Dewey was led to make his well-known distinction between "having" and "knowing" in experience. In *Experience and Nature* Dewey put the distinction as follows: "There are two dimensions of experienced things: one that of having them, and the other that of knowing them so that one can have them in more meaningful and secure ways."[8] For Dewey there is only one kind of knowing, scientific knowing, which is reflective and inferential.

Smith is sympathetic to Dewey's concern not to confuse "having" with inferential knowing. Moreover, he shares the concern about immediacy; insofar as knowing is a dimension of experience, it cannot be construed as standing over against it as an immediate judge. Nevertheless, Smith, in considering the role that nonreflective experience has played, for example, in religion in the history of human culture, sees something problematic in pushing the having-knowing distinction too far. As he sees it, to say that no "knowing" occurs in "having" drives a wedge in the middle of Dewey's notion of experience—a wedge he probably does not want to have. It creates the possibility for the very kind of dichotomy that Dewey most often sought to overcome.

In pushing the distinction too far, Dewey, or readers of Dewey, might arrive at a view that denies certain aspects of the self's having of experience. Smith uses the case of knowing forgiveness through undergoing it: "I agree with Dewey that the pervasive qualities of situations that mark out 'having *an* experience' must be 'had' but I contend that in undergoing an experience of forgiveness, for example, we 'know' what the quality of this experience means in and through having and no controlled inquiry is involved."[9] Dewey's fear of the immediate led him to work around the issue of a cognitive element in having. On the one hand, he clearly denied experimental knowing to the dimension of "having"—a denial with which Smith is in full agreement. On the other hand, his descriptions of experience often seemed to involve cases like the case of forgiveness above. For Smith, experience seemed to disclose the fact that persons often find themselves knowing things without conducting controlled inquiry. Thus, he sought for a way to deal with this fact within a Deweyan framework of experience.

In responding to Beth Singer's review of *Purpose and Thought*, Smith developed a line of reasoning he had taken some years earlier in *Reason and God*. He began by acknowledging his agreement with Dewey that there is no immediate experience: "All experience contains meaning of some sort and all meaning implies determination and discrimination. This means that were there totally immediate experience, it would remain fully inarticulate even for the self who has it" (*RG*, 181). Inasmuch as knowing is a dimension of experience, it follows that there can be no immediate knowing. If our options are only immediate knowing and knowing by controlled inquiry, moreover, Dewey is right in asserting the exclusiveness of experimental knowing. Sensing the tension this places on the self's experiencing of a kind of cognitive having, Smith seeks to outflank the dilemma.

"In the theory of knowledge," Smith argues, "the dogma tells us that every cognition is either an immediate apprehension or intuition or it is an inference" (*CS*, 31). That is, the given options are knowing that is absolutely immediate with no semiotic mediation and knowing that is inferential in the sense of being an intentionally controlled inquiry. Smith fails "to see that the alternative is exhaustive" (*CS*, 31), and he adduces as evidence a case in which two persons encounter each other:

> Consider two selves encountering each other in conversation; to begin with, each is directly *present* to the other in the sense that it is both highly artificial and non-empirical to say that each "infers" the existence of the other as a mind from signs, because the only signs that could count in this regard would be perceived as expressions of meaning and intent which are themselves *already presupposed* to be expressions of a sign-using being, i.e., a mind. (*CS*, 31)
>
> The experience in the case of both selves is direct, i.e., it is of someone actually present and not inferred, but the reason I do not say that this direct experience is immediate is that we understand, know, interpret each other's meanings *only* mediately through signs in the context. (*CS*, 31)

Thus Smith marks off a realm of direct experience. The selves are neither immediately transparent to each other as centers of intention, nor do they exercise a controlled inquiry to arrive at a hypothesis of the other's selfhood. The direct experience carries with it, in the having, a cognitive dimension; there is acquired meaning in the having that is direct but not immediate, that is mediated but not inferred.

While Smith acknowledges that the cognitive dimension of direct experience in his sense "has yet to be worked out," we can turn to his discussion of interpretation to obtain a heading. Following Royce, Smith distinguishes interpretation from perception and conception inasmuch as one can both perceive and conceive some sign without being able to interpret it. This is particularly the case, for example, in our encounter with other selves as in the instance above. Insofar as a self is neither merely the qualitative content of a perception nor the abstract universal of a conception, the mediating function of interpreting is required to account for the experience of knowing and understanding others (*SS* 321–23). Moreover, while interpretation is clearly not immediate because of its involving signs, it is also not equivalent to an inferential process narrowly construed. Even if one did, as would be highly unusual, infer another's existence in experience from a set of premises in a specific situation, there would be a remainder of meanings not captured by the inference. As Smith argues, interpreting in direct experience means that we read the "import," the meaning, of an encounter; we do not merely describe or explain it (SS, 33). The difference is crucial. In his discussion of knowing God in *Experience and God* Smith pinpoints the location of interpretation's role in direct experience:

> On the one hand, he [God] is not immediately apprehended because he is known only in and through the medium; on the other hand, he is not inferred because he is *present* in the medium and the apprehension of that presence is something different from the logical process of inferring the divine existence by starting with some fact as a basic premise. (*EG*, 83)

In sum, the experienced situation is more complex than intuitionism, empiricism, or Dewey's having-knowing distinction allows.

Thus, Smith at once uses Dewey's reconception of experience to renew discussion of direct cognition and uses the tradition's interest in direct cognition to alter the angle of Dewey's perspective. While the discussion of direct cognition and interpretation requires development, it seems to me an important avenue of inquiry for two reasons. First, and most fundamentally, it responds better to the experiencing self's lived situation than does a hard and fast division between knowing and "having." The second point of import of direct experience is that, as a reconceived account of knowing by acquaintance, it has further implications for what Dewey called "know how."

The idea that persons can acquire know how is crucial not only to Dewey's overall theory of experience but to understanding experience itself. One can know how to handle horses, build a stone wall, and so on. This is of course an old philosophical concern as Socrates' analogy of teachers and horse trainers attests. However much controlled inquiry may be involved in cases of acquiring know how, it seems evident that it is not the only cognitive factor. Smith's account of direct experience suggests a way of getting at this without recourse to immediacy. Nor is this merely a philosopher's problem. One result of misreading Dewey's intent in the having-knowing distinction has been a kind of scientism undergirding the development of public affairs in the United States. This is nowhere more evident than in the teaching of teaching where "knowledge" of teaching is reduced to the content, hypothetical and factual, of "scientific" studies of society. While Smith's perspective does not advocate the overthrow of reason, his notion of direct experience offers a way of reintroducing artfulness to human endeavors without returning to some version of absolute intuition. Not only does it provide the possibility of present, direct apprehension of meaning, it allows for past knowings and habits and their relations to remain cognitively alive in the present situation.

The fact that Dewey can be misread in the direction of scientism does not result only from the ambiguity of the division between having and knowing. It stems rather from his more general inattention to the self, and in particular to the self's interiority. Despite his belief in the self as agent and in the primacy of education, Dewey focused primarily on public, social reconstruction, on institutional reform, as the appropriate route to ameliorating life. Even in some late writings such as "The Democratic Faith and Education" where Dewey appeals to human ideals, desires, and understanding, there remains a feeling that he is coming at them publicly, from the outside.[10] As Smith puts it, for Dewey "The hindrances to human progress are largely in the public world, the surrounding environment, not within ourselves; we must look rather in the external world if we are to modify the shape of things, remove obstacles to growth and liberate the forces of progress." (*SA*, 144). Smith, in refocusing on the self in experience, sought to temper, though certainly not to eliminate, the importance of public progress (see *PT*, 88). This is nowhere more evident than in his recovery and reconception of the notion of self-realization.

## THE SELF AS SELF-REALIZING

On Smith's view, insofar as a self is a center of intention and purpose, her movement into the future is her primary concern. Being a self is to be making oneself in accord with one's overarching purpose. In a discussion of the nature of a person's willing, Smith puts the point as follows: "In willing its realization, first through a life plan and subsequently through the actions and efforts required to bring it to fruition, the person at the same time gives expression to a commitment or investment that is essentially a form of self-identification."[11] This conception of the self sets the stage for discussion of the moral aim of life and in this connection we hear an echo of self-realization theories of ethics in the work of idealists such as F. H. Bradley, A. E. Taylor, and Brand Blanshard. Nevertheless, Smith's notion of self-realization is transformed by its being interpreted through his reconception of experience.

The first difference from traditional views of self-realization is that the very precariousness of experience, and therefore of the self's experiencing, precludes a narrow and closely fixed conception of purpose and its fulfillment. Telic activity as the self's work *in* experience cannot be of the sort in which one has a fixed role in the scheme of the cosmos. Indeed, Smith responds to Bradley and Hegel in direct fashion:

> As we can see from the concrete or objective moralities to be found in Hegel's philosophy and in Bradley's *Ethical Studies*, the realization of the individual and the moral demands thus entailed all too readily fall back into the pattern represented by "my station and its duties." (BW, 29–30)

One's station and duties, whatever they might be and insofar as they are not abstractions, will meet resistance in experiential encounter. To hang on to them tenaciously and without adjustment to situations is to become a mechanism, not a self. Such a fear is at the heart of Bertrand Russell's well-known description of "the rational man" as "that inhuman monster." As Smith suggests, the diversity of experiential encounter demands that the search for and the fulfillment of one s purpose must be creatively undertaken: "A life plan, in the nature of the case, will be general in the sense of being open to novelty, creativity, and ensuing possibilities in the course of its realization" (*BW*, 29).

Let me develop Smith's suggestion through an example. Suppose one takes as part of one's purpose or plan, "to be a teacher." Simple *identification* of oneself as a teacher might occur if one gets the proper degrees, clothes, external affections, and so forth; such accoutrements may exist as cultural parameters for being a teacher. However, one's purpose is not fulfilled. Experience teaches us that teaching itself is a creative response to other selves. It involves interpreting their purposes, interests, and awarenesses; it involves adjustment and reaction in light of our own general purpose. All of this requires not a strict realization of a narrowly conceived telos, but a breadth of knowledge and know how at work in experiencing under the guidance of a general purpose. Indeed, Smith's identification of purpose as general suggests a further point: that the purpose itself will develop over time in response to experiential encounter. While Smith does not make this point explicit, it seems to me to be in concert with his description of self-realization, and it calls forth Dewey's emphasis on growth as well as Peirce's notion of "developmental teleology." It is a line of thinking in Smith's work that warrants further attention.

Smith's reconception of experience transforms not only the end and process of self-realization but its enactment as well. For Smith, self-realization occurs through acts of willing. While this seems an obvious point, Smith's attention to the experience of willing reveals an important shift away from the simple war of reason and impulse that, for example, Blanshard describes in his account of rational self-realization.[12]

First, in connection with our earlier discussion of direct experience, it seems apparent that willing is no more a highly intentional reference to a specific purpose in all its instances than knowing is always a result of controlled inquiry. Insofar as self-realization is developmental, we see the self in experience as bearing with it habits of intention and direction—in Smith's terms, its experience of "me" and "mine." Nor are we to construe habits as mere parts of one's character; rather, the self is shot through with habits of intention and direction as Smith reminds us in his many descriptions of the self's multiplicity (see BW and SU ) .

Moreover, as Smith describes, when willing is more self-consciously intentional, it is still not simply a matter of reasonableness dominating impulse. Willing involves several dimensions beyond purpose: preference, power, and perseverance (*BW*, 27).[13] To focus on the first of these as exemplary, Smith maintains that the presence of preference, as "a judgment expressing a grading of priorities," is extensive in acts of willing (*BW*, 32). However, it becomes significant in those cases ordinarily called "moral dilemmas," for in these cases preferring must occur blindly. Reason is sometimes simply impotent. As Smith argues: "If it were true, as I believe it is not, that reason, in some imperious sense, could of itself guarantee a total harmony and absence of conflicts between goods and obligations, living the good life would be a far less strenuous affair than it actually is." (*BW*, 32). In short, then, it is not the case that self-realization is simply "up to us" as rational beings fulfilling a clear duty. There is, Smith says, a tragic dimension revealed when willing is limited to blind preference or choice. And this tragic dimension results directly from the precariousness of experiential encounter.

While self-realization in Smith's hands obtains a more experiential flavor than its idealist counterpart, it is also important to see that Smith's insistent attention to self-realization serves as a corrective to Dewey. Again, the difference is primarily one of emphasis and tone. Indeed, as Smith points out, there is "every reason to believe that the unification and self-realization of the person as a whole remained for Dewey a central value" (*PT*, 193). The problem is that Dewey's marginalizing of the self led him to ignore or distort certain features of the self in experience.

Let me address this issue first by pointing to a fundamental agreement between Smith and Dewey. They agree that a crucial aspect of self-realization is the active engagement of the self in the reconstruction of society and cultural meaning. As Dewey put it in describing the role of education: "We must think and act upon the assumption that public education has a positive responsibility to shape those habits of thought and action which in turn shape organized conditions and social action."[14] However, for Smith self-realization has a twofold objective: "On the one side, it is an effort to realize the good as the self-fulfillment of the individual; on the other, it is the aim to make some contribution to the human community in accordance with the interests we have and the unique endowments we have inherited." (*BW*, 27). Smith resists Dewey's tendency to marginalize *self*-realization in order to focus on community realization. Moreover, he resists Dewey's tendency to cast solutions to problems in scientific and institutional terms. "Not all human problems," Smith argues, "are directly a matter of overt and external control of things; some of them have to do with the interpretation of individual life and its purpose" (*RG*, 111). Smith locates these differences experientially.

In his discussions of the self Smith repeatedly illustrates that the self encounters in experience not only an environment but itself as a dimension of that environment. A person is able to interpret himself: "In being selves we are able to arrive at indispensable data by directing attention to what we think and do. In this sense we are in a 'privileged position' for self knowledge" (*SU*, 145).

Such self-encounter serves as the arena for the self's dialogue with itself: "What Dewey did not see," says Smith, "is that the individual has an inner life of his own which is itself *social* in character just because it is an endless dialogue of the self with itself" (*SA*, 129). It is in this process of self-encounter that the moral dimension of the experience of self-realization emerges, for the self becomes a problem for itself and can threaten to fragment the wholeness of the person (*PT*, 89). Smith illustrates this point in his description of *conative* doubt: "The self feels an opposition within itself resulting from a sense of incongruity or incompleteness" (*EG*, 103, see also *RG*, 111–12). The self thus faces itself with the question of "what to do?" And this question in turn leads to the question, "to what purpose?"

In brief, then, the moral dimension of self-realization develops as the self comes to interpret and to know itself. However, the moral request for internal adjustments of the self is not experientially complete. It in turn calls forth the religious dimension of experience: "The religious dimension comes into view when we encounter in our own selves a peculiar question and concern, the question and concern for the quality of our life and our world *taken as a whole*" (*RA*, 60). It is at this juncture that a more serious rift between Dewey and Smith begins to appear.

On the one hand, in *A Common Faith* Dewey does admit that while there is no such thing as religious experience there is "a religious aspect of experience."[15] On the other hand, Dewey refused to talk in terms of ultimate purpose, opting instead to talk of "imaginative ideals." Smith points to Dewey's own commitment to democracy and intelligence as revelatory of something deeper and more comprehensive in experience—a sense of the religious that Dewey, perhaps because of his inattention to *self*-realization, falls short of addressing. Smith addresses this point in two ways. First, he argues that the moral dimension is inadequate without the religious dimension: "Just as surely as moral criticism implies moral standards, so moral standards themselves imply some view concerning the final destiny of man" (*RG*, 200). Second, Dewey's account is inadequate to the full sense in which human endeavor seeks not only knowledge but inspiration:

> In encountering ourselves, however, and in reflecting on the fact of our being in the world at all, we come to realize that our total life is problematic in the sense that we stand in need of a purpose for being, a self-integrating power that makes self-realization possible in a situation constantly threatening us both from without and from within. (*RA*, 60–61)

Thus, for Smith the experiential trajectory of self-realization discloses more than what Dewey was willing to admit. Regardless of how one describes them, imaginative ideals as the work of finite minds do not seem to do justice to the experiencing of mystery and commitment. In pragmatic terms, Dewey's account of the religious in experience is akin to replacing wine with grape juice. This rift between their views is a complex one, and it is not possible to provide a just treatment of it here. Suffice it to say that, as Smith sees it, coming to the religious dimension by way of interpreting the self as self-realizing *in* and *through* experience allows us to see, in Peirce's sense, the reality of the dimension. Coming at it, as Dewey does, from a scientifically-driven outlook subjects the religious dimension to a genetic reduction and instrumental reading that are inadequate to experience itself.

Smith's recovery of self-realization in light of experience reconceived not only alters the idea of self-realization but returns to philosophical discussion within the bounds of contemporary pragmatism questions of the self's internality and the moral and religious dimensions it discloses. As in the case with direct experience, this is a recovery in two directions, and it forges a continuity in the American tradition where many are wont to force a division.

## CONCLUSION

The features of the recovery of direct experience and self-realization resulting from Smith's attention to the self as the heart of experience I take to be representative and suggestive. Smith's replacement of the self seems to be a significant development in the history of American thinking. Dewey's pragmatism has a tendency to begin to blur the edges of evaluative distinctions, to democratize the elements of nature. Smith's work, in reaching back to insights of Edwards and Royce, reminds us that the very human problems that Dewey sought to ameliorate have a way of coming back to us not as the result of institutional mismanagement but through the direct encounter of ourselves in experience. They surprise us with the force of their significance not unlike the premature loss of a loved one. In considering the self in experience, Smith has hit upon a central problem in American pragmatism.

That Smith's work occurs when pragmatism is being reconstituted as neopragmatism under the influence of the linguistic turn and a narrowly empirical conception of experience makes it significant also as an alternative way of developing pragmatism. Those working in the American tradition will do well to follow Smith's lead in general if not in particular. While it does reveal insights that demand attention, neopragmatism seems on the whole unable to get out from under the program of analytic philosophy and thus fosters a kind of philosophical regression that seems more likely to develop "stagnantism" than pragmatism in the long run. However, Smith's work calls forth a dialogue of ideas and insights that exemplifies the developmental character of philosophical recovery.

## NOTES

1. John E. Smith, "The New Need for a Recovery of Philosophy," in *The Spirit of American Philosophy: Revised Edition* (Albany: State University of New York Press, 1983), 231. Hereafter *The Spirit of American Philosophy* will be cited in the text as *SA*.

2. John E. Smith, *Reason and God: Encounters of Philosophy with Religion* (New Haven: Yale University Press, 1961), 109. Hereafter *Reason and God* will be cited in the text as *RG*.

3. John E. Smith, *Experience and God* (New York: Oxford University Press, 1968), 36. Hereafter *Experience and God* will be cited in the text as *EG*.

4. John E. Smith, "The Reconception of Experience in Peirce, James and Dewey," in *Pragmatism Considers Phenomenology*, ed. Corrington, Hausman, and Seebohm (Lanham, MD: University Press of America,

1987), 86. Hereafter this essay will be cited in the text as *RE*. See also *RG*, 109–11.

5. John E. Smith, *Religion and Empiricism* (Milwaukee: Marquette University Press, 1967), 44. Hereafter *Religion and Empiricism* is cited in text as *RA*.

6. John E. Smith, "Is the Self an Ultimate Category," in *Philosophy, Religion. and the Coming World Civilization: Essays in Honor of William Ernest Hocking*, ed. Leroy S. Rouner (The Hague: Martinus Nijhoff, 1966). Hereafter The essay is cited as *SU*. See also Smith, *Purpose and Thought: The Meaning of Pramagmatism* (Chicago: University of Chicago Press, 1984 [1978]), 95. Hereafter *Purpose and Thought* will be cited in the text as *PT*.

7. John E. Smith, "Signs, Selves and Interpretation," in *Contemporary American Philosophy*, ed. John E. Smith (New York: Humanities Press Inc., 1970), 324. Hereafter this essay is cited in text as *SS*. Here and elsewhere Smith develops his account of the self at length. Of particular interest is Smith's description of knowing selves by way of interpretation. However, the limited scope of this project prevents further inquiry in that direction. Also, for a more extended treatment of Smith's view of "experience," see Dale M. Schlitt, "John E. Smith on Experience," *Philosophy and Theology* 2, no. 2 (Winter 1987): 105–123.

8. John Dewey, *John Dewey: The Later Works. Volume I*, ed. Jo Ann Boydston (Carbondale: Southern Illinois University Press, 1981), 379.

9. John E. Smith, "Comments on Beth J. Singer's 'John E. Smith on Pragmatism,'" *Transactions of the Charles S. Peirce Society* 16, no. 1 (Winter 1980): 30. Hereafter cited in text as *CS*. This same issue arises in Dewey's well-known exchange with Benedetto Croce. In her review of *Purpose and Thought*, to which Smith is responding here, Beth Singer points to ways of recovering a noetic element through Dewey's notion of perception. While her point is well taken, it remains the case that Dewey never wholeheartedly admitted to anything like a belief in direct experience and on many occasions appeared to deny its possibility. Smith seems to me right in identifying this as a serious ambiguity in Dewey's work, and I take his response to be not a refutation of Dewey so much as a way of reading the ambiguity in a way that will maintain Dewey's insights about experience.

10. John Dewey, *John Dewey: The Later Works. Volume 15*, ed. Jo Ann Boydston (Carbondale: Southern Illinois University Press, 1989), 251–60.

11. John E. Smith, "Being and Willing: The Foundation of Ethics," *The Journal of Speculative Philosophy: New Series*, 1, no. 1 (1987): 27–28. Hereafter "Being and Willing" is cited in text as *BW*.

12. Brand Blanshard, *Reason a Goodness* (New York: Humanities Press Inc., 1961), 409–446 in particular. In fairness to Blanshard, his account of this war is much more subtle than many earlier versions, and although he operates without a reconception of experience, his compelling style and use of examples nearly overcomes the omission.

13. I refer the reader to *BW* or Smith's phenomenological apology for the alliteration.

14. Dewey, *John Dewey: The Later Works. Volume 2*, 235.

15. Ibid., Volume 9, 10.

Lewis S. Ford

# Whitehead's Distinctive Features

## PRELIMINARY OBSERVATIONS

American philosophy could simply mean philosophy done on American soil, but such a broad categorization would be unhelpful, at least in this century, where so many different kinds are practiced. More particularly it has been taken to refer to the philosophizing growing out of the seminal writing of Charles Sanders Peirce and William James. This certainly includes the trajectory of pragmatism, but if it is so restricted to pragmatism, most of the contributions of Josiah Royce, and all of those of George Santayana, would be ignored. Let us consider instead a cluster of interrelated trajectories, one of which would be pragmatism, another Whitehead's metaphysics. It appropriates the earlier concern with radical empiricism, dynamism and process, fallibilism, weaving them into a coherent synthesis. Several, including John E. Smith,[1] have defended Whitehead's inclusion in American philosophy.

However, Whitehead was an Englishman, spending most of his life in Cambridge and London, before coming to Harvard in 1924, at 63. But then he was not a professional philosopher, having taught nothing but mathematics in England. Harvard was the setting of his philosophical career, both for teaching and for writing. True, he had written three books on the philosophy of nature in England, but the expansion of his thinking into metaphysics had to await the Lowell Lectures, delivered in Boston, February 1925, and later incorporated into *Science and the Modern World.*

It is true that William Ernest Hocking has written that "his speculative structure, which came to fruition during his American years, was already well advanced in its main outlines" in England.[2] Yet the metaphysics sketched out in those Lowell Lectures of 1925 are exceedingly meager.[3] What Whitehead achieved over the next four years was the constant, intense revision of this sparse beginning. Hocking may have inferred that because Whitehead was not influenced very much by his immediate colleagues he must have brought it all with him from England. What he brought from England are all the historical, literary, scientific, and philosophical influences chronicled in *Science and the Modern World*. Its metaphysical development was primarily an exercise in self-criticism.

Whitehead's reading in philosophy in England was quite informal, except for Kant, whose transcendental aesthetic (since it pertained to space, time, and mathematics) was practically memorized. His knowledge of Aristotle and Hegel was largely derivative from secondary sources and personal contact with Lord Haldane and McTaggart. The debate between proponents of internal and external relations may have influenced him, although Hartshorne has more explicitly resolved the issue within process circles by his asymmetrical relations than Whitehead has. Again, the evolutionary theorists such as Bergson, Smuts, and C. Lloyd Morgan should have had same impact, although George Lucas has found less than might be expected.[4]

It makes less sense to place Whitehead in the tradition, say, of Bradley or of the evolutionary theorists, than as successor to James and Dewey. Moreover, it is in terms of the comparative impact on British and American philosophy that Whitehead's identity as an American philosopher becomes most evident. As far as we know, his impact on British philosophers was practically nil. Here he has not lacked for champions, most notably, Charles Hartshorne. Hartshorne is not so much a disciple of Whitehead as an independent thinker with a remarkably similar agenda, but he has indefatigably defended Whitehead's cause over many decades.[5]

It is a curious fact that while Whitehead's philosophy continues to enjoy considerable interest from philosophically minded theologians, it has come to be largely neglected by American philosophers. Yet his major work, *Process and Reality: An Essay in Cosmology* devotes only fourteen pages to theism, even though it was first presented as the Gifford Lectures in natural theology.

In contemporary Germany the situation is reversed: there is growing interest among the philosophers, but the theologians, still laboring under Karl Barth's interdict against natural theology, shun process thought.

If in America, theologians cultivate Whitehead's philosophy but philosophers neglect it, why should this be so? The strong interest of theologians in process thought easily explained: Here is a comprehensive philosophy informed by relativity physics which is also a radical critique of traditional theism while still being intrinsically theistic, affirming a transcendent source of value and novelty. Whitehead redesigned theism in such a way as to counter some of the basic atheistic objections, especially those concerning divine power and evil.

## REASONS FOR PHILOSOPHICAL NEGLECT

Philosophers have neglected his thought for two primary reasons. He has become quite unfashionable in many philosophical circles because of his commitments to metaphysics and to theism. Later an we will examine various idiosyncrasies (such as his tiny occasions and pansubjectivity), contingent objectionable features which perhaps could be corrected, but which are quite characteristic of his philosophy.[7]

### *Theism*

Philosophy over the years has tended to became a secular substitute for religion, and many shy away from anything explicitly and intrinsically theistic, although recognizing the great systems of the past that were theistic. However, classical theists, such as Thomists, often leave process theism alone because of its apparent unorthodoxy.

God is distinctively required because every concrescence or process of becoming, without which no actuality could be, depends on an an initiating aim for its subjectivity, and this aim can only have a transcendent source. While nontemporal in many aspects, this God temporally experiences the world in its on-goingness, as it becomes actual.

Many find Whitehead's theism objectionable and seek to treat it as a contingent idiosyncrasy. It is certainly conceivable that a naturalistic variant is possible. The real issue is whether such attempts can be both coherent and reasonably similar to Whitehead's thought. Donald W. Sherburne's "Whitehead without God"[8] is perhaps the most well known, but I question whether the target of his attack is Whitehead's own position rather than William A. Christian's interpretation of it.[9] More recently, however, George Allan has made a very telling argument for Whiteheadian naturalism that must be respected.[10]

*Metaphysics*

Metaphysics has been buried by its detractors at least since Kant, but it has a peculiar resilience. As the study of the necessary features of reality it must be a perennial undertaking. Unless everything is absolutely contingent, in which case the contrast between the necessary and the contingent will have no meaning, there are necessary features to be studied, no matter how abstract and arcane. Philosophy as the disciplined use of free imagination in the quest for knowledge is particularly suited for the metaphysical enterprise. Its structure is invariant. As William James remarked, the world cannot take a holiday from its sway. In order to notice a metaphysical principle we need to contrast it with some imagined alternative.

Martin Heidegger often gives the impression of seeking to replace metaphysics by ontology. He argues that metaphysics has concentrated on the Being of particular beings, thereby neglecting what may be called "primordial thinking," the thinking of Being as such. By limiting itself to a science of first principles specifying the generic features of all beings, metaphysics has been unable to discern the Being out of which these beings arise.

We accept these distinctions and also the limitation on metaphysics that they impose. Metaphysics without ontology may be ultimately empty, neglecting its final source, but ontology without metaphysics is hopelessly vague, for we lack the means of articulating what issues forth from this source. Besides, Whitehead's *Process and*

*Reality* is not simply a metaphysics; it contains a very minimal, though quite usable, ontology as well. The Category of the Ultimate, of creativity, one, and many, analyzed the final conditions underlying all acts of becoming whereby anything comes to be that is. While the particular beings are analyzed according to the generic structures of metaphysics, this ultimate generation of the beings comes from the Being of ontology.[11]

Besides Heidegger, Richard Rorty has urged a return to the pragmatism of Dewey.[12] Pragmatism is particularly strong in avoiding foundationalism, as Richard Bernstein has shown with respect to Peirce.[13] Peirce argued that we are justified in holding a belief to be true which we do not now have reason to doubt, recognizing that future situations may require us to revise the belief. Whitehead holds to just this sort of fallibilism. Reviewing his own achievement in *Process and Reality*, he remarks: "There remains the final reflection, how shallow, puny, and imperfect are efforts to sound the depths in the nature of things. In philosophical discussion, the merest hint of dogmatic certainty as to finality of statement is an exhibition of folly."[14] The subject matter of metaphysics pertains to what is everlastingly necessarily so, but this does not apply to our beliefs about metaphysics, which are perhaps more open to doubt than our beliefs pertaining to other disciplines.

While it is being recommended to us for its fallibilism, pragmatism also has its metaphysical side. Sandra B. Rosenthal carefully examines this aspect in *Speculative Pragmatism*.[15] The affinities with Whitehead's philosophy are evident. Without too much exaggeration, his endeavor could be called the metaphysics growing out of the pragmatic movement.[16]

To be sure, the sort of metaphysics Whitehead advocates is quite different from the classical metaphysics Kant, Heidegger, pragmatists, and many others have rejected. Classical metaphysics, Rosenthal notes, "is a history evincing positions that systematically denied or rejected the sense of temporality, creativity, novelty, fallibilism, pluralism, perspectivalism, and openmindedness—in short, the key dimensions of speculative pragmatism—in favor of the eternal, the fixed, the final, the certain, the absolute spectator grasp, the ultimate completion, the perfected whole."[17] Certainly Whitehead's thought seeks to include these elements of temporality, creativity, novelty, and fallibilism, although perhaps not perspectivalism as here understood. Even so, each actual occasion is a perspective upon the world, and the concept 'world' must always be understood indexically.

## STRENGTHS

Many have turned away from metaphysics because they deemed that it had pretty much exhausted its novelty, so that the quest for novelty requires us to search out alternatives to metaphysics itself, whether logical positivism, analysis, phenomenology, Heidegger, deconstruction, or whatever. Except for pragmatism, which was less insistent in its rejection of metaphysics, these alternatives began to appear on the scene about 1930. The last metaphysics to have already established itself by that time would be Bradley's absolute idealism, if not Hegel's. If the history of metaphysics is arbitrarily ended at that point, Whitehead's strong sense of interlocking coherence, whereby all the basic elements reciprocally require each other, would be lost, as well as many novel insights.

This is the first comprehensive metaphysics built on relativity physics and evolution which seeks to make room for experience within nature. The first concern led Whitehead to find a suitable replacement for the customary elements of scientific materialism (space, time, and matter) in terms of objects and events, while the second concern seeks equal justice for matters such as value and novelty.

One consequence of relativity physics is that contemporaries cannot causally interact. How then is perception possible, for we seem to perceive what happens simultaneously with ourselves? Whitehead analyzes the perception as constituted by two kinds of relations: (a) largely subconscious causal relations whereby past actualities produce data for the present perceiver; (b) relations projecting that data upon the contemporary field. These relations are nearly simultaneous for things close by, but become important for very distant things, such as stars which have already disintegrated before their light could reach us.

This means that we perceive causation, although these perceptions are on the fringe of our clear and distinct awareness. They are dull, massive, indistinct, but suffused with causal power. Our vivid perceptions, those exhaustively analyzed by Hume, are the contemporary projections. Hume is correct in finding no causation, for contemporaries do not causally interact. However, he restricted his analysis to only one kind of perception.[18]

The concept of 'prehension' enables us to span the gap between science and phenomenology. Prehension is a generalization of perception as 'apprehension', where the 'ap-' has been removed to indicate that this relationship is not necessarily conscious. It is any 'taking account' of another. Thus if *A* causes *B*, then *B* prehends *A*. So both the causation of science and the perception of phenomenology can be linked together by this useful concept.

We may state this basic schema another way: if (object) *A* causes *B*, then (subject) *B* prehends *A*. Or if (past) *A* causes *B*, then (present) *B* prehends *A*. The relation of subject and object, so problematic ever since Descartes treated *res cogitans* and *res extensa* as two different kinds of actuality, can be resolved by treating them as two different temporal aspects of the same actuality. The causal-prehensive relations between objects and subjects are asymmetrical, external to the object but internal to the subject. This strategy gets around the difficulties associated with either symmetrically internal (Bradley) or symmetrically external relations (Russell).

The subject is generally considered to be enduring, having many acts of perception and action. In contrast, Whitehead considers it to be momentary (as in Buddhism). Each act of subjectivity is restricted to one act of perception. Subjectivity has to do with the process of present becoming, whereby the many elements appropriated from the past by prehensive grow together in concrescence to form one determinate unity. At the outset the way these prehensions are to be unified is quite indeterminate, while at the conclusion this is fully determinate. The act of becoming is thus clearly delimited, and it is atomic, not divisible into smaller acts. If it were, a smaller act coincident with an incomplete phase of the larger ought to be able to render the phase of the larger determinate, whereas any incomplete phase by the theory of concrescence must be indeterminate.

Whitehead describes this process in terms of becoming, but it is not becoming in the ordinary sense of the tree's leaves becoming red. That presupposes an underlying substance whose properties change. For Whitehead, there is no underlying being, for the being only comes to be at the end of concrescence. I prefer to use the term *creation* for this process, understanding it in a immanent, pluralistic sense as the self-creation of occasions out of the many actualities of the past as guided by a novel possibility as to its final unity. Here 'creation' must be purged of its usual connotations.

'Self-creation' is the deepest meaning of freedom and shows us a way to reconcile freedom and causal determinism. No situation can lack causal influences in the form of past actualities, for then there would be nothing to unify. However, unless the subjective input is negligible, the multiplicity of past actualities provides no way for its own unification. The subject determines how it shall be unified; this is element of self-creation. Thus no matter how determined and determining the past shall be, there is always room for present self-determination.

This temporal understanding of past objectified occasions and present subjects also helps us to understand the relationship between repeatable universals and unrepeatable particulars. As Richard Rorty writes, "The distinction between unrepeatable entities and repeatable entities is simply, for Whitehead, a distinction between present actual entities and past actual entities."[19] The concrescence is irreducibly particular as unrepeatable because only that act of unification can bring together that particular past actual world. Once objectified as past being, however, an actuality can be ingredient in any subsequent act of becoming.

## THE ADVENTURE OF WHITEHEAD'S OWN PHILOSOPHIZING

I have briefly sketched some of the strengths of Whitehead's metaphysics, particularly those pertaining to his qualitative analysis of time. The next strength I allude to is of a very different order. It is clearly a very distinctive feature.

*Process and Reality* is a notoriously difficult text. In part, to be sure, this difficulty simply reflects the complexity of the position he is seeking to expound. Yet it is also due to the peculiar way in which he presents his position. Characteristically, Whitehead proceeded by criticizing and modifying his earlier positions, even in same cases during the process of composition of his works. Traces of earlier positions remain. For he lacked a virtue the consistent author needs, the willingness to be bored by one's own ideas. Once he had written something meant for publication, he retained it, even though in the meantime his own conceptuality may have been transformed many times over.

C. D. Broad has noted that Whitehead often admits detailed reasons and arguments for his positions.[20] As the secondary literature indicates, such reasons are not difficult to come by. Yet there was a reason why Whitehead would feel constrained *not* to use them. Since he is usually criticizing his own earlier position, he would only be calling attention to passages he had implicitly abandoned even while explicitly retaining them. Usually he justified such retention by inserting prefatory material designed to persuade the reader to interpret it in line with later theory.[21]

The Lowell Lectures of 1925, which present a metaphysics of objects and events suitable for the philosophy of nature of his earlier books, form the early stratum of *Science and the Modern World.* It is overlaid by the epochal theory of becoming, which leads to quite different results in the chapters "Abstraction" and "God."[22] Thus within the same book are two comprehensive theories, one based on continuously divisible events, the other on occasions which cannot be subdivided in their actuality.

In *Process and Reality*, there is a major shift, for part 2 for the most part has the process of becoming (concrescence) start from being, whereas parts 3 and 5 have becoming result in being. In the first theory, which has now been rigorously worked out by Jorge Nobo,[23] being is the basis for becoming; in the later theory being is the outcome of becoming.

By a compositional analysis quite similar to biblical source criticism it is possible to uncover the levels of composition in *Process and Reality* and compare them. It is possible to follow the adventures of Whitehead's own ideas as he shapes them in place. We can be present at the birth of new ideas and can see him exploit a wealth of unanticipated insights. In short, we can know more about how Whitehead developed his ideas than about how any other major philosopher might have proceeded.

Because of the difficulties with the text, the first major task of Whiteheadian scholarship has been to systematize its presentation. Before tackling *Process and Reality*, one is well advised to consult Ivor Leclerc's excellent introduction[24] or William A. Christian's careful analysis.[25] Christian distinguishes between Whitehead's pre-systematic and systematic passages, and concentrates on the latter. This enabled him largely to ignore the earlier theory in favor of the latter.

The final result of Whitehead's continued inquiry is remarkably consistent and coherent. The beauty of the system and the challenge of making it intelligible and accessible have enlisted the efforts of a generation of scholars. Now that we know how that system was put together, however, I propose we explore its diversity, both the diversity of the positions which Whitehead espoused as he was working his way along, and the diversity of modifications that might be proposed to overcome its remaining idiosyncratic features. The coherence of Whitehead's central system still allows experimentation in concept and application on peripheral issues without damage to the core. To be sure, we must discern what is basic and what is inessential.

## NEGATIVE FEATURES

While some of Whitehead's distinctive features are decided strengths, others are more problematic. Some have formed a major barrier to the assimilation of his philosophy. We shall consider four such "negative" features: the eternal objects or transcendent forms, temporal atomicity, the "pre-Kantianism," and more particularly the alleged panpsychism. These negative features are considered to be objectionable by many.

To be sure, what counts as objectionable lies in the eye of the beholder. Even if most philosophers find these features objectionable, Whitehead still could be correct. For that may be the way reality is, as I previously argued with respect to eternal objects[26] and pansubjectivity.[27] Nevertheless, neglect of Whitehead will continue if many find these features to be unacceptable. So I will try an alternative strategy here, drawing upon the fallibilistic and open-ended nature of Whitehead's project, to show how revisions or explanations eliminating these features might be possible. It is hoped that this will help facilitate the larger task of recovering American philosophy.

What follows is a sketch of how Whitehead's philosophy might be revised with respect to the first two features, exploring the last two more fully. The third, on pre-Kantianism, needs more of a explanation than any revision.

### *Eternal Objects*

Many have urged the elimination of eternal objects, Whitehead's democratic version of Plato's Forms, beginning with Everett W. Hall.[28] Such eliminative versions usually have difficulty accounting for novelty, which is one of the major reasons Whitehead retained them. When first introduced, objects and events were simply an alternate way of analyzing nature, replacing the usual space, time, and matter. Nature was constituted by spatiotemporal volumes, some of which had characteristics (i.e., objects). There were two kinds of objects: enduring objects which characterized events through some temporal stretch; and etenal objects such as sensa whose natures were independent of their spatiotemporal instatiations. In the initial version of *Science and the Modern World* there were only immanent eternal objects, only those ingredient in the events they characterized. They were reconceived as also transcendent as a result of the introduction of the theory of epochal becoming, which transformed the final version of *Science and the Modern World*, and necessitated the introduction of God as the principle of limitation.[29]

The eternal objects were essential for Whitehead's conception of God as their ultimate synthesis and for the provision of the initial aims guiding all actual occasions. However, their eternality became dispensable once Whitehead conceived God as also temporal.[30] For this invites the project of conceiving God as purely and solely temporal, thus placing God wholly within the horizon of temporality. A purely temporal God may have no need of eternal objects, and in fact, God's existence even could be incompatible with their presence.

Moreover, according to the ontological principle, Whitehead grounds all actualities, both in terms of their existence and in terms of their nature, in becoming. Eternal objects are also so grounded with respect to their existence, that is, their spatiotemporal instatiations, but not with respect to their nature. Yet we are told that "there is no justification for checking generalization at any particular stage."[31] Only the eternal objects defy the ontological principle; only they form an anomaly.

Yet how can that which is eternal come into being? How can it be an instance of becoming? They can if they only *appear* to be eternal. If an "eternal" object abstracts from its emergence, it would betray no trace of its origin, and would appear to have been from time immemorial.

I only mention this possibility here,[32] for the project of reconstructing a way of emergence for these objects is beyond the scope of this chapter, particularly one that can give an adequate account of novelty.

*The Tiny Occasions*

The next feature and the fourth primarily concern the application of Whitehead's philosophy to the world. George L. Kline points out: "What is problematic in Whitehead's position, it seems to me, is not his ontological atomism, but the precise relationship between the evanescent individual units of living process (concrescent occasions) and the relatively stable selves, persons, and things of the macro-world. This is a portion of his speculative system which Whitehead himself left relatively undeveloped."[33]

The objection to temporal atomicity is properly directed to the size of these occasions. Though they are considerably larger than Leibniz's infinitesimals, they are all very small. At first this is just the weak side of the correlation of subjectivity with the present, objectivity with the past. For this to be so, the present must be more than an instant yet have the definite boundaries of an indivisible quantum. Also it must be atomic as an act of becoming, for only the outcome is fully determinate. If it is a process of increasing determinateness, any initial portion would lack the determinateness of the outcome of the whole.

Also there must be an order of very small occasions to explain every change whatsoever, since change is the difference between successive occasions. Having introduced this order, however, Whitehead has no way of permitting larger occasions that might include these smaller occasions within themselves. For according to relativity physics contemporaries cannot causally influence each other. It would thus seem that he is thereby limited to very small occasions.[34] For an occasion including another would be its contemporary and so could not prehend it.

If we modify this account, however, by permitting larger occasions to influence included occasions by ways other than prehension, it may be possible to get around the difficulty. A smaller, included occasion can act just like a past occasion with respect to the larger occasion that includes it if the smaller occasion becomes determinate before an extended initial phase of the larger one is no longer causally influenced by its past. We can then distinguish between simply past occasions and included occasions by this modification: in its initial phase the included occasion participates in the purposing (subjective aim) of the larger occasion.

This should be possible because both occasions, in the initial stages of their concrescing, have no barriers against each other. The smaller could share in the aim of the larger. Each could then develop the aim in its own autonomous way in later phases. Thus the smaller is affected by the larger occasion, but in a mode different from the simple efficient causation of physical prehension. Because this modification is perfectly general with respect to inclusive/included occasions, it should permit the building up of more and more inclusive occasions to meet the demands of all natural beings.[35]

### *Whitehead's "Pre-Kantianism"*

Some philosophers, particularly continental philosophers,have taken exception to Whitehead's remark that his philosophy is "a recurrence to pre-Kantian modes of thought." In one sense this is true, for while both philosophies order and unify perceptions into fully articulate experience, Kant's perceptions derive from Hume's atomistic impressions, whereas Whitehead's prehensions refer to the past actualities themselves. Yet while this clarifies one contrast with Kant, it hardly explains the pre-Kantian modes of modern thought, which were as representational as Kant.

With respect to the history of philosophy, we must remember that Whitehead was an amateur, having formally studied and taught mathematics to the age of sixty-four. When he came to teach philosophy at Harvard in 1924, a scant five years before the publication of *Process and Reality*, he resolved to improve upon his desultory reading by studying the modern greats: Descartes, Locke, Hume. Perhaps also Kant, but he had already studied sections of Kant's first *Critique* quite closely, particularly those pertaining to space, time, and the philosophy of mathematics.

He thought his own philosophy would diverge from these thinkers, "But a careful examination of their exact statements disclosed that in the main the philosophy of organism is a recurrence to pre-Kantian modes of thought."[36] In context we recognize that "pre-Kantian" tells us nothing about Kant, being only a shorthand way of referring to early modern philosophy. As Whitehead notes at the outset of his preface, "These lectures are based upon a recurrence to that phase of philosophic thought which began with Descartes and ended with Hume."[37]

When we compare his claims with the writings of the pre-Kantians, notably Locke, it is difficult to discern that they were saying the same thing, or even anything reasonably close. For example, Whitehead frequently cites his indebtedness to Locke for the notion of "time as a perpetual perishing."[38] But Locke shows no particular perspicacity with respect to time, nothing like Plato's sense of "that which is always coming into being and perishing and never really is."[39] Most probably Whitehead's own insight about the perishing of subjective immediacy with the attainment of objective immortality took place while he was reading Locke on time, and he generously read that insight into Locke. Thus the close correlation Whitehead found with Locke and others may be more due to what he was able to read into the texts than what is in the texts themselves.

A characteristic word of Locke is *constitution*, used in the sense of a component in the make-up of a thing. But Whitehead was apt to interpret the word dynamically as the bringing together of elements into a whole, hence as synonymous with concrescence. This figures into the dispute over the meaning of "its being is constituted by its becoming."[40] If Locke's 'constitution' was read as 'concrescence,' it is no wonder Whitehead saw his affinities with Locke above all. In his estimate, "The writer who most fully anticipated the main positions of the philosophy of organism is John Locke in his *Essay*, especially in its later books."[41]

Thus his "recurrence to pre-Kantian modes of thought" has more to do with Locke than with Kant, but it has been unfortunate, because it obscures some important ways how Whitehead was affected by Kant. Often Whitehead, stimulated by his reading of Kant, was able to achieve something creative in his own philosophizing. The issue does not in the first instance depend on how accurately Whitehead read Kant.[42]

Both made careful analyses of experience as a process of unification whereby many precepts were conceived together as a whole. It is proper to conceive of concrescence as the synthesis of the manifold of perception. Where Kant used his categories to analyze experience in contrast to reality, Whitehead's categories are equally categories of experience and of actuality, since each actuality is an instance of experience.

Though Whitehead does not express himself in this way, we might consider him to have made the transcendental turn, in that all nonlogical necessity has its origin in the subjective experience of constituting objects. The categoreal conditions governing concrescence, the necessary rules determining every act of becoming, form the counterpart to Kant's categories of the understanding.

The reason the two philosophies look so different is that Whitehead also has objective necessity, but all objective necessity is derivative from subjective necessity. The Whiteheadian notion of object identifies the two extremes of the Kantian epistemological process, the thing-in-itself, that shadowy source for the bare precepts, and the final fully constituted object. This identity is possible because the terminus of the private subjective process achieves the determinate unity necessary for a being, a publicly accessible object. In Whitehead's language, subjective immediacy perishes in order to be objectively immortal. Becoming ceases in the attainment of being.

Kant cannot make this identification (which could enable him to by-pass all those problems concerning the thing-in-itself) because he assumes that the subject endures. Even with his very austere notion of the transcendental unity of apperception, Kant has not stripped his subject of all unnecessary presuppositions. Only if the subjective act is momentary, thus matching the process of objectification, can the subjective and objective be seen as aspects of the same act. Subjectivity is the private process, which results in (and thereby ceases in) the public product, which in turn can influence subsequent subjective processes.

### *"Panpsychism"*

Besides his theism and metaphysics, many philosophers are put off by Whitehead's alleged panpsychism. The combination of panpsychism and tiny occasions reminds many of a latter-day Leibniz. Yet Whitehead rejected many cardinal features of Leibniz's thought, not least his reliance upon God to unilaterally create the pre-established harmony. Whitehead had been an atheist most of his mature life (from about 1897 to 1925) because he could not stomach the notion of an omnipotent creator. He became a theist only because the doctrine he could affirm did not entail that God was creator. Moreover, if panpsychism means a pluralistic idealism such that all is ultimately mind, Whitehead is not a panpsychist. All of Whitehead's occasions are physical as well as mental, which he came to see were subjective in their present immediacy but objective in their pastness. (Even this degree of panpsychism was not his doctrine in his earlier writings, such as *Science and the Modern World*, despite some appearance to the contrary.)[43]

Though the exclusive emphasis on mind is foreign to Whitehead, he does finally affirm pansubjectivity, the claim that all primary actualities, actual entities, enjoy subjectivity. This was not yet his view in the earlier parts of *Process and Reality*, before the major shift. Then Whitehead affirmed a two-step process of becoming for every actuality, a fluency of transition establishing the original datum, and a fluency of concrescence flowing from that original datum.[44] The first act of becoming is not subjective, for all subjectivity is vested in concrescence, which was not possible until after the original datum was constituted.

Yet because Whitehead interpreted temporal atomicity to mean that "the act [of becoming] is not extensive, in the sense that it is divisible into earlier and later acts of becoming,"[45] he later reconceived the occasion so that there would be only a single act of becoming. Then each concrescence took account of or physically prehended all causal influences impinging on it, before unifying them into one determinate whole.

If all primary actualities were subjective, then the next factor in Whitehead's program would be to devise a metaphysics of subjectivity. He had access only to his own subjective immediacy, but that could be purged of all contingent elements, such as consciousness. Some existentialist philosophers seek to give subjectivity a metaphysical status, yet at the same time treat it as if it were a contingent feature, since it does not apply to all primary actualities. A metaphysics of subjectivity entails a pansubjectivity. Reduced to its bare essentials, subjectivity is merely present immediacy. Since all acts of becoming enjoy present immediacy in their origination, all enjoy subjectivity, although every occasion we can ever experience lies in our past as objective.[46]

We can discern at least three levels of subjectivity for Whitehead: (a) active receptivity; (b) responsiveness; and (c) consciousness. What is often regarded as passivity in perception is here reconceived as active receptivity.[47] Yet this is merely random activity without responsiveness to purpose. Whitehead felt that subjectivity entailed such responsiveness, especially for the realization of any novelty.

Novelty is not merely what is different; it must in some sense be better, if only in the sense of being new, that is, of standing in a temporal contrast to that which has been. A new/old contrast, when initially proposed, has a vividness often worn away by repetition. For then the new becomes old and there is no effective old/old contrast.[48]

Whitehead devised nine categoreal conditions for concrescence, the process of growing together the many prehensions of past actualities into one determinate feeling. These conditions also serve as the minimal conditions for novelty. Initially, the primary responsibility for novelty was placed on reversion, which is the subject's ability to entertain possibilities cognate to those which it derived from the past.[49] But it is not clear how primitive occasions can conceive of possibilities transcending their experience, and how they can discern which alternatives to follow, especially in their initial stages. So this theory was revised by the introduction of an initial purpose or subjective aim modifiable by the subject from a transcendent source of novelty.[50] Subjects differ from objects in that they can be affected by alternative possibilities and by especially interesting novelty.

Novelty is essential if the world is to be conceived as thoroughly evolutionary, for it is the importation of order into the world. Whitehead notes that "the non-evolution of matter has been a tacit presupposition throughout modern thought.'[51] If matter could evolve out of prior occasions, these nonmaterial occasions would have to lack the stability of character which a series of material occasions of matter would inherit from each other. Perhaps nonmaterial occasions would simply transmit what they receive, without affecting it in any way. But in any case, in order to develop into material occasions, they would have to receive and entertain the novelty of "material order." For some to be receptive to novelty, Whitehead reasons, all must have the potentiality of receptiveness and hence possess the conditions for novelty.

That all occasions are capable of novelty is affirmed at least as early as *Religion in the Making*.[52] The claim is justified in the Category of the Ultimate:

> "Creativity" is the principle of novelty. An actual occasion is a novel entity diverse from any entity in the "many" which it unifies. Thus "creativity" introduces novelty into the content of the many, which are the universe disjunctively. The "creative advance" is the application of this ultimate principle of creativity to each novel situation which it originates.[53]

In these last paragraphs I have been presenting Whitehead's argument for pansubjectivity, insofar as it *pertains to novelty*. Many besides him are convinced we cannot derive novelty merely from efficient causation, for then we are simply deriving the new from (chance) combinations of the old. The new must be entertained in order to be actualized, and only subjects are sensitive to new alternatives. However, is Whitehead correct in claiming that all actual occasions must have the potentiality to respond to novelty just because some do? Some must, at all levels of evolution (otherwise there could be no creative advance), but the subjectivities of their successors may simply atrophy through lack of use.

While subjectivity may be necessary for novelty, it may not be needed for that which is utterly devoid of novelty, having lost whatever novelty its ancestors had. Whitehead assumes that every actuality has some degree of novelty; at least he offers no theory as to what is not novel. We might sketch such a theory for him.

That which is utterly devoid of novelty would be totally derived from the past, hence causally determined. We could still conceive it as an occasion having (physical) prehensions, but it would be devoid of any subjectivity, including subjective forms and aims, as well as conceptual feeling. This would resemble Whitehead's original theory of prehension, whereby every event was constituted out of its prehensions of every other (past) event.[54] These prehensions together would constitute the nonnovel occasion for what it is.

Consider one kind of nonnovel occasion: material occasions. If there is an evolution of matter, there would be material societies evolving from occasions of empty space. Such evolution would require some sort of very minimal subjectivity which could be affected by the novel possibility of materiality, for this possibility would never have been actualized before in that environment.

Whitehead, using all the resources of his cosmology, interprets matter in terms of "corpuscular societies," which are strands of enduring objects. The defining characteristic of the personal society of each strand is passed down from occasion to occasion, providing each with the stability we associate with matter.[55] We may think of the subjective aim as being involved in this process, but it need not be: the defining characteristic may be nothing more than the dominant persistence of the past occasions of the society, which give the present occasion its persistent identity amid all the other causal influences impinging upon it. All these influences, however, including the dominant influence of the past society, are physically prehended in the usual manner.

The transition from an occasion of empty space, where all influences are equally and impartially prehended, to a material occasion, where the influence of the prior material occasion predominates, requires novelty and hence subjectivity, the capacity of the occasion as a whole to respond to possibility. Once the novel step is taken, however, successor occasions can lapse in routine. Any vestige of subjectivity falls into disuse; no longer needed, it simply vanishes from that type of occasion.

One precondition for subjectivity is that the occasion as a whole be able to act. In the nonnovel occasion this is impossible, for the parts, the various prehensions of the past, alone determine the outcome. There can be neither active receptivity in the ordering of the prehensions, nor responsiveness to alternative possibilities if there is only one possible outcome.

Naturally much more needs to be said about these nonnovel occasions, but a sketch will have to suffice for the present. If these occasions account for all (atrophied) inorganic entities, subjectivity could be restricted to the organic ones. While it is difficult to draw the boundary between subjectivity and nonsubjectivity, some sort of limit seems called for to render a doctrine of pansubjectivity reasonable to most.

## CONCLUSION

Partly by focusing upon the place of novelty in nature, Whitehead has succeeded in relocating the place of subjectivity. In our anthropocentric bias we tend to identity subjectivity with human mentality. Then pansubjectivity looks like the projection of humanity on inanimate things. By persistent inquiry into the place of mind in nature Whitehead discovered that it was not mind but subjectivity that needed to be reconceived. The basic causal relation between two actualities was seen as a generalization from perception, allowing for the pole opposite the cause to actively contribute to the total impact of the relation. Subjectivity could now be understood as active receptivity. If so, mentality means the response to novelty, physical activity the response to the old, to tradition.

This chapter underscores this orientation of subjectivity to novelty. Subjectivity is essential for novelty and hence for any evolutionary emergence, not just for humans. Whitehead would urge us to see objective actuality as past subjectivity. Yet since everything we encounter can only be past and objective for us, we should not expect to have any direct access to this past subjectivity.

To be sure, on my emendation there could be no metaphysics of subjectivity, for there would be nonnovel and hence nonsubjective occasions. That is one of the strengths of unlimited pansubjectivity, not available to its restricted versions.

Because of the fallibilistic character of Whitehead's philosophizing, as witnessed by his own constant revision of basic principles, we should not think of it as some static monolithic structure that has to be either accepted or rejected in toto, but as an array of close variants derived from a common vision. The variants need not be Whitehead's own, for we should explore additional ones, possibly overcoming features felt to be idiosyncratic such as those discussed here.

## NOTES

1. John E. Smith, *The Spirit of American Philosophy* (New York: Oxford University Press, 1963), 163f. He was one of my first philosophy teachers his first year at Yale and directed my dissertation (on Tillich). He was a gifted teacher who generously gave of his time in conversation with an inquiring undergraduate.

2. William Ernest Hocking, "Whitehead as I Knew Him," in *Alfred North Whitehead: Easays on His Philosophy*, ed. George L. Kline (Englewood Cliffs, N.J.: Prentice-Hall, 1963), 8.

3. See my *Emergence of Whitehead's Metaphysics* (Albany: State University of New York Press, 1964), chapter 2. Hereafter, *EWM*.

4. George Lucas, *The Rehabilitation of Whitehead* (Albany: State University of New York Press, 1989), chapter 4. Evolutionary theory, by its very nature, must concentrate on such major transitions as nonlife to life, from the physical to the mental. If there are such transitions, it must have been possible for the world to have existed without life or mentality. Then these become contingent features abstracted from a rigorous metaphysics.

Yet Whitehead may be understood to be framing a general theory concerning the possibility of emergence itself. Every actuality can be conceived as an instance of novel emergence.

5. For an exploration of their differences, see *Two Process Philosophers: Hartshorne's Encounter with Whitehead*, ed. Lewis S. Ford (American Academy of Religion, AAR Studies in Religion, 1973), and more recently, my essay "Hartshorne's Interpretation of Whitehead,"

*The Philosophy of Charles Hartshorne*, ed. Lewis E. Hahn (The Library of Living Philosophers, vol. 21; LaSalle, IL: Open Court Press, 1991).

6. This interest can be sampled in two recent collections: *Whitehead's Metaphysics of Creativity*, ed. Friedrich Rapp and Reiner Wiehl, (Albany: State University of New York Press, 1990), and *Natur, Subjektivitaet, Gott: zur Prozessphilosophie Alfred N. Whiteheads*, ed. Helmut Holzhey, Alois Rust and Reiner Wiehl (Frankfurt am Main: Suhrkamp Verlag, 1990). For a contemporary estimate by a professor of philosophy at Heidelberg (Wiehl): "Whiteheads spekulative Kosmologie . . ., die als das bedeutendste Gedankengebaeude einer Metaphysik des 20. Jahrhunderts angesehen werden muss" (*Natur*, 210).

7. Here I offer a brief comment, referring the interested reader to the fuller account given in my "Afterword: A Sampling of Other Interpretations," in *Explorations in Whitehead's Philosophy* ed. Lewis S. Ford and George L. Kline (Fordham University Press, 1983), 305–345. Hereafter, *EWP*.

There I also defend pansubjectivity as a positive feature, but treat it here as a negative feature. It is really both. It must be defended as a necessary feature of every actual entity. At the same time, there is an idiosyncratic, contingent feature, which concerns whether everything we regard as actual should be conceived in terms of active actual entities having the potentiality of novelty.

8. Donald W. Sherburne, "Whitehead without God," *Process Philosophy and Christian Thought*, ed. Delwin Brown, Ralph E. James, Jr., and Gene Reeves (Indianapolis: Boobs-Merrill, 1971), 305–328.

9. See my essay, "An Appraisal of Whiteheadian Nontheism," *The Southern Journal of Philosophy* 15/no. 1 (July, 1977), 27–35.

10. George Allan, "The Primacy of the Mesocosm," in *New Essays in Metaphysics*, ed. Robert C. Neville (Albany: State University of New York Press, 1986), 25–44.

11. I have discussed these issues further in "Whitehead and the Ontological Difference," *Philosophy Today* 29, 2/4 (September 1985), 148–55.

12. It is worth remembering that in his pre-analytic days Rorty wrote a particularly insightful essay arguing that Whitehead was the first to solve the problem of universals and particulars that Aristotle introduced: "Matter and Event," in *Explorations in Whitehead's Philosophy*. (*EWP* 68–103).

To be sure, in a subsequent article he argued that Sellars had also solved the problem in a way which avoided metaphysics: "The Subjectivist Principle and the Linguistic Turn," in *Alfred North Whitehead: Essays on His Philosophy*, ed. George L. Kline (Englewood Cliffs, N.J.: Prentice-Hall, Inc. 1963), 144–5. Yet this is small gain if the proposed alternative in "ordinary language" turns out to be more complicated and less intelligible than Whitehead's account.

13. Richard Bernstein, "Pragmatism, Pluralism, and the Healing of Wounds," *Proceedings and Addresses of the American Philosophical Association* 62, no. 3 (November 1989), 5–18.

14. Alfred North Whitehead, *Process and Reality* (New York: The Free Press, 1978), xiv. Hereafter, *PR*.

15. Sandra B. Rosenthal, *Speculative Pragmatism* (Amherst: University of Massachusetts Press, 1986).

16. I owe this point to George Allan of Dickinson College.

17. Rosenthal, *Speculative Pragmatism*, 195.

18. This contrast between perception in the mode of causal efficacy and perception in the mode of presentational immediacy is worked out in *PR*, 2:4 and 8 (*PR*, 117–26, 168–83), and in *Symbolism, Its Meaning and Effect* (New York: Macmillan, 1927).

19. Richard M. Rorty, "The Subjectivist Principle and the Linguistic Turn," in *Alfred North Whitehead: Easays on His Philosophy*, ed. George L. Kline (Englewood Cliffs, NJ: Prentice-Hall, 1963), 139.

20. C. D. Broad, "Alfred North Whitehead (1861–1947)," *Mind* 57 (April, 1948), 139–45.

21. Much of this, except for the diversity and the extent of the insertions in *Process and Reality*, is documented in *EWM*.

22. See my essay "Whitehead's First Metaphysical Synthesis," *International Philosophical Quarterly* 17, no. 3 (September, 1977), 251–64, or *EWM*, chapter 1.

23. Jorge Nobo, *Whitehead's Metaphysics of Extension and Solidarity* (Albany: State University of New York Press, 1986). See also my examination of Nobo in contrast with the traditional interpretations based on Whitehead's later theory in "Recent Interpretations of Whitehead's Writings," *The Modern Schoolman* 45, no. 1 (November 1987), 47–59.

24. Ivor Leclerc, *Whitehead's Metaphysics: An Introductory Exposition* (Lanham, MD: University Press of America, 1958).

25. William A. Christian, *An Interpretation of Whitehead's Metaphysics* (New Haven: Yale University Press, 1959).

26. Lewis S. Ford, "Whitehead's Differences from Hartshorne," *Two Process Philosophers: Hartshorne's Encounter with Whitehead*, ed. Lewis S. Ford (American Academy of Religion: Studies in Religion, number 5, 1973), 58–83.

27. See note 6.

28. Everett W. Hall, "Of What Use Are Whitehead's Eternal Objects?" (1930), reprinted in *Alfred North Whitehead: Essays on His Philosophy*, ed. George L. Kline (Englewood Cliffs, NJ: Prentice-Hall, 1963), 102–16.

29. See *EWM*, 1–21, 67–70, 101–7.

30. Ibid., 227–29.

31. *PR*, 16.

32. See my essays on "The Creation of 'Eternal' Objects," *The Modern Schoolman* 71/3 (March 1994) 191–222 and on "Temporality and Transcendence," in *Hartshorne, Process Philosophy and Theology*, ed. Robert Kane and Stephen H. Phillips (Albany: State University of New York Press, 1989), 151–67, particularly 153f.

33. George L. Kline, "Concept and Concrescence," in *Hegel and Whitehead: Contemporary Perspectives on Systematic Philosophy*, ed. George R. Lucas, Jr. (Albany: State University of New York Press, 1986), 143.

34. This is the ultimate basis for Robert C. Neville's criticisms of Whitehead with respect to enduring personal identity and the texture of human life in "Contributions and Limitations of Process Philosophy," *Process Studies* 16, no. 4 (Winter 1987), 283–98. He argues that Whitehead's account "can render no clear distinction, among the decisive moments with which the person is connected in tight causal or dialogical ways, between those within the person and those outside the person" (289). Further, while he acknowledged social, historical, and cultural structures, "he did not tie them to his model which thus appears as an atomism too dependent on promissory notes about connective tissues" (292).

35. This issue is explored more fully in "Inclusive Occasions," in *Process in Context: Essays in Post-Whiteheadian Perspectives*, ed. Ernest Wolf-Gazo (Bern/Frankfurt: Peter Lang Verlag, 1988), 107–36.

36. *PR*, xi.

37. Ibid.

38. See my *The Emergence of Whitehead's Metaphysics*, 1925–1929. (Albany: State University of New York Press, 1984), 194f, 208f.

39. *Timaeus*, 28A.

40. *PR*, 23, at (ix).

41. Ibid., xi.

42. Whitehead did not even read Locke, his favorite, very accurately. See the able essay by Rainer Specht, "Whitehead's Interpretation of Locke in *Process and Reality*," in *Whitehead's Metaphysics of Creativity*, ed. Friedrich Rapp and Reiner Wiehl (Albany: State University of New York Press, 1990), 34–56.

43. See my essay tracing out the stages of Whitehead's development "From Pre-Panpsychism to Pansubjectivity," in *Faith and Creativity: Essays in Honor of Eugene Peters*, ed. George Nordgulen and George W. Shields (St. Louis: CPB Press, 1987), 41–61.

44. *PR*, 210.

45. Ibid., 69. This well could be the pivotal passage for the major shift from becoming based on being to being as the product of being. For a more complete analysis of this shift, see *EWM*, chapters 8 and 9.

46. For a further defense of pansubjectivity, see my afterword in *EWM*.

47. See my "Whitehead's Transformation of Pure Act," *The Thomist* 41, no. 3 (July, 1977), 381–99.

48. As Whitehead remarked in a larger context, "The use of philosophy is to maintain an active novelty of fundamental ideas illuminating the social system. It reverses the slow descent of accepted thought towards the inactive commonplace" (*Modes of Thought* [New York: The Free Press, 1938, 1968], 174).

49. *PR*, 249f. Whitehead later found that this category was superfluous and could be abolished: *EWM*, 219–27.

50. See *EWM*, 219–27.

51. *PR*, 95.

52. "The birth of a new instance [of actuality] is the passage into novelty. Consider how any one actual fact, which I will call the *ground* can enter into the creative process. The novelty which enters into the derivate instance is the information of the actual world with a new set of ideal forms. In the most literal sense the lapse of time is the renovation of the world with ideas" (*Religion in the Making* [New York: Macmillan, 1926], 113f).

53. *PR*, 21.

54. See *EWM*, 23–31.

55. *PR*, 34f, 99f.

Richard Hocking

# Emergence and Embodiment: A Dialectic within Process

## OUR SYNOPTIC PROGRESS

Imagine living in an intellectual climate of cleansing skepticism. Imagine that the prevailing interest among philosophers has come to focus on special issues, taken one by one for sharp analysis, many of these concerned with the mind's tools. In such a time, the synopsis of philosophical experience might well be out of fashion.

In such a time, one might look for the survival from a remoter past of certain majestic systems of thought. For example, there might be lingering traces of one or another of the three great synopses of classical antiquity: that of extreme pluralism in the tradition of Democritus, that of extreme monism in the tradition of the Stoics, and that of duality in the blended tradition of Plato and Aristotle. Such antique achievements of systematic thought might even be fostered, in a skeptical time, simply out of a museum fondness for early works, like abandoned churches.

Imagine further that there have arisen two newer currents of systematic thought, each of them refreshingly novel and each persisting against probability when we consider the intellectual milieu. The simple persistence of two such original forms of systematic thought in an adverse climate argues that they are disclosures of some kind of comprehensive necessity in the structure of philosophic experience.

But a prompt correction is obviously called for. This is not imagining but remembering, remembering the recent past through which our elder colleagues have lived. The two fresh currents of systematic thought are alike in taking the flux of time and the creative advance of the world seriously. But they stand in a certain polar contrast to each other in that one focuses on the ongoing of nature and the other focuses on the ongoing of history. The former has come to be known as process philosophy and evokes in our minds thoughts of evolutionary doctrines and the scientific genius of a Darwin or a Mendel in the great coming of age of the biological sciences. The latter recalls romantic history and the paradoxical freedom movements and revolutions of the two hundred years past, finding expression in the dialectic of freedom or simply the philosophy of history. It becomes apparent that a characteristic theme of cosmological process philosophy is the principle of emergence. A comparably persistent theme of philosophical reflection on history and freedom is the principle of embodiment. Both of these systems of thought are philosophies of process, however unrelated their lines of development happen to have been. How should they stand to each other in a wider universe of discourse?

My purpose here is a double one. In the first place, I aim to explore, through examples, the contrasts and even disjunctions which apparently separate these two currents of thought. In the second place, I shall put forward the thesis that the emergence form and the embodiment form of process philosophy require each other in an on-going complementarity without loss of distinction and without reduction of either to an element of the other. We cannot rest content with an either-or in a situation that confronts us with an unstable lack of coherence. Our obligation to the wider range of philosophical experience is to discover (not invent) the categorial frame which shows the purpose of such a polarity.

## EMERGENCE AND EVOLUTIONARY COSMOLOGY

Philosophers for whom emergence is a major principle seem especially at home in a period in which biology came of age. The theme of biological evolution runs strong, for instance, in the writings of Bergson, Peirce, James, and Dewey. Whitehead, who finds his scientific sources preeminently in field physics and relativity mechanics, coupled with introspective psychology, moves in harmony with the great age of biology when he offers his doctrine of "actual occasions" as a kind of microbiological living fecundity. And Charles Hartshorne's gifted avocation in ornithology is altogether becoming to his philosophy of nature's innovative process.

The association of the principle of emergence with process philosophy was, we know, brought to the fore by Samuel Alexander with his acknowledged debt to Lloyd Morgan and Morgan's theory of emergent evolution. The principle has become the general possession of process thinkers, albeit under diverse names.

Lloyd Morgan cites, as an instance of emergence, the forming of crystals in a solution. They arise as radical novelties; "they were not actually there, or any where, prior to such emergence, and yet did not come 'out of nothing' for they come into being out of the cooling liquid." Similarly with Alexander, an emergent is an ontologically new thing which arises whenever certain configurations or complexes or Gestalten are achieved. "The existence of emergent qualities . . . is something . . . to be accepted with the 'natural piety' of the investigator," he writes, adding with heroic candor: "It admits of no explanation." "A being who knew only mechanical and chemical action could not predict life; he must wait till life emerged in the course of Time."[1]

The etymology of the word *emergence*, from its Latin usage, suggests waters out of which surprising forms spring. The diving loon surfaces on a New England lake. Morgan and Alexander have elaborated the term to mean that a radically unpredictable being emerges from something which could not be its cause.

Given this context, consider three other modern philosophers whose thought widens the reach of the emergence principle: Bergson, Peirce, and Nicolai Hartmann.

The Bergsonian *élan vital* has become virtually a commonplace in the thinking of our century. The noun *élan*, aptly chosen by Bergson, is related to the verb *s'élancer*, "to shoot forth," "to spring." "To spring" and "to emerge" are akin. We recall Bergson's vivid account of the stream of life energy, never two instants the same, inventively encountering and flowing around obstacles, all of which are the remnants of past life. The *élan* evolves, engendering the successive novelties of instinctive life and intelligent life and intuitive life. Who knows what further new creations the future may hold?

In the treasure house of Peirce's literary fragments we find everywhere the principle of spontaneity, or chance, or firstness, which is life. Peirce welcomes Darwinian evolution, in which doctrine "the only positive agent of change . . . is fortuitious variation." "The absolutely first . . . must be fresh and new. . . . It must be initiative, original, spontaneous and free." "When we gaze upon the multifariousness of nature we are looking straight into the face of a living spontaneity." So, this spontaneity, with "its characteristic innocence," is first in the universal process, underlying all evolution of interactions and lawfulness, all ascending grades of individuality; emergence under another name.[2]

Nicolai Hartmann's philosophy of nature expounds a doctrine of ontological levels. Things have their proper places in strata which are largely dependent on underlying strata, but in part are autonomous. In the ascending scale, the strata comprise, in succession, things material, living, conscious, and cultural. Evidence of any "ontological dependence" from above there is none: nothing like St. Thomas's "finitude from above." Higher strata derive their diminished allotments of strength from the material basis of things, which is the sole source of strength. (Cf. Santayana.) However, there *is* novelty "upwards." Each higher stratum exhibits its characteristic accession of freedom, a freedom which "rests on the emergence of a categorial novelty." The familiar unexplained novelty runs through the whole scheme of this "metaphysics from below." The emergence principle is manifest.

In an evolutionary cosmology, relying on the principle of emergence, novel variation everywhere throughout the cosmos is a first. It is that which, in Darwinian fashion, arises to be selectively restrained by all environments, sometimes for a good called "growth." The unending wealth of variation is an assurance that all ecological niches will be duly filled in time. An emergence cosmology thus offers an open future in the world process with always the prospect of better things.

## EMBODIMENT AND HISTORICAL CONCRETENESS

In turning to the theme of embodiment from that of emergence, our attention moves from the perspective of an evolutionary cosmology to that of history. The maturing of philosophical reflection on history happens to have kept pace, during the romantic period and since, with the coming of age of the biological sciences. The historical consciousness is likewise dealing with process. History is the process of thought-filled action of individuals and communities living through achievements, successes, failures, tragedies, exploitations, and rebirths. When we recall the three great dialectical philosophers of history—Hegel, Marx, and Kierkegaard—we find in all three the emphasis on the progressive embodying of freedom in concrete circumstances, be it politically, economically, or religiously. All three find in the historical process a striving for continuity of action. The urge for continuity presses through the ironies, the paradoxes, the apparent contradictions, and the proclaimed absurdities of active experience. Not surprisingly, all three are dialectical thinkers about history for two reasons. The historical consciousness appears as a struggle to sustain continuities, continuities of traditions, technologies, families, religions, and policies. But continuity is forever being menaced by the opposite of continuity, the accidents of history. "'Accidents will happen" (to quote a favorite aphorism of Prof. J. W. Miller of Williams College).

One may say of "dialectic" that a historical situation becomes dialectical when a person or a community commits itself in action to embodying a fraction of the whole of concrete freedom, taking it to be the whole. The process of history is such that the dogmatically limited situation will, sooner or later, be overwhelmed by experiences which it failed to include. The movements of thought-filled action will be, in principle, toward a widening of the horizon to embody freedom in an ampler situation.

For this dialectical reason, embodiment is a principle of reflection and hence of explanation, unlike emergence which, as Alexander said, "admits of no explanation."

More recent spokesmen for the principle of embodiment include Royce in America, also Dewey in certain respects, Collingwood in England, and Marcel in France.

How is the principle of embodiment expressed in Royce's thought? Consider his ethical doctrine of loyalty to "causes" which widen the scope of loyalty. Royce's term *cause* refers to any actual joint effort which aims to embody some good, small or great; (the rescue of a child in a matter of minutes, the vocation of a religious order over centuries). Causes are concrete plans of shared action; they are unique histories. Loyalty to a cause is the individual embodiment of a chosen duty. And "loyalty to loyalty," Royce's concrete "categorical imperative" (as distinguished from Kant's formal one), expresses the duty to act on increasingly compatible causes. Over a life time, every individual and community may achieve ethical embodiment through a growing harmony of unique causes in a progressively more concrete and social whole.

Turning from ethics to metaphysics, we find that embodiment is the essential ingredient of Royce's "Fourth Conception of Being" in a way quite in keeping with his ethical position. His central metaphysical thesis asserts that to be is to be the full and unique embodiment of a plan of action. His careful formulation runs: "What is, or what is real, is as such the complete embodiment, in individual form and final fulfilment of the internal meaning of finite ideas."[3] Here is the basis for interpreting history in terms of concrete freedom progressively realized.

There is to be found in Dewey's thought also an expression of the theme of embodiment as a historical principle. It is presented in his respect for all human arts, fine and humble, especially and democratically the latter. It is also implied in his sustained revulsion from classical slavery and modern approximations thereto. The entire culture of tools and technology, which is in effect the history of technology, draws his interest. "By its nature technology is concerned with things and acts in their instrumentalities, not in their immediacies." "A tool is a particular thing, but it is more than a particular thing, since it is a thing in which a connection, a sequential bond of nature, is embodied."[4] Dewey is recognizing ways in which evolutionary linkages in nature are drawn into the embodying process of history. Dewey's "pragmatic technology" is, lately and properly, receiving new attention.

In Collingwood's well-known part 5 of *The Idea of History*, we come again upon the distinction of history from the natural course of events in terms of the idea of "action." "An action is the unity of the outside and the inside of an event," he writes, and "the inside of an event . . . can only be described in terms of thought."[5] It follows that to be aware of history is to be aware of thought-filled action. "Our knowledge that human activity is free has been attained only through our discovery of history." Action is embodied in one situation after another, each with its own pattern of compulsion. "The freedom that there is in history consists in the fact that this compulsion is imposed upon the activity of human reason not by anything else, but by itself." "The hard facts of the situation" for any historical agent "are the hard facts of the way in which he conceives the situation."[6] This is a way of understanding history which binds the time-spanning autonomy of thought to the temporal uniqueness of actions which embody thought. The mature historical consciousness of present action is united with the habit of thoughtful re-enactment of relevant past actions. The reflective character of the embodiment principle as a principle for understanding history could hardly be more explicit.

Finally, the voice of Marcel in his ironical form of communication, the diary, is symbolic of a calculated Socratism. He gives us his individual history as a dialogue with himself which others are implicitly invited to share. His vocation is to trouble the thinking community of precisely this epoch, not to construct a philosophical system for any and every epoch. In the vein of Socrates, he can write, "The world we live in . . . rests wholly in an immense refusal . . . the refusal to reflect." Marcel explores the historical itinerary of a great return from *le monde cassé* of our time to the hoped-for and dawning world of in gathering and recuperation. He holds the mirror up to our present stage of partial reflection, calling it but "first reflection" (*réflexion première*), which is the world of scientific "objectivity," bureaucratic impersonality, and technological dehumanization. From this he guides us to the recuperative stage of profound "second reflection" (*réflexion seconde*), which recovers the feel for the intersubjective world of creative fidelity, concrete freedom, and the joyful certitude of being at home in the entire cosmos. Second reflection is the new Socratic recollection (*receuillement*), "the philosophy of the concrete," a historical journey in being.[7]

We shall rely further on Marcel's insight in the conclusion of this exploration.

## POLARITY: AN INEVITABLE PHILOSOPHICAL EMBARRASSMENT

Given these two kinds of process philosophy, we return to our question: How should they stand to each other? Their separated development hitherto has been partly a geographical accident in that the evolutionary cosmology has flourished greatly in English-speaking countries, whereas the more dialectical reflection on history has been strongly developed on the European continent. Apart from that contingency, there is the more pertinent separating factor: that the two principles of emergence and embodiment under discussion are distinct, each pertaining, it seems, to distinct categorial frames which are partly in polar opposition to each other. Is it becoming to philosophical discourse to let such a gap stand unbridged or to leave two such bodies of philosophical experience uninclosed in an ampler categorial frame?

It is to the credit of Adolph Portmann, Swiss ecologist at Basel, to have directed special attention to this polarity as an embarrassment for biologists. He does so by warning that the biologists's term *evolution (entwicklung)* has, in usage, two distinct meanings, one of which does not belong to biology but to history. *Menschliches Tun* (human action) realizes the evolution of history in which every situation and action brings forth complete novelty unconditioned by any underlying biological influence. From within human historical experience, the "how" of the evolution of novelty is known firsthand. For biology, the "how" of the rise of novelty in organic nature is unknown. Biologists and prehistorians, between them, try to make a continuum of the two evolutions where there is none. They fail. Between the two efforts there persists "a dark zone of silence" (*eine dunkle Zone des Schweigens*).[8] Portmann urges biologists to understand the free actions of history in order to make up for their lack of access to the biological how. He does not resort to the emergence principle. He declares for a more radical polarity.

It is tempting to overcome polarity by absorbing history into the vaster process of nature's evolution. This is Dewey's temptation. He writes: "Only as science is seen to be fulfilled and brought to itself in intelligent management of historical processes in their continuity can man be envisaged as within nature and not as a supernatural extrapolation."[9] Portmann, as a natural scientist, would warn against this reduction. Marcel would call it the all too pervasive "réflexion première." Historicity, thus naturalized, loses its distinctive qualities of hope and failure, anxiety and mystery.

The converse temptation is to absorb evolutionary cosmology into history on the historian's terms, as Collingwood does in *The Idea of Nature*. Here we have, not so much a philosophy of nature as rather the historian's interpretation of earlier thinkers' hypotheses about nature. The sense fades of the majestic ontological endurance of the natural process, its infinities large and minute, its endless variety and variations, its "blessed unconscious thinghood" (to borrow John Findlay's phrase).

The embarrassing polarity resists reduction either way. It calls for finding the significance of this polarity within a wider enclosure of philosophical experience.

## COMPLEMENTARITY: THE NEXT STATE OF PHILOSOPHICAL EXPERIENCE

We return to Marcel's exploration of embodiment ("incarnate being"), finding there his proposal of a passage through a sheer polarity to a resolving complementarity of these two philosophies of process. (Let Marcel represent especially well the group of continental thinkers, including Heidegger, Sartre, Ricoeur, and Merleau-Ponty.)

When Marcel takes, as the "central datum" for all metaphysical reflection, the "I" who reflects, this is deceptively close to Descartes's *cogito*; but when he insists that 'I am *my* body' is prior to 'I have *a* body,' the situation is wholly changed. 'I am *my* body' is not objective, but concrete; it is not a problem, but a serious mystery. 'Mystery' means something so immediate, concrete, and inalienable as to be authoritative over all objectivity. "The mysterious and the ontological are identical." One must add 'with others,' for the space-time of all bodily process is public and outward and the field for real behavior. I am my body with all others. Marcel's "Here I am" is vividly expressed: "Existence and the exclamatory awareness of existence cannot really be separated."[10]

What follows? Here the already emphasized historical imperative for continuity asserts itself in experience. My body is my local situation in the unbounded manifold of everything. "For me all existence is constructed on the model of and in prolongation of the existence of my body." "Prolongation" is a continuum of a kind with all history and yet is the cosmos. It encloses the chance series of discontinuous emergents while remaining a history-like continuity. For each historically embodied and reflective agent, I am situated in the entire bodily universe as my home. "My body is in sympathy with things," he writes, "I am really attached to and really adhere to all that exists, to the universe which is my universe whose center is my body." The French word *foyer* is rich in associations of warmth and domesticity. The entire world of things is, in this sense, our foyer, in English "our hearth and home." (Cf. also Merleau-Ponty.)

Marcel signals, with this insight, the end of the long Cartesian dualistic headache more completely and more unambigously than does Dewey's revolt against dualism, because here we find no messages, no signs, no subject-object relations to displace or substitute for the immediacies of embodiment which sustain them all.

Thus far, by widenings of experience, the embarrassing polarity begins to soften in the direction of a more philosophically responsible complementarity of the two perspectives on process. The perspective of emergence is experienced as an "upward" way of unintended discontinuities and infinite variations. The perspective of embodiment is experienced as an inverse, let us say, "downward" way of intended historical continuity and sustained enclosure. The evolutionary emergence of the new is everywhere. The historical embodying of the new is everywhere. The upward way and the downward way are such that each is the rest of experience for the other in a dialectic within process. Conjoined they may count as a probing of the words of Heracleitus, the obscure, who said long ago, "The way upward and downward is one and the same" (Diels, 60.).

## NOTES

1. Samuel Alexander, *Space, Time, and Deity*, vol. 2 (New York: Dover Edition, 1966; original, New York: Macmillan, 1920), pp. 46–47.
2. See Peirce's "Architecture of Theories," in *Collected Papers*, vol. 6, pp. 11ff.
3. Royce, *The World and the Individual*, vol. 1 (New York: Dover, 1959); original edition New York: Macmillan, 1899) p. 339.
4. John Dewey, *Experience and Nature* in *John Dewey: The Later Works*, vol. I, 1925, edited by Jo Ann Boydston (Carbondale: Southern Illinois University Press, 1981), p. 101.
5. R.G. Collingwood, *The Idea of History* (Oxford: Clarendon Press, 1946) p. 213.
6. Ibid., p. 317.
7. Gabriel Marcel, *Creative Fidelity* (New York: Farrar and Strauss, 1964) pp. 22–23.
8. Adolph Portmann, *Biologische Fragmente zu einer Lehre vom Menschen* (Basel: Benno Schwabe, 1951), p. 19.
9. Dewey, op. cit., p. 130.
10. Gabriel Marcel, op. cit., pp. 17ff.

## REFERENCES

Alexander, Samuel. *Space, Time, and Deity*, Vol. 2. New York: Dover Edition, 1966; original edition, New York: Macmillan, 1920.

Bergson, Henri. *Creative Evolution*. Translated by Arthur Mitchell. New York: Henry Holt, 1911.

Collingwood, R. G. *Essay on Philosophical Method*. Oxford: The Clarendon Press, 1933.

———. *The Idea of History*. Oxford: The Clarendon Press, 1946.

Dewey, John. "Experience and Nature," in *John Dewey: The Later Works*, Vol. 1, 1925. Edited by Jo Ann Boydston. Carbondale: Southern Illinois University Press, 1981.

Hartmann, Nicolai. *New Ways of Ontology*. Translated by Reinhard C. Kuhn. Chicago: H. Regnery, 1953.

Hickman, L. "John Dewey's Pragmatic Technology," in *Journal of Speculative Philosophy*, 5/2 (1991).

Marcel, Gabriel. *Being and Having*. Translated by Katharine Faffer. Boston: Beacon, 1951.

———. *Creative Fidelity*. Translated by Robert Rosthal. New York: Farrar and Strauss, 1964.

———. *Metaphysical Journal*. Translated by Bernard Wall. London: Rockliff, 1952.

Miller, J. W. *The Philosophy of History*. New York: Norton, 1981.

Peirce, Charles S. *The Collected Papers of Charles Sanders Peirce*, edited by Charles Hartshorne and Paul Weiss, vol. 6. Cambridge: Harvard University Press, 1936.

Portmann, A. *Biologische Fragments zu einer Lehre vom Menschen*. Basel: Benno Schwabe, 1951.

Royce, Josiah. *The World and the Individual*, vol. 1. New York: Macmillan, 1899.

———. *The Philosophy of Loyalty*. New York: Macmillan, 1908.

Whitehead, Alfred North. *Introduction to Mathematics*. New York: Henry Holt, 1911.

———. *Process and Reality: An Essay in Cosmology*. New York: Macmillan, 1929.

Zaner, Richard M. *The Problem of Embodiment*. The Hague: Nijhoff, 1964.

Donald W. Sherburne

# The Goldilocks Syndrome: On Philosophical Aspirations That Are Too High, Too Low, and Just Right

Goldilocks had a terrible time: What with porridge that was either too hot or too cold, chairs that were too big, too soft, or too fragile to bear her weight and beds that were too soft or too hard, she was one lucky kid to finally secure a decent meal and a good rest. Philosophers are faced with an analogous sort of difficulty in our time, especially when contemplating the "recovery of philosophy" in the wake of the many cross-currents and cross-winds that have buffeted it in recent decades. Just where should philosophical aspirations be aimed? John E. Smith's career (the philosophical interests embedded in that career) exemplifies the tensions and polarities faced by philosophy today as it seeks to recover a sense of its possibilities and limits. Most assuredly one of the great teachers of his time, Smith has taught such divergent philosophical figures as Kant, Hegel, Royce, and Dewey with such brilliance, passion, and insight in each case that it is virtually impossible in each particular instance to doubt that NOW Smith has arrived home, NOW his philosophical aspirations have made contact with their proper object. But where is "home" for Smith? It is hard to say. Just as Goldilocks had a terrible time with a huge bed and chair on the one hand, and a tiny bed and chair on the other, so Smith seems unwilling to bed down either on Hegel's humongous four-poster, or on the straw mat Dewey has spread in the corner. Goldilocks knew the too big, too hot, too hard and the too little, too cold, and too soft when she encountered them, and she also knew the just right. My concern in this essay is to articulate considerations which bear on the too high, the too low, and the just right when it comes to philosophical aspirations.

Nathaniel Lawrence, in his last little book on Whitehead, makes some interesting comments about the word *speculative* as it ought to be understood in the phrase "speculative philosophy." As he notes, in ordinary discourse the word *speculative* has a rather chancy ring to it. We say that one speculates in the stock market, meaning that one plays a hunch, one guesses, that the market will go up or down. But the word *speculative* in the phrase *speculative philosophy* has nothing to do with all this, Lawrence asserts. He points out that the Latin root from which our word *speculative* derives is the word *specula*, which means literally a watchtower. A watchtower is a high place from which an army sentry, for example, can get a good view of the surrounding terrain, seeing more than can be seen from the ground and being able to put what is seen in proper perspective. Speculative philosophy is the business of building an intellectual watchtower firmly enough anchored so that it will support us, but high enough so that, from the vantage point of its platform, we can do such things as see over the walls that separate academic disciplines from one another. When we accuse someone of not being able to see the woods for the trees, we are suggesting that the person ought to get a perspective on the matter at hand which is a little more all-encompassing, which is to say that we are urging the person to mount a somewhat higher *specula* from which the outline of the whole forest will become apparent. Metaphysics has often been described as the attempt to discover how things hang together, which can be understood in the current context as being the effort to get up high enough to see the lay of the intellectual land spread out about one.

Now we have a beginning in the search for the too high, the too low, and the just right in the context of the philosophical aspirations. We want to get high enough so that we can distinguish the contours of what we experience as the fundamental problematic, the woods, about which we have a concern, but we are nervous about getting any higher than we need to because we want our watchtower to be as firmly anchored as possible on solid ground—those of us in the American tradition concerned about the recovery of philosophy in America are very sensitive to the fact that the higher the watchtower one builds, the shakier and more unsteady it becomes. John Dewey knew this well. Dewey is a fascinating figure to consider in this context, and for three reasons: (1) the attraction he holds for John Smith, always tempering the enthusiasm which Smith easily develops for more speculatively inclined philosophers; (2) the debate about who really is entitled to don the mantle of pragmatism which centers on the different understandings of what is important in Dewey held by Richard Rorty on the one hand and such as Ralph Sleeper, Richard Bernstein, and Abraham Edel on the other; and (3) Dewey's account of how he sees his own philosophical work related to and differentiated from that of Alfred North Whitehead, thc philosopher whom I am convinced is the watchtower masterbuilder of the modern era. Dewey is very nervous about getting very high off the ground. His ambivalence fuels the differences in the way Sleeper reads him—as abandoning the term *metaphysics* but never giving up the project of the *Logic* and the *Theory of Valuation*—and the way Rorty reads him—as abandoning not only the term, but also the project that that term had originally identified. It seems clear that Dewey does see philosophy as engaged in a search for the generic traits of experience. It is also clear that this search involved a process which resulted in the "purification" of experience, which seems to mean that it brings about some degree of systematization of experience. Dewey distrusts system and yet needs system. You cannot get at the generic traits of primary experience without some abstraction and some systematization, that is, without at least a little bit of a watchtower. In Dewey's notion of transactional inquiry, events have to be transformed into objects before they can be manipulated back into the form of events that perhaps enable us to deal more effectively with our environment. Dewey recognizes that there are secondary discourses derived from primary experience, and he identifies science as being one such secondary discourse. The systematization of science occurs pretty close to the ground, and Dewey seems at ease with this healthy, necessary, useful sort of systematization in no small part because it exhibits a continual readiness to loop back to primary experience, to reform and redirect it.

But any sort of watchtower higher than this makes Dewey very nervous, primarily, I gather, because Dewey fears that, in building a substantial watchtower, philosophy would come to consider itself as providing an intellectual report from the outside upon an external subject matter which philosophy viewed as complete and finished in itself, as a landscape viewed from a high tower is considered compete and finished in itself. (See Dewey's contribution to the Schilpp volume on Whitehead, 659.) Dewey protested against the idea that philosophy is a finished set of meanings, a formal, static, "foundational" product of abstract philosophical analysis. If the watchtower is kept very, very low, then philosophy is not viewed as statically and abstractly over against experience, delineating once and for all the generic structures of experience, but, rather, as anchored *in* experience, as just one more part of experience. It is as though Dewey knew he needed a specula, a watchtower, but wanted it low and so small only one foot could rest on it so that the other would constantly be balancing the whole by touching and pushing away from solid ground—touching and pushing, touching and pushing with that one free foot. When Dewey is looking at one foot, the one on his stepstool of a specula, Sleeper encounters the real John Dewey; when Dewey is looking at the other foot, when it is flat on the ground, Rorty encounters his John Dewey, the Dewey who at the end seemed about to abandon even a mere stepstoolish specula.

Richard Rorty's Dewey puts me in mind of the circus high diver who came home to his wife one night in terrible shape, covered with bandages and splints. He explained his awful condition as follows. He had been diving off a forty-foot tower into two feet of water for some time and cranked the act up a notch by going to fifty feet and only using one foot of water. He finally perfected the show by diving sixty feet into a damp rag. Then on this particular night some scoundrel had wrung out the rag! I gather that a lot of people feel as though Rorty has "wrung out the rag" on Dewey the philosopher. Sleeper seems to be content if we agree to leave one or two feet of water in the tank, but my impression concerning John Smith is that he is reluctant to believe that you can really survive a forty- or fifty-foot drop into only one or two feet of water. Given my two metaphors, the critical questions become, How deep the water? How high the watchtower?

As indicated above, using the watchtower metaphor, one wants to get high enough so that one can distinguish the contours of experience as the fundamental problematic, high enough so that one can trace the outlines of the woods around. What one experiences as the fundamental problematic conditions everything. I want to describe that problematic as I experience it, and show how, given that starting point, I understand the significance of the debates over Dewey's intentions and accomplishments, as well as the import of the directions being explored by Rorty. So this is the time to abandon nursery tales, metaphors, and funny stories and speak as plainly and directly as possible.

*The* problematic, *the* issue for philosophy, *the* challenge for our era is, in my judgment, the challenge to do justice to human being at the same time that human being is understood as a part of nature. Paul Weiss once commented, "Three philosophers have done justice to man as a part of nature—Aristotle, Hegel, and Whitehead." What may well have been a casual observation for Weiss has bounced round and round inside my head until it has come, for me, to frame the very character of the philosophical enterprise. Pierre Teilhard de Chardin helped cement Weiss's observation in its position of centrality when I encountered his claim to the effect that no one could ever philosophize responsibly without taking into account the doctrine of evolution. Science in its many dimensions seeks to tell us about, to do justice to, the world; psychology, psychiatry, phenomenology, existentialism, social and political thought, art, drama, and poetry seek to tell us about, to do justice to, human being, both in the singular and collectively; but it falls to philosophy to try to put them together, to do, in Weiss's words, justice to man *as a part of nature*. The genius of Aristotle, that which justified the habit in a later time of referring to him as "The Philosopher," was that he generated a set of categories that not only permitted him to handle the old Eleatic dilemmas about change and becoming, but also allowed him to analyze nature and human nature in the same terms. The Copernican revolution tore those categories for understanding nature away from us irrevocably and bequeathed to subsequent philosophy the challenge to complete the Copernican Revolution by finding a way to do for the post-Copernican age what Aristotle did for the classical period—discover a set of categories compatible with the best contemporary scientific understanding of nature, which would be adequate to the richness of our immediate experience of our human reality and furthermore would exhibit that human reality as part and parcel of the wider reality from which it emerged and within which it is set. The genius of

Whitehead is that he accepted the challenge to complete the Copernican revolution and succeeded in articulating the central features that any adequate response to the challenge must exhibit.

To return to Dewey, it is fascinating to find Dewey, in his essay in the Schilpp volume on Whitehead, beginning the article by stressing the degree to which Dewey finds that he and Whitehead share the same "background and point of departure" (645). Dewey describes this shared background and point of departure as the belief in the central importance of the ideas

> that experience is a manifestation of the energies of the organism; that these energies are in such intimate continuity with the rest of nature that the traits of experience provide clews for forming "generalized descriptions" of nature . . . and that what is discovered about the rest of nature (constituting the conclusions of the natural sciences) provides the organs for analyzing and understanding what is otherwise obscure and ambiguous in experiences directly had. (645)

Dewey's "intimate continuity with the rest of nature" is just another formulation of Weiss's "do justice to man as a part of nature." Here is Dewey again:

> The idea that the immediate traits of distinctively human experience are highly specialized cases of what actually goes on in every actualized event of nature does infinitely more than merely deny the existence of an impassable gulf between physical and psychological subject-matter. It authorizes us, as philosophers engaged in forming highly generalized descriptions of nature, to use the traits of immediate experience as clews for interpreting our observations of non-human and non-animate nature. It also authorizes us to carry over the main conclusions of physical science into explanation and description of mysterious and inexplicable traits of experience marked by "consciousness." (647–48)

After stressing again and again his agreement with Whitehead on such matters, Dewey concludes his segment on shared background and point of departure with a surprisingly strong statement: "For I believe that only by means of a view of the same general nature as is involved in this position can philosophy escape the road it has been following, a road which demonstrably has led to a dead end" (649).

More about philosophy having been on a road leading to a dead end in a moment. First I wish to make two comments concerning

Dewey's misgivings, expressed later in this same article, about Whitehead's mode of philosophizing. In the first place, Dewey is hung up on Whitehead's early achievements in mathematics. It would appear that Dewey cannot help but think that Whitehead models the philosophical enterprise upon the mathematical enterprise. Dewey finds the language used by Whitehead in describing "the task and office of philosophy" suggestive of "the kind of structure exhibited in pure mathematics" (656–57). For Dewey this leads to "the assimilation of the proper subject-matter of philosophy (the constitution of nature) to that of mathematical theory" (657–68). Here Dewey has been misled by Whitehead's reputation as a mathematician and by what I suspect is the strong likelihood, for which there is some evidence, that Dewey had not read Whitehead's *Process and Reality*, but drew his response to Whitehead entirely from his reading of *Adventures of Ideas*. Early in *Process and Reality*, however, Whitehead attacks Descartes and all others who attempt to assimilate the methodology of philosophy to that of mathematics:

> Philosophy has been misled by the example of mathematics. . . . The verification of a rationalistic scheme is to be sought in its general success, and not in the peculiar certainty, or initial clarity, of its first principles. . . . Philosophy has been haunted by the unfortunate notion that its method is dogmatically to indicate premises which are severally clear, distinct, and certain; and to erect upon those premises a deductive system of thought.
>
> But the accurate expression of the final generalities is the goal of discussion and not its origin. . . . The primary method of philosophy is descriptive generalization. Under the influence of mathematics, deduction has been foisted onto philosophy as its standard method, instead of taking its true place as an essential auxiliary mode of verification whereby to test the scope of generalities. (8, 10.)

To go back to the Goldilocks theme, Dewey tries out Whitehead's orientation, and although he likes much about it, he finds its aspirations to be too high, in no small part because of what Dewey perceived, at least to a degree inaccurately, as its structural similarity to the method of mathematics.

Now to my second comment concerning Dewey's misgivings about Whitehead's philosophy. This suggests that one of the reactions Dewey has to Whitehead reveals that Dewey's philosophical aspirations are too low. Toward the end of his Schilpp article, Dewey makes the following revealing observation:

> It is one thing, marking to my mind a great advance, to see and say that there must be something homologous in the material of physical science and that of feeling, ideas, emotion and enjoyment as they occur in human experience. But for the purpose of discovery of better possibilities and the criticism of what exists all that is needed in the way of homology is correspondence of functions. Insistence upon identity of content tends, I believe, to obscuration of what is philosophically important. (660)

For Dewey, what is "philosophically important" is the criticism of what is, and this in the way and at the level which focuses attention on the "discovery of better possibilities." Now it is hard to be against "better possibilities," just as it is hard to be against America, motherhood, and apple pie! Dewey has no monopoly on wanting to loop back to primary experience with the aim of improving things. In fact, I have argued elsewhere that part 4 of Whitehead's *Adventures of Ideas* is the process of articulating the "formulated aspirations" which emerge from Whitehead's philosophy of organism; it is this process which constitutes the way that his metaphysics loops back to primary experience with the aim of correcting and improving it—the notions of truth, beauty, zest, adventure, and peace are technical terms embodying these formulated aspirations as Whitehead conceives them to be capable of reshaping the character of our experience. The difference between Whitehead and Dewey is that Whitehead thinks that he will not be equipped to loop back to primary experience until he has acquired the sort of knowledge metaphysics is capable of generating, whereas Dewey thinks that philosophy gets in trouble once it sees itself as generating a kind of knowledge. In the Schilpp article Dewey stresses that a philosophy of experience will see itself as a form of experience, as within experience, within any sort of report it itself may issue about experience. Such a philosophy of experience

> will not take itself to be a kind of knowledge. It will not be concerned with just reporting and "explaining" in a coherent way the things that are valid in past experiences. It will concern itself with the conditions under which they have arisen for the sake of being better able to form plans by which they may be reinforced and expanded. . . . Report, even in the most systematic fashion, of subject-matters and contents . . . will be subordinated to determination of what will follow in consequence of them. (659)

The problem with Dewey as I see it is that in backing away from philosophy as productive of knowledge, from the idea of building anything more than the most stepstoolish specula, he leaves his key ideas dangling in the wind, ungrounded. Wherefore "valid"? Howso "better"? Whitehead builds a higher specula, but that venture into ontology gives him a much less ambiguous voice when he does (as in part 4 of *Adventures of Ideas*) complete the loop back to primary experience. This is at least part of what I suspect Roy Wood Sellars had in mind when, in that same Schilpp volume (425) he wrote: "To me the high value of Whitehead's thought is ontological. It is a serious alternative to any form of materialism. In this respect it is far more stimulating than any traditional form of experientialism, such as Dewey's, which never really grapples with ontology."

Some pages back I quoted Dewey to the effect that the background and point of departure he shared with Whitehead was the only position which would let philosophy escape the dead-end road it had been following. I promised to come back to this point and will do so now. Dewey's comment about "the dead end road" was made fifty years ago, which serves to put the current discussions about the end of philosophy in perspective. Whitehead also, more than *sixty* years ago, was engaged in similar reflections. I will put Whitehead's comments in juxtaposition with Richard Rorty's move toward a post-Philosophical culture. The analysis will focus upon the relationship between epistemology and metaphysics. But first, I need to make one important observation about my perception of the fundamental assumption underlying Rorty's disengagement from Philosophy. (I use the capital "P" to reflect Rorty's distinctions and meanings.)

From Rorty's perspective, everything discussed up to now is irrelevant, and so is what is to follow. His fundamental assumption cuts the ground out from under my claim that the task of philosophy is to do justice to man as a part of nature. Rorty, who was intensely involved some decades ago in the debates within philosophy of mind concerning the identity theory, appears to me to have ended up simply assuming a behavioristic materialism. This certainly entails that human being is a part of nature, but from my perspective, and most clearly from the perspective of someone such as, say, Sartre, this assumption does not *do justice to* man, even though it places human being smack in the middle of nature. Having made this assumption, Rorty can be rather cavalier about what philosophical issues no longer seem interesting. Whitehead at one point observes that there is no more fascinating subject for study than scientists motivated by the purpose of showing that there are no purposes. For better or for worse, that wry jest by Whitehead is never far from my mind as I watch Rorty pursue his purpose of bringing the era of Philosophy to a close. But now, to the question of Whitehead, Rorty, and the end of Philosophy.

The opening sentence of Whitehead's magnum opus, *Process and Reality*, tells us that Whitehead looked quite self-consciously down that very road so recently traveled by Rorty, saw with great clarity where that road leads (or should we say, does *not* lead), and quite unambiguously articulated the alternative to Rorty's kamikaze impulses. I will explicate the meaning of that sentence by drawing out key aspects of the context within which it must be understood. In the process, the contrast with the path taken by Rorty should become quite clear. What Whitehead knew, and Rorty overlooked, can be summarized in the phrase *all epistemological difficulties are only camouflaged metaphysical difficulties.* When Rorty finds his epistemological difficulties overwhelming, insuperable, he bails out of the philosophical game; when Whitehead encounters the same epistemological stone wall, he knows full well, as does Rorty, that there is no point in continuing to bang his head on that impenetrable barrier, but he also knows, and this is what Rorty overlooks, that there is a way to back up and reorient the philosophical enterprise which will quite neatly circumnavigate the region of the wall. In the paragraphs which follow I will adumbrate Whitehead's alternative to Rorty's suicidal proposal and will advance some considerations designed to enhance the plausibility of Whitehead's project.

That extremely illuminating first sentence of *Process and Reality*, which is actually the first sentence of the preface, goes as follows: "These lectures are based upon a recurrence to that phase of philosophic thought which began with Descartes and ended with Hume" (xi). That sentence seems simple enough, but just let the sound of its meaning begin to reverberate through the echo chamber which is *Process and Reality* and that meaning thickens and deepens considerably. A good way to begin that thickening and deepening process is to scrutinize carefully two words which occur in that opening sentence: *recurrence* and *ended*. I will begin with the latter, *ended*.

Clearly, Whitehead believes something ended with Hume, and he labels that something a "phase of philosophic thought." Rorty thinks that something ended with Sellars, Quine, Davidson, and others, but he labels that something not *a phase* of philosophical thought, but Philosophy itself! I strongly suspect that Whitehead and Rorty are witnessing to the end of the same thing. The basic disagreement concerns what that thing, which is ending, is. That Rorty can see what is ending as Philosophy, while Whitehead sees it as only a phase of philosophical thought, is possible at least in part because they differ over the question of whether all epistemological difficulties really are only disguised metaphysical difficulties. I wish to turn now to some materials which will shed light on this radical divergence between the views of Whitehead and Rorty.

I begin with one of my favorite passages in *Process and Reality*, what I refer to as the "O Bottom" passage .

> All modern philosophy hinges round the difficulty of describing the world in terms of subject and predicate, substance and quality, particular and universal. The result always does violence to that immediate experience which we express in our actions, our hopes, our sympathies, our purposes, and which we enjoy in spite of our lack of phrases for its verbal analysis. We find ourselves in a buzzing world, amid a democracy of fellow creatures; whereas, under some disguise or other, orthodox philosophy can only introduce us to solitary substances, each enjoying an illusory experience; "O Bottom, thou art changed! what do I see on thee?" (*PR*, 49–50)

This passage has a clear association with our phrase *and ended with Hume*. The phrases *modern philosophy* and *orthodox philosophy* are equivalent in scope to the phrase *that phase of philosophic thought which began with Descartes and ended with Hume*. What Whitehead is clearly saying is that if you start with the Cartesian notion of substance, a something that requires nothing other than itself in order to exist, and then let that understanding color your use of the notions of a subject and a particular, then there is an unbridgeable gap between the verbal analysis and the character of immediate experience. The verbal analysis is no more isomorphic with experience than is the ass's head of Shakespeare's Bottom with the head his friends are accustomed to seeing on his shoulders! The Cartesian starting point leads inexorably to the Humean dead end, where all relations are external and there is not a shred of evidence upon which to ground inferences involving causal connectedness. Whitehead notes that the acceptance of this starting point

> led to the collapse of Descartes' many substances into Spinoza's one substance; to Leibniz's windowless monads with their pre-established harmony; to the sceptical reduction of Hume's philosophy, a reduction first effected by Hume himself, and reissued with the most beautiful exposition by Santayana in his *Scepticism and Animal Faith*. (PR, 48)

In short, what Descartes began in his role as the father of modern philosophy, Hume ended in his role as the ultimate epistemological skeptic.

We are now ready to redirect our attention to what I see as an absolutely fundamental philosophical difference between Whitehead and Rorty, namely, their perceptions of the relationships between epistemological and metaphysical difficulties. First, an explanation. One verbal pattern Whitehead uses to point to the problem generated by the Cartesian orientation is to say that starting with the notion of a substance as requiring nothing but itself in order to exist, and also understanding human knowers to be substances, guarantees that one will never find a connection between the experience of individuals on the one hand, and the structures of the external world on the other. With that point firmly in mind, we need to look at the passage in which Whitehead most clearly articulates his understanding of the relationship between epistemological and metaphysical difficulties.

> All metaphysical theories which admit a disjunction between the component elements of individual experience on the one hand, and on the other hand the component elements of the external world, must inevitably run into difficulties over the truth and falsehood of propositions, and over the grounds for judgment. The former difficulty is metaphysical, the latter epistemological. But all difficulties as to first principles are only camouflaged metaphysical difficulties. Thus also the epistemological difficulty is only solvable by an appeal to ontology. (*PR*, 189)

Here is our great divide. Whitehead is convinced that claims about the know*er* precede claims about know*ing*. That is, whenever one is faced with intractable epistemological problems, one must go back and reexamine all the presuppositions built into the account that one gives about what, in the context of that difficulty, are the structures of the knowers with the problems. That is why Whitehead believes that it is only a phase of philosophic thought which came to an end with Hume.

*Recognizing the intractability of Hume's problem is a signal to go back to the initial metaphysical assumptions of that phase of philosophical thought and explore how those assumptions generate presuppositions about the nature of knowers*.

This point brings me to the second key word of that opening sentence of *Process and Reality*, *recurrence*. The recurrence envisioned, and executed, by Whitehead, is the act of returning to the Cartesian assumptions with the aim of isolating just those assumptions about the nature of know*ers* which, within that Cartesian realm of discourse, compromise the very possibility of know*ing*. As the "O Bottom" passage has made clear, it is the connotations grouping around the notions of subject, substance, and particular which, as they shape and form the Cartesian understandings, cut off the possibility of defending knowledge claims. Whitehead's response to this recurrence is not to sit around paralyzed, wringing his hands, reduced simply to indulging in edifying discourses. Rather, it is to roll up his sleeves and so some Philosophy, do some metaphysical tinkering with that notion of a knower which defeated the possibility of knowing. As a result of this metaphysical activity, Whitehead created the category of an actual entity. The whole point behind the way Whitehead created this category of an actual entity was to end up with the notion of a particular, a subject which was *not* cut off from other things, requiring nothing but itself in order to exist, but which was, to the contrary, the *process of integrating other things into a unique mode of togetherness*. Other things, gathered together in a novel synthesis, is just what an actual entity is. An actual entity is not the sort of thing which requires nothing but itself in order to exist; quite to the contrary, without other things to serve as data for its conformal phase, the notion of an actual entity is incoherent, empty, void. *Substance*, a something requiring nothing but itself in order to exist, has in Whitehead's hands, given way to *process*, to the process-integrating-other-entities-from-a-perspective which is an actual entity. Such an actual entity, unlike the "orthodox philosophy" of the "O Bottom" passage, could never "introduce us to solitary substances, each enjoying an illusory experience" precisely because each actual entity is, in its very nature, social, related, out there in the middle of the "buzzing world, amid a democracy of fellow creatures."

It is not my purpose here to elaborate upon the notion of an actual entity. Rather, I wished merely to point out that the creation of the category of an actual entity is Whitehead's response to the same conditions and conclusions which lead Rorty to abandon Philosophy. Whitehead recognizes with absolute clarity that Hume has shown that Descartes' assumptions about the nature of the knower lead inexorably to skeptical conclusions about knowing. But what Whitehead knows, and Rorty overlooks, is that "the epistemological difficulty is only solvable by an appeal to ontology." The fundamental insight driving Whitehead's response to orthodox philosophy is the insight that epistemological difficulties are only camouflaged metaphysical difficulties, that metaphysics undergirds epistemology, that paradoxes and dead ends in the domain of knowing entail faulty assumptions in that domain of thought which specifies what it is to be a knower. Unhampered by any a priori terror at the thought of doing metaphysics, unhampered by the restricted vocabulary imposed upon the philosophical enterprise by the epistemological dogmatism of the last half century, Whitehead never for an instant contemplates abandoning philosophy. To the contrary, with clarity and simplicity he tells us, toward the end of the preface of *Process and Reality*, that our task as philosophers is "to frame a scheme of ideas, the best that one can, and unflinchingly to explore the interpretations of experience in terms of that scheme" (*PR*, xiv). Rorty has told us that some such schemes fail; Whitehead, quite aware of that, has told us what we must then do, and has himself taken a good shot at doing it.

Do I mean to suggest that Whitehead's work as it stands completes the Copernican revolution, finalizes our understanding of human nature while exposing its connectedness to the wider nature which supports it? Of course not. I have my problems with Whitehead's conceptuality. I find the concept 'God' puzzling and its role in the larger scheme incoherent. I waffle in my own mind about the importance of eternal objects—should I follow Charles Hartshorne in down-peddling their significance, or should I struggle over and over with that monumental chapter on abstraction in *Science and the Modern World* in search of a better way of appropriating its many insights? Exactly what are the physicists, chemists, and biologists proposing this week which might suggest new ways of grasping the character of that wider nature of which human nature is a part? So much is unsettled. And yet Whitehead's basic notion of the actual entity, with its prehensive, relational structure does seem to me to point the way toward the specula needed in our time if we are to complete the Copernican revolution by finally exhibiting in a coherent, logical, applicable, and adequate set of concepts how what is can be, that is, how the richness of human nature can be understood as integrated with nature. John Smith brings a world of philosophical experience, subtlety, and insight into his retirement years. And yes, he does bring with him a teasingly peripheral interest in, and knowledge of, Whitehead's achievements. By making some connections here between Dewey, Whitehead, and Rorty, perhaps I will have encouraged him, during the richly productive years of retirement that we all wish for him, to work toward the articulation of a specula that is neither too high nor too low, but just right—and quite possibly Whiteheadian in more than a minor way.

## REFERENCES

Lawrence, Nathaniel. *Alfred North Whitehead: A Primer of his Philosophy*. New York: Twayne Publishers Inc., 1974.

Schilpp, Paul Arthur, ed. *The Philosophy of Alfred North Whitehead*. In The Library of Living Philosophers. New York: Tudor Publishing Company, second edition, 1951.

Whitehead, Alfred North. *Process and Reality*, Corrected Edition. New York: The Free Press, 1978.

Merold Westphal

# Philosophy as Critique and as Vision

> *The practice of philosophy, since the end of the nineteenth century, has taken place within a greatly altered cultural context. The magnitude of this change has required philosophy to redefine its theoretical function and its relation to other cultural activities. But Western culture has also suffered from the decline in philosophical vitality. Philosophy exists to meet the native human demand for the integration of knowledge. The cultural need for cognitive integration has remained unsatisfied while philosophy adapted to its new historical situation. Serious doubts now exist whether that need can be met, whether philosophy or any human activity can order and unify the extraordinary pluralism of our time.*
>
> —McCarthy, *The Crisis of Philosophy*

If we would speak of the recovery of philosophy in America, it is important that we avoid romantic nostalgia about the "good old days." The notion of recovery refers to something lost, in this case, presumably a world in which philosophy was an important part of a culture that, in turn, was an important part of a society. What is to be recovered is a world in which ideas have consequences, in which the institutions and practices of a people are shaped by a shared life of the mind in which philosophy plays a weighty role.

One reason for not lapsing into such nostalgia too quickly is to avoid overestimating the degree to which the world of "classical"

American philosophy was such a world. Perhaps Dewey had a more directly visible impact on educational practices than any single contemporary philosopher has; but we need to remember that the "pragmatic" dimension of the American character is not so much an affinity for the philosophical subtleties of the great pragmatists as an aversion toward abstract analysis of the sort that distinguishes any philosophy from accounting, science, and engineering.

Another reason to restrain any impulses toward nostalgia that we may feel is to avoid a misleading focus on the distinctly American features of our philosophical status quo. For it may well be that generic features of modernity are more important than any specifically American traits. This, at any rate, is what is suggested by the reference to "Western culture" in the quotation that begins this chapter.

What philosophy needs to recover is not some glorious past, however good the "good old days" may have been. What it needs to recover is itself. It needs to become philosophy.

This way of speaking is perhaps less paradoxical than it sounds. Some verbs, such as *to run*, are task words, while others, such as *to win*, are achievement words. While the latter designate a state of completion, the former signify an ongoing process, an activity not yet at its *telos*.[1] Whether *to be* is a task or an achievement verb depends on how it is qualified. Platonists, for example, would insist that to be temporal is a task, that only the eternal simply is what it is and that everything else is trying to be something it never fully is.

For present purposes, a weaker thesis will work. We can concede, for the sake of argument, that some temporal things, such as cabbages, simply are what they are, but that others, such as kings, are not. To be human is always an unfinished task, and in this case, to be is always to become. Since philosophy is a human activity, to philosophize is always to be on the way toward philosophy. In such a frame of reference, presupposed here, there is no paradox in saying that philosophy needs to recover itself, meaning that philosophy needs to become philosophy.

But just what is it that philosophy is trying to become? Perhaps no better answers can be found than the ones found in the Platonic dialogues. There was pre-Socratic philosophy, to be sure. But insofar as philosophy has played a significant role in Western culture, that role begins with the dialogues. This beginning is not the *arche* for which Greek philosophy sought, the conceptual equivalent of the primordial perfection portrayed by myth. Like all historical beginnings, this one arrived too late to begin, since the party has always already started. Nor can any convincing claims for perfection be made for the dialogues, either in the sense of infallibility or in the sense of completeness. They are nevertheless a good place for us to join the conversation that has already begun about the recovery of philosophy.

My thesis here is that in the dialogues Socrates teaches us that philosophy is critique and Plato teaches us that philosophy is vision. The relationship is dialectical, for the two sides need to be simultaneous in spite of the radical difference between them, the difference, for example, between Socratic ignorance and irony on the one hand and Platonic myth and metaphysics on the other. Critique without vision is nihilism, while vision without critique is despotism. Philosophy is dangerous because when it fails to be sufficiently dialectical it ends up in the service either of nihilism or of despotism (unless it has lost its vitality completely by failing to be either critique or vision).

For Socrates, critique is Janus faced. One the one hand, it is directed toward the Athenian establishment. Socrates asks embarrassing questions *about* the great heroes of the Athenian empire (did they make Athens better or only richer and more powerful?), and equally embarrassing questions *to* his contemporaries who bask in the glory that was Athens. The latter include the business community (artisans), the media (poets), and the politicians, whose replies to Socratic questioning reveal again and again the gap between instrumental expertise and wisdom.

On the other hand, Socrates is critical of the cultural avante-garde, including the new scientific materialists and especially the sophists. Neither tradition nor technique can be trusted to the point of escaping cross-examination. If his message to the Athenian establishment is that culture without critique is complacency, his message to the cultural avant-garde is that critique without commitment is cynicism. It is entirely in the spirit of Socrates that Kierkegaard describes sophistry as "the perpetual life-and-death struggle of knowledge with the phenomenon in the service of egotism" and as "the wild and dissolute thrashing about of egotistical thought."[2] This is the essence of cynicism.

A complacent social mainstream and a cynical cultural elite. This description of what Socrates was up against was not a bad account of the West before the fall of the Berlin wall, the dissolution of the Warsaw

Pact, and the decline, if not the disintegration, of the Soviet Union. But in the midst of the celebration of having won the cold war, it has become, if anything, more profoundly characteristic of who we are. The complacency of social institutions which take their non-Communist modernity to be the sign of their ultimacy is challenged only by a cultural postmodernism that always flirts with cynicism and sometimes is seduced into it.

If philosophy is to become itself in such a context by learning to practice Socratic critique, it will have to be very direct and concrete. Philosophy is never a first-order activity. If it were, it could never be either reflection or critique. But it lives in the constant danger of so falling in love with the "meta" spheres in whose ether it flourishes that it loses touch with the reality of everyday life.

During the early seventies, I went to hear one of my colleagues give a lecture to incoming frosh as part of a series on recent developments in various disciplines. My colleague told them that philosophers had spilled a lot of ink discussing the meaning of such terms as *justice*, and what criteria there might be, if any, for distinguishing justice from injustice. This left little time, he pointed out, for discussing what kinds of actions and institutions might actually be just. It left Americans, at least, free to continue assuming that since the pledge to the flag says we are a nation of liberty and justice for all, the plain evidence to the contrary could be ignored.

Then, he said, a guy named Rawls wrote a book, *A Theory of Justice*, in which he tried to argue that social institutions of this sort were just and others unjust. Although he himself belonged to the philosophical tradition in which ethics had been all but eclipsed by metaethics, he celebrated this return to a more nearly first-order question.

I say "more nearly" because, while I join in celebrating the Rawlsian return from metaethics, I am not sure it is the return to a critique as direct and as concrete as the Socratic. There can be no doubt that the ongoing debate spurred by Rawls' book has happily transgressed the boundaries of the sometimes all too clubby philosophical profession. But it is not so clear that it has really gotten outside the academy. Scholars from a variety of disciplines juxtapose their theories to his, and at times, although the debate is about the world in which real people live, it seems almost as removed from that world as the metaethical debates of earlier decades.

The point is not to challenge the legitimacy of theory; it is rather to challenge theory to complete itself by bringing its generalities into unambiguous contact with the particularities of everyday life. For example, when I read the *Gorgias* with students in their first philosophy class, I first try to help them see that Socrates views the sophists as those who gain wealth and/or power by practicing techniques of persuasion untied to truth or insight. Then I ask them who the sophists are in contemporary society. Consistently and without coaching, they identify three groups: lawyers, advertisers, and politicians. While they are both able and, when asked, willing to make this connection, they are not particularly eager to do so. For it has a concreteness and directness that is disconcerting. It is no longer someone's theory that is challenged but practices, professions, and lifestyles that some of their parents practice and to which some of them aspire themselves.

Some students, having no personal or family links to law or advertising, are not especially bothered by a Socratic analysis of these parts of their world; but all of them have been taught that as part of democratic America they are the last best hope of the world. I do not feel it is my job to shield them from the disturbing question of the degree to which American democracy is founded on sophistry. Just the opposite.

Similarly, when we read the *Republic*, I ask them to apply the critique of democracy developed there to American politics as they know it to see how well it fits. They have little trouble seeing the point of the allegory about those who think that the skills required of a sea captain are those of seizing and retaining control of the wheel, with or without the skills of a navigator.

I call Socratic critique direct and concrete because its bearing on the familiar practices and institutions of daily life is blatant. That is, of course, what got Socrates into trouble. His critique was addressed so unambiguously to certain practices and professions that those engaged in them felt personally threatened. He gave them the gift of a mirror in which, had they been willing to look, they might have learned both a specific and a general truth. The former is that at least some features of their own practices were highly questionable. The latter is that practices in general are not justified by being widespread and taken for granted in a particular social milieu. Social complacency[3] is one thing, rational validity another.

Some might respond by suggesting that I am confusing philosophy with journalism. To this charge perhaps the best response might be to plead guilty. For what *we* might learn from Socrates is that the distinction between philosophy and journalism that seems so self-evident to us is anything but self-evident in itself. It may well be that philosophy cannot recover itself without leaving the secure womb of theoretical abstraction for the dangerous world of everyday concreteness. In that case we might have to paraphrase Plato by saying that until philosophers become journalists or journalists become philosophers,[4] the "last best hope of the world" will be a society of flag-worshipping warriors eager to impose its "new world order" on others although it is itself ravaged by drugs and crime, homelessness and hopelessness, illiteracy and superliterate sophistry, and a division of wealth that makes a joke out of every theory of justice.

No doubt it will never be easy to practice critique in the style of Socrates. It will always require more courage than many of us have. Still, it might seem as if the path is easier for us that it was for him. We are, after all, as he was not, heirs of an Enlightenment that Kant was able to summarize in that famous footnote:

> Our age is, in especial degree, the age of criticism, and to criticism everything must submit. Religion through its sanctity, and law-giving through its majesty, may seek to exempt themselves from it. But they then awaken just suspicion, and cannot claim the sincere respect which reason accords only to that which has been able to sustain the test of free and open examination.[5]

Surely Socratic critique is less likely to be judged a capital offense among us than in ancient Athens, and to that degree we have a certain advantage over Socrates. But we must be careful not to exaggerate it. For, in the first place, enlightenment, as defined above, is anything but ubiquitous among us. A dogmatic and uncritical spirit is by no means rare.

In the second place, and more important, even where the Enlightenment has prevailed, we have no unambiguous advantage over Socrates. He had the difficult task of asserting the rights of reason against tradition and of *logos* over *mythos*. We have the no less difficult task of affirming critical reason in the face of the Enlightenment *mythos* about the *logos*. That myth has become a tradition which, in purporting to define reason, becomes a form of dogmatism.[6]

The name of this myth is instrumental reason or calculative thinking.[7] It is not entirely uncritical, for by its utilitarian canons anything that is not the effective (read: successful) and efficient (read: of minimal cost) adaptation of means to ends is judged to be irrational. The dogmatic moment comes in equating canons of effectiveness and efficiency with rationality. Two types of questions are thereby excluded a priori from the realm of rational discourse: questions about what ends we should seek[8] and questions about which means are permissible (as distinct from effective and efficient) in their pursuit. But these two questions, the one about the good and the other about the right, define the entire domain of ethics. Instrumental reason dogmatically excludes ethical discourse from the realm of reason.[9]

Among the more powerful analyses of instrumental reason are those of Jacques Ellul and Jürgen Habermas. In his powerful trilogy, *The Technological Society* (1954), *Propaganda* (1962), and *The Political Illusion* (1965), Ellul shows how for the technological mindset that modernity has become, questions of ends are simply replaced by questions of means and the possible becomes the permissible, even the necessary.

In the title essay of *Technik und Wissenschaft als "Ideologie"* (1968) and in two of the included essays,[10] Habermas begins his critique of decisionism (the moral equivalent of emotivism) and lays the foundation for his later analysis of modernity as built upon the "colonization of the life-world."[11] Where Ellul notes the way modern society under the spell of instrumental reason propagandizes itself, Habermas reflects on the ways in which technology and science have become the ideology of modern society, that to which society appeals for its basic legitimation. Efficiency and effectiveness become the norms by which society evaluates itself. Just as the meter bar at the Bureau of Standards cannot be more or less than a meter in length, so instrumental reason, itself the definition of reason and thus the criterion of all else, is beyond critical questioning.

Habermas notes the consequences for ethics. Sounding almost like Kierkegaard, he writes, "Technological consciousness reflects not the sundering of an ethical situation but the repression of 'ethics' as such as a category of life. . . . The ideological nucleus of this consciousness is the *elimination of the distinction between the practical* [ethical] *and the technical*."[12]

Now, perhaps, it is somewhat clearer why being heirs of the Enlightenment is no unambiguous advantage over Socrates so far as critique is concerned. Just to the degree that the preceding analysis fits, modernity is a double mystification. Its legitimation discourse is a self-selected propaganda (Ellul) or an ideology that disguises the true nature of our practices (Habermas). But in its celebration of itself as critical reason, modernity turns out to be not only a first order false consciousness, but also the systematic masking of that fact.

The implication for any future philosophy that would come forth as critique is clear. Not only do we face the birth trauma of moving from the womb of theoretical abstraction to the concreteness of everyday life; when we get there we encounter *both* personal and institutional practices that do not wish to be cross-examined *and* the ideological systems of discourse that serve as their propaganda while operating under the alias of critical reason. It becomes necessary not only to question, for example, the practices of image management in personal, economic, and political life, but also to challenge the deeply entrenched habits of instrumental reason that make it all seem so sensible and which give to the experts in image manipulation the place that should go to the wise.

It is clear that if philosophy can recover itself only by rediscovering Socratic critique, the task will be no easy one. It will have to learn to ask unwelcome questions about practices that are taken for granted in everyday life and about the background beliefs that make them seem beyond questioning. And it will have to learn to carry out both of these tasks more or less simultaneously so as never to lose sight of the cognitive embeddedness of the practices on the one hand and the practical import of belief systems on the other.

But this is not the end of our difficulty. Two other issues posed by Socratic practice make the task even more daunting. First, there is the question whether critique has any relation to its targets than a critical one. If it does not, the suspicion of cynicism will be high. In any case, unwelcome questions are easier to dismiss if they are perceived to come from an enemy rather than a friend, and a critic whose only relation to that which is questioned is critical will inevitably be viewed as an enemy. There is a "love it or leave it" mentality that is all too willing to take any critical questioning as a sign of hatred and ingratitude.

The result of Socrates' trial no doubt illustrates this point. Up to that time he had failed to show the love and loyalty to Athens that he subsequently demonstrated in the events recounted in the *Crito*. What this suggests is that if critique is to have any chance at all of getting a serious hearing, the critic not only will have to be but will also have to be seen as a friend. Critique will have to be rightly seen as grounded in love for its targets and in loyalty to a lifeworld that is shared with one's opponents. Since the positive relationships must be both reality and appearance, this will be extraordinarily difficult.

Socrates proved his loyalty to Athens, after it was too late, by choosing to suffer violence rather than employ it. The same can be said for Jesus, Gandhi, and King after him. It may be that there is an important, even an essential, link between philosophical critique and nonviolent activism, especially in a world in which violence seems to be the means of choice for "good" and evil alike. I shall not argue for that conclusion here, but only suggest that it deserves more attention than it usually gets.

However, the recovery of Socratic critique requires some solution to the problem of being ruthlessly critical without either being or seeming to be merely ruthless. The image of Jesus weeping over Jerusalem shows the required posture, but such a posture neither can be nor can seem to be posturing.

Finally, there is the question of critique's relation to itself. If it is important that there be a positive relation between critique and its targets, it is just as important that there be a negative relation between critique and itself.[13] In other words, critique must be self-critical. Critique that is arrogant, that takes itself to be absolute, invites its opponents to respond in kind; for the philosopher who assumes infallibility or purports to see the world *sub specie aeternitatis*, so far from providing a principal objection to the ultimacy of the finite actually serves as a model for that absolutizing of the relative he or she purports to oppose. Critique must be humble as well as loyal.

The Socratic critic must never forget Socratic ignorance. It must serve as a constant reminder of the philosopher's limits. By itself, however, it is not enough. Even if we assume, as I do, that the historical Socrates consistently professed only the love of wisdom and never wisdom simpliciter, he often comes across in the dialogues as arrogant and as much more disposed to cross-examine the answers of his interlocutors than his own mode of questioning.

Moreover, if we assume, as I do, that the recovery of philosophy entails vision as well as critique, we will have to go beyond Socratic ignorance to make positive proposals. This is the point, it seems to me, at which Plato becomes an important corrective to Socrates.[14] Finding the proper balance between the courage to venture speculative vision and the humility to do so tentatively (not timidly) is no childish task. If we would be heirs of Socrates we must be willing to accept as part of his legacy the perennial problem of uniting tough critique that is not disdainful with bold vision that is not dogmatic.

I turn now to the second part of my thesis, the role of vision in the Platonic dialogues as a guide for the recovery of philosophy. If critique without vision is nihilism, then Socratic critique is inherently unstable, wavering between the cynicism Aristophanes finds it to be in *The Clouds* and the speculation into which Plato turns it in the middle dialogues. The recovery of philosophy, as I envisage it, requires the dialectical union of Socrates and Plato, irony and myth, critique and metaphysics.

I do not mean here the self-mediation in which one of the opposites presides over the negotiation with the other and unites it to itself as a mastered moment within its own project. I mean rather the mutual mediation in which each of the opposites simultaneously opens itself to the claims of the other and addresses its own claims to the other.[15] The "result" of this process will be less adequately described as reconciliation than as tension,[16] and it will be the ability to sustain this tension that is the measure of philosophy's self-recovery.

The image of a good marriage might be helpful here, for it is the image of a relation in which difference is rendered fruitful by avoiding two extremes, divorce and engulfment. If the typically "male" self is a separative self that stresses independence and self-sufficiency to the point of risking isolation and estrangement and the typically "female" self is the soluble self that stresses union and belonging to the point of risking absorption and even dissolution,[17] then philosophy's self-recovery can take neither as its model. Critique and vision cannot be divorced from each other, nor can either allow itself to be *aufgehoben* or teleologically suspended by the other.

It is clear from the political character of critique that philosophical vision will also have to be political. Philosophy is an intrinsically political activity, at least if it takes the Platonic dialogues as its point of departure. Here it may be particularly easy to remember that a point of departure is not an *arche*, for Plato's political vision is not one we are likely to be entirely comfortable with. We need not give the dialogues as wooden and uncharitable a reading as Popper does in *The Open Society and its Enemies* to be a bit nervous about Plato's proposals for censoring the stories told to children and for structuring the family relationships of the guardians, to mention but two obvious examples.

If, however, we are willing to approach Plato's political vision both with charity and with humility, it might still prove fruitful in the contemporary search for philosophical self-recovery. (The attentive reader will have noted that charity is here added to the virtues of humility, loyalty, and courage that seem to be built in to our project. These are moral, not intellectual virtues, but they keep presenting themselves as indispensable to the intellectual task we have set for ourselves.)

The possibility that Plato's political vision might inform ours stems from his refusal to take democracy's self-congratulation at face value. The Athenians seem to have been as proud of their democracy as we are of ours, but in the central books of the *Republic*, for example, and not just in the "Socratic" dialogues, Plato insists on asking tough questions about the cash value of those democratic institutions. In other words, his vision grows out of critique.

But it is more than critique, for Plato does not just locate the hard questions and ask them; he makes concrete proposals for their solution. These proposals are his political vision. Let us look briefly at three of these, (1) the philosopher-king, (2) the "extended" family of the guardians, and (3) the censorship of children's stories.

Plato saw as keenly as we can see today what the results are when the ability to gain and maintain political power is the only effective requirement of political leadership. He thought that democracy was better than tyranny, or, in other words, that elections are to be preferred to coups. But his political vision grows out of the insight that this difference can very easily be overrated. For neither necessarily involves the serious attempt to entrust political power to those either with wisdom or with the self-control to place the common good over private advantage. (He would have found the concept of a 'private good' incomprehensible, at least so far as the *vita activa* is concerned.)

The idea of the philosopher-king is his proposal to make the possession of these virtues the *sine qua non* of political power. We may find his aristocracy of virtue elitist. But I want to suggest that the charitable reading of the *Republic* at this point goes like this:

> Here's a real problem, and here's my solution. If you don't like it, find a better one. But be sure that unless you solve this one, your democracy will be only marginally superior to tyranny. And note well. If you take democracy as seriously as you say you do, this is not just a problem about holders of public office; for in democracy ultimate power is entrusted to the people as a whole, and every citizen will need to possess these virtues.[18]

Beyond the specifics of the philosopher-king proposal, or better, at its very heart, is a vision of the essential link between wisdom and moral virtue on the one hand—neither of which is reducible to or derivable from the instrumental expertise of calculative thinking—and a healthy society on the other. The "end of ideology" ideology,[19] whatever its descriptive power, is the fatal hope that Plato's vision on this point has become obsolete. I call this hope "fatal" because its offspring is death, death to community, death to justice, and sooner or later, death to the planet. Just to the degree that we are beginning to sense this, philosophy begins to recover itself and its Platonic heritage.

A similar reading can be given, to the "extended family" among Plato's guardians. It is not difficult to be offended by this proposal at a number of points. But if we are as eager to learn as to refute (or to sustain our reputation as politically correct by being for family values and against eugenics), we will see in Plato's vision both a concern about the politically problematic character of private interests and an insight into the family as an important locus for the same. Unless the family (clan, tribe, race, class) can be surpassed (or extended) with "brotherhood from sea to shining sea," the republic will be in trouble.

And it will not do just to sing about it loudly on ceremonial occasions. That kind of patriotism is the sort of self-congratulatory complacency that is the target of Socratic critique. It cannot be the dialectical partner of Platonic vision. Something has to be done quite realistically to increase the inclusive power of family and decrease its exclusive power, so that we cease to see "them" as outside the scope of our concern and see "them" no longer as "them" but as "us," as our sisters and brothers, mothers and fathers, daughters and sons. Once again, in a democracy this concerns not just the proximate rulers, the politicians, but the ultimate rulers, all the people.[20]

If meant literally and not ironically, Plato's solution is crude indeed. But his vision of a society that says of those we now call burdens, "He's not heavy; he's my brother," is a vision we can ill afford to abandon. Our own hope that economic prosperity could be the glue that holds us together has proved at least as crude as Plato's proposal (taken literally), for our prosperity has never been able to transcend the injustice and poverty it presupposes.[21]

I turn finally to the question of censorship. Once again we find it repugnant, and for good reason, to think that the state should dictate the stories to which children are exposed. And once again there is depth to Plato's vision that our quick rebuttals overlook. Plato sees, as we are beginning to rediscover, the close link between narrative and character formation;[22] and he recognizes the decisive importance of early influences.

If we think for a moment about the narratives our own children are brought up on via television and the movies and the way they define human life in terms of sex and violence, we might begin to suspect that once again Plato has identified a problem from which we cannot escape. Here is my solution, he says, seriously or ironically. If you do not like it, find a better one.

His political vision at this point as before consists not so much in the arrangements he suggests as in the insight that society cannot flourish when the narratives that shape its collective and personal identities are of just any sort. Good people and good institutions require good narratives that do not merely entertain but sensitize, inspire, and challenge. To our secular and pluralistic society this is a frightening thought. It suggests, though it need not, moralizing and indoctrination. But the alternative we have adopted has become a nightmare of ever increasing terror.[23]

Plato's vision is unequivocally political, and those who would make it their point of departure for the recovery of philosophy will be challenged to cultivate political vision. But Plato's vision is not merely political. It insists on placing politics in a metaphysical context. If Socratic critique refuses to let current political practices be self-validating, Platonic vision refuses to let political practice as such be self-sufficient.

Introducing metaphysics into politics is doubtless as dangerous as introducing morality into education, and we would do well to listen carefully to the chorus of warnings that will come quickly and loudly in response to this suggestion. However, the problem is that just as there is no morally neutral education, there is no metaphysically neutral politics. Metaphysical assumptions will be at work in our politics whether we like it or not. The only question is whether they will be overt or covert, reflective or unreflective, defensible or indefensible.

In any case, metaphysics can be (even if it often has not been) humble. It can refuse to resort to violence or propaganda in seeking to make its point, assuming with the Socrates of the *Gorgias* that it is better even for the truth to suffer evil than to do it. While on the one hand it need not be intolerant, we should note that the putative purifying of politics from metaphysics is not an automatic defense against dogmatism and indoctrination.

Another objection to mixing political and metaphysical vision is that the point of doing so is epistemologically erroneous. The idea is that metaphysics as pure science should somehow provide foundations for politics that will be changeless and certain. But the collapse of the foundationalist project in general undermines this specific hope as well.

No doubt that is true, but the argument is an *ignoratio elenchi*. For the point of placing politics in a metaphysical context is not, as some, including Plato, have sometimes thought, turning politics into a rigorous science. The point is rather, as Plato also thought, to be reminded that neither this actual state nor any ideal state of counterfactual human devising, is or can be the ultimate reality. The voice of the people is not, even in principle, the voice of God.[24]

In practical terms this means that politics must always be asking about the limits of its freedom and its creativity. It must be asking about givens, the "nature" that it must take into account as it sets up its art, its nurture, its conventions. This does not mean that nature must be conceived in any particular fashion, for example, as static, or as hierarchical. It may very well be that *nature* is not the best name for the boundaries within which politics operates. Taking Plato as a point of departure need not mean identifying metaphysics with Platonism, as the names of *Augustine* and *Whitehead* should be sufficient to remind us.

Another practical consequence of this view of the linkage between politics and metaphysics is that the latter can never be purely speculative, if by speculative we mean theory for theory's sake. It is contemplative, to be sure, and a Platonically inspired recovery of philosophy will welcome the dialectical tension between the *vita activa* and the *vita contemplativa*. But contemplation in the Platonic sense is radically different from speculation as just defined. For Plato, if not for Aristotle, contemplation is inseparable from *phronesis*, is necessarily linked to personal and to political formation. If Socratic critique teaches us that epistemology must never be separated from the ethico-political questions that originally give it birth, Platonic vision teaches us the same thing about metaphysics. When it comes to the primacy of practical reason, Kant is just another (important) footnote to Plato.

One of the least conspicuous acts in John Smith's long and distinguished career was giving to us an English translation of Richard Kroner's (very) little but (very) valuable book, *Kant's Weltanschauung*.[25] It has the primacy of practical reason as its theme.

It may well be that this theme is the unifying key to the astonishing and at times exasperating diversity of Smith's philosophical activity. Whether exploring the Christian tradition, explaining German idealism, expounding American Pragmatism, or, for that matter, entering the lists of philosophical politics on behalf of philosophical pluralism, his goal was always to bring epistemological and metaphysical reflection back from their speculative exile to their contemplative home. In doing so he has left his own distinctive mark on the recovery of philosophy in America today, both in the writing and in the teaching for which he volunteered and in the professional politics to which, like a certain figure in the *Republic*, he found himself drafted.

We are deeply in his debt.

## NOTES

1. Gilbert Ryle makes this distinction throughout *The Concept of Mind* (New York: Barnes and Noble, 1949).

2. *The Concept of Irony: With Constant Reference to Socrates*, trans. Lee M. Capel (New York: Harper and Row, 1965), 63, 176. In the same spirit, he writes (113–14) that ironic negativity "is a sickness insofar as it is unable to tolerate the absolute except in the form of nothingness."

3. It is worth noting here that complacency was as characteristic of the cultural avant-garde as of the Athenian establishment. The sophists were as given to self-congratulation as, for example, Euthyphro and Anytus in the *Meno*.

4. This formula is not meant to exclude the possibility that critique will have religious origins, arising in the person of the prophet as well as of the philosopher. It seems to me that it is part of the task both of the church and of the academy to bite the hand that feeds it by offering courageous critique of every status quo. That we would do well to think of philosophers on the model of the Hebrew prophets is my thesis in the first chapter of *Kierkegaard's Critique of Reason and Society* (Macon, GA: Mercer University Press, 1987).

5. *Critique of Pure Reason*, A, xi.

6. See Max Horkheimer and Theodor W. Adorno, *Dialectic of Enlightenment*, trans. John Cumming (New York: Continuum, 1982, and Jürgen Habermas, "The Entwinement of Myth and Enlightenment: Max Horkheimer and Theodor Adorno," in *The Philosophical Discourse of Modernity: Twelve Lectures*, trans. Frederick Lawrence (Cambridge, MA: MIT Press, 1987).

7. While the former phrase is associated with Horkheimer and Adorno, the latter comes especially from Heidegger. For his analysis see first of all *The Question Concerning Technology* translated by William Lovitt (New York: Harper & Row, 1977) and *Discourse on Thinking*, translated by John M. Anderson and E. Hans Freund (New York: Harper & Row, 1966). Later Frankfurt School thinkers such as Marcuse and Habermas draw on both of these traditions.

8. This question includes the question of the relative priority of ends, seeking to identify the better and the best as well as the merely good.

9. See Alasdair MacIntyre's bitter complaint about this legacy of the Enlightenment in the opening chapters of *After Virtue* (Notre Dame, IN: University of Notre Dame Press, 1981). He notes that what is in effect emotivism in ethics is far more prevalent than the logical positivism that gave it that name.

10. For English translation, see the final three chapters of *Towards a Rational Society*, trans. Jeremy J. Shapiro (Boston: Beacon Press, 1970).

11. In the second volume of *Theory of Communicative Action*, 2 vols., trans. Thomas McCarthy (Cambridge, MA: MIT Press, 1984, 1987).

12. *Toward a Rational Society*, 112–13, his italics. Cf. 103, where in consort with Claus Offe he sees government restricted to administration. "*Practical substance is eliminated.* . . . [Contemporary politics] eliminates practical questions and therewith precludes discussion about the adoption of standards." (his italics).

13. This implies that critique, like the self in Kierkegaard's *Sickness unto Death*, is a relation (both negative and positive, toward its world) that relates itself to itself. What is in focus here is the quality of that self-relation.

14. Simultaneously, of course, Socrates must be a corrective to Plato to assure that the speculative moment not succumb to hybris.

15. I am drawing here on William Desmond's concept of 'mutual' or 'metaxological' mediation as skillfully developed in *Desire, Dialectic, and Otherness: An Essay on Origins* (New Haven: Yale University Press, 1987) and in *Philosophy and Its Others* (Albany: State University of New York Press, 1990).

16. In other words, Kierkegaard prevails over Hegel about the nature of philosophy.

17. These categories are developed with considerable power in Catherine Keller, *From a Broken Web: Separation, Sexism, and Self* (Boston: Beacon Press, 1986). A philosophy that learns to live the tension between its negativity and its positivity might be in a good position to contribute to our better understanding of ourselves as gendered selves. Then again, it might be the other way around. Only as we learn the mutual mediation of our gendered otherness will we be able to render the tension between critique and speculation fruitful. Most likely the relation between these two challenges to find the metaxological middle is a circular one, each presupposing the other and, in turn, nourishing it.

18. One advantage of this reading is that it reduces the question whether Plato is serious or ironical about his proposals to a merely scholarly question, whose resolution is unnecessary to a serious philosophical reading.

19. See *The End of Ideology Debate*, ed. Claim I. Waxman (New York: Simon and Schuster, 1968). Those who espoused the end of ideology are precisely those whom Habermas has in mind in speaking about science and technology as ideology.

20. John Rawls has built this motif into the very fabric of his theory of justice, arguing that without fraternity there can be no genuine

liberty and equality. See *A Theory of Justice* (Cambridge, MA: Harvard University Press, 1971), 100–108. That Michael Sandel overlooks this feature of Rawls' theory suggests that his much-discussed critique is based on a misreading. See *Liberalism and the Limits of Justice* (Cambridge: Cambridge University Press, 1982).

21. Here I suppose it is Marx who triumphs over Hegel on the nature of a rational society. See note 16.

22. The work of Stanley Hauerwas on this topic is of central importance, not just for ethics but for politics as well.

23. I recently saw a poster made by young children in their church school class. Under the heading, What Our Parents Do For Us, they had listed a variety of things. What struck me was the first item mentioned: "They let us watch TV."

24. This is the point at which Habermasian politics is, it seems to me, insufficiently Platonic. But this is not to acknowledge that it is, as it claims to be, postmetaphysical, for the claim that the human conversation is, in principle and as a regulative ideal, the Truth, is to make a very strong metaphysical claim. It excludes every theism, every pantheism, and the eschatological humanism that envisages the possibility of an actual human community whose voice would be divine.

25. Richard Kroner, *Kant's Weltanschauung*, (Chicago: University of Chicago Press, 1956).

Errol E. Harris

# All Philosophy as *Religionsphilosophie*

Throughout its history philosophy has primarily been concerned about itself. What is philosophy? Is it a distinct discipline with a subject matter of its own? Or is it no more than a distinctive method of criticism and scrutiny of the contents and methodology of other sciences? Questions of this ilk have bedecked the portals of the Hall of Philosophy from the earliest times. In recent decades, the prevalent opinion has favored the second alternative, that philosophy is no more than a method of analysis, although there has been less agreement as to what is to be analyzed. For some, it has been language, for others concepts, and for yet others the two have been seen as one and the same; and in all cases the subject matter has been supplied by other sciences and disciplines and by common experience. Or philosophy has been restricted to logic and methodology reflective upon the special sciences, but without any peculiar content of its own.

A long tradition, however, supported by etymology, has identified philosophy with the love of wisdom and the pursuit of truth. "What is truth?" asks the cynical Pilate, but this question, posed directly and not rhetorically, marks the serious quest of the philosopher. For Plato, it was The Good, what makes all things intelligible and the mind intelligent;

for Augustine, in the Platonic tradition, it was God. If this tradition is followed, philosophy is recognized as the reflective contemplation and conceptual clarification of what is worshipped in religion. This indeed is Hegel's view, although it is commonly misunderstood and misinterpreted, especially by those who accuse (or applaud) him for elevating philosophy above religion, who convict him of intolerable hubris, or who commend him for enlightened atheism.

It would be true to say of Hegel's position that he regarded all philosophy as religionsphilosophie.

## I. RELATION BETWEEN PHILOSOPHY AND RELIGION

Kierkegaard accused Hegel of making the ridiculous claim that he could comprehend the infinite in his philosophy and of ranking human philosophy above religious faith. The appropriate Christian attitude he maintained, was to acknowledge humbly the limitations of the human intellect making the leap of faith into the dark to find the redeeming power of divine Providence and love. It is written: "For my thoughts are not your thoughts, neither are your ways my ways, saith the Lord. As the heavens are higher than the earth, so are my ways higher than your ways, and my thoughts than your thoughts." (Isaiah, 55, 8.9).

Such criticism of Hegel, however, reveals a failure to comprehend or to appreciate his position aright. He not only recognized but also insisted upon the limitations of the human intellect, as understanding; but he pointed out (specifically in his criticism of Kant) that to recognize such limitations the mind must already have passed beyond them and have risen to the stage of speculative reason. Kierkegaard's strictures remain within the confines of the understanding, and his objections are typical of its thinking. For the understanding separates and holds apart what are legitimate distinctions as if they were separable absolutes. So it separates the finite from the infinite, setting the latter in an unattainable beyond, leaving God as an abstract and empty name, the true meaning of which we cannot know. But this, Hegel argues, simply converts God to another finite, while it ignores the exhortation of Christianity to know God: For they shall all know me, from the least of them unto the greatest of them, saith the Lord," (Jer. 31, 34; Heb. 8, 11).

Speculative reason recognizes the spurious nature of the false infinite that is no more than a perpetual removal of the limit beyond the particular point reached, so that the result remains endlessly finite, and it recognizes the true infinite to be the whole, in principle and of necessity complete in itself and self-sustaining, which is the source of the existence and is immanent in the nature of all finites, including the human mind. This whole is the truth, the proper object of philosophy, but (as the true infinite) it is equally, and by the same token, the object of religion, apart from which philosophy would be impossible, because there would be no awareness of truth, and consequently no philosophy.

Accordingly, so far from exalting philosophy above religion, Hegel makes it conditional upon religion and sees all philosophy as the philosophy of religion. This thesis is nothing new. Something very like it has been brilliantly maintained by Emile Fackenheim, and abundant evidence for its truth has been mustered in Quentin Lauer's admirable exposition of Hegel's conception of God, in his book of that name.[1] My object in what follows is no more than to try to elaborate, from what Hegel actually writes, an argument that he does not explicitly state, in support of a position that he undoubtedly held.

## II. SPIRIT'S KNOWLEDGE OF ITSELF AS SPIRIT

For Hegel philosophy is absolute knowing, that is, Spirit aware of itself as spirit, and that again is religion: *"Die Religion nämlich ist Wissen des Geistes von sich als Geist . . ."* (Religion is, namely, Spirit's knowledge of itself as spirit).[2] Philosophy, he tells us in the preface to *Phenomenology*, is not simply the love of wisdom but the knowledge of the truth as scientific system—the true form in which the truth exists. And the truth is the whole.[3] Moreover, the whole is the Absolute, culminating as Absolute Spirit, which is God, and God, as Augustine had long since declared, is truth. So we find Hegel, throughout his philosophical writings, referring to his subject matter in theological terms. In *Phenomenology* he constantly speaks of the Absolute as *das Göttliche*, and refers, whether in criticism of other theories or in advocacy of his own, to *Göttlichkeit* as what the theories are about.[4]

The Logic, he says, is "God in his eternal essence, prior to the creation of Nature and finite spirit;"[5] and in the very first paragraph of the *Encyclopaedia* he tells us that the object of philosophy is common with that of religion: "they both have the truth as their object, and indeed, in the highest sense, that God is the truth and He alone."[6]

Nature is the Idea in the form of other being (or externality), what Schelling called "petrified" (and others "frozen") intelligence. *Der Gott aber bleibt nicht versteinert und verstorben, sondern die Steine schreien und heben sich zum Geiste auf.*[7] The previous portion of the same *Zusatz* is a sustained exposition of the relationship of Nature to God. The place of Nature within the whole, he says, is determined by the fact that the Idea posits difference and otherness within itself, "so that God remains equal to Himself [at home with himself] in his [self]determination; each of these moments is itself the whole idea, and must be posited as the divine totality."[8]

The *Geistesphilosophie* traces the dialectic of subjective and objective mind and unites them in Absolute Spirit, ending with a long quotation from Aristotle's *Metaphysics* (that he himself calls "theology") describing God as active reason.[9]

Contrary to common opinion, Hegel's system culminates in religion, the final moment of Absolute Spirit, philosophy, being nothing more (nor less) than the philosophy of religion. It simply identifies content with form, subject matter with method. Hegel invariably insists that the content of art, religion, and philosophy is one and the same (namely, God or Truth), the only difference being their appropriate forms; but in the case of philosophy, content and form coincide in the thinking study of thinking, which, in the last resort, is God as active reason. So philosophy, as the self-awareness of spirit, is the consummate religion, though not in the form of representation, as we find it in the New Testament, but in the form of the concept, as set out in the third part of the *Religionsphilosophie*. The final sections of the *Logic* and the *Philosophy of Spirit* state this formally, but the final part of the *Philosophy of Religion* sets it out in its concrete substantiality,[10] as do also (more concisely) the final chapters of the *Phenomenology*.

The dialectic, as we all know, repeatedly recapitulates earlier categories in new and developed forms. This occurs, not only throughout the *Logic*, but similarly (if less obviously) in the *Naturphilosophie*, as well as in the *Geistesphilosophie*. It is therefore not surprising that we find similar recapitulation in the *Religionsphilosophie*, the phases of which correspond primarily to the major logical phases of Being. Essence, and the Concept, and also to those of the *Geistesphilosophie*.

Religion is an activity of the spirit, so the categories of Nature feature within it only implicitly, in suppressed and symbolic appearances. But Nature plays an important and indispensable part, not only in the religion(s) of Nature, but also as represented in the second person of the Trinity in the Christian revelation.

Religion as it appears in history (its *Erscheinung*), is the self-awareness of spirit immanent in human experience (as *Erlebnis* and *Erfahrung*). In its emotional and representational aspects it belongs to subjective mind; in its ritual and institutional forms it is a feature of objective mind; and in its ultimate self-awareness, as revealed religion, it is absolute—the Christian Trinity. In each and all of these phases, it recapitulates the dialectic of the Concept, which is the formal structure at once of subjective experience, of objective reality, and of self-conscious reflection. And this is what is set out *in extenso* both in the system as a whole and in the *Religionsphilosophie*, its culminating phase.

Religion in human experience is the awareness of the relation of human nature to God, to the divine nature, that is, to the whole, or Truth. It is the revelation of the truth to the human mind. Spinoza maintained that revelation occurs in two forms, through the intellect and through the imagination.[11] And Hegel agrees in principle. Revelation through the intellect takes place (as it does for Spinoza) in philosophy in general, and in the *Logic* in particular (the Idea being God in his eternal essence, prior to Nature and finite spirit). Revelation through the imagination is (for Spinoza) prophecy and, likewise, for Hegel representative religion, the universal moments of which are set out in the first part of the *Philosophy of Religion*. The second part reviews and sets in their dialectical relationships the forms representational religion has taken in the course of its historical development; and their consummation, the revelation of the immanent truth, is expounded and explained in the third and final part. Thus revealed religion in its representational form is religion proper, and the philosophy of religion is its theology. Philosophy, if it ever calls religion in question, does so only in order to establish its content (God) as the ultimate truth.

## III. *RELIGIONSPHILOSOPHIE* AS CONSUMMATION

Hegel is quite explicit in the introduction to the first part of the *Religionsphilosophie* that philosophy and religion coincide. Philosophy, he says, only explicates itself so far as it makes religion explicit, and so far as it makes itself explicit, it explicates religion. "So religion and philosophy fall together in one; philosophy is in fact itself the worship of God (*Gottesdienst*), is religion . . . Philosophy is identical with religion."[12] But it differs from what one usually calls "religion" in the peculiar style and manner in which each is concerned with God.

Philosophy is the conciousness of truth as Idea, the truth in thought, the concrete concept of which is a unification of opposed categories. It busies itself with thought determinations (*Denkbestimmungen*), not simply with intuitions (*Anschauungen*) or representations (*Vorstellungen*). However, religion is the consciousness of the truth as the total object of speculative reason, as absolute and self-determinate, concretely universal. Its object is not merely the whole as thought, but, at the same time as actual and active in the world and individual consciousness—not just "God in His eternal essence," but the living God, the Creator of the universe. In short, the object of religion is Absolute Spirit uniting the Idea and Nature. But this could just as well be a description of the entire content of the *Encyclopaedia*, in short, of speculative philosophy.

However, the ordinary worshipper asks for "the meaning" of all this, meaning not the concept (e.g., of God), but its representation. Without some representation the ordinary worshipper finds the thought content hard to grasp. It then becomes the task of the *Philosophy of Religion* to explicate the meaning of the representation of God entertained.

In the introduction, Hegel says all this by way of explaining the place of the *Religionsphilosophie* in the system of philosophy as a whole; and what he says amounts to a virtual identification of it with the third division of the *Geistesphilosophie*, on Absolute Spirit. Yet, as is well known, this division in the *Encyclopaedia* includes art and philosophy as well as religion, so how are we to understand this explanation?

Here, as elsewhere, Hegel treats his subject matter as the divine substance and views art as the sensuous expression of *das Göttliche*, of the objects of religion; so aesthetics becomes, in effect, part of the philosophy of religion. Philosophy, he says in the concluding paragraphs (572–77), is the unity of art and religion in which the sensuous form of the first and the representative form of the second are united and raised to self-conscious thought: "*Dieses Wissen ist damit der denkend erkannte Begriff der Kunst und die Religion.*" (This knowledge is thereby the thinking, cognized Concept of art and religion *Enz.* 572).

He declares that the content of religion and philosophy are the same, he inveighs against the spurious philosophy of the understanding, known as "rationalism," which claims to discover contradictions in the exposition of the faith, that arise only in consequence of the inadequate representations through which it is expressed; and he upholds "the conceiving reason" and genuine philosophy, "the content of which is speculative and thus religious." Then after a long defense of philosophy against the accusation of pantheism (with which we have become familiar from earlier passages), he ends with an account of philosophy, much like that outlined above, but now in terms of the three major syllogisms, that were set out previously in the Logic, in which each of the main divisions of the *Encyclopaedia* mediates the transition from one to another. In effect, therefore, philosophy again turns out to be the philosophy of religion.

The whole, or concrete universal, that is in the final outcome Absolute Spirit, is a self-representative system, dialectically structured, like a fractal curve in complex dynamic systems theory. In whatever range it is examined, and on whatever scale, it discloses a similar configuration. In the Logic, the moments of the Concept are Being and Essence, but within the doctrine of Being, quality, quantity, and measure stand in corresponding relations one to another. So, in Essence, do identity, difference, and ground; and these reappear at the level of the Concept, as universal, particular, and individual. On the larger scale of the entire system, Idea, Nature, and Spirit are mutually related as are Being, Essence, and Concept, as identity, difference, and ground, or as universal, particular, and individual. It is thus only to be expected that the same structure should reappear in the culminating phase of the system, the philosophy of religion.

That philosophy begins with "its universal content, the as yet veiled concept of religion itself, that God is the absolute truth, the truth of everything, and that religion alone is true knowledge." Its first task is to develop scientifically (i.e., philosophically) the notion of God that is present in all religious experience, but is still, for the intellect, an abstract name. God is for *religionsphilosphie* what Being is for Logic, the immediate, initially unmediated, universal. At this level of the dialectic, however, God has to be defined as the absolutely true, the absolutely concrete universal, which comprehends everything, contains its particulars in itself, and gives them subsistence, differentiating and specifying itself by its own inherent activity and power. God is, in short, at once Absolute Idea and Absolute Spirit manifesting itself in Nature and human mentality.

The essence of religion is its self-reflective phase, the reflection of spirit into itself in its self-differentiation and self-specification. It now presents itself as the relation of God to his creation, the naturally generated human personality—the relation of human consciousness and of the human person to God. What Hegel calls "the necessity of religion" is proved by its establishment as the inevitable outcome of the dialectic of consciousness itself and of its object. The next phase of the philosophy of religion is thus a phenomenology of religious experience, recapitulating at the appropriate level the earlier categories of subjective spirit, and by implication those of the philosophy of nature of which spirit has proved to be the truth.

The outcome of this dialectic is the apprehension of an affirmative relation of finite to infinite spirit, the concept of 'religion' as this relation, and more, as the self-relation of Absolute Spirit to its other; and yet more, as the idea of spirit relating itself to itself, or the self-consciousness of Absolute Spirit. Absolute Spirit sets itself as its own object, thus limiting itself and implicating finite consciousness (in which subject and object are also thus distinguished).[13] It posits itself as finite consciousness, mediating itself through it in order to become knowledge of itself. Thus religion is the knowledge of the divine spirit, of itself through the mediation of finite spirit. The relation of the divine and the human, which is the essence of religion is, in this way, explicated so as at once to define it speculatively and to prepare the ground for the account of the Incarnation to be given in the final part of the *Religionsphilosophie*.

In this context Hegel explicitly refers to "the activity and movement of the idea of Absolute Spirit in itself," whereby it makes itself object and self-subsistent as opposed to the concept, in the form of the natural world. While this self-diremption is one moment, the other is the return of this object, through its own process to its source. Spirit is self-appearing to itself, and the appearance is Nature, but not merely as phenomenon; it is also the process to its own appearance to itself in human experience. Within the religious consciousness this is represented as the heavens declaring the glory of God, and God as the Lord of the world.

What we have been given here is then virtually a retracing of the dialectic of the *Phenomenology* and the *Encyclopaedia*, but in the context of the final phase in each case. Process and end overlap, the latter sublating and encompassing the former. The philosophy of religion displays itself as the whole of philosophy *aufgehoben*.

The third moment of the Concept, as such, is individuality; so the concept of religion likewise has a third phase in which its subjectivity is objectified. In the introduction Hegel wrote: "*der Geist, der nicht erscheint, ist nicht*" (there is no spirit that does not appear). Objectification of the subjective is a theme that recurs consistently and systematically throughout Hegel's philosophy; so here again subjective religion, like subjective mind, expresses itself in objective configurations, as cult, in the forms of creed, ceremonial, and church. This is the unity of God (as universal) and humanity (as particular) in the religious community inspired by the holy spirit (individual). The cult is the impregnation of social life and custom with religious conviction and practice, and is, in fact, the latent motif of the whole philosophy of objective spirit, as becomes evident in this section of the philosophy of religion. Not surprisingly, then, the first part of the *Religionsphilosophie* ends with a lengthy discussion (echoing that in no. 552 of the *Encyclopaedia*) of the relation between church and state.

Accordingly, we have here a recapitulation, not simply of the appropriate logical categories, but also of those of Objective Mind, within the framework of the consummatory phase of Spirit, as such, in which all prior moments have been sublated, that is, preserved while having been superseded and transformed.

## IV. RELIGION AS ESSENCE

We are told in *Enzyclopädie* (no. 114) that the Doctrine of Essence is the most difficult part of the Logic, because, Hegel says, it (especially) contains all the categories of metaphysics and science (meaning by "metaphysics" the old-style dogmatic metaphysics). It is indeed the most difficult, not only for the reason given, but also for reasons more profound and intrinsic to the dialectic. Essence, as we are also told in this context, repeats the categories of Being, but now as relative, as reflected into themselves. Its categories become twofold, each consisting of a pair of complementary and interdependent aspects, so that we have to grasp the significance of their mutual relation as well as their relation to prior and posterior categories that are likewise double.

Further, the categories of Essence are those of the understanding (i.e., of science and metaphysics), which is that stage of thinking that characteristically abstracts, analyzing its objects and holding the distinguished elements apart, oblivious of their mutual interdependent relationship. Accordingly, each category can be interpreted both concretely, as a necessary and legitimate moment in the dialectic of the

Concept, and abstractly, as applied by the understanding. Logic, therefore, at once expounds them as they are generated by their inherent dialectic and criticizes them as abstractly understood. Criticizing them from the viewpoint of the Concept, it anticipates by implication what is to follow, while it also reflects what has gone before. It is by reason of such complexity that Essence becomes the most difficult part of the Logic.

Much the same is true of the second part of the *Religionsphilosophie* and for the same reasons. It corresponds to the Doctrine of Essence in the *Logic*. It deals with the self-specification of religion, its different historical manifestations, its particular determinate forms. It relates to the first part, therefore, as particular to universal, as it should, so far as religion, qua Absolute Spirit, has sublated the categories of the Concept. But while the concept of religion is immanent in each and every actual, historical religion, none expresses it adequately; and they advance dialectically, progressively approaching in degree the consummate religion that is to be expounded in part 3. It is, so to speak, the essence of which they are the adumbrating appearances (as the Concept is in principle the essence that appears in reflection upon Being). For this reason, however, they are also false appearances (*schein*), and, while their legitimacy as phases of religious development is to be established, they are concurrently criticized for their inadequacy. They are each, at the same time, the actual existence of religion (*dasein*), religion *an sich*, but not yet *für sich*—not yet *Geist für den Geist*. Accordingly, part 2 is the most difficult, the most complicated, and by far the longest part of the *Religionsphilosophie*.

Further, determinate religion relates to the concept of 'religion' as Nature relates to the Idea: it is its externalization. And the position of Nature is ambivalent. It is at one and the same time a return to the immediacy of Being, yet is self-external and reflected into itself as other, revealing its essence in otherbeing, and itself as the outer appearance of an inner energizing principle that progressively emerges (in organism) as life and mind.

Likewise, just as the Idea immanent in Nature impels natural processes back to its own self-realization in Spirit, so religion begins with the immediate and self-external, but develops the idea (*vorstellung*, representation) of its object in the direction of the spiritual. Religion has the absolute Idea (God) as its intentional object, and, in the first instance, the divine is represented as the immediate object of perception—Nature (which is the Idea in the form of otherbeing). It is Nature, not as mere phenomenon, or natural feature of the environment, but as imbued with a sacred presence. This representation, however, proves inadequate to the Truth which religion takes its object to be, and it develops next to a still natural, anthropomorphic projection of the Idea, as embodied Spirit, as the Lord, or as diverse super-human representations, of beauty, virtue, and power, in gods like those of the Greeks.

Moreover, as Nature, in its self-externality, fails to conform to the ideal dialectical configuration, displaying what Hegel calls "*ohnmacht*," so determinate religion divides into tetrads, as much as into triads, and Hegel seemed uncertain of the precise delineation of its internal phases, arranging them differently in the successive expositions that he presented in different lecture courses. At the same time, it has to be borne in mind that Hegel explicitly and emphatically denies (in *Wissenschaft der Logik*) that the dialectic is a rigid triadic mold into which everything must be forced in defiance of the facts. What can be related triadically can also be analyzed into diads or tetrads, depending on what one seeks to emphasize. Again, in the intervals between the successive lecture courses, Hegel was learning more about the religions he was discussing, benefiting by recent historical and archeological discoveries, and new studies in comparative religion, so that he quite naturally changed his assessment of some of the religions concerned, and, in consequence, his views about their dialectical relationships. Nevertheless, the logical structure of the exposition of this part of the *Religionsphilosophie* remains intact in all the differing versions, despite internal rearrangements and displacements of particular topics.

It is not my aim in this chapter to discuss the detail of Hegel's treatment of the various determinate forms of religion. For my purpose it is sufficient to point out that in explaining their historical relationships, and those of their intellectual and symbolic content and its interpretation, Hegel is, in effect, engaged upon the philosophy of history in one of its special aspects. At the same time, the philosophy of history, as Hegel presents it in its own right, also turns out to be philosophy of religion. History is the record of human action, which in essence and principle is responsible rational conduct; so historical progression is dialectical, and its aim or "end" is freedom. But freedom, in the fullest sense, is "the service of God"—the full realization by spirit of its ultimate destiny, the reconciliation and atonement of the human spirit with absolute Spirit. So the philosophy of religion—and particularly of the specific religions which occur, and as they appear in history—is continuous with, and is a necessary phase of, the philosophy of history generally.

It is significant that the dialectic of Objective Spirit, having proceeded through the phases of *Sittlichkeit* to the organization of the State, moves to the philosophy of history, while both the consideration of the State and that of the concept of religion end with a discussion of the relation between civil authority and religion. The *Rechtsphilosophie* thus becomes, through the medium of the philosophy of history, a propaedeutic to the *Religionsphilosophie*.

## V. ABSOLUTE RELIGION

Why did Hegel not treat of Christianity under the heading of determinate religion? It is, surely, historical like all the rest; it is organized and has an institutional structure; it has its cult, with ritulalistic practices, its ceremonies and celebrations. But these facets of religion have already been dealt with in the first part, as moments in the concept of religion; and although they are exemplified in each determinate religion, Hegel's object in part 2 is not just to illustrate this fact, but to demonstrate the inner dialectic by which each determinate form, through its inadequacy to its concept, demands supplementation by its opposite, so that these particular exemplifications of religion develop to the point at which, on the one hand, the Eastern religions have driven to its extreme the abstract idea of absolute truth, and, on the other, the Western religions have pressed to its denouement the deification of the finite in the person of the Roman emperor. Here all diversity is blurred in the Pantheon; in the exaltation to divinity of finite purpose as such, the tryanny of imperial caprice nullifies all finite aspirations to personal freedom; all finite desires are suppressed (e.g., in Stoicism); and that infinite grief, the dark night of the soul, is reached, through which finite spirit must go in order to attain to final atonement with the infinite. At this point in history "the time has been fulfilled" and absolute truth is revealed in the advent of Christ. It is the exposition of this final truth that is to be set out in the third and last part of the *Religionsphilosophie*.

Christianity is the religion in which the concept of 'religion' has become object. It is that religion in which the relation of humanity to

God, what religion is by definition, has become its own object, namely, in the Incarnation. It is thus the fulfilment of the concept, not merely subjectively, but in objective reality, *coram populo*, existing in actuality for all to see. It is, therefore, in fact, treated as a determinate religion, but as that determination which is at the same time the actualized universal, at home with itself in its other. Hence it is the Truth, absolute and revealed.

The object of religion is Truth, the absolute Idea, God, in His eternal essence; but the Idea is the identity of subject and object, which is here represented in the identity of Christ, as human and finite, with God as infinite and divine. It is the identity of finite spirit, incarnate in man, with infinite spirit, God, incarnate in Christ. Each is self-conscious, each is conscious of the other as object, and each is conscious of the other as identical with self. This absolute unity in difference of God and Man Hegel identifies as eternal Love. The identity is now set out as mediated by its essential moments of universality, particularity, and individuality, as it was (qua Concept) in the *Logic* and (qua Absolute) in the *Encyclopaedia* as a whole. And its exposition in the *Philosophy of Religion* runs parallel with both of those expositions at once.

> That is ever the way of all science: first the concept, then the determination of the concept, the reality, objectivity, and finally this, that the first concept is object to itself, is for itself, becomes objective to itself, relates itself to itself. That is the way of philosophy. First the concept of the conceiving science; this concept we have. The last, however, is that the science itself grasps its concept, this concept is for itself. (*Philosophie der Religion*, 3:1)

In short, all philosophy is what the philosophy of religion is, and especially is re-enacted in the final part, the theory of the absolute, the fulfilled, the revealed religion. It is here that "the science itself grasps its concept," and the concept, which is, in its fulfilment, the Truth (God in his eternal essence), is for itself.

The content of part 3 makes this abundantly clear. God, the Truth, the Absolute Idea, alienates himself from himself, making himself, as other, his object; that is, he creates the natural world, and within it humanity. So Nature returns through its own inner dialectic, to spirit, but in the first instance, finite spirit. Thus God reveals himself first in Nature:

> The heavens declare the glory of God; and the firmament sheweth his handiwork. (Ps. 19)
>
> The earth is the Lord's and the fulness thereof; the world and all that dwell therein. (Ps. 24)

But in the fullness of time, when the human spirit has developed to the appropriate point in its history, God reveals himself in his true form as Spirit, in the person of Christ, uniting in one, both finite and infinite Spirit, which then continues to dwell in the holy community, as objective religion—in the church, where the concept of religion has become its own object.

All this has been presented in the extended system of philosophy: the Idea in the Logic, its self-diremption and appearance in the form of otherbeing in the philosophy of nature, and its becoming aware of itself and objectifying its self-awareness in history in the philosophy of mind. Culminating in absolute Spirit, this self-awareness and self-objectification takes the forms of art and religion, the philosophy of which is finally the philosophy of religion, the whole of philosophy.

This "*Gang in aller wissenschaft*" presents itself in the third part of the *Religionsphilosophie* in three phases: the Realm of the Father (Idea), the Realm of the Son (Nature), and the Realm of the Spirit, disclosing the philosophy of religion as the whole of philosophy become aware of itself as object, the object being that of religion—Truth, in the sense that God, and God alone, is the truth. And this Truth is the identity of identity and nonidentity: the atonement of God and natural man in Christ (who is the spiritual head of which the church is the body).

The self-diremption of the universal—its self-specification into the diverse particular embodiments of its own self-development as its other, and its final identification of itself with this other—is the persistent and repetitive structure of the dialectic of spirit throughout its course. And this is what is shown to be the essential nature of the triune God of the absolute, the revealed, religion. The Holy Trinity is thus the implicit content of, and therefore what is actually foreshadowed by, every triad in the dialectic. For Hegel, religion (in particular the Christian religion) is the presupposed foundation and intrinsic essence of all philosophy; and the entire *Encyclopaedia of Philosophical Sciences*, culminating in the *Religionsphilosophie* is the demonstration *in extenso* of this inner inspiration.

So, for Hegel, philosophy does not take precedence over religion, but is dependent upon it, while in the philosophy of religion both are identified. The philosophy of religion is, qua Concept, what religion itself is, qua representation; and philosophy as a whole, and in its detail, is a presentation, as knowledge, of the Holy Trinity worshipped in the Christian religion. It is the knowledge of God, of which Isaiah sang: "The earth shall be full of the knowledge of the Lord as the waters cover the sea."[14]

## NOTES

1. Cf. Emile Fackenheim, *The Religious Dimension of Hegel's Philosophy* (Bloomington: Indiana University Press, 1967); Quentin Lauer, *Hegel's Concept of God* (Albany: State University of New York Press, 1982).

2. *Vorlesungen über der Philosophie der Religion*, 3, Jaeschke, v. 5, p. 104.

3. *Phänomenologie*, preface.

4. Ibid.

5. *Science of Logic*, introduction.

6. *Enzyclopädie der Philosophischen Wissenschaften*, no. 1.

7. *Enzyclopädie, Zweiter Teil*, no. 247, *Zusatz*.

8. Ibid.

9. Cf. *Enzyclopädie*, no. 552, where Hegel identifies the concrete content of faith as spirit, "the absolute determination of which is active reason."

10. In the passage quoted above from the *Religionsphilosophie*, Hegel explains that religion is spirit's knowledge of itself as spirit but that merely subjective knowing is limited and so insubstantial. Truly infinite self-knowledge is concrete, as realized in Absolute Spirit.

11. Cf. *Tractatus Theologico-Politicus*, ch. 1.

12. *Religionsphilosophie*, 1, introd., A, 2, 1.

13. Here there is a distinct echo of Fichte.

14. Isaiah, 11:9.

Carl G. Vaught

# Theft and Conversion: Two Augustinian Confessions

The recovery of philosophy in America is not the same as the recovery of American philosophy. The first of these phrases challenges us to focus our attention on fundamental philosophical questions, while the second asks us to acknowledge our debt to the classical American philosophers. In this chapter about theft and conversion in Augustine's *Confessions*,[1] I shall be concerned primarily with the first rather than the second of these tasks; but in turning to it, I shall also attempt to remain true to what John Smith has described as the spirit of American philosophy.[2] This spirit requires us to develop a rich account of human experience,[3] forces us to face philosophical problems that cannot be reduced to narrow issues of logic and language,[4] and presupposes that our reflections ought to make a difference, not only in theory, but also in practice.[5]

If it is true that Smith never loses sight of human experience as the touchstone of philosophical reflection,[6] it is equally clear that his own attempts to recover philosophy in America reach their richest expression in the intersection between religion and philosophy in his thinking.[7] Hegel may have been mistaken when he claimed that religion is the region where all the enigmas of the world are resolved;[8] and indeed, having cited this surprising remark of the greatest modern philosopher,

Smith himself insists that religion has become an enigma in the contemporary world.[9] Yet this teacher, philosopher, theologian, and historian of philosophy also knows that religion is the place where the deepest and the most perplexing philosophical questions arise.[10] My reason for turning to the themes of theft and conversion is to honor Smith by focusing on enigmatic questions that make a difference in human experience, but I also do so with the conviction that these enigmas raise questions about the relation between God and the soul that demand our deepest reflections. Thus, I am happy to join my teacher in exploring problems at the place where religion and philosophy converge, not because they are fashionable, but because they are fundamental.

Augustine's *Confessions* is the locus classicus for the perplexing problems before us;[11] but as anyone who struggles with the text will soon discover, the *Confessions* itself is a difficult book. For most students, there are too many prayers, too much self-flagellation, and too much philosophy. What other book begins by praising the greatness of God and ends with an account of the nature of memory, the problem of time, and the hermeneutics of creation? Where else can we find an autobiography about the sins of infancy and about an adolescent act of mischief that becomes an obsession? Who besides Augustine pictures sexuality as a boiling caldron that seethes and bubbles all around him? In book 7, he describes a mystical experience in which he sees the unity of God with a trembling glance. In book 8, he depicts his conversion to Christianity when he puts on a new garment that he calls "Jesus, the Christ." And in book 9, he recounts a mystical experience with his mother, dominated by conversation and auditory metaphors rather than visual images and as a consequence, unparalleled in the mystical tradition. The *Confessions* expresses a range of feelings that transcends language, but it also reflects a powerful capacity for discursive discourse. Unlike most philosophers, Augustine can feel deeply and speak profoundly in the same sentence. Indeed, his book poses difficulties for interpretation because it unites what most professional philosophers try to separate.

How shall we respond to a book as rich and complex as this? What approach should we take? What questions should we ask? What answers should we expect? What purpose should undergird our enterprise? Without trying to answer these questions prematurely, at least this much should be clear from the outset: we cannot plunge into the *Confessions* without calling ourselves into question. Augustine speaks as a psychologist, a rhetorician, a philosopher, and a theologian; but he speaks most fundamentally from the heart. If we are unwilling to probe the depths of our souls, we will never understand Augustine; for he makes insistent demands upon his readers that we trace out the path he has traveled in our own spiritual and intellectual development.

This is nowhere more evident than in Augustine's account of the two most important events in his spiritual development. The first is the pear-stealing episode in which he falls away from God (2: 9–18); the second is his conversion to Christianity in which he finally comes back home to the house of his father (8: 28–30). The theft takes place in an orchard near his home in Tagaste; the conversion occurs in a garden in Milan; and taken together, these two episodes stand side by side as mirror images, the second of which overcomes the defects of the first. Yet the pear-stealing episode not only points beyond itself to the garden in Milan, but also raises fundamental questions about the aesthetic, ethical, political, and religious aspects of human experience. These lenses filter and give us access to Augustine's existential situation, but they also bring us face to face with one of the most puzzling philosophical problems we will ever encounter. Our task in the first section of this chapter is to confront this situation and to struggle with the problems it raises.

## THE PEAR-STEALING EPISODE

Augustine generates the context for the pear-stealing episode by describing his adolescence: first, he says he needs someone to gather him up from the fragments into which he has fallen; then he claims he wants to love and to have someone to love him; and finally, he exclaims, "I was tossed to and fro, wasted and poured out, and I boiled over in my fornications" (2: 2). At the age of sixteen, while his father struggles to raise the money so he can continue his education, Augustine spends a holiday from school, walking "the streets of Babylon" with his Babylonian friends (2: 8). Late one night, after their games are over, they participate in a theft that seems innocent on the surface, but that epitomizes their fragmented condition (2: 9).

The details of the story are deceptively simple. Augustine and his friends steal pears from a neighbor's tree. They slip under the fence, shake and rob the tree, and slip away again with an enormous load of pears, barely tasting them before dumping them out to the swine (2: 9). What could be more innocent than this? Almost everybody does it.

Adolescent acts of mischief happen as a matter of course; it is not surprising that Augustine participates in one; and most of us would admit that we have engaged in similar acts ourselves. Yet this is precisely the point. The pear-stealing episode is not simply Augustine's story, but also our own. What *is* surprising is not that the reader stands on common ground with Augustine, but that in sharing it with him and in understanding the significance of our actions, we enter a forbidden place that brings us face to face with one of the deepest mysteries of the human predicament.

The most obvious thing to notice about the pear-stealing episode is its aesthetic significance. Though the pears he steals are not as good as the ones in his own vineyard, and though nothing about their color or flavor draws him to them (2: 9), Augustine admits that they are pleasing and attractive. This gives the stolen fruit a positive place in the order of creation, allowing what beauty it has to reflect the beauty of God. Nevertheless, the crucial point is Augustine's insistence that he cannot explain the pear-stealing episode from an aesthetic point of view. He pilfers something he has already in sufficient measure, and of much better quality, and says that the motive for his act is not a desire to savor what he steals. Rather, he steals the pears simply to enjoy the theft itself.

Augustine's description of the episode makes it sound like a crime rather than an aesthetic phenomenon; and for the saint who is once a Manichaean, it is. Manichaeans believe that trees spring from the semen of demons and are a rich source of particles that have escaped from the Kingdom of Light. A Manichaean would never pluck their fruit; and even if he did so accidentally, he would ask one of the Manichaean elect to ingest it to release the light. From a Manichaean perspective, giving the fruit to an animal would increase the disgrace of the crime, embedding the goodness of the particles in it in creatures lower in the chain of being than trees. When he reminds us that the theft occurs at night as the powers of darkness reign, the episode becomes even more reprehensible for a man who has been a Manichaean for nine years. It is understandable that some commentators have traced Augustine's horror of the event to the years he spends absorbing Manichaean cosmology.[12]

However persuasive this interpretation may be, Augustine places his initial description of the episode within an ethical framework rather than within a cosmological context. From the outset, he insists that a theft is not only a violation of the positive law the Ten Commandments codify, but also an encroachment on the deeper natural law God has written on our hearts. The attitude of a professional thief confirms this: he will not tolerate the theft of his possessions by another, and even a rich thief will not permit a poor one to steal from him. Augustine admits that he wants to steal from his neighbor's tree because of his contempt for appropriate behavior and that stealing the pears pleases him and his friends because it is forbidden (2: 9). Thus, he characterizes the theft as a violation both of natural and of positive laws and as an act of pleasure in stealing forbidden fruit, generating the expectation that he might try to explain it in ethical terms that have aesthetic implications.

Yet having begun to move in an ethical direction, Augustine quickly undermines this kind of explanation. First, he suggests that there is no moral reason for stealing the forbidden fruit: he is neither poor nor hungry, nor is this a case of stealing bread for starving children. The theft he commits is a gratuitous act that does not point beyond itself but has an inherently negative character that he loves for its own sake. As he formulates the point, there is "no inducement to evil but the evil itself" (2: 9). Second, Augustine's evaluation of the act mentions shame rather than guilt, insisting that he is "seeking nothing from the shameful deed but shame itself" (2:16). If guilt is a moral category, and if it is sometimes associated with the aesthetic delight we take in doing what is forbidden, shame drives deeper, exposing us for what we are rather than for what we do. Finally, Augustine suggests that if the act were primarily ethical, it would involve a preference for a lower to a higher good. In moral contexts, we explain a crime by pointing to a desire for something good that overrides our commitment to something better (2: 11); but in the pear-stealing episode, there is no logical space for excuses. In stealing the pears with his adolescent companions, and in finding his sole gratification in the act itself, Augustine falls into a bottomless pit that lies beneath unethical behavior.

The political dimension of the theft surfaces in Augustine's reference to the companions with whom he commits it. As he says himself, "The bond of human friendship has a sweetness of its own, binding many souls together" within a larger community (2: 10). Indeed, friendship arises from an orientation toward common objects of affection, making it understandable that Augustine says seven times that he would have never stolen the pears alone. Perhaps the explanation for the pear-stealing episode is communal and hence political in the traditional

Aristotelian sense. Might he not simply blame his behavior on others, suggesting that when they say, "Let's go, let's do it," he cannot resist (2: 17)? Evocative language is often the penultimate cause of political action, sweeping our isolated individuality up into collective action that reflects the will of a larger community.

Having claimed that he would not have stolen the pears without his friends, Augustine seems to embrace this political explanation of his action. He underscores the point by insisting that he still recalls how he felt about this then: "I could not have done it alone" (2: 16). This allows him to conclude that he loves the act, not only for itself, but also because of the companionship of the accomplices with whom he commits it. Yet at the last moment, he rejects this conclusion with these puzzling remarks:

> I did not, therefore, love the theft alone—yet indeed, it was only the theft that I loved, for the companionship was nothing. What is this paradox? . . . Had I at that time loved the pears that I stole and wished to enjoy them, I might have done so alone. . . . *But since the pleasure I got was not from the pears. it was in the crime itself, which a group of us joined in sin to do* [my emphasis] (2:16).

It is not surprising that Augustine finds a paradox here. He says that both the act and the companionship are nothing. But how can the nothingness of a community of friends enhance a negative act? Presumably, this community is both positive and negative at once. Stealing the pears would not be possible apart from the community. Yet every member of the group is to blame. The theft Augustine commits presupposes the bond of friendship, but every participant is responsible for shattering it.

Augustine's reference to his fellow sinners points beyond a political context to a distinctively religious dimension we must explore if we are to come to grips with the deepest dimension of the pear-stealing episode. One indication of this is that we can scarcely read the story without being reminded of the theological framework it presupposes and of the abyss into which Augustine falls in re-enacting a familiar biblical drama. Yet since he refers to his pleasure in stealing the pears, calls it a crime, and claims that companionship enhances his enjoyment of it, we must not abandon the aesthetic, ethical, and political explanations of his behavior for a religious interpretation that fails to take them into account. What we need is a way of understanding the episode that is sufficiently rich to incorporate these other dimensions, driving the aesthetic, ethical, and political facets of the act to a higher explanatory level.

As a preliminary step, let us isolate the most obvious religious implications of Augustine's narrative. First, the pear-stealing episode reminds us of an original garden where Adam and Eve face an absolute prohibition. God gives them all the fruit they need, but he demands that they not eat fruit from a tree he has reserved for himself. When they refuse to obey, they reach beyond their natural limits to encroach on the divine mystery.[13] Second, Augustine and his friends transform an orchard of innocence into a garden of willfulness. In the process, they not only place themselves beside Adam and Eve in the Garden of Eden, but also pitch the pears they steal to the hogs (2: 9). In doing so, they stand beside the Prodigal Son in the hog trough, eating the husks of their adolescent enthusiasm with the swine. Finally, Augustine's most penetrating account of the sin the pear-stealing episode epitomizes characterizes it as a negative act he performs gratuitously. As he says over and over: "I stole the pears, not for their sake, and not for my sake, but for the act's sake." The end of the act is not beyond it, but the act itself. Stealing the pears does not express a desire for determinate objects that bring satisfaction. Rather, it is an act of the will that turns back upon itself, pointing toward the frozen abyss of the bottomless pit.[14]

It can scarcely be denied that Augustine's obsession with this adolescent episode seems excessive. Both the act and his description of it display a lack of moderation. A Neoplatonic response to the problem would reject Augustine's concept of sin and would recommend moderation and education to cure the psyche. Insofar as the problem is a question of the body, it demands moderation; insofar as it is a problem of the soul, it requires education. The journey from the cave to the sunlight expresses the Platonic solution to the problem of the disoriented psyche, directing our attention away from adolescent acts of mischief toward the intelligible conditions that bring stability and liberation to the soul.[15]

Nevertheless, Augustine rejects this solution to the problem of the fragmented soul because he believes that neither insight nor wisdom can resolve it. When he plucks forbidden fruit, he falls into an abyss that separates him from God, moves from will to willfulness along the vertical axis of his experience, and is unable to reverse this fateful transition through moderation or education. Taming the body will not transform the will that motivates his actions (8: 20–21); and though he understands the value of education, embracing it without reservation simply accentuates the pride with which he pursues his professional ambitions (1: 31).

When Augustine and his companions steal the pears, they seek to become infinite. If Augustine and his friends had stolen the pears to eat them, it would have been a finite act. If they had stolen them to respond to a craving several bites would satisfy, it would have been a bounded episode. Stealing pears in either case would embed the act in a determinate context that would make it intelligible and would permit Augustine and his friends to make excuses for their behavior. However, when they steal the fruit simply to be stealing it, their theft becomes an infinite act that separates them from God.

Augustine appeals to pride as a perverse imitation of God to make the pear-stealing episode intelligible (2: 14). This explanation allows him to bring aesthetic, ethical, and political considerations to bear upon what would otherwise remain an exclusively theological account.

> Did I wish, if only by a gesture, to rebel against thy law, even though I had no power to do so actually—so that, even as a captive, I might produce a sort of counterfeit liberty, by doing with impunity deeds that were forbidden, in a deluded sense of omnipotence?
>
> Could I find pleasure only in what was unlawful, and only because it was unlawful? (2:14)

The crucial words in this quotation bring aesthetic, ethical, political, and religious considerations together. By moving from pleasure, through law, captivity, and counterfeit liberty, to deeds that are forbidden and that generate a deluded sense of omnipotence, Augustine establishes a comprehensive framework within which to approach the act that continues to perplex him.

What more can be said about the childish prank that Oliver Wendell Holmes ridicules and refuses to adjudicate,[16] but with which Augustine continues to struggle at the concluding stage of his argument? The sinner, the saint, and the confessor gives the answer by claiming that since "the theft itself was *nothing*, I was all the more wretched in that I loved it so" (2: 16). Combining this quotation with the earlier claim that the companionship of his accomplices is also *nothing* leads to the heart of Augustine's problem. The saint, looking back upon his sin, trembles as he faces the abyss of the two *nihils* with which his recollection of the pear-stealing episode confronts him.

Aesthetic, ethical, political, and religious considerations converge in Augustine's explanation of the act; and he brings these dimensions together when he says, "But since the pleasure I got was not from the pears, it was in the crime itself, enhanced by the companionship of my fellow sinners" (2:16). Pleasure, crime, companionship, and sin stand together in Augustine's pantheon of explanatory principles. He also mobilizes these principles when he claims, "We laughed because our hearts were tickled at the thought of deceiving the owners, who had no idea of what we were doing and would have strenuously objected" (2: 17). The laughter that delights them is aesthetic, deception is ethical, ownership is political, and since the ultimate owner of the vineyard is God, deceiving the owners has inescapable religious implications. Nevertheless, the problem of nonbeing, both in the act he commits and in the companionship he shares, remains at the center of his perplexity, inviting us to make a final effort to plumb the depths of his predicament. Indeed, Augustine suggests that the two *nihils* and the relation between them stand at the center of his problem by asking at this juncture, "Who is it that can explain it to me but God, who illumines my heart and searches out the dark corners thereof?" (2: 16). Only the one who creates the world *ex nihilo* can illuminate the darkness that results from Augustine's fateful attempt to embrace the absolute nothingness from which he emerges.

The theft of the pears from his neighbor's tree allows Augustine to experience absolute nonbeing, for his account of the episode is an experiential indication of his awareness of radical absence in human experience. The Neoplatonic return of the soul to its origins transcends the relative nonbeing of finitude, but it does not erase the sin that separates it from God. The restlessness of the psyche increases the likelihood that it will try to become infinite and make the transition from will to willfulness. Bound by its limitations, it cannot succeed; but in attempting to do so, it becomes a negative reflection of its creator by seeking to return to the nothingness from which it is created.

Sin is a stain that defaces the psyche more deeply than aesthetic, moral, or political distortions; for in stealing the pears, Augustine tries to infinitize himself. The self-transcendent structure of the psyche makes it possible for him to reach for God; but in the pear-stealing episode, he attempts to become infinite in his own right. In this case, he tilts so radically in the direction of infinitude that he tries to become divine, seeking to become infinite without qualification. In the process, he turns away from God and plunges toward the abyss of absolute nonbeing.

There are three forms in which absolute nonbeing appears as a crucial element in the *Confessions*. First, when Augustine commits himself to the doctrine of creation *ex nihilo*, the nothingness from which he comes is absolute in the sense that it does not stand over against God either as an independent or as a derivative principle. If it were the first, God would not be infinite because nonbeing would impose limits upon him; and if it were the second, the nonbeing in question would be relative rather than absolute. This first kind of nothingness is *metaphysical* and is the absolute abyss from which God brings creatures into existence by a spontaneous act of speaking. Second, when Augustine speaks of evil as a privation of goodness, the evil in question is the limit of a continuum of corruption, which can be approached, but never reached. This second kind of nothingness is both *ontological* and *epistemic*, for it asks us to posit a continuum and to approach a limit that can never be reached from a merely reflective point of view. The ontological continuum exists independently of consciousness, but our attempt to reach its limit is impossible from an epistemic perspective. Finally, when Augustine describes the pear-stealing episode as a negative act he performs for its own sake, the nothingness to which he points is a form of absolute nonbeing he can embrace only by engaging in a performative act. The sin in the face of which he shudders is an act that breaks beyond the ontological continuum of corruption, the limit of which can be approximated but never reached by reflection alone. This third kind of nonbeing is *volitional*, and Augustine seeks it by leaping into an abyss that points to the possibility of a permanent separation from God (2: 9).

The nothingness of creation, the nothingness of privation, and the nothingness of sin are not the same. The first is a metaphysical condition that makes creation *ex nihilo* possible. The second is an ontological and epistemic condition that makes it possible for us to presuppose and to understand a continuum of beings, arranged in a descending order of corruption. The third is a volitional condition Augustine embraces when he leaps beyond the limits of corruption and attempts to return to the nothingness from which he comes. The locus of nonbeing in this third case is an act and not a content, and it is to be distinguished from the nothingness of creation *ex nihilo* by the fact that the direction of the performative act that typifies it is a radical inversion of the act of creation that brings the world into existence. In this case, as in so many others, the volitional orientation of the person rather than ontological considerations about its nature is the fundamental issue. The being of God is prior to the metaphysical sense of nothingness; the knowledge of God is prior to the ontological and epistemic sense of nothingness; and the will of God is presupposed by the volitional sense of nothingness Augustine embraces in the orchard with his adolescent companions.

Augustine claims that both the act he commits and the companionship he shares are nothing. Since this assertion presupposes absolute as opposed to relative nonbeing, and since the nonbeing in question is volitional rather than metaphysical, ontological, or epistemic, we can begin to understand the struggle Augustine undergoes in trying to articulate the significance of the pear-stealing episode. Radical nonbeing cannot be characterized discursively or placed within a systematic framework as a categorial principle. This suggests that no dialectical relation between being and nonbeing makes the act in the orchard intelligible and that we cannot understand it as a structural element in a philosophical system. When we turn our attention from Augustine to his relation with his friends, we face a similar difficulty: on the one hand, both the episode and the companionship are nothing; on the other, there is something about adolescent friendship that makes stealing possible. Yet how can we reconcile these claims without finding a third term that binds them together and without relativizing the absolute nonbeing both of the act and of the companionship by giving them a place within a larger unity?

Augustine makes a final effort to evade this problem by suggesting that stealing the pears is an occasion for laughter that reaches into the hearts of himself and his companions, that it allows them to deceive the owners who do not know what they are doing and would resent their actions if they did, and that it permits him to derive pleasure from the fact that he does not engage in the act alone (2: 17). Yet when he asks why companionship is essential, and when he suggests that it might be important only because no one laughs when he is alone, he replies that though this is usually so, it is not always the case. Indeed, individuals are sometimes overcome with laughter when they are alone, if something very funny affects their senses or strikes their mind (2: 17). Apparently, laughter and the enjoyment it seeks point to the blessedness of paradise rather than to the misery of perdition; and Augustine insists that he never would have moved from one to the other without falling into the abyss he shares with his friends.

Augustine drives to the end of his analysis of the pear-stealing episode by claiming that the act expresses his love for two things that are insubstantial: first, he loves the episode itself; then he loves the companionship he shares in participating in it. The first is a negative act rather than a substance; the second degenerates from a community of friends into a community of thieves. In both cases, absolute nonbeing in its volitional guise surfaces as an inescapable dimension of the human situation. In the first instance, Augustine falls away from his origins as an individual; in the second, he falls away from them as a participant in a negative community. This suggests that the chasm into which he falls is not only volitional and performative, but also individual and communal. Our final task in considering the pear-stealing episode is to confront this mystery.

The community in which Augustine participates is not negative from the outset. Friendship defines the nature of an emerging individual, where, for an adolescent, to be is to stand alongside others in a positive community. Augustine is being true to his friends when he says that he would not have stolen the pears without them. He is correct in considering the possibility that they are to blame for his behavior, and he is also accurate when he describes the delight he takes in the companionship of others. In both cases, he needs the recognition and support of his friends if his act is to have aesthetic, moral, or political significance. However, this way of formulating the issue focuses too exclusively on mutual recognition and social solidarity.[17] The crucial point is not that Augustine needs recognition and support, but that the pear-stealing episode would have been impossible as a volitional act apart from the community in which it is embedded. Yet this raises a problem about how we can understand the role of the community in the theft without robbing Augustine and his companions of their individuality. This problem drives us beyond a dialectical interplay between the individual and the community to a dialogical relationship in which they "stand alone together."

Though the pear-stealing episode begins in a community of friends, it unfolds as an act Augustine and his friends commit alone. When he plucks the forbidden fruit, he individuates himself; and as his friends join him, they individuate themselves as well. These acts of individuation disrupt their bond with each other and transcend both aesthetic delight, ethical proscriptions, and political companionship in a process of spiritual degeneration. What begins as a community of friends ends as a community of individuals. In Augustine's words, the result of the theft is not friendship, but "unfriendly friendship," (2: 17) where this kind of friendship is as negative as the acts it presupposes. Before he steals the pears, Augustine enjoys the companionship of his friends; but as the act unfolds, both he and his comrades abandon this positive community by individuating themselves. Augustine's problem arises within a community of friends, but it also points to a situation in which negative individuation generates a disjunctive collection of individuals.

There is a subtle relation between the theft and the community in which it occurs. At the beginning, Augustine is part of a community of adolescent companions, but in the theft and the "unfriendly friendship" that sustains it, he does not find anything positive. Both the theft and the companionship are nothing. Each member of Augustine's adolescent community acts alone, though they act alone together. Once more, two volitional "nihils," one of which is individual and the other of which is communal, come to the center of our attention.

At the deepest level, what connects Augustine with his companions is not aesthetic enjoyment, ethical defiance, or political solidarity, but the fact that they engage in the same negative act. A community is not a collection of individuals, a cluster of persons held together by a social contract, or a hierarchy of different classes of beings bound together by a noble lie, but images of God who bind themselves together so they can take delight in common objects of affection. In the biblical tradition Augustine's analysis of the pear-stealing episode presupposes, to be human is not only to be created in the image of God, but to be created with other finite beings where shared affections are oriented toward the ground of their existence. When God says, "Let us make man in our own image," he points to the positive interplay among the persons of the Trinity;[18] and it is our common orientation toward this positive community which our life together is intended to reflect.

To be a member of a community is to bind oneself to others, and we often take delight in the playful companionship of our friends. Yet in the pear-stealing episode, we disrupt the bond that binds us together by engaging in a collective act that tears us apart. Indeed, the bond breaks when Augustine loves the theft alone; it reappears when every member of the group is oriented toward the same end; but this final bond merely reflects a communal act of self-accentuation that every member of the group expresses. What begins as a community of friends bound together in an act of adolescent mischief degenerates into a collection of individuals because the object that binds them together is *nothing*, permitting both Augustine and his companions to undergo a process of negative individuation that dissolves their companionship into nothingness as well. In this case, a community of wills becomes a community of willfulness, where its members scatter as the collective act in which they engage comes to completion.

From both spatial and eternal points of view, this incident reflects the biblical account of the Fall: Adam and Eve are both members of a community, but they fall away from harmony with one another when they rebel against God. Satan tempts Eve to steal forbidden fruit; Eve plucks the fruit from the tree of the knowledge of good and evil and gives it to her husband to eat; and both Adam and Eve blame someone else for their predicament. Adam tells God that Eve is to blame because she gives him fruit he would not have stolen himself. Eve replies that the Serpent deceives her and that she would never have stolen it alone. We can almost hear them saying, "I did it because of the companionship of my accomplice."[19] Yet at the most profound moment in the story, it is as if God replies, "It is only the theft you love. The companionship is nothing."[20]

At the outset, the members of Augustine's community stand in a positive relationship that reflects the dialogical interplay among the persons of the Trinity; but as the theft unfolds, this positive community degenerates into its negative reflection. Indeed, even the acts of the members of this negative community reflect one another, generating an imagistic relation between Augustine and his companions that binds them together. This relation unifies them because each member of the group is oriented toward the same end and participates in a process of self-accentuation that is a collective phenomenon. However, the negative community that emerges from this collective act inverts the community of friendship with which Augustine begins. In the process, the community becomes a negative reflection of its members, where the only bond that connects them expresses the nothingness of their efforts to imitate God (2:14).

At the crucial moment, Augustine and his friends say, "Let's go, let's do it" (2: 17). This evocative utterance expresses the intention of Augustine and his companions to act in unison. In chanting it together, every member of the group commits himself to the community they share. These words also issue quite naturally in the act, for there is no question in this case of a separation between intention and action. On this occasion, the intention and the action merge because language is not a verbal affair cut off from the action, but the performative act that initiates the action itself.

Augustine and his friends masquerade as divinities; for in saying, "Let's go, let's do it," they imitate God. However, this utterance is a symptom of perverse imitation that inverts the original act of creation. In the first case, "Let there be light" generates a new world;[21] in the second, "Let's go, let's do it," refuses to let things be (2: 17). The first utterance emerges from a trinitarian community and expresses the harmony the created order imitates. The second emerges from a positive community of friends but degenerates into its negative reflection. The first community reflects the act of creation that brings it into existence; the second expresses the isolation of the individuals into which it fragments. This isolation is masked initially by the aesthetic fact that Augustine and his friends laugh because they are deceiving the owners, by the ethical fact that they wish to do harm "from impulses of mirth and wantonness," and by the political fact that they crave "another's loss without any desire for one's own profit or revenge." However, when someone says, "Let's go, let's do it," both Augustine and his friends are "ashamed not to be shameless" (2: 17). Shame of this sort points to the loss of the self, breaks the communal bonds that give an individual's existence social significance, and emerges from the abyss of volitional nothingness that has annihilation as its natural consequence. Nonbeing of this kind can only erupt within a community because it presupposes a shared "object" of negative affection; but when it does, it threatens to destroy both the community and the individuals who participate in it. In response to his own fragmentation and to the dissolution of the adolescent community of which he is a part, Augustine says on more than one occasion that he must move from *avertitur* to *convertitur.* Having been created good, but having been averted from God to embrace the nothingness from which he comes, the thief must be converted, so he and his friends can stand together in a community that is responsive to the love of God.

In attempting to describe and grapple with this episode, we must not override the presence of mystery in it. At the conclusion of his story, Augustine is correct in asking, "Who can unravel such a twisted and tangled knottiness (2: 18)?" Sin can never find a place within a structural analysis or a dialectical articulation of the human situation. Nevertheless, Augustine's unrelenting narrative makes it clear that he understands the most important implications of his act. His story depicts what his reflections suggest, carrying us to the center of the human predicament. The Loeb edition of the Latin text captures the pathos of Augustine's situation by printing the final paragraph about the theft as an inverted pyramid (2:18).[22] On this page, we see a vivid picture of his contraction into frozen isolation:

> I fell away from you, O my God, and in my
> youth I wandered too far from you,
> my true support. And I
> became to myself a
> wasteland.

## THE CONVERSION EXPERIENCE

As Augustine understands the concept, sin is an infinite attachment to a finite good rather than an appropriate attachment to what is infinite (1: 31); and in the discussion of the pear-stealing episode, he suggests that it reaches its most extreme expression when he performs a negative act for its own sake (2: 9) The pear-stealing episode creates a predicament from which Augustine is unable to extricate himself; and it produces what a later Augustinian monk describes as "the bondage of the will."[23] Bondage of this kind separates us from God, paralyzes the soul, and destroys the community in which it is embedded; but on certain occasions, it also generates a quest for redemption that mobilizes the same lenses though which we have filtered Augustine's predicament. It is to this aesthetic, ethical, political, and religious quest for deliverance that we now turn.

The salvation Augustine pursues is not identical with knowledge: intellectual salvation presupposes that to know the good is to do it, while the transformation of the will requires the reversal of infinite self-accentuation. Augustine's deepest difficulty is not the problem of finitude, but the problem of fallenness; his fundamental predicament is not the problem of ignorance, but the problem of willfulness. Thus, his most important task is to pursue the pathway that leads beyond an epistemic framework to the grace of God and to answer Paul's question, "Who shall free me from the body of this death?" (8: 12).[24]

Before he undergoes what is usually described as his "moral conversion," Augustine claims that his intellectual conversion is complete. He has already participated in a mystical experience that brings a dozen years of intellectual conflict to a culmination, moving up the Neoplatonic ladder and beyond it, catching a glimpse of God as *He who is*, and responding to this mystical intuition by exclaiming,

> Thy words had stuck fast in my breast, and I was hedged round about by thee on every side. Of thy eternal life I was now certain, although I had seen it "through a glass darkly." And I had been relieved of all doubt that there is an incorruptible substance and that it is the source of every other substance. Nor did I any longer crave greater certainty about thee, but rather greater steadfastness in thee. (8: 1)

The steadfastness Augustine seeks is moral rather than intellectual because it is temporal rather than eternal. At this stage of his journey, he does not seek more light, but a reorientation of his will that will bring what he does into accord with what he knows. This is a practical rather than a theoretical problem, justifying the conviction that Augustine's conversion in the garden in Milan has an ethical dimension. My only hesitation about embracing this view is that it suggests that the transition from the intellectual to the moral conversion is more continuous than it is. If to know the good is to do it, it is only a matter of time before knowledge leads to appropriate action. However, on this point, Augustine breaks decisively with the Neoplatonic tradition: his moral conversion is practical in the strongest possible sense, pointing to the fact that it is a volitional way of crossing a chasm that the intellect can never bridge.

The depth of Augustine's moral predicament is reflected in the claim that even after his intellectual conversion, sexuality poses an intractable problem. He is still "tightly bound by the love of women," and for this single reason his "whole life is one of inner turbulence and listless indecision" (8: 2). Augustine's preoccupation with his sexual impulses is a familiar theme in Augustinian studies,[25] and it is an convenient way to make the point that the problem he now faces is moral rather than intellectual. However, the root of his problem is not that he is enslaved by sexuality, but that he is addicted to a way of acting that reflects the bondage of his will. It is this fact about himself that moves Augustine beyond his intellectual conversion to seek the stability that can emerge only from the conversion of his will.

With this motivation in mind, Augustine goes to Simplicianus, the spiritual father of Ambrose, to recount his wanderings; and when he mentions that he has read certain books of the Platonists Victorinus has translated, the old man congratulates him (8: 3). Yet instead of engaging Augustine in philosophical discussion about Neoplatonic themes, he encourages him to become a Christian by telling him about the conversion of Victorinus, the scholar and rhetorician whom he had known in Rome. This elderly man had been a rhetorician of enormous power and influence, had been the teacher of many senators, and had been a worshipper and a defender of idols for most of his life; but Simplicianus tells Augustine that despite all this, he had abandoned his worship and defense of idols to become a Christian (8: 3–10).

As Augustine listens to the story, he wants to imitate his predecessor. In the pear-stealing episode, he attempts to become divine by imitating omnipotence (2: 14); now he wishes to return to God by imitating the transformation of another (8: 10). Since Augustine is a rhetorician, it is appropriate that he should seek to imitate a person who represents what he is and what he wants to become. It is also unlikely that he fails to notice the name of the person he wants to imitate. "Victorinus" points to victory and, by implication, to the conquest of the predicament from which Augustine needs to extricate himself.

Though Augustine longs to imitate Victorinus, he cannot do so, and he tells us why by describing the chain of the will that has enslaved him so long:

> The enemy held fast my will, and had made of it a chain, and had bound me tight with it. For out of the perverse will came lust, and the service of lust ended in habit, and habit, not resisted, became necessity. By these links, as it were, forged together—which is why I called it a "chain"—a hard bondage held me in slavery. (8: 10)

The remedy for this kind of bondage, and for the addictions that express it, requires more than the freedom of the will that makes ethical action possible. It also requires the grace of God that transforms the entire person.

The transition from will to willfulness leads from lust, through habit, to necessity. In doing so, it moves beyond the finite-infinite structure of the person who has been created in the image of God toward an infinity of its own that seeks to transcend its limitations and to leave its finitude behind. The explanation for the presence of evil is not two competing principles, as the Manichaeans maintain; nor does it simply reflect the privation of the good to which Neoplatonists call our attention. In the human realm, the problem of evil expresses itself most profoundly in the opposition between freedom and bondage; and in describing the contrast between them, Augustine speaks about two radically different directions in which the will develops:

> But that new will which had begun to spring up in me . . . was not able as yet to overcome my former willfulness, made strong by long indulgence. Thus my two wills the old and the new, the carnal and the spiritual were in conflict within me; and by their discord they tore my soul apart. (8: 10)

As Paul says in the Book of Romans, "the flesh lusts against the spirit, and the spirit lusts against the flesh";[26] and as Augustine suggests in the passage before us, he understands this opposition from his own experience (8: 11).

It is tempting to equate the distinction between the flesh and the spirit with the more familiar contrast between the soul and the body. The struggle at the center of Augustine's being would therefore become a conflict between these two sides of the person. Yet when Augustine contrasts flesh and spirit, he is not distinguishing two parts of the person, but describing two directions in which the person can develop in relation to God. The contrast between flesh and spirit is not the distinction between soul and body, but an opposition between two directions in which the entire person can develop.[27] Sins of the flesh are both bodily and mental, and they reflect the distorted will of the individual who engages in them.

At this stage of his development, Augustine can no longer claim that he is uncertain about the truth. Nevertheless, his flesh binds him to the earth, and he carries the baggage of the world about him as if he were asleep. He says, "Your love satisfied and vanquished me; my lust pleased and fettered me (8: 12). On all sides, God shows Augustine that his words are true; but even though he is convicted by the truth, he can only reply with the drowsy words: "'Presently; see, presently. Leave me alone a little while.' But 'presently, presently,' had no present; and my 'Leave me alone a little while' went on for a long while." Augustine concludes, "I was in captivity to the law of sin that is in my members" (8: 12);[28] and he exclaims in the familiar words of the Apostle Paul, "O wretched man that I am! Who shall deliver me from the body of this death but thy grace alone, through Jesus Christ our Lord?" (8: 12)

Before the transformation Augustine longs for occurs, a friend visits his house; and when they sit down and begin to talk, the visitor notices a book lying on a gaming table in the garden (8: 14). When he picks it up and finds that Augustine has not been reading a textbook of rhetoric, but a letter of the Apostle Paul, he looks up with a smile (8: 14). Ponticianus is a Christian, but he has no idea Augustine has been considering becoming one as well. As a way of trying to persuade him to do so, he tells him the story of Anthony, a well-educated and well-respected Egyptian monk who has embraced Christianity and lives in the desert (8: 14).

Anthony's biography has been instrumental in the conversion of two secret service agents of the emperor. This episode occurs in a garden where they read while they wait for the emperor to attend the gladiatorial games (8: 15). It is not a coincidence that the book that prompts the recollection of this episode is lying on a gaming table and that one of the stories his friend relates mentions the circus. Augustine, the rhetorician, is preparing his readers for the most important moment of his life, generating an aesthetic context in which his conversion unfolds.

The most comprehensive way to make this point is to notice the subtlety with which Augustine constructs his narrative. He builds his account around a series of examples, nesting them inside one another like Chinese boxes. Augustine does not know why Ponticianus has come to visit him, but the letter of Paul on the table provides the context for their conversation. This conversation, and the larger story of Augustine's spiritual development, includes the narrative of Ponticianus about the conversion of Anthony. This leads, in turn, to the account of the conversion of the secret service agents. The artistry of Augustine's story expresses itself in concentric circles that are related to one another in a descending order of comprehensiveness: Augustine's *Confessions*, the story of Ponticianus, the story of Anthony, and the story of the secret service agents. The first contains the second, and the second contains the third and the fourth. In this self-reflexive way, Augustine is spinning a web of words that will eventually raise a question about the way out of the labyrinth.

An interplay between aesthetic unity and religious transcendence is central to Augustine's intentions, and this interconnection surfaces in the structure of his narrative. The series of concentric circles and the aesthetic circularity it represents presupposes a transcendent dimension that stands over against it. Not knowing what Ponticianus wants with him generates a dimension of indeterminacy that surrounds Augustine's story, and this story includes other stories as elements of itself. However, the story also points beyond itself to a source of power that breaks into it from beyond the human realm. The book on the table finally frees Augustine from the aesthetic circularity of his narrative by addressing him directly; and when this occurs, God reveals himself as a source of power that transcends the human realm.

The aesthetic element of Augustine's narrative is sustained by repeated references to entertainment. Ponticianus finds the letter of the Apostle Paul on a gaming table, and this becomes the occasion for his story about Anthony and the secret service agents. The agents of the emperor also find a book about Anthony while the emperor is watching the gladiatorial games, and it is this aesthetic context within which their conversion occurs (8: 15). These references to recreation suggest a radical contrast between two ways of reading the *Confessions*: Is it an aesthetic and rhetorical game Augustine is playing with his readers, or does he intend to contrast the gaming table and the diversions of the emperor with the book on the table and with the conversions of the secret service agents that stand in contrast with them? In the conversion experience Augustine is about to relate, a question also arises about whether what prompts him to read the text he carries from the table into the garden is a children's game or the voice of God. Augustine knows the difference between aesthetic and religious experience, and he moves from the first to the second as his narrative begins to reach its culmination.

The subtle rhetorician makes the transition from aesthetic circularity to religious transformation by saying that while his friend is speaking, God turns him toward himself. In doing so, God approaches him from behind, does not allow him to hide his shame, and sets him face to face with himself so he can see how ugly he is (8: 16). Religious alienation sometimes produces aesthetic and moral disfigurement, and this seems to be so in Augustine's case. When Augustine tries to turn his gaze away, his friend continues his narrative (8: 16). Then God opposes Augustine to himself and forces him to look at himself so he can see his iniquity and hate it. Augustine knows his sin, but acts as though he does not, winking at it and trying to forget it. Finally, he plays a game of his own by praying, "Grant me chastity and continence, but not yet" (8: 17).

At this decisive moment, Augustine turns inward to continue his struggle. Yet on this occasion he does so not to have a mystical experience, but to face the fragmentation of his will (8: 18). Augustine's earlier intellectual conversion is not sufficient to transform his heart because it does not address the opposition between flesh and spirit or enable him to come to grips with the bondage of his will. This self-transcendent being who has attempted to become infinite for so long is now at war with himself (8: 19), and he must first confront his internal conflicts directly if he is to hear the voice of God that will address him from beyond the garden wall.

When Augustine turns inward, he experiences bodily changes over which he has no control. He also describes their common predicament to his friend, Alypius, first by asking a series of questions, then by comparing their situation unfavorably with the joy of others who are much less sophisticated, and finally by suggesting that they are bound together in the same kind of "unfriendly friendship" he had experienced so long ago in the pear-stealing episode (8: 19). At this juncture, Augustine scarcely knows what he is saying, and he flings himself away from his companion as Alypius gazes at him in silent astonishment. Yet in doing so, he does not sound like himself; and his face, eyes, color, and tone express his meaning more clearly than his words (8: 19).

There is a garden attached to the house where Augustine and Alypius are living, and the turmoil in Augustine's heart drives him out into it, where no one can interrupt him. Yet Alypius follows him step by step, and they sit down as far away from the house as possible (8: 19). Once more, Augustine, the rhetorician, is at work: the house beside the garden points to the center of his soul; and in moving away from it, he turns away from himself. The young man is angry with himself for not obeying the will of God, and even his bones cry out for him to embrace it. The distance he must travel to do so is not as far as he has traveled already in moving from the house to the garden. Yet what he needs to make the journey in this case is "a strong and single will"; and what he must learn to transcend is "a changeable, twisting, fluctuating will, wrestling with itself while one part falls as another rises" (8: 19).

Bodily movements express Augustine's agitation and the separation from himself that threatens to tear him into pieces.

> In the very fever of my indecision, I made many motions with my body, like men do when they will to act but cannot, either because their limbs are bound or weakened by disease, or incapacitated in some other way. Thus if I tore my hair, struck my forehead, or entwining my fingers, clasped my knee, these I did because I willed it.
>
> Yet I did not do that one thing which seemed to me infinitely more desirable, which before long I should have power to will . . . with a single will. For in this, the power of willing is the power of doing; and as yet I could not do it. Thus my body more readily obeyed the slightest wish of the soul in moving its limbs at the order of my mind than my soul obeyed itself to accomplish in the will alone its great resolve. (8: 20)

Augustine's predicament is so fundamental that it implicates his entire being: both the voluntary and the involuntary parts of his nervous system respond to it; and like Achilles in the *Iliad*, he tears his hair, seeking relief from his desperate predicament (8: 20).[29] Behind this act is a literary tradition with which Augustine is familiar and over which he exercises rhetorical control. Nevertheless, his erratic behavior suggests that his problem lies deeper than the power of his intellect. Originally finite, and now fallen, Augustine seeks redemption; and what requires transformation in this case is not only his soul, but also his body. If this is to occur, he must engage in a performative act in which willing and doing are the same. Like the Prodigal Son, who demands his inheritance prematurely and squanders his possessions so tragically, Augustine needs to go back home.[30]

Augustine attempts to reach the goal he seeks by saying, "Let it be done now; let it be done now" (8: 25). In doing so, he attempts to move toward redemption through a performative utterance. In the act of creation, utterance and act are identical.[31] In the pear-stealing episode, "Let's go, let's do it," precipitates the action (2: 17). However, on this occasion, performative discourse is unable to achieve its result (8: 25). A chasm opens up between the transformation Augustine seeks and the power of his will to achieve it. This does not imply that Augustine's will is not an indispensable factor in the conversion experience he is about to describe. However, his conversion cannot result from an act of his own, but must reflect the fact that the finite-infinite structure of the psyche has become receptive to the grace of God.

All the while his friend, Alypius, keeps close beside him, awaiting the outcome of his agitation in silence. Yet when Augustine finally admits his incapacities, the storm breaks and the tears come. He leaves Alypius behind to be alone in another part of the garden, abandoning the negative community in which both of them stand. He flings himself on the ground under a fig tree, and when the decisive moment comes, it occurs in solitude. Alone in the wasteland, Augustine abandons his willfulness and opens himself to a source of power that lies beyond himself (8: 28). This does not mean that he renounces either his will or his friends, but that he is willing to stand alone before God. In this moment of solitude, he finally exercises the will of absolute receptivity rather than the willfulness of self-accentuation.

A wall surrounds the garden in which Augustine stands, and he has no visual access to what lies beyond it. Yet from the house beyond the garden wall, he hears the voice of a child, whose gender he is unable to determine. The voice chants, "*Tolle, lege,*" "*Tolle, lege,*" "Take and read," "Take and read." Augustine's first response to what he hears is not active, but reflective. He ceases to weep and asks whether he has ever heard these words before as part of a children's game. His life has been a sequence of diversions, and when the decisive moment comes, he wants to know whether it is aesthetic or religious. If it is the first, he remains a pagan rhetorician; if it is the second, he can respond to the grace of God. Augustine longs for deliverance, but he will not accept a routine occurrence as an expression of divine intervention. Only when he realizes that he has never heard these words before does he act as if the voice of the child is the voice of God (8: 29).

Augustine's inability to determine the gender of the child who chants God's message not only places its words beyond sexuality, but also points to the place where God speaks to the fragmented heart. When he hears the voice from beyond the garden wall, it punctuates the Neoplatonic circularity of the soul's conversation with itself; and he moves into the vertical space between God and the soul where he can finally respond to the voice that addresses him there.

Augustine returns to the bench where Alypius is sitting and snatches up the book he has left there. He opens it and reads the first paragraph he sees. In Romans, Paul says, "Not in rioting and drunkenness, not in chambering and wantonness, not in strife and envying, but put on the Lord Jesus Christ, and make no provision for the flesh to fulfill the lusts thereof" (8: 29).[32] Then Augustine says, "I wanted to read no further, nor did I need to. For instantly, as the sentence ended, there was infused in my heart something like the light of full certainty and all the gloom of doubt vanished away" (8: 29).

This episode is the turning point of the *Confessions*, and its decisive impact upon Augustine's life is undeniable. To understand it, listen first to the words that come from beyond the garden wall. The words Augustine hears are two Latin imperatives, *tolle, lege*, "Take up and read." However, we can also translate the passage, "Destroy and read." *Tollo* is irregular, and its principle parts are *tollo, tollere, sustuli*, and *sublatum*. As Hegel points out in the *Phenomenoloy*, sublation has four stages: it means to take up, to destroy, to move beyond, and to embrace in a higher unity. The Latin *tollo* carries this significance as well. God not only asks Augustine to take up a book, but also to put off his old nature and accept transformation by something new.

Nevertheless, there is a crucial difference between Hegelian *Aufhebung* and Augustinian sublation. Hegel insists that when we destroy and move beyond an earlier stage of our experience, we must preserve what is essential at a higher level. By contrast, the salvation Augustine seeks demands that he abandon his willful nature and become a new creation. In this case, there is nothing to preserve. Augustine must accept a rupture in the flow of his natural consciousness that reflects the original discontinuity of creation *ex nihilo*. The content of the verses he reads reflects this demand. Paul's point is that Augustine must put off the negative dimension of his nature and put on a new garment, destroying his past so the passion that drives him can embrace the peace of God.

Most interpreters assume that the crucial part of the passage from Romans is the one that tells Augustine to abandon the lusts of the flesh. It is easy to argue that his conversion requires the repudiation of the body and the return of the soul to its origins. If this is so, his Christian conversion is a disguised redescription of his earlier conversion to Neoplatonism. However, an adequate interpretation of the episode requires us to take the entire passage into account.

Paul urges him to put aside rioting and drunkenness, chambering and wantonness, and strife and envying. The first two defects do not apply to him. The second pair points to sexual indulgence and is clearly pertinent to his situation. But strife and envying are also defects that continue to plague him. Augustine not only labors under "the chain of sexual desire," but also under "the slavery of worldly business." This forces us to broaden our conception of Augustine's predicament.

We must not restrict our attention to sexuality, but must drive beyond it to the moral, political, and religious slavery that constrains him. In the Epistle to the Romans, the flesh stands in contrast with the spirit and is not identical with the body. References to the flesh are Paul's way of pointing to the willfulness of the human situation. The lusts of the flesh transcend the body and point to the will that separates itself from God. These lusts not only include sexual desire, but also the strife and the envy that disrupt Augustine's journey toward God.

Putting off the lusts of the flesh stands in contrast with putting on Christ. Yet what are we to say about the central injunction from Romans that tells us to "put on Christ" (8: 29)? Most interpreters pass over it without comment, but unless we can interpret this passage, it will become an incantation. If it does, one could scarcely blame a philosophical audience for ignoring it and for assuming that the earlier Neoplatonic vision is superior to the Christian conversion. However, this phrase is the heart of Paul's admonition and points to the central role of the incarnation Augustine has been trying to comprehend. Unfortunately, an abysmal failure to understand how he does so prevents most interpreters from illuminating the most important episode in the text.[33]

In the phrase *Put on Christ*, the words *put on* translate *induo. Induo* sometimes means to put on a costume, but it also describes the moment when a Roman boy becomes a man by receiving a toga from his father. Augustine assumes many guises, not only in childhood and adolescence, but also throughout his intellectual development. Now he must put these earlier stages behind him if the old costumes are to become a new creation. The need for a new creation leads us to the center of Augustine's transformation. However, the most perplexing part of the story concerns the words that finally make redemption possible. These words are the scandal and the stumbling block that tell Augustine to put on "Jesus, the Christ."[34]

What can a philosopher say about this injunction that will allow us to uncover its significance? How can Augustine's conversion to Christianity give us access to a place that unaided philosophical reflection can never reach? Earlier Augustine says that all that remains to make his intellectual conversion complete is an adequate understanding of the incarnation (7: 24). Now he finally achieves a tacit understanding of it when he hears words that not only transform his life, but also provide a solution to his deepest problem.

The incarnation inverts the relation between the finite and the infinite dimensions of the psyche. Because the soul is an image of God, it is both finite and infinite.[35] However, it deals with this fact by denying its limitations and by attempting to become divine. In the Garden of Eden and in the orchard of Augustine's neighbor, human beings storm the gates of heaven through self-accentuation. Both Adam and Eve and Augustine and his adolescent companions fall away from God by embracing their own willfulness. By contrast, the incarnation involves a transition from the infinite to the finite. It demonstrates that infinitude need not detach itself from what is finite, but can embrace it as a realm in which it can express itself fully.

When Jesus prays, "Let this cup pass from me," he turns away from death. Yet the crucial fact about his prayer is that he also says, "Nevertheless, not my will, but thine be done."[36] In this moment, the incarnation reaches its richest expression. Here we see a picture of what it means, not for finitude to infinitize itself, but for the infinite to accept limitations. The verses Augustine reads demand that he accept the reversal of the natural consciousness, embracing a new way of living in which infinite power and intelligible structure receive a finite expression. The will that had been willful for so long now becomes a will again. Freed from the bondage of the will, Augustine accepts infinitude as a gift of God's grace.

The new garment Augustine puts on replaces the garments worn by adolescent thieves. It also takes us back to the original garden that makes the pear-stealing episode possible. Adam and Eve try to hide from God by clothing themselves in fig leaves. When he comes walking in the garden, he asks "Where are you?"; or more literally, he inquires, "Why are you where you are?"[37] Adam speaks for them both by answering with an excuse, but the fig leaves they wear cannot camouflage their negative condition. God tells them to take off the clothes they have made; and in exchange, he provides new garments of his own making.

God places garments of skin around his children; and as they wear them, Adam and Eve can talk with him again.[38] Augustine also puts on a new garment that brings him back into relation with God; and it is this new clothing that he calls "Jesus, the Christ." The finite being who has sought to become infinite for so long undergoes a radical inversion; and when he puts on Christ, he finally embraces the finite place where infinity expresses itself fully.

The conversion of Augustine's will from infinite self-accentuation to finite self-acceptance occurs in private. However, he does not remain isolated, but quickly returns to his friend to tell him about his conversion (8: 30). In this way, Augustine recovers his relation to the community. The community he now embraces is not friendship with adolescent companions, but it also differs from the community of thieves in which every member stands alone. It is a new kind of community in which Augustine and his friends stand alone, but stand alone together.

Alypius responds to Augustine, not by commenting about what has happened to him, but by telling him what has happened in his own case (8: 30). The events he describes occur simultaneously with the more famous episode on the other side of the garden. Yet these separate events do not remain separate. After Alypius tells Augustine what he has experienced while he has been alone, he asks to see what Augustine has been reading. When Augustine hands him the book, Alypius finds that the next sentence is uniquely appropriate to himself. It says, "Him that is weak in the faith, receive."[39] When Alypius responds to these words, he also becomes a Christian, thereby joining Augustine within a community that does not cancel his individual integrity (8: 30).

The conversion of Alypius is derivative upon the experience of Augustine. This is appropriate; for throughout the *Confessions*, Augustine has been the teacher and Alypius the pupil (6: 11). However, both conversions display their own uniqueness, and each reflects the character of the one who undergoes it. There is enough content in the source Augustine touches for more than one. The conversion of Alypius is not as dramatic as Augustine's; but because Alypius interprets his situation as an example of weakness of will, there is a connection between them.

In the case of Alypius, fallenness expresses itself in weakness rather than in self-accentuation; in the case of Augustine, this same predicament expresses itself in erotic power rather than humility. However, in both instances, the grace of God inverts the structure of the soul. The transformation of Alypius differs from the conversion of Augustine, but it has the same internal structure: the weakness of Alypius becomes the strength to accept a divine gift, and the strength of Augustine becomes the weakness to accept his limitations. The same inversion that has transformed Augustine transforms Alypius as well; and when this occurs, the internal structure of their separate experiences binds them together.

When their conversion is complete, Augustine and Alypius tell Monica what has happened; and when they explain how it has occurred, she leaps for joy. She also praises God for being able to accomplish more than she could ever ask or think. As Augustine says,

> For thou didst so convert me to thee that I sought neither a wife nor any other of the world's hopes, but set my feet on that rule of faith which so many years before thou hadst showed her in her dream about me. And so thou didst turn her grief into gladness more plentiful than she had ventured to desire, and dearer and purer than the desire she used to cherish of having grandchildren of my flesh.

Again, Augustine tempts us to give a Neoplatonic interpretation of his intentions by emphasizing that his conversion turns him away from marriage and forces Monica to abandon her desire for grandchildren. However, this narrow reading of his conversion suppresses other elements of it that are more important. Augustine not only forsakes "the chain of sexual desire" and "the slavery of worldly business," but also takes his stand upon the rule of faith about which Monica had dreamed. Faith in Christ stands at the center of Augustine's conversion; and despite her desire for him to achieve professional success by marrying a Roman heiress (6: 23), finding Augustine on the rule of faith is the single aspiration Monica cherishes more than having grandchildren (8: 30).

A Christian community emerges from this foundation. It is not a collection of role players like the adolescent community with which Augustine begins, nor is it a negative community in which participants become isolated from one another. Rather, it includes an indefinite number of individuals that image one another in relation to God. The imaging relation that binds them together creates an analogical unity. Augustine, Alypius, Monica, and other members of this new community are identical in certain respects, but they are also different. The living logos that the text makes accessible does not cancel their differences; for though it is rich enough to individuate them, it also gives them common ground in relation to God. In the present case, this richness creates a new community, where the identity and difference that defines it sustains the interaction of its members.

The infinite must become finite to allow the finite order to come to itself. In some cases, we must abandon our desire to become God; in others, we must exchange our weakness for God's strength; and in still others, we must give up our longing for grandchildren. Monica, Alypius, and Augustine, who have been friends before, become friends within a new kind of community. In this new community, each member stands alone; each experiences the grace of God in his own way; and each stands alongside one another as a unique intersection between God and the soul.

This convergence brings wholeness to Augustine and his companions. It also allows them to participate in a community that both binds them together and holds them apart. The community that emerges is neither simply a collection of individuals, nor a larger whole that subsumes and engulfs them. Rather, it is a community of participants that presupposes analogies between vertical and individuating experiences with God. This community is compatible with the unity of the person in contrast with the dualism of soul and body; for it is the entire person who stands together with others within an analogical nexus.

Friendship is a crucial thread that runs throughout the *Confessions*. It begins in adolescence, appears in a negative form in the pear-stealing episode, and contracts into the frozen isolation of an adolescent wasteland. Now friendship resurfaces, generating an imagistic relation that grounds a new kind of community. Friendship of this kind presupposes that those who have stood alone before God stand together.[40] The pear-stealing episode leads from a positive community of friends to a negative community of isolated individuals. By contrast, conversion leads from individuating experiences with God to a community that not only holds its members apart, but also binds them together. In the final analysis, this is not only a promissory note about an eschatological future, but also a down payment on what Augustine means when he points beyond the city of men to the city of God.

NOTES

1. I have presented earlier versions of this chapter at several institutions: the Graduate Christian Forum at Cornell, the Convocation Lecture Series at Bethel College, the Distinguished Lecture Series at Baylor, the Philosophy Department Colloquium at the University of Essex, the Faculty of Divinity in the University of Edinburgh, the "D" Society at Cambridge, and the School of Philosophy at the Catholic University of America. I want to thank those who attended these lectures for comments and criticisms that helped me sharpen some of the issues in this final version.

2. John E. Smith, *The Spirit of American Philosophy* (New York: Oxford University Press, 1966).

3. Smith makes this point most clearly in his defense of a theory of experience that is broader than that of the British Empiricists. See John E. Smith, *Reason and God* (New Haven and London: Yale University Press, 1961), 174–83, and *Experience and God* (New York: Oxford University Press, 1968), 21–45.

4. Smith formulates the point by discussing the opposition between philosophical demonstration and experiential evidence. And he attempts to give reason an appropriate place in philosophy and theology by distinguishing between "formal" and "living" reason. See Smith, *Experience and God*, 109–120.

5. Ibid., 161–62.

6. Ibid., 22, 100.

7. Ibid., 3–20.

8. George Wilhelm Friedrich Hegel, *Lectures on the Philosophy of Religion*, vol. 1, ed. Peter C. Hodgson and trans. R. F. Brown, Peter C. Hodgson, and J. M. Stewart (Berkeley, Los Angeles, London: University of California Press, 1984), 83.

9. Smith, *Experience and God*, 3.

10. Smith, *Reason and God*, ix–xiv.

11. The standard critical edition of the text is St. Augustine, *Confessionem libri XIII.* Ed. Martin Skutella, rev. Lucas Verheijen. Corpus christianorum, Series latina, vol. 27. Turnholt: Brepols, 1981. The translation I use is *Augustine: Confessions and Enchiridion*, trans. Albert C. Outler (Philadelphia: Westminster Press, 1955). This translation combines the literal and poetical dimensions of the text better than any other.

However, Outler sometimes makes mistakes, and I have tried to correct these at the appropriate places.

12. L. C. Ferrari, "The Pear-Theft in Augustine's *Confessions*," *Revue des Etudes Augustiniennes* 16 (1970): 234–37.

13. Gen. 3:1–19.

14. The clearest picture of this conception of the abyss occurs in *The Comedy of Dante Alighieri: Hell*, trans. Dorothy L. Sayers (Baltimore: Penguin Books, 1949), 32, 22–39. However, Augustine anticipates the description when he says, "[But] thou hast melted away my sin as if it were ice" (2. 15).

15. Plato, *Republic*, vol. 2, trans. Paul Shorey (Cambridge: Harvard University Press, The Loeb Classical Library, 1969), 514a–521b.

16. See the reference to Holmes' remark in Peter Brown, *Augustine of Hippo* (Berkeley and Los Angeles: University of California Press, 1967), 172.

17. This is one of the mistakes in what is otherwise a brilliant and very helpful book. See Colin Starnes, *Augustine's Confessions: A Guide to the Argument of Confessions I–IX* (Waterloo, Ontario: Wilfrid Laurier University Press, 1990), 44–45.

18. The word *God* in the Hebrew text is plural. As Augustine recognizes (13: 32), this becomes explicit semantically as well as syntactically in Gen. 1:26. There God says, "Let us make man in Our image."

19. Gen. 3:12–13.

20. Ibid. 3:14–19.

21. Ibid. 1:3–5.

22. *St. Augustine's Confessions*, vol. 1 (Cambridge: Harvard University Press, The Loeb Classical Library, 1977), 94.

23. *Martin Luther: Selections from His Writings*, ed. John Dillenberger (Garden City, NY: Anchor Books, Doubleday & Company, Inc., 1961), 166–203.

24. Rom. 7:24.

25. See W. M. Alexander, "Sex and Philosophy in Augustine" *Augustinian Studies* 5 (1974), 197–208.

26. Gal. 5:17.

27. The best discussion of the relation among these crucial terms can be found in Reinhold Niebuhr, *The Nature and Destiny of Man*, vol. 1 (New York: Charles Scribner's Sons, 1941), 150–240.

28. Rom. 7:23.

29. *The Iliad of Homer*, trans. Richmond Lattimore (Chicago and London: The University of Chicago Press, 1951), 18. 26–27.

30. Lk. 15:18–24.

31. John 1:1–3.

32. Rom. 13:13.

33. I intend this indictment to be quite general. However, I will postpone a detailed citation and discussion of the relevant texts.

34. I Cor. 1:23.

35. The finitude of the soul expresses bodily, mental, and volitional limitations. By contrast, the infinite dimension expresses its capacity for self-transcendence. The soul is not only an individuated being, but also an individual who can reach for God. In the Christian tradition, the positive interplay between finitude and infinity defines the human situation.

36. Matt. 26:39.

37. Gen. 3:9.

38. Gen. 3:21.

39. Rom. 14:1.

40. In spring 1992, thirteen philosophers came to Penn State for a week to study the *Confessions* with me. We thought and talked until we were exhausted; but in the process, the text opened up in ways that none of us could have anticipated. Some of the papers from graduate seminars in 1989 and 1991 about the *Confessions* and the conference in 1992 appear in a two-part issue of *Contemporary Philosophy* 15, nos. 1 and 2, 1993. This collection of essays relates the *Confessions* to themes at the center of contemporary philosophy; and the chapters in this volume are important because they move the discussion of Augustine beyond familiar philological, historical, and theological considerations to the heart of his personal and philosophical intentions. I owe the phrase I use here to one of my students, Janice Stabb, whose chapter in this collection is entitled, "Standing Alone Together: Silence, Solitude, and Radical Conversion."

Robert Cummings Neville

# American Philosophy's Way around Modernism (and Postmodernism)

If the "modern" period in philosophy can be said to have started singly in the seventeenth century with the development of mathematical physics and the spread of its paradigms by analogy far beyond science, it cannot be said to have had a single development. Yet there is a common textbook story of the development of modern Western philosophic thought. The story begins with Descartes and branches into his rationalist successors, Spinoza and Leibniz, and his empiricist correctors, Hobbes, Locke, and Hume. Kant combined the two branches with his transcendental turn, which delegitimated all philosophy of nature and empirical approaches to ethics, politics, and aesthetics, rendering philosophy a discipline to analyze and ground all first-order discourses. The romantics, including Hegel, Schelling, and Kierkegaard, reacted against Kant's limitations for philosophy and practiced philosophy in ways that blew past those limitations with speculation, intuition, imagination, or faith.

The romantic reaction could not sustain itself in an age that gave supreme legitimacy to science, however, and by the end of the nineteenth century philosophy had become one of several methods associated with modernism. It could be an ideological instrument for change (Marx), a subversive weapon for exposing deceptions, particularly bourgeois deceptions (Nietzsche, Freud), or a second-order discourse that analyzes and attempts to justify the first-order discourses that directly engage the world (Husserl, Wittgenstein the logical positivist, Wittgenstein the language analyst). Modernism in philosophy has been identified with the last set of approaches, those seeking to ground other ways of knowing the world, and postmodernism, taking the subversive approach unto its own, has attacked the modernist philosophies. Jacques Derrida and Richard Rorty are postmodern philosophers with great learning and craft.[1]

The likelihood of any one intellectual event ramifying itself in only one way, with only one stream of development, for four centuries is extremely small. We should expect modernism to be only one development in the late modern period, to be paralleled by many others. In fact, there should be many streams branching off, some to sink out of sight, perhaps to re-emerge later in new configurations, others to go their own way, growing or diminishing, finding subcultures in which to flourish and paralleling the more recognized streams. Literary or academic politics might try to obscure any but some favored stream; this in fact is what happened when many European philosophers came to the United States after World War I, insisting that the story from early modernity to modernism, thence to postmodernism, is the only story to be told. Other stories can be told, however, that shift the values of the major players and lift up other ideas for their importance.

The thesis of this chapter is that the American tradition is to be understood by a story subtly different from that told above about the rise of modernism. By the "American tradition" is meant the New England philosophy exemplified in Jonathan Edwards in the eighteenth century, Ralph Waldo Emerson in the early nineteenth, the pragmatists (Charles S. Peirce, William James, John Dewey, George Herbert Mead) of the late nineteenth and early twentieth, and the process philosophers (Alfred North Whitehead and Charles Hartshorne) and other speculative metaphysicians of the twentieth century.[2] The American tradition is itself internally diverse with many streams; for instance, the pragmatists were contemporaries and differed from one another as they learned from one another. The variety is even greater among our own contemporaries.

The focal point for understanding the American tradition's way around modernism is its developing treatment of experience. John E.

Smith has called this the "reformed conception of experience" and contrasted it with the "classical empiricism" associated with Locke and Hume and reacted to by Kant, Hegel, the phenomenologists, and other twentieth-century modernists. The argument of this chapter will be first to analyze Smith's interpretive distinction, to explore it in the prepragmatic philosophies of Edwards and Emerson, to elaborate Peirce's self-conscious separation of his approach from the Kantian agenda, to show how the modernist concerns, determined as they are by the Kantian agenda, are only of tangential interest to the fruitful deployment of American thought, and finally to indicate the parochial character of much postmodern criticism. That is, the legitimate target of postmodern criticisms does not include the main themes of the American tradition. On the one hand, the postmodern criticisms seem to be a century late in developing a non-Kantian agenda, and on the other hand, they seem to be wildly wrong in attempting to delegitimate speculation and direct philosophic engagement with the world.

## THE AMERICAN ALTERNATIVE: A RECONSTRUCTED THEORY OF EXPERIENCE

John E. Smith has pointed out that "experience" is the main theme of modern philosophy, similar in its importance for modernity to the ideas of cosmos in the ancient Greek world or God in medieval thought.[3] He distinguishes the modern senses of empiricism from the ancient Greek. Aristotle, so often called an "empiricist" in contrast to Plato's "idealism" or "rationalism" (all categories vainly applied to the ancient world!), took experience to be the result of repeated encounters with the same or similar things, yielding a knowledge distinctly inferior to more theoretical knowledge of causes. The chief importance of experience for Aristotle, Smith points out, is in practice, in learning to act with "art."[4] But experience is never normative for rational understanding in Aristotle's thought.

By contrast, experience in the modern period becomes the normative center both for reason, with its theoretical structures and inferences, and for practice. Smith writes:

> The valid and permanent contribution of modern empiricism, as Hegel made so clear, was its insistence that every man should see and feel himself present with every item of knowledge he is expected to accept. This demand meant a rejection of tradition and authority as grounds for the

> fixation of belief and appealed instead to the encounter with the world which each individual enjoys. The problem that immediately arises, however, can be expressed in the question: What is experience and how is it to be understood in its generic character?[5]

Smith distinguishes within the modern period between the "classical" empiricism of Locke, Berkeley, and Hume and the subsequent modern variants, most of which attempted to broaden the classical notion of experience, including logical empiricism, linguistic empiricism, pragmatic empiricism, and radical empiricism.[6] Husserlian phenomenology and Bradleyian idealism could also be included in this list.[7]

Smith principally focuses his discussions of experience, however, on the "reconstructed" theory developed by the American pragmatic tradition of Peirce, James, and Dewey. The argument of the present essay is that there is a larger development of the "reconstructed" approach in American thought, extending back to Jonathan Edwards, and that the tradition as a whole constitutes a decisive alternative to the modern-through-modernist/postmodernist story.

In his analysis of the reconstructed theory of experience, Smith has brought out four major features.[8] First, experience is not to be conceived as something that happens within the mind of an individual as in classical empiricism but is an interaction of the experiencing self with the experienced world, an "organic togetherness" of world and self. Second, experience is not the passive reception of data by the subject, but involves the subject's interpretive interaction with the world; experience is the result of interpretive engagement of the world. As a consequence, experience is not an absolutely truthful presentation, undistorted by human interventions, from which conclusions might be read off with certainty. Rather, the cognitive claims to be derived from and within experience are fallible. Third, the normative character of experience comes not from infallible sensations or other such data but from the process in which interpretations are corrected in the relational and purposive activity of experiencing. What is normative is less the having of a singular experience than being experienced at engaging some subject matter or activity.

Fourth, Smith calls particular attention to what he terms the "intensive quality" of experience, or what we might term its valuative character. This has two sides. On the one, things are experienced as valuable, and this value-quality is intrinsic to the experience of them.

Experience is thus realistically aesthetic and moral. Experiences not only appreciate discriminable objects but also integrative qualities of situations; they are "poignant or dull, decisive or trivial." On the other side, the values of things experienced are taken into the interpreter and qualify the interpretation itself. The self responds so as to value things in specific ways. This is true also of the integrative qualities of situations, to which we might respond with anxiety.

In summary, Smith has pointed out that experience, according to the reconstructed theory, is (1) a matter of interactive engagement, (2) interpretive, (3) corrective, in process, of antecedent expectations, and (4) aesthetic. The following sections shall attempt to show how these ideas developed in the American tradition and how they constitute an alternative to the classical conception of experience that led to modernism.

## EDWARDS AND EMERSON

Jonathan Edwards was the last of the great American Puritans, a key player in the enthusiastic Great Awakening of the eighteenth century, and a rhetorical opponent of freedom of the will. Ralph Waldo Emerson was his century's most famous Unitarian, an opponent of organized religious movements, and the most florid proponent of free spirits prior to Bubba Free John. In these and other respects they represent opposite extremes in the American cultural tradition. All the more significant, then, is their commonality with respect to the four features that will go to make up the reconstructed understanding of experience. Charles Peirce is the pivot for that reconstructed understanding, and therefore the reading of Edwards and Emerson is retrospective, and a bit reconstructive, from the classical pragmatic perspective which was a distancing of philosophy from Kant. Edwards and Emerson can be read as anticipations of the reconstructed view from the standpoint of their own historical situations.

Edwards (1703–1758) was contemporary with Hume (1711–1776); his great *Treatise concerning Religious Affections* appeared only seven years after Hume's *A Treatise of Human Nature*.[9] Yet because of distances he knew nothing of Hume and responded instead to John Locke and the earlier generation of Cambridge Platonists as his intellectual milieu.[10] In his early book, or set of notes, *The Mind*, Edwards was an idealist of a sort very close to the position developed by George Berkeley.[11] If that were the main text, no case could be made for Edwards' anticipation of the four points of the reconstructed theory of experience save the fourth. In those notes he began the development of his aesthetic theory that being consists in excellence and that excellence is a matter of proportion and harmony.[12] Excellence is a function of objective characteristics of things and is not imposed by the individual mind. Furthermore, mental perception of things always includes a grasp of their agreeableness or disagreeableness, insofar as we catch their true excellence. Edwards developed this notion of excellence as intrinsic to existence and a first-order object of cognition all his life; see, for instance, its role in the discussion of the "tenth sign" in the *Religious Affections* and in his moral theory in *The Nature of True Virtue* (1755).

With regard to the other marks of the reconstructed theory we must look to Edwards' major discussion of experience as a normative touchstone, namely, the *Religious Affections*. The main plot of that book has two steps: first, to argue that true religion consists in holy affections and, second, to argue that we can discern something of the difference between truly holy affections and their counterfeit. His situation was the defense of religion as a matter of affections against those who would argue that the only important religious question is God's judgment, with no personal transformation or sanctification involved. On the other side, he had to defend the location of religion in the affections, that is, in what and how well a person loves, against the "enthusiasts" in the Great Awakening who, like New Age religionists today, regarded how religious emotions feel to oneself as the only thing that matters. Salvation for Edwards consists in a certain kind of personal excellence that in turn consists in the quality of one's love of God and all that depends therefrom.

The affections themselves constitute the main part of life and involve many kinds in addition to the religious. Human response to the excellencies of things is affectionate and arises from engaging them. Edwards sharply distinguished real affections from "mere wouldings," unexpressed intentions, intentions not acted upon. To be a person of "mere wouldings" is to be incomplete, in fact a human failure. Genuine experience, for Edwards, is engaged and affectionate, a prototype of the pragmatic point about experience as interactive engagement.

Further, Edwards believed that the novelty in experience is not sheer given sense data—although some of the early writings can be interpreted that way. Rather, what is learned new in engagement is an improved way of seeing with the categories we already have. Conversion, for instance, consists in a "new sight" that comes from God; but this new sight provides no new propositional knowledge if one had read the Bible before. Rather, the new sight shows the truth and proper understanding of the Bible and the proper affectional response to it. Whereas Locke had emphasized new data that transform the index of items in consciousness, Edwards emphasized the transformation of the heart: with divinely given new sight, we are able to love God with true affection and in that love understand God's true beauty and excellence. Precisely because the new sight is not an experiential datum but a new quality of behaving affectionately, the new sight is not infallible. Or rather, it is always open to doubt whether the new way you look at things is the true new sight or something that misses the mark. The "signs" of true religious affections that Edwards discusses are important because they give clues as to the authenticity of the sense that one has the new sight and true affections. The fallibility of experience is the second point of the reconstructed theory. Edwards' discussion of the devil's ability to counterfeit signs of true affections is as subtle as any pragmatic discussion of fallibility, and his ultimate appeal, like Jesus', is pragmatic: test the fruits of alleged holiness.

From this follows Edwards' anticipation of the third point of the reconstructed view, namely, that experience learns through the correction of expectations in ongoing behavior, not through finding a new positive datum. Experience does indeed learn new things, both in the mundane affairs of the world and in divine ones. Edwards by no means anticipated Peirce and Dewey's careful formulation of the idea of hypotheses to which the world can say no. But he did understand that the novelty in learning consists in improving or correcting previous intelligent behavior, particularly with respect to how to value things.

For all the idealism of much of Edwards' language, his view of experience was that its nature can be discerned in the differences it makes to the way we live, public differences that the community can observe even if it cannot make sure judgments of the heart. The connection between the inner content of experience and its expression in behavior is not merely an inferential one, but is intrinsic to the nature of the person as such. We are what and how we love, and that is in the actual loving. Ever the theologian, Edwards believed that this view of experience was a proper expression of the doctrines of creation and incarnation. If God is really to create the world, and not merely think about it as some idealist theories might have it, then the religious action is in the persons created. And if God is really to enter the world, it must be by a real residence in and transformation of the finite creature, respecting the finitude of human affections but filling them with the divine object.

With these points, Ralph Waldo Emerson (1803–1882) was in agreement. Exactly a century younger than Edwards, he was part of the great romantic reaction to the scientific attempt to limit reality to the measurable. From Kant (wonderfully misread), Hegel, Goethe, and Coleridge, Emerson learned the power of the notion of imagination. In his hands, it was transformed into a metaphysical theory of the Oversoul. Not an Absolute of which we are all different parts, Emerson's Oversoul was a great universal spirit that found particularity in individual persons with their historically different settings. Communication between persons on the important levels was a movement from one particularity to another through the medium of the Oversoul in each soul. From one point of view, Peirce had very few changes to make in Emerson's conception of the relation of finite souls to the Oversoul to develop his idea of the community of investigators. Formally, Peirce's community is a discursive version of Emerson's Oversoul. A fascinating story remains to be told of the transitions from Edwards' God of divine glory in whom people live as expressions of glorious excellence, to Emerson's Oversoul, to Peirce and Royce's great community, down to Dewey's notion of community religiously unified by the sublime quality depicted in *A Common Faith*.[13]

With regard to the topic of experience, Emerson wrote an essay with precisely that title.[14] Like most of his essays, this one is intuitive and imaginative rather than didactic and expository. Furthermore, it was written two years after the death of his son, and much of the essay is a function of what was learned from that "experience." Pre-eminently, Emerson held to the first of the four traits of the reconstructed approach to experience: interactive engagement.

Emerson analyzed experience in terms of seven themes, each but the first related dialectically as a corrective to its predecessor. He lists his themes at the end: "Illusion, Temperament, Succession, Surface,

Surprise, Reality, Subjectiveness—these are threads on the loom of time, these are the lords of life."[15] His first point is that we are born in the middle of things, awaking, as he put it, as if in the middle of a staircase with stairs below we seem to have ascended and stairs above stretching out of sight. "Where do we find ourselves? In a series of which we do not know the extremes, and believe that it has none."[16] Moreover, the interpretation we place on our affairs might be wholly mistaken when matters out of sight are taken into account; hence, our concrete life with its built-in interpretation might well be an illusion in the larger context. So much for the second of the reconstructive themes: experience is all interpretive. Emerson appreciated the vast importance of temperament, and wrote that "life is a train of moods like a string of beads.[17] Were our temperaments not successive, they would put us in bondage, and even their succession is a problem for freedom. Attempts to settle things intellectually rest on the surface and do not engage the real powers of nature. Rather, we should admit to our deep instincts and seize our muscular work in the midrange of activities. Life consists of power and form, wrote Emerson, and a stress on either one out of balance with the other will evoke a surprise correction. Reality shows itself against all illusions when we get out of balance. The third point of the reconstruction is decisively emphasized by Emerson in his theory of nature as the great teacher. The Fall of Man, said Emerson, consists in "the discovery we have made that we exist."[18] Ever after, we understand that our experience is all mediated, not undistorted immediacy, and are often inhibited by self-consciousness of subjectivity. The predicament of human experience is to break through the mediations of subjectivity so as to engage life with vitality. Emerson quotes Mencius to the effect that vigor in life is a participation in the principle of vigor in the universe, a restatement of the doctrine of the Oversoul.[19] The importance of vigor or vitality is that it is Emerson's "sign" of aesthetic excellence, his version of Edwards' "signs" of true religious affections, fallible like Edwards' signs but the indwelling of actual divinity, the true spirit of the Oversoul. From Nietzsche onward, readers have known that Emerson's vision was based on the aesthetics of power and form. Hence, his version of divinely derived excellence that Peirce would refine in his doctrine of intrinsic value, that which is good in and of itself, as the actualization of concrete reasonableness.[20]

The sources of the pragmatists' reconstruction of the notion of experience in terms of interactive engagement, interpretation, correction of ongoing activity, and aesthetic definitions of being and value, lie powerfully expressed in Edwards and Emerson. Those writers both reflected underlying sensibilities in sections of the American character and helped to actualize the sensibilities. The pragmatists, especially Peirce, brought them to professional philosophic formulation. We need not rehearse the classic pragmatic expressions because Smith has done it so eloquently. Rather, we shall now examine how Peirce directed the American tradition around the modernist movement that arose contemporary with his work.

## PEIRCE'S REJECTION OF KANT

Peirce, of course, thought of himself as a Kantian in most respects, writing about Kant frequently and claiming to derive pragmatism from Kantian inspirations.[21] He defined his philosophy as "critical commonsensism," in which title the "critical" refers to Kant's *Critique of Pure Reason* and the "commonsensism" refers to the Scottish common sense school.[22]

The commonsense part turns out to be far the most important. As is well known, Peirce construed ideas as the "leading principles" for actions, and he construed actions as formed with the generality of habit.[23] Experience, for Peirce, is the human engagement with the world in which worldly realities correct the general habitual structures in actions. Generality in habits has the form of signs, and thus all actions are structured with signs in interpretive relations to one another. Actions in turn are oriented by purposes. The anticipations involved in actions, which can be corrected by the brute givenness of reality when mistaken, are always with respect to intentional or purposive orientations that interpret the situation in selective respects. Peirce's is no crude pragmatism; for him, the most important issues of life are those involved with determining what purposes are worth having.

There is no way, on Peirce's view, to separate mental representations from concrete actions formed by interpretive structures. The most abstruse reflection on abstract ideas is just as much an action formed by interpretive structures as walking to the store to buy milk. Thus there is no way in Peirce's theory to register Kant's problem of how to infer from the subjective order of representations wholly within consciousness to an objective order; this is the crucial topic of the *Critique of Pure Reason* as focused in the "Second Analogy." For Peirce, there can be no question of how we can know the external world because there is no inner consciousness to which a world might be external. In fact, consciousness itself is not an important category for Peirce. Rather, for Peirce the relevant questions are whether this belief about the problem of the one and the many is correct and whether that road is the one to take to the milk store. For Peirce there is no *epistemological* question of how we can know, only questions about whether putative knowledge is correct.

Of course, as a matter of curiosity it is important to inquire about the nature of knowledge itself and to frame hypotheses about that, testing the hypotheses against other things we know and comparing them with alternatives. Although consciousness as an empistemological category is not important for Peirce, self-consciousness as an intellectual practice is very important. This is what is left of reflexive Kantianism in the "critical" part of "critical commonsensism." But criticism in this sense is not the specific kind of criticism Kant associated with the transcendental deduction. It is simply the kind of self-reflection associated with philosophy since the critical conversations of Socrates.

The crux of Peirce's rejection of Kantian transcendentalism has to do with hypothesis itself. Kant accepted hypotheses in science, but not in philosophy. He argued, in the "Discipline of Pure Reason" toward the end of the first *Critique*, that even scientific hypotheses do not make sense unless philosophy, in a nonhypothetical, fundamentally certain way, can define *possibility*. By defining possibility Kant meant defining what it means to be an item in the real world, what hypothetical representations might be, and what might count as evidence for or against an hypothesis.[24] This is a classic statement of foundationalism: no claim to knowledge can be trusted, in science or elsewhere, unless we can show with certainty how it is possible and what might be right or wrong about it.

Against this Peirce simply held that a higher level hypothesis can explicate the kind of knowledge at stake in lower level hypotheses. The theory of hypotheses, habits, leading principles, and so forth, is itself a philosophic hypothesis that needs to defend itself on many fronts. Peirce rejected the chain analogy of argument, that an argument is as strong as its weakest link. Rather, he used a rope analogy—an argument has the cumulative strength of many different strands of reasoning and evidence. High-level philosophical hypotheses about knowledge and action are to be defended with many strands of argument and, once they have come to seem the easiest and most natural way to think, are not to be doubted except insofar as one can find concrete reason to doubt them. Speculative metaphysics, for Peirce, is the deliberate effort to find reason to doubt our most general hypotheses. Peirce was in no doubt about the ability of the philosophic community to develop plausible hypotheses about how knowledge is possible; he had a good one himself.

## A WAY ROUND MODERNISM

If thinking is continuous with other forms of behavior, if knowledge is a problem of learning through experience rather than inferring from inner representations to an external world, and if all knowledge is fallible, even the knowledge of how knowledge is possible, then there is no reason to move to the problematic of philosophical modernism. Foundationalism, and the problems of epistemology, are simply not serious problems.

Modernism in philosophy cannot be defined in any easy or innocent way. But the various forms of philosophical modernism seem to agree in holding that philosophy should itself be self-grounding in the sense of being able to authenticate its own sources and not be dependent upon nonphilosophical materials, except accidentally. Modernist philosophies also agree in saying that it is their business to analyze and assess, so as to ground or delegitimate, claims to knowledge in all other fields. Negatively, modernist philosophies agree that the history of philosophy is not an intrinsic part of philosophy, but rather of intellectual history, and that first-order philosophies such as philosophy of nature, of politics, and so forth should really be handed over to the sciences. One need only read Husserl's defense of the transcendental standpoint in *Ideas* or his concerns about the "crisis of the European sciences" in the book of that name to see an illustration of philosophic modernism. G. E. Moore's reduction of philosophy to the analysis of common sense, or Russell's emphasis on logic, or logical positivism, or the early Wittgenstein's logical picture theory, or the late Wittgenstein's analysis of integral life worlds all attempt to be self-grounding and foundationalist. Richard Rorty is right to criticize all of them as being fixated upon the problem of finding certainty about knowledge of the external world and virtually reducing philosophy to epistemology.[25]

The force of Peirce's distancing of himself from Kant was to establish a philosophic agenda that does not need to register the foundationalist problems of epistemology. There is no need to obtain certainty before proceeding, only always to make one's beliefs vulnerable to correction.

At a stroke, therefore, the American tradition whose early moments Peirce summed up and whose later development he stimulated has an answer to the deconstructionist postmodern critics. *Logocentrism* is a seriously bad name if it refers to unchanging systems rigidly believed to have been established with certainty and grounding the possibility of other things. For then indeed those people and views marginalized and delegitimated by the "central" idea do need to have the venue changed so that their perspective is recognized. On a pragmatic fallibilist view, however, an idea ought always to be kept vulnerable to correction by the things it misses. Those marginalized ideas need to prove their worth, of course, and are not to be approved simply because they are "the oppressed." They might in fact be rejected because they are bad ideas. On the other hand, such a rejection should always be vulnerable to correction by a learning procedure that does not prejudice the case. Deconstruction is right to call attention to what is left out or distorted. American pragmatism long ago called for the constant testing of the balance of the perspectives within which critical correction and learning take place.

The chief negative point of postmodern deconstruction is its rejection of metaphysics or speculative philosophy. It might indeed be right to reject metaphysics as defined by modernism, which also rejected metaphysics. But the speculative philosophy in the American tradition, from Edwards down to our contemporaries, is fallibilist and utterly non-Kantian. It is metaphysics in a different sense from that attacked by Kant who insisted on a different kind of certainty, transcendental rather than metaphysical. The postmodern deconstructionist critiques of speculation are simply wide of the mark with regard to the rich American speculative tradition because they do not know the American story. They suppose that only Heidegger's story about metaphysics is true, yet Heidegger's is a very narrow and ignorant approach in light of the American tradition.

As mentioned earlier, the contemporary heirs of the American tradition are extremely diverse. Perhaps the following is a rough classification. On the one hand, there is a naturalist stream running from Peirce to Dewey and Santayana to Justus Buchler to David Weissman. On the other hand, there is a dualist stream, often both with theological and with scientific interests, focused in Whitehead with variants in Hartshorne, Robert S. Brumbaugh, John B. Cobb, Jr., Donald Sherburne, and George Allan. In between are less easily classifiable figures such as Paul Weiss, John E. Smith, William Desmond, Charles Sherover, David L. Hall, Carl G. Vaught, Cheng Chung-ying, Tu Weiming, Stephen David Ross, and Brian John Martine.

Despite their differences, all these thinkers hold one or another version of the four traits identified by Smith as characteristic of the reconstructed theory of experience. All in one way or another find a basic orientation in American pragmatism, however they might have developed it. And in this situation in which these latest contributors to the American tradition are defining themselves as an alternative to modernism/postmodernism, there is another set of common traits.

First, these thinkers all take the interpretation and criticism of historical philosophers to be an internal part of philosophy itself. Not merely as intellectual history, but as part of identifying, defining, and justifying one's own position, it is necessary to come to terms with the history of philosophy's many stories.

Second, these thinkers are peculiarly open to philosophic engagement with representatives of the Chinese and Indian traditions. At a time when modernist and postmodernist philosophers tend to define philosophy as itself a Western cultural phenomenon, and thus capable of relating only to its Western forms, these thinkers have taken the field of philosophy to include anyone interested in the topics with a deep tradition of reflection to contribute. Many have done serious scholarly work outside of Western philosophy, and there is a growing movement in the group to take the worldwide philosophic situation as the only context for philosophic work. Two of those listed above would count themselves principally as Chinese philosophers, although their contact with Western philosophy is through the sympathies of the American tradition.

Third, perhaps as a generalization of the previous point, most in the group would agree that philosophy of culture should hold the central orienting place that modernism and postmodernism would give to epistemology. Thus philosophy should learn from all other humanistic and scientific disciplines and should extend its reflections to contribute to those disciplines where possible. Philosophic conversation naturally requires conversation with nonphilosophers, at least with those who are not philosophers in any professional sense. Philosophy should address human problems most generally and should get at them through whatever cooperative means are available. Philosophy of culture seems to be the approach that monitors the scale of philosophic thought.

Fourth, following from the above is a general uneasiness among these thinkers about viewing philosophy as a profession, as profession is ordinarily defined. Although there is a legitimate guild character to academic philosophy, consisting in knowledge of arguments and positions, philosophy is not true to itself unless it goes far beyond the guild. Philosophy is cross-disciplinary as well as cross-cultural, for most of these thinkers.

Fifth, for all these thinkers, philosophy is legitimately speculative. Although some concentrate more on philosophy of culture or interpreting the history of philosophy than on speculation themselves, all honor the genre and construe it as central to the synoptic wisdom philosophy is supposed to offer. While rejecting the modernist view that philosophy should be foundationalist, this group of American thinkers believes that the most basic issues about which speculation thinks contain the most practical categories of all, categories that subtly affect everything in the human response to life.

This chapter has argued that the American tradition as described herein offers an alternative to modernism/postmodernism. Doubtless there are other alternatives, surely among the contemporary philosophies of East Asia and India. The genius of the American tradition consists in its reconstruction of the classical notion of experience, as Smith has analyzed the point. That classical notion found its problematic set in stone by Kant, and modernism flows directly from that. The reconstructed notion indicates how limited Kant's agenda is and how to get around it to more interesting topics about which human life needs wisdom.

## NOTES

1. Derrida's seminal book is *Of Grammatology*, trans. Gayatri Chakravorty Spivak (Baltimore: The Johns Hopkins University Press, 1976); Rorty's is *Philosophy and the Mirror of Nature* (Princeton: Princeton University Press, 1979).

2. Despite the fact that speculative metaphysics was supposed to be extinct after the modernist critique, impressive bodies of work, and a distinguished list of students, have been produced by thinkers such as Brand Blanshard, Robert S. Brumbaugh, Justus Buchler, John Findlay, Errol Harris, F. S. C. Northrop, Kenneth Schmidts, John E. Smith, and Paul Weiss. For examples of the work of the next generation, see the authors in *New Essays in Metaphysics*, ed. Robert C. Neville (Albany: State University of New York Press, 1987), or those in this book. I have discussed some of the variety of recent American philosophy—American in the sense being defined here—in *The Highroad around Modernism* (Albany: State University of New York Press, 1992).

3. See *Religion and Empiricism* (Milwaukee: Marquette University Press, 1967), 1ff.

4. See Smith, *Themes in American Philosophy* (New York: Harper, 1970), 44ff.

5. See Smith, *Purpose and Thought: The Meaning of Pragmatism* (New Haven: Yale University Press, 1978), 79.

6. For this list, see *Religion and Empiricism*, 3.

7. See Smith, *Themes in American Philosophy*, 49.

8. The following discussion is taken from *Reason and God* (New Haven: Yale University Press, 1961), ch. 9, pp. 179–181. Dale M. Schlitt has reviewed the development of Smith's discussions of the reconstructed theory of experience beginning with the early book *Royce's Social Infinite* (New York: The Liberal Arts Press, 1950); see Schlitt's "John E. Smith on Experience," in *Philosophy & Theology* 2, no. 12 (Winter, 1987), 105–123. Unfortunately, Schlitt stops with Smith's *Analogy of Experience* (New York: Harper, 1973), thus missing some of the most sophisticated later studies, chief of which is the 1978 *Purpose and Thought*. There is a more serious drawback to Schlitt's discussion, however, namely, his own idealist agenda. He wants to develop Smith's work in the direction of "idealist concerns . . . for structure and totality" (Schlitt, 121). This agenda seems to lead him to seek out a dichotomy in Smith between the mental and the real, a dichotomy Smith's interpretation of experience is supposed to surmount but does not until the very latest writings. Schlitt supposes a mentalist theory of "interpretation" and thus, when Smith writes of experience *and* interpretation, takes Smith to be contrasting them even though the same writings say that interpretation is part of experience. For the early Royce, such a

dichotomy might be useful. But both the later Royce and the "early Smith" were well acquainted with the writings of Charles Peirce in which interpretation is explained as action, the action of employing and modifying habits. Interpretation is thus not "mental" in any sense that contrasts with the real world but is more like the form of the human side of the interaction that constitutes experience. Interpretation for Peirce is not phenomenalistic but is equated with the activities of investigation and inquiry, activities the proper subject of which is the community; that this lay behind Royce's theory is the major thesis of Smith's *Royce's Social Infinite* (see, for instance, p. 27). While not wanting to argue that Smith's thought has failed to develop from its early themes, I do want to stress that on the alleged relation of subjective mentality to real objects within experience, Smith has been a Peircean from the beginning. That same Peircean background would also make Smith hesitant about moving toward idealist concerns for totality. Peirce was an evolutionist who argued that the universe is quite disconnected but that certain parts of it have a tendency to generalize and reach out to seek connections with other parts; in Peirce's later thought this was expressed as *agape*. At best, Peirce could conceive of totality only with reference to the *intention* to achieve a complete interpretation on the part of the community in the infinite long run. Royce, who had been a strong devotee of totality early in his career, for instance in *The Religious Aspect of Philosophy* (New York: Houghton Mifflin, 1985), moved toward a nontotalistic Peircean view in his late philosophy, for instance *The Problem of Christianity* (New York: Macmillan, 1918), where the totality registers as the ideal community toward which the actual community moves intermittantly as motivated by the intentional structure of loyalty; see Smith's introduction to the 1968 University of Chicago Press edition of *The Problem of Christianity*. For another view of Smith's theory of experience, see the chapter by Douglas Anderson in the present volume.

9. Edwards' *Treatise* (Boston: Kneeland and Green, 1746); Yale Edition, ed. John E. Smith (New Haven: Yale University Press, 1959); Hume's *Treatise* (London: Noon, 1739).

10. On the background for Edwards' approach to experience, see John E. Smith's introduction to the Yale edition of *Religious Affections*. For a wonderfully comprehensive introduction to Edwards see John E. Smith's *Jonathan Edwards: Puritan, Preacher, Philosopher* (Notre Dame: Notre Dame University Press, 1992).

11. See Leon Howard's *"The Mind" of Jonathan Edwards: A Reconstructed Text* (Berkeley: University of California Press, 1963).

12. See the references in Howard's text to existence and excellence, for instance, and the discussions of substance.

13. John Dewey, *A Common Faith* (New Haven: Yale University Press, 1934).

14. "Experience" is in his *Essays: Second Series* (1844). It is available in *The Complete Essays and Other Writings of Ralph Waldo Emerson*, ed. Brooks Atkinson (New York: Modern Library, 1940), 342–64. Subsequent citations are from this edition.

15. "Experience," 362.

16. Ibid., 342.

17. Ibid., 345

18. Ibid., 359.

19. Ibid., 357.

20. See *The Collected Papers of Charles Sanders Peirce*, ed. Charles Hartshorne and Paul Weiss, vol. 5 (Cambridge: Harvard University Press, 1934), book 1, lecture 5, "Three Kinds of Goodness."

21. Peirce, *Collected Papers*, vol. 5, paragraph 1.

22. Ibid., book 3, chs. 2 and 3.

23. Albeit "well known," the reader might want to check Peirce's texts; the fifth volume of the *Collected Papers* is a good locus that contains most of the important themes and the seminal papers. The best commentaries on these points are by John E. Smith; see his discussions of Peirce in *Reason and God, Themes in American Philosophy, The Spirit of American Philosophy*, and *Purpose and Thought*. I have analyzed some of the points here in greater detail, with close citations of passages from Peirce, in *The Highroad around Modernism* (Albany: State University of New York Press, 1992), ch. 1.

24. See the *Critique of Pure Reason*, B: 797–98.

25. In his *Philosophy and the Mirror of Nature* (Princeton: Princeton University Press, 1979). I have criticized Rorty's analysis for its extremely biased approach to American philosophy. He rightly sees that Dewey has abandoned epistemology, but he believes that this also entails abandonment of the entire speculative tradition in American thought. See my introduction to *Highroad around Modernism*, and elsewhere.

John E. Smith

# Philosophy in America: Recovery and Future Development

Gratitude for bounties received can, happily, be expressed in more ways than one, starting with the simple and heartfelt *saying* of "I thank you" and reaching to the condition of *being* thankful and, since this is not a static condition, it coincides with showing gratitude in ways that go beyond the saying. A favorite expression of Jonathan Edwards evoked by his discussion of what he called "holy practice," was "It is much easier to get 'em to talk like saints, than to get 'em to act like saints." Saints aside, the talking and the acting are both necessary, the latter being the validation of the former. Hence I begin by saying thanks to all those who have contributed their ideas and convictions in the chapters that make up this volume which is presented to me. Some are former students with whom I shared and have continued to share over the years philosophical and religious ideas, and others are long-term associates in the philosophical quest; *all* are members of what Royce called a "community of interpretation," a community made one by our dedication to the cause of sustaining constructive philosophy over years when the climate of opinion was, to say the least, more like that of a winter storm than a summer shower ending with a rainbow.

Our common cause may be described through a distinction proposed many years ago, but which I here adapt to a different purpose. It was said that there are three types of philosophy, the philosophy of "nothing but," the philosophy of "something more," and the philosophy of "what's what." I believe that the import of each type is clear enough, but I would suggest that the fundamental conviction of those represented in this volume is that "what's what" *is* "something more"! Philosophy betrays its heritage if it goes in for reductionism because the articulation and illumination of experience which is the goal of reflective thinking, cannot contain less than that with which we started. If the splendor that falls on castle walls belongs to our direct experience, it must still be there at the end of analysis and not be transformed into wave lengths. As for what's what, if that means the need to portray what we encounter with accuracy, the quest for "what's what" is essential. If, however, it means trying to understand things solely in terms of so-called instantaneous and present fact as in the protocol sentences of positivism, then this is a false quest because many thinkers have shown that the complexities of the world, its processes, novelties, and possibilities cannot adequately be construed in terms of present, sensible, atomic fact. Those who are said to be looking for something more do so because they have seen the error of nominalism and hence insist on the need to discover—I believe the words are Paul Weiss's—"what there is beyond the things that are."

All the chapters in this volume, different and distinctive as they are, represent illuminating, reflective thinking about fundamental philosophical questions, and in this sense they are *exhibiting* the recovery of philosophy, which is our common theme, and not merely talking about its possibility. In the comments that follow, I shall aim to keep this point constantly in mind. Since the chapters are of several types, I cannot treat all in the same way. Some put questions to me, whether explicitly or implicitly; others are on themes in which I have been interested but whose authors do not direct questions to me. In either case, I shall try to respond in the way that seems, to me, most appropriate.

## RESPONSE TO GEORGE R. LUCAS, JR.

George Lucas in "Philosophy's Recovery of Its History" deals effectively and incisively with the use and abuse of the distinction—it need not be attributed to anyone since it has been a dominant assumption for decades—between those who are "doing" philosophy and those who are supposedly engaged merely in dealing with its history. To the extent that this distinction is viable at all, it can be validated only in the grossest terms. We can, for example, recognize the fundamental difference between the work of a Wolfson and that of a Peirce. I choose this illustration because each did distinguished work, and hence no question arises about one ranking higher than the other. Wolfson is the monumental scholar seeking to recapture the thought of Spinoza, to show its background in the tradition, to elucidate his central concepts in great detail and to present us with Spinoza *an sich*, so to speak, and apart from the use of his thought in the philosophical agenda of others. In Peirce we have a thinker who was breaking new philosophical ground in metaphysics and logic, offering novel insights into the nature of inquiry and the history of science, and laying the foundations of semiotics. Apart from his meticulous study of the works of Duns Scotus whose critique of nominalism he greatly admired, Peirce was not working as an historian of philosophy. A similar comparison might be made of H. J. Paton's work on Kant; no one has surpassed Paton in his efforts to get Kant "right" as a preliminary to any critical discussion, but with the exception of his excellent and neglected book on the philosophy of religion, Paton did not embark on a philosophical quest of his own. To fill in the comparison, Peirce was indebted to Kant for certain features of his own thought, but, despite his claim that he could recite the *Critique* from memory, many of Peirce's comments on Kant show that he had no special concern to get Kant "right." What is the point of the comparison? Simply that in such obvious cases it is possible to distinguish between Wolfson and Paton as doing historical work and Peirce as essentially engaged in constructive philosophy. Even as we say that, however, we must not forget Hegel's insight that the *historian* of *philosophy* has to be engaged in *philosophy*, otherwise no comprehension of the subject matter is possible. So much for the gross distinction between the historian of philosophy and the constructive philosopher.

Sometimes the distinction between "doing" philosophy and historical interpretation is made in terms of those who are discussing issues "systematically" and those who are merely talking about what others say. Here, of course, the distinction breaks down, as Lucas has rightly seen, because if one is talking about Wittgenstein, Quine, or Davidson for example, that counts as philosophy proper—even if one is only expounding their ideas for a journal article—whereas if one is talking about Descartes or Aristotle one is a historian. The truth is that in both cases the talk is about what *others say*, and indeed how could it be otherwise if philosophy is that "conversation" it is now reputed to be, or is supposed to become.

Lucas' paper is rich in thought and, like his other works, shows a remarkable ability to present trends and developments in philosophy in a distinctly *philosophical* way so that this chapter itself becomes a fine example of how philosophy uses its history. Considering the over-all trend in philosophy starting with Kant's first *Critique* in 1781 and ending with Reichenbach's *Rise of Scientific Philosophy* in 1951, Lucas rightly concludes that the aim was to rid philosophy of its "historical and speculative concerns" and establish it as a respectable discipline with a subject matter of its own and a definable method to be used by specialists for whom the history of philosophy is no more than a comedy or, better, a tragedy of errors. I heartily applaud Lucas' perception that the "managerial, administrative class" in charge of the modern university welcomes this view of philosophy since it makes possible the "assessment" both of faculty and of departments in precise and measurable terms—efficiency, progress, and quantitative productivity. I would add that this conception of philosophy is attractive to administrators because it helps to dispel the uneasiness many of them feel in the face of a subject that baffles them.

Lucas is right on the mark when he points out that the consensus concerning method and subject matter in philosophy has come apart in the past two decades and that what he calls "methodological anti-historicism" was dealt a heavy blow by Quine's "Two Dogmas" and Kuhn's *Structure of Scientific Revolutions*, followed by Rorty's *Mirror* and MacIntyre's *After Virtue*. I need not rehearse the sequel: Lucas has done that very well. However, I would like to underline two points in his conclusions; first, that at present there are clear signs that philosophy is recovering its history, and, second, that, as a result, we may hope to see reversed the priority previously accorded to "*episteme* and unreflective *techne*" over *sophrosune*, *phronesis*, and *sophia*.

Naturally, I am grateful to Lucas for attributing to me some role in the attempt to recover, especially in the case of the classic American thinkers, the historical roots of the tradition they established. As he rightly sees, my efforts were not directed to embalming the past, but rather to recovering for present purposes those ideas which seemed to me most important for recovering philosophy itself from the analytic doldrums and the Babylonian captivity of empiricism. Thus, for one example, the great emphasis I have placed on the reconstruction of the conception of experience in these thinkers was for the express purpose of highlighting the total inadequacy of classical empiricism and of pointing out the fact, unnoticed by most analytic philosophers, that many are still taking that empiricism for granted, but substitute for Hume's association of ideas the machinery of modern logic. I regard the making of that point a matter of philosophy and not only of history.

## RESPONSE TO KUANG-MING WU

I remember Kuang-ming Wu very well when he was a student at Yale and again when he was a lecturer in the department offering an introduction to Chinese philosophy which soon drew a large roomful of students. I much appreciate his generous comments about my relation to him as a teacher. "The Spirit of Pragmatism and the Pragmatic Spirit" makes a significant addition to the East-West dialogue in philosophy and the effort to reach understanding across cultural boundaries. I believe that Wu's distinction between the spirit of pragmatism which he finds in American thought and the pragmatic spirit that pervades Chinese thought is essentially sound. The two are different, and yet they are in the same vein and complement each other. I should point out that in my comparison of the thought of Wang Yang-ming and that of the pragmatists, I was purposely stressing *convergences* of experience and of interpretation in the belief that such convergences offer strong evidence for the continuity of experience when, as in this case, the thinkers were totally independent of each other. It is similar to the situation in which Peirce and DeMorgan, prior to their correspondence, each say independently that the classical syllogism is based on one triadic relation—if *aRb*, and *bRc*, then *aRc*. In stressing these convergences, however, I did not mean to imply that there are no differences between the whole tenor of Chinese thought and patterns of thought to be found not only in the pragmatists but in Western philosophy in general. Wu has nicely focused these differences without losing sight of the affinities that exist. I believe that he is right in taking note of the theoretical distance that characterizes much Western thinking and which, if he is correct, appears even in attempts to overcome it. Thus he contrasts the pragmatic emphasis on handling things with the Chinese aim of "living in/with nature revered as Heaven," and suggests that, while

Peirce and Royce, for example, were concerned to relate the particular and the universal, Chinese thought focuses primarily on the concrete particular in order to find the generality it exhibits. If I understand him correctly, Wu believes that both Peirce and Royce gave priority to the universal and then sought to include the particular within it, whereas Chinese thought works the other way around. This is too large an issue to be joined here; suffice it to say that Wu puts the difference in question best when he says that for the Chinese the concept "is a scene, a compressed story" or a generalized concrete, and this is surely different from the main drift of Western logic. Wu presses the point further when he declares that "in China thinking is not formal abstract theorizing, but a sensitive discernment of the many-layered meanings of a concrete experience." In emphasizing this contrast, however, Wu seems to forget that the pragmatists would not agree that thinking is no more than "formal abstract theorizing," nor would it be correct to say that they had no regard for capturing the "many-layered meanings" of concrete experience. Numerous examples would be relevant at this point; I shall choose two that seem to me the most perspicuous. In the analysis of the stream of thought in his *Psychology*, James insisted that the person is "always interested more in one part of its object than in others, and welcomes and rejects, or chooses, all the while it thinks." And he went on to point out that it is impossible for us to distribute our attention "impartially" over a number of impressions. What is this if not the recognition that the interests and selective attention of the individual person are at work in all thinking activity?

Dewey's account in *Art as Experience* of what it means to have *an* experience, one with its own pervasive quality and individual unity as distinct from the more or less inchoate experience that happens continuously solely in virtue of the fact that we are live creatures interacting with the world and other people. Philosophers, Dewey claimed, have invariably spoken of experience at large or in general and thus have failed to take note of certain individualized experiences which we often call "real" and say to ourselves "that was *an* experience." An experience—*that* meal we had in the Paris restaurant, *that* storm we encountered crossing the Atlantic—has a pervasive quality such as being sublime, terrifying, delightful, or poignant, which bestows on it a unity and makes it memorable, an episode marked off from the ordinary run of things.

I do not mean to deny the significant distinction Wu draws between Chinese and Western thought. What I wish to point out is that his belief in the need to combine the spirit of pragmatism found in the American thinkers with the pragmatic spirit in Chinese thought can be enhanced by emphasizing the fact that the pragmatists were making their own criticism of abstract rationalism in thought when they broadened and deepened the scope of experience and insisted on its esthetic integrity.

## RESPONSE TO THOMAS P. KASULIS

The teaching and learning situation is subtle and often baffling, especially for the teacher who needs to know something at least of what is getting across to students. I have long had a sense that students are not learning more than a fraction of what one is trying to teach, but that in the dynamics of the exchange they are actually learning much that one is not explicitly trying to teach at all. Under the circumstances I am very grateful for help from Thomas Kasulis whose chapter begins with three points which have guided his philosophical thinking about religion and which he believes that he learned from me. Whether he is right or not, I recognize these points at once as ones I continued to stress throughout my teaching career. The first is the primacy of experience for determining the interpretative categories and leading principles that structure an inquiry. The aim, as Kasulis rightly says, is to avoid ruling out matters of experience because of too narrow or inadequate categories. To take an example at random, the contribution of mythological speech to the interpretation of experience was completely lost on those who regarded myth as no more than a "primitive" form of something else, usually either science or philosophy. My emphasis on experience, moreover, is not a matter of philosophical principle alone; it is a living prescription as well. Kasulis is right when he recalls that I suggested his going to Hawaii and Japan to learn Japanese and thus have a direct encounter with the religion and the culture. Advice of this sort stems from my approach to teaching, which Kasulis sums up by saying that I do not try to fit students into my own mold and that I help them to find the "problematic"—what they can best do or that they are really interested in doing—within themselves. I have long had the idea—which was reinforced by Royce's conception of Being as the fulfillment of a purpose—

that each human being has some special talent or capability that needs to be developed or "led out" of the person. I have often coupled that idea with the belief that such talent is unique so that if it is buried or allowed to wither away, the community no less than the individual suffers a permanent loss. What I find inspiring and gratifying in Kasulis's working out of his own "problematic" is that to which it finally led. Because of the philosophical adventure I encouraged him to take, he writes, "I find myself in communities of discourse that barely existed a quarter century ago. One of these is the community of 'Buddhist-Christian' dialogue" (40–41).

The second point, the intrinsically social or communal character of religious thought and practice, leads us to ask of a religious utterance, to what audience is (was) it addressed? The aim is not, as James seems to have thought, to disregard or undervalue religion in individual life, but rather to adhere to the fact that the existence of some form of community is a trait of every religion we know. In fact, as both Royce and Peirce pointed out, an individual comes to a religion initially through the community in which the tradition has been preserved.

The third point concerns the fact, indeed the inevitability, of pluralism, both in our own country and throughout the world. There are different views, different experiences, and different interpretations, and I frankly do not understand how these realities could have escaped the notice of anyone who has lived in America, which is, and ever has been, a nation of nations. It is important that Kasulis calls attention to both sides of the coin; pluralism can indeed mean conflict, but it also is an important means whereby we are led to reflect on our own assumptions. I can recall my introduction as an undergraduate to the Eastern religions and my thinking that Taoism was quite bizarre in its quest for a truth that cannot be named. It was not until further study and my participation in the East-West conferences in Honolulu that I became aware of how bizarre Christianity with its creation out of nothing and crucified Saviour might appear to Buddhists and Confucians. I do not believe that it is possible to, so to speak, think your way into the needed perspective; it can come about only through actual exchange between people who are committed to the religions involved, and that means going beyond scholarly study. If I may appeal to another anecdote, a television discussion with Prof. T. R. Murti who was representing Buddhism led me to *see* the truth of what I have just said. We were conversing as committed adherents of different religions, and his question to me was,

How can a being who is created be in any sense free? In the situation, I realized vividly what a stumbling block the Christian idea of creation is to Buddhists, and at the same time I had the sense that, despite the many differences that divide Christians, the many mansions are in the same house, and those differences seemed far less formidable than the Buddhist challenge from outside the house altogether. I shall return to the point shortly in connection with Kasulis's account of what goes into the Christian-Buddhist dialogue in which he is engaged.

Kasulis is actually presenting us with an analysis of the experience and form of expression characteristic of religion. However, he is doing so not in general terms, but in the light of what is needed if the novel sort of interreligious dialogue in which he is engaged is to succeed. There is no need for me to rehearse his theory since it is clearly set forth and, most important, is thoroughly informed by the *practice* involved both in the religions themselves and in the dialogue across boundaries as well. However, I would like to single out several points for special emphasis.

I think Kasulis is right to begin by rejecting the simple dichotomy between viewing religious statements either as universal truths, objective and publicly verifiable after the fashion of empirical inquiry, or as the expression of subjective feelings or sentiments. I agree further that it is a mistake to suppose that one can avoid these two extremes by declaring that religious expression is *sui generis*, because it is then isolated from all other forms of discourse and experience. His solution is to seek an alternative to the false dichotomy, and he finds it in the conception of an objective but not publicly verifiable knowledge that can be attained only through "praxis in a specific community" (45) For Kasulis, religious knowledge is closer to the way a parent knows a child or to the way a connoisseur evaluates a wine than either is to the way a scientist knows a natural phenomenon. The distinction echoes James's pointing to the fact that in many languages there are parallel words for "knowing" where one signifies objective information, what he called "knowledge about," and the other signifies what is apprehended through direct experience or personal undergoing, what James called "knowledge by acquaintance." To take but one of many examples, the German *wissen* means theoretical or scientific knowledge, while *kennen* means what we come to know in a first-person way through participation and encounter. I agree with Kasulis that religious expressions are largely of the latter sort, but I believe there is more interpenetration than he seems to allow. However, this is not the place to argue that point; the important matter is to see how this approach contributes to the interreligious dialogue.

His main point is that religious truths have to be communicated by what he calls "intimation" within a community and the basis of this truth cannot be expressed directly; it can be intimated to those within the tradition, but never made fully intelligible to those outside. However, Kasulis does not believe that interreligious communication becomes impossible on this account, but rather that it alerts us to the difference between truth *within* a tradition and truth *about* a tradition. The former requires intimation, while the latter requires discursive explication. In pursuing the conditions for dialogue, Kasulis makes what I believe is a most fruitful distinction between three dimensions in which religious discourse takes place. First, there is the circle of religious practice in which intimation is primary.[1] Second, there is the discourse of critics—scholars such as historians, philosophers, anthropologists and so on—who, although they cannot teach outsiders what can be apprehended only through practice, can inform outsiders about the training and the practice of those who most fully understand the intimations belonging to the community. Third, there is what Kasulis calls "metacriticism" of which his chapter is an example, and it concerns itself with a general theory of what truth means in a religious context.

The function of this three-level conception is to provide some measure of what can and what cannot be communicated across boundaries, and thus help to avoid misunderstandings that arise from the supposition that we are communicating on a given level when as a matter of fact that is not what is happening. The illustration given by Kasulis concerning the approaches of D. T. Suzuki and Nishitani Keiji in their treatment of Buddhism throws a great deal of light on this matter. According to Kasulis, many metacritical theorists have come to regard religion as irrational and without truth because the critics upon which they are based confused intimations with discursive explanations. Thus, he claims, inaccurate metacritical interpretations of Zen Buddhism are to be traced to Suzuki's failure to be clear about his aim; was he describing how nothingness is discussed intimately in Zen practice, or was he attempting to explain what nothingness means to Zen Buddhists? Kasulis thinks the confusion led to a picture of Zen as rejecting all concepts and theories. By contrast, Nishitani is said to have a critical standpoint at the boundary of Zen which would not lead to a view of Zen as irrational.

I believe what Kasulis says about Suzuki provides me with the key to clearing up what puzzled several of us so much upon the occasion of an entire afternoon's discussion with him about the meaning of self in Zen. If I may resort to one more anecdote, the occasion was a meeting of the East-West Philosophers Conference in Honolulu some thirty years ago. Through the good offices of Dr. Richard De Martino, it was arranged to have a meeting with Dr. Suzuki, Professor John Findlay, and myself. In the course of the discussion, Findlay and I found that we understood what Suzuki was saying to us about the no-self emphasis in Zen, and he and I sought to confirm this understanding by asking each other questions; to the best of our knowledge Suzuki seemed to find no fault with our conversation. However, when either of us addressed comments directly to Suzuki in an effort to express our understanding of some point, Suzuki invariably responded by telling us that we had not grasped the point. Could it be that we understood him when he was, to follow Kasulis's distinction, attempting to explain Zen Buddhism to outsiders, but that in telling us that we had not understood he was referring in his own mind to how no-self is intimated in Zen practice? If this had been the case, I think it would help to explain what Findlay and I experienced.

## RESPONSE TO GEORGE ALLAN

George Allan calls attention to the contrast I drew in my presidential address to the APA, "The New Need for a Recovery of Philosophy," between an irrelevant philosophy that is no more than a war between philosophers and a philosophy that recovers itself by making a concerted attack upon problems arising from our efforts to maintain a life that is human. Allan rightly proposes to enlist philosophical resources in the effort to deal with one of the current critical problems facing education in America today—the explosive debate about a canon of studies and the claims of multiculturalists. I believe that his essay "Modernism, Postmodernism, and the Pragmatic Recovery of an Educational Canon" is an excellent illustration of constructive philosophy at work in combining clear thought, good sense, and the concern which the pragmatists had for defusing dualisms and dogmatically opposed positions, what Royce called "dangerous pairs" when confronting each other without a mediator. In a measured way, Allan wisely seeks to lay hold of what is at issue between the canonists and the noncanonists as a prelude to finding a way in which justice can be done to the interests of both sides. Citing the original idea of Matthew Arnold via the paraphrase of William Bennett, Allan points out that the guiding idea of canon is "the best that has been said, thought, written and otherwise expressed about the human experience." Allan then goes on to focus on the principal objections raised by the noncanonists; first, there is the charge that this canon is too exclusively Western in content, and, second, but more important, is the claim that the idea of a canon itself is illegitimate because it represents the perpetuation of an order which was imperialistic, colonial, patriarchal, and exclusionary. In short, the proposed canon must be deconstructed so that its cultural roots will be exposed as representing the privileged over the unprivileged member of society. Allan views the argument as a dispute about two conceptions of reality; the canonists contending that it is organized hierarchically with essential and accidental elements, and their opponents claiming that no such distinction holds because all things are related interdependently. For a resolution of the problem, Allan turns to William James's idea that, since we cannot just "copy" the world and there would be no point in it if we could, the alternative is to accept the fact that objective factors and human factors interpenetrate in all of our efforts to form a coherent picture of ourselves and the world we inhabit.[2] Thus the world can have more than one "edition," and each is limited and fallible. Allan understands a canon in this Jamesian sense so that it becomes a framework or orientation teaching us what it means to be a human being, or, as he puts it, "A culture's educational canon is an orientation program for membership in its community." Allan concludes that the wisdom of the modernists is found in their realization of the need for interpretative frameworks "and the prudential value in having canonical ones."

On the other side of the ledger stands the wisdom of the postmodernists, which Allan sees expressing the truth "that there is no natural hierarchy to things, that people, deeds and ideas are all born equal. Each concrete thing is just what it is." The task is to recognize the uniqueness—the special voice—in all that goes into "the unending world chorale." Accordingly, Allan insists that, since America is "a conjuries of ethnicity," each group deserves equal representation in any educational curriculum aimed at introducing the nation's heritage to the younger generation. But he rightly warns us that "education in a postmodern mode must do more than celebrate difference; it must come to terms with its necessarily hegemonic implications."

In an attempt to reconcile the competing views, Allan once again, and quite rightly, appeals to James's idea that new truth has always to be joined to "the whole body of other truths already in our possession," so that old opinion and new fact are married by new truth, with, in James's words, a "minimum of jolt and a maximum of continuity." The canon, for Allan is the "old opinion," and "the new fact" stands for all the new cultures the postmodernists want to see represented on the educational menu. As Allan insists, however, there must be a framework within which this marriage function can be realized and that is provided by the stock of truths already in our possession. To deny the old opinion is to leave us without a framework into which the new can be incorporated.

If I may add a footnote to Allan's fine discussion, I would suggest that the very idea of recognizing and, hopefully, of achieving a harmony of different cultural voices in one society finds its modern roots in the Enlightenment and its cosmopolitanism; such a harmony can be brought about in America only if the nation—all ethnic groups—becomes more conscious of and remains committed to the Enlightenment ideals that played so large a part in the founding of a democratic government wherein every group is represented and the rights of all are protected. Hence it must be kept in mind that part of the modernist canon authorizes the protests of those who regard it as exclusionary and oppressive. What is not so clear is whether these protesters themselves stand in traditions dedicated to equal representation for all ethnic groups.

## RESPONSE TO DOUGLAS R. ANDERSON

Douglas Anderson's chapter, "John E. Smith and the Heart of Experience," is such that no one could ask for a more accurate, sympathetic, and yet critical interpretation of his or her writings. He goes beyond exposition to critical reconstruction and provides a living illustration of Kant's idea that others may understand us better than we understand ourselves. No matter how circumspect and self-critical we may be, the critical *alter* ego is never "*alter*" enough; we need the *other* consciousness, the perspective of another self, who alone can provide the view from beyond. To begin with, I believe that Anderson is correct in connecting my view of the self with the new conception of experience developed by the American thinkers. I cannot stress too often how many things fell into place for me in connection with the entire development of philosophy since the British empiricists when I first read Peirce's incisive argument to show that we are not intuitively aware that the immediate content of apprehension is confined to our own minds. Thus the problem of reaching the "external" world—Russell spent a lifetime trying to do so—vanishes; there is nothing still to be reached since we are already there in the midst, as Peirce would say, of the independent "reals." As Anderson rightly perceives, the further development by Dewey of experience as a public affair led me to wonder whether full justice was being done to individual experience, hence my concern for placing the self at the heart of experience. But, as Anderson notes, I had no thought of recovering the self as an isolated subject; I have too high a regard for community to fall into atomic individualism. On that note we can explain what Anderson calls the "general trend in pragmatism" to downplay the role of the individual. Leaving James aside, Peirce, Royce, and Dewey stressed the importance of community not so much to demote the individual as to attack the individual*ism* that has long been prominent in the American temper. I believe this distinction is very important, even if it is not always appreciated; it is one thing to cherish the uniqueness and protect the rights of each individual, but it is quite another to think of an individual as a totally self-sufficient and self-enclosed unit for whom relations with others are purely extraneous.

Anderson's discussion of the having/knowing distinction drawn by Dewey accurately reflects my uneasiness when the distinction is pushed too far. I agree with Dewey's concern to challenge the identification of experience with knowledge as we find it in Locke and Kant, and I understand that Dewey's distinction is meant to deal with the problem. The question, however, is whether this solution does not depend on limiting knowledge to the outcome of controlled inquiry so that no room is left for any sort of knowing within experiences had. Consider my example of having or undergoing an experience of forgiveness at the hand of someone to whom we have done an injustice. Are we not justified in saying that in this experience we "know" the meaning of forgiveness, how difficult it may be to grant and often more difficult to accept, and yet it seems quite inappropriate to suppose that any controlled inquiry is involved? Anderson correctly points out that I sought to deal with the problem, first, by denying the dogma that every cognition is either an immediate apprehension (intuition) or an inference, since the alternative is not exhaustive, and, second, by drawing a distinction between "immediate" and "direct" experience; the latter is neither immediate nor inferred. His treatment of my example of direct experience—two individuals in conversation—is acute and to the point, especially in his noting the crucial difference between *interpreting* the meaning or "import" of an encounter and describing or explaining it. My uneasiness in the face of Dewey's "scientism" stems from his confining "knowing" exclusively to the outcome of controlled inquiry; the latter is a public affair which is not continuous with the direct experience I aim to preserve. It is not without importance that, with the exception of parts of *Human Nature and Conduct*, Dewey's problematic situations are invariably found at the interface between organism and environment, and this seems to leave out the organism's becoming a problem to itself. In short, there is little place for those situations where the self is at odds with itself as described by James in the divided self and the sick soul. The truth is that for many at present the disorders of a self out of joint loom as the most problematic of all the situations we face.

I believe it is important that Anderson should emphasize my ideas about the self and self-realization (he is right about my harking back to Edwards and Royce) in the context of Dewey's thought because it highlights Dewey's tendency to back away from or try to avoid certain ideas uncongenial to his naturalism. This tendency is nowhere more evident than in his treatment of the self. In response to Gordon W. Allport's contribution to *The Philosophy of John Dewey*, Dewey writes, "I am obliged to admit what he says about the absence of an adequate theory of personality."[3] Dewey goes on to explain, "In a desire to cut loose from the influence of older "spiritualistic" theories about the nature of the unity and stability of the personal self (regarded as a peculiar kind of substantial self) I failed to show how natural conditions provide support for integrated and potentially equilibrated personality-patterns."[4] I believe the point is clear, and I shall not join the issue further; suffice it to say that Anderson has laid hold of an important lacuna in Dewey's thought, and I hope that he is right in saying that my approach to the self opens up a positive dialogue with prospects for a renewal of philosophy as compared with the current neopragmatism that seems still caught in the linguistic turn and in the old empiricism.

## RESPONSE TO LEWIS S. FORD

In "Whitehead's Distinctive Features," Lewis Ford makes an excellent contribution to the task of locating Whitehead on the American philosophical map at the same time that he seeks to explain why Whitehead, whose thought has generated much interest among philosophically inclined theologians, has been neglected by philosophers. To begin with, I believe Ford is correct in placing Whitehead in the tradition neither of Bradley nor of the evolutionary philosophers—Bergson, C. Lloyd Morgan—but in the line of James and Dewey. On this view, Whitehead's metaphysics would form one trajectory and pragmatism another with obvious affinities—radical empiricism, dynamism and process, and fallibilism. Ford finds that Whitehead's insistence on the need for metaphysics or systematic philosophy and his commitment to a form of theism are stumbling blocks for many contemporary philosophers; Ford's aim is to reinterpret these features, firm in the belief that they are essential to Whitehead's thought. I can lay no claim to a knowledge of Whitehead's cosmological scheme such as that possessed by Ford, Sherburne, Kline, Neville, and others. However, what I do know leads me to agree with Ford that the theism is not extraneous, nor is it expendable because God has numerous functions in Whitehead's cosmic scheme. In addition to providing an aim for subjectivity, God also furnishes the principle of limitation without which becoming or the creative advance would not issue in definite results. Hegel made a similar point when he claimed that, unless it is true that something *has become*, we are left with no more than endless becoming without a determinate outcome.

As regards metaphysics, if it is valid to define metaphysics as having to do with the necessary features of existence, metaphysics cannot be avoided by retreating into an empiricism in which everything is absolutely contingent, because, as Ford rightly points out, Whitehead insisted that contingency depends for its meaning on the contrast term, or necessity. Ford sets forth clearly the many strengths of Whitehead's thought in the belief that these features should be taken more seriously by philosophers because of their contemporary relevance. If one considers the following list of salient points in Whitehead's writing, it is hard to understand why he has not had more influence on current thinking. His scheme pays close attention to scientific theory in the form of evolution and relativity physics; he reworked the meaning of perception in the sense of apprehension, omitting the "ap" and adopting the idea of "prehension" so that the relation is not necessarily conscious, and hence the gap between science and direct experience is bridged; he reconceived the relation between subject and object so that the Cartesian polarity of thought and extension is overcome and the two are to be regarded as different temporal aspects of the same actuality. The result is that, on Whitehead's view, the causal-prehensile relations between objects and subjects become *asymmetrical*—external to the object, but internal to the subject. Ford says this is the strategy for avoiding the problems raised by Bradley's symmetrical internal relations and Russell's symmetrical external relations. Bradley, it will be recalled, declared the concept of 'relation' one that is "riddled with contradictions," by which he meant the infinite regress that breaks out as the result of his claim that in *aRb*, the *R* itself has to be related to the *a* at one end and the *b* at the other. It was Hartshorne, I believe, who described Bradley's view as like a door that has hinges both on the left and on the right, and Russell's as like a door that has no hinges at all.

For Ford, these and other features of Whitehead's process philosophy—creativity, self-creativity, coherence, and consistency—represent his positive contributions. Ford, however, is also aware of certain Whiteheadian doctrines that have led to uneasiness among philosophers—the eternal objects, temporal atomicity, the "pre-Kantian" turn, and pansubjectivity. In each case Ford takes pains to show how these ideas work in Whitehead's cosmology and he rightly confronts critics by saying, in effect that something more is demanded than objections, namely, the need to understand the problems the above ideas were meant to resolve and to consider what alternatives you have to propose.

## RESPONSE TO RICHARD HOCKING

Richard Hocking's chapter, "Emergence and Embodiment: A Dialectic within Process," bears his trademark; it is a perceptive marking out of a distinction which, while it may seem obvious after being noticed, is likely to have been passed over or conflated by those less discerning. In this case the distinction in question concerns two trajectories within the course of process philosophy—the ongoing of *nature* and the passage of *history*—whose identities may be lost if we think only in general terms about process, growth, development, or creativity. It is especially noteworthy that Hocking finds these "two newer currents of systematic thought" persisting despite the adverse climate generated by the tension between an analytic approach that excludes synopsis and the viewpoint which says that the great synoptic visions of the past cannot be written off as just so much error. I agree with Hocking in his conclusion that the persistence of these two original forms of systematic thought under the circumstances "argues that they are disclosures of some kind of comprehensive necessity in the structure of philosophical experience."

Identifying cosmological process philosophy with *emergence* or the appearance of radical novelty, and reflection on history and freedom with embodiment, Hocking traces the patterns of both in order to show that regarding them as polar opposites is an error, since neither can be reduced to the other, and, what is more important, they are not independent, but require each other in what Hocking calls "an on-going complementarity." He presents the case so convincingly that it would be impertinent of me to rehearse it. I would, however, like to add a footnote that adds further confirmation. Polarity, as Hegel and Peirce saw, makes integration between the opposites impossible, for it is dyadic and leaves each side totally different from and independent of the other. This was the flaw in Descarte's polarity of thought and extension; there is nothing in the nature of either which allows a relational foothold for the other. Hocking has thus added a new dimension to process thought by calling attention to the dialectic of nature and history which exists *within* process philosophy. One consequence is that it is now possible to see a hitherto neglected affinity between such thinkers as Peirce and Dewey on one side and Marcel and Collingwood on the other.

## RESPONSE TO DONALD W. SHERBURNE

I appreciate Donald Sherburne's chapter, "The Goldilocks Syndrome," both for its insights—the comparison between Dewey and Whitehead on philosophy as knowledge, for example, is illuminating —and its invitation to make clearer what, in his language, is "home" for me, which I take to mean my philosophical position. For a start, let me say that I understand how this question arises for someone who has heard me expound and interpret such thinkers as Kant, Hegel, Royce, and Dewey with such a concern to "think their thoughts after them" that I must have appeared successively as a Kantian, an Hegelian, a Roycean idealist, and a Deweyite. With the wisdom of hindsight—if indeed it is that—I have two comments to make on Sherburne's perception. First, it has been my long experience that in American colleges and universities professors are expected to *teach* their subjects, whereas in many universities in other countries professors discharge their duties chiefly by *leturing* (G. E. Moore's seminars always began with his reading a long paper unaccompanied by any concern for whether his hearers comprehended it or not). Second, philosophy has a special involvement with its own history because many philosophical problems are persistent and reappear in every period so that a dialogue with past thinkers is unavoidable. Despite this fact, however, philosophy is or should be a creative enterprise, one that continually transcends its past in the efforts of philosophers to lay hold of new problems while also attempting to find new solutions for old perplexities.

Let me now attempt to show the implications of the foregoing two comments for my own situation. Important as teaching undoubtedly is, and the concern to present major thinkers to students through the texts and in terms they can understand, it is also inhibiting in the sense that the teacher often has to keep his or her view of an issue in abeyance in order to achieve the desired results. Those who merely lecture—leaving the major part of the work to the student—have the clear advantage that they can more readily keep their own thought intact. One would, of course, like to think that there is some ideal, middle ground, and indeed there may be, but I am less concerned with resolving that problem than with the fact that in being committed to teaching and in having a broad range of interests, I found myself doing too much teaching and covering too much territory during almost four decades of teaching at Yale. One result—it is reflected in Sherburne's essay—was that my own philosophical position was never made as explicit as it should have been. Before making a brief attempt to redress that balance, I wish to add something to what I said above about the involvement of philosophy with its history.

When I was a student in the Department of Philosophy at Columbia, the approach to the subject was determined for the most part by two features that were prominent in the thought of Dewey. One was the belief that the most significant and relevant philosophers of a given period were those who responded most successfully to the challenge posed by the most fundamental problematic situation confronting them at the time. The second feature was Dewey's tendency to deal with philosophical issues by an historical or even a genetic account of the conditions under which they arose, the counterpart in philosophy for that stage in the pattern of inquiry which he called "locating the problem." While I believe there is something sound in both these features, I am also aware of their limitations. The pattern of challenge and response is readily illustrated by the thought of Locke and Kant each of whom was attempting to interpret the implications of the new universe of Newtonian science for the entire range of human experience. It was for them a matter of making clear the consequences of leaving behind the qualitative and thoroughly organic cosmos of Aristotle and entering into the mechanical world of Newton. The risk in this approach is two-fold; it can mean limiting philosophy to a commentary on the culture and a turning away from systematic thought, and it can mean conceiving relevance to the problem at hand too narrowly and hence to the neglect of what is ultimately important but not so easy to grasp in the immediate situation. Some insurance against both risks is to be found in the pursuit of what Peirce at his ironic best called "useless knowledge" or the basically theoretical questions in the sciences and the speculative dimension in philosophy.

The risk attached to understanding philosophical problems through historical origins also is two-fold; one can become so completely involved in trying to understand a particular philosopher's view that critical appraisal is omitted, or one can become a party to writing unreliable and over-simplified history in the process of interpreting a philosophical trend. Dewey's *The Quest for Certainty* is a case in point; while the underlying thesis is clear and well presented—the need to recognize the reality of change and becoming over against the static and the fixed, the need to accept the fallibility of our knowledge over against the lure of certainty, the need to stop trying to avoid the precariousness of existence by becoming attached to a timeless realm of Being—it is nevertheless true that Dewey exaggerated the priority assigned to theory over action in Greek thought, and he too readily identified metaphysics with the hypostatization of the objects of thought into a transcendent realm.

The point of this excursion is to show the influence on my own work, teaching and writing, exercised by the Columbia tradition and its emphasis on historical analysis. Sherburne witnessed some of the consequences of this influence when he attended my seminars dealing with the major philosophers he mentions and where he found it difficult to detect my own positions on the issues discussed. However, there was, another factor in the philosophical situation at that time which must be taken seriously. Those who regarded themselves as "doing" philosophy and not engaged merely with history—what Ryle described on one occasion as "philosophy without footnotes"—were dealing mainly with special professional "puzzles" such as that of the existence of other minds or fueling the epistemology industry with the question of how to reach the "external world." In comparison with philosophy of that sort, the study of Kant, Hegel, Royce, Dewey, and Peirce represented a much richer diet and, although it was unfashionable, many of us saw in this supposedly mere history a philosophical importance far in excess of anything to be found in the analytic establishment.

Against this background, I should like to answer Sherburne's question about what is "home" for me more directly through a brief philosophical autobiography. For many years I could say, along with Kierkegaard, "Kant is my philosopher." I read all of Kant's major writings over a number of years of study with Richard Kroner, whose little book *Kants Weltanschauung* I translated and to whom I owe a great deal. I believe that I absorbed much from the transformation that Kroner was undergoing at the time. For many years he had been the Editor of *Logos*, the international Hegelian journal, and was obviously under the spell of Hegel, but after coming to America he made his own version of "zurück zu Kant," and wrote a number of books declaring the primacy of moral and religious faith over metaphysics and especially over Hegel's panlogism. However, things changed when I began to study Hegel on my own. Two points in Hegel's critique of Kant were uppermost for me; first was the idea that philosophy cannot have an "introduction" or a preliminary examination of thought in the transcendental way, because an examination of the categories of thought requires that we see them at work in the analysis and articulation of actual subject matter and not only as "idling," so to speak, in the understanding. I took Hegel to mean that, while the idea of appraising an instrument prior to its use is sound in itself, when the instrument is thought, the transcendental approach is inadequate. Hegel's second criticism—that Kant ceased being a critical philosopher and became dogmatic (in Kant's own sense) when he claimed that understanding provides the standard for all knowledge so that reason is reduced to the limited task of providing unities for a content that comes to it solely from without—seemed to me correct and relevant far beyond discussions of Kant and Hegel, since it means that philosophical interpretations are to be judged in their own terms as philosophy and not as empirical science.

I do not see myself, as Sherburne suggests, caught between Hegel and Dewey, for, while I am indebted to both for important insights, I have strong reservations about Hegel's having obscured the surd character of existence (in Peirce's language, letting thirdness swallow up secondness) and about Dewey's scientism and naturalism. Nevertheless, I welcomed Dewey's reconstruction of the meaning of experience and his charge that the "epistemology industry" was being kept alive by repeating the errors of British empiricism. Dewey, moreover, was consolidating the belief that philosophy must set out from experience and fill it with the light of reflection without the need for some preliminary justification assuring us that philosophy is a viable enterprise after all. I cannot exaggerate how much I appreciated Dewey's essays "An Empirical Survey of Empiricisms" and "The Need for a Recovery of Philosophy."

They showed how "unempirical" the conception of experience held by the British empiricists really was and also how philosophy might be reoriented through the broad and rich understanding of experience developed by Dewey along with Peirce and James. However, my impression is that most philosophers in Britain still have not grasped this critique of their own tradition, chiefly because of an almost congenital antipathy to pragmatism.

With this help from Dewey and by going back to my earlier interest in Royce through whom I was introduced to Peirce and James, I began—probably in the early sixties—to turn away from the European thinkers and in the direction of the classical American thinkers. It seemed to me odd, and it still does, that these original thinkers should have been so neglected by American teachers and students in favor of Heidegger, Wittgenstein, Husserl, and the British linguistic philosophers. I shall not try to explain the situation here; I shall say only that a major factor was a failure of many philosophers in America to act as if they believed in that self-reliance Emerson thought was the basis of the American spirit. Instead, many philosophers expressed embarrassment that pragmatism was "soft" and no match for positivism, the schools of analytic philosophy, and the phenomenology of Husserl. There were those who did not think James important until they discovered that

Husserl had underlined passages in James's *Psychology* and still others who began to take Peirce seriously only after European philosophers such as Appel touted his Kantian lineage and showed interest in his semiotics and work in formal logic.

I began to read Peirce in depth, and I soon became aware of the experience and good sense behind his insights, expressed not only in his pragmaticism but in his metaphysics of synechism, tychism, and agapism. I regard it as a great mistake to suppose that the "real" Peirce is in the logic, while the metaphysics is just so much window dressing. I am in total agreement with his formula that reality is independent of what this or that individual, or any finite collection of them, may think it to be, but not independent of thought in *general* (taken in Peirce's realistic sense). I believe that this formula, as I tried to show in "Community and Reality in Peirce," effectively overcomes the traditional opposition between idealism and realism by preserving the element of truth in each while steering clear of the one-sidedness that keeps either from being the whole truth. The independence feature plus Peirce's stress on secondness do justice to the *existence* and *insistence* of what is encountered, while the dependence factor makes it possible for us to understand the intelligibility of reality so that knowledge is neither something merely accidental nor a miraculous occurrence that defies comprehension. Peirce's idea of the *general* is central to his entire outlook. However, I believe, that the connection this idea does have with "Scotistic realism" must not lead us to suppose that Peirce was offering an account of "universals." The latter term was, for him, essentially a logical term, whereas generals he regarded as *dynamic* patterns conditioning action and which themselves evolve. Generals are the stuff of Thirdness, law, order, and intelligibility, all of which find embodiment in the reality of community and in the spread of ideas that makes up a "climate of opinion." The reality of generals, moreover, spells the doom of positivism and atomistic empiricism and indeed of all attempts to construe reality in terms of wholly determinate particulars.

My most basic dissent from Peirce's metaphysics is what I consider his exaggeration of continuity, which in turn led him to express doubts whether there are any individuals at all. I certainly agree with his claim that the boundaries between things and between persons are *vague* (a notion of inestimable importance for Peirce), but does this mean that there are no boundaries at all? It may be, however, that he was exaggerating in his denial of individuals and that he meant to claim only that there is nothing that is *absolutely* individual.[5] I welcome his theory of signs as the way beyond the opposition between immediacy and mediation; pure immediacy without meaning apprehended and expressed through a sign would be dumb and inarticulate, while if reality were identical with a system of signs, we would lose the existence or brute element in the world which immediacy signals. Given the emphasis placed by Hegel on development—becoming—and, even more, the body of evidence upon which evolutionary theory is based, I am convinced that a metaphysics of process and events is inescapable. Whitehead, of course, has made an important contribution to such a metaphysics, and I am not one who shrinks from his panpsychism. However, I believe that Peirce's idea that the material of the cosmos was from the outset capable of taking on habits is the best way of making clear why the physical, the organic, and the mental cannot be kept in non-communicating compartments. His combination of order, chance, and creative love or attraction is superior to mechanistic interpretations of evolution, on the one hand, and to excessively "creative" accounts on the other. I stand with Peirce and James on the matter of freedom being dependent on real possibility as a mode of being. Is it not striking that "The Doctrine of Necessity" and "The Dilemma of Determinism," so utterly different in their mode of argumentation, should, nevertheless, aim to support the same conclusion—the reality of real possibility.

I hope that this sketch may help to indicate, at least in a few essential points, where home is for me on the philosophical map. I do not know whether I can succeed in expressing this home in terms of the figures of the watchtower and the water. It would seem that the tower would have to be high enough to allow for comprehending the principles necessary for the interpretation, in Whitehead's phrase, "of everything that happens." This means, among other things, that a tower from which one can see nothing more than matter of fact is too low. As for the water, I suppose it would have to be as deep as the well of experience which can have no bottom assignable in advance, because only with such depth can we have any assurance that what we see from the tower is comprehensive and coherent enough to interpret that content adequately. In any case, I am sure that Dewey would agree with me that two feet of water is far too little!

The figure of the watchtower is a useful way of expressing the nature of reflection since it also serves as an indicator of its scope. If one has a low tower of vision, there is not much to be seen, but if one goes too high, the world of experience will fade away and we shall be left seeing—what shall we say?—only the clouds. Sherburne may well be right in claiming that Whitehead is the "watchtower master builder" in our era, but I think he is entirely right in saying that Dewey was nervous about getting very high off the ground. I would not illustrate this point, however, by citing the conflicting views of the late Ralph Sleeper and Rorty about Dewey and metaphysics. Dewey's nervousness was prompted by the naturalism that led him away from certain conclusions. I have previously taken note of Dewey's response to the charge by Allport that he did not have an adequate theory of human personality. In accepting the criticism, Dewey said that he was determined to avoid the "timeless ego" of T. H. Green. But surely avoidance cannot be the best path to reaching a positive view. One should indeed shun a position which there is good reason to doubt, but otherwise avoidance becomes purely ideological. Something similar can be found in Dewey's interpretation of religion; his outlook was controlled by an overriding concern to avoid the "supernatural," something he conceived in simplistic terms and never confronted a sophisticated version of what it might mean to "transcend" nature.

## RESPONSE TO MEROLD WESTPHAL

Merold Westphal's chapter, "Philosophy as Critique and as Vision," rightly begins by asking what sort of recovery is meant when we speak of the need for a recovery of philosophy. I agree with his contention that such a recovery should have nothing in common with nostalgia for the good old days, including the period of the classical American philosophers. The desired recovery is of philosophy itself as the reflective activity aimed at integrating knowledge and experience and resulting in a unified picture of ourselves and the world. For Westphal, philosophy must combine criticism and vision, and he finds the model of the former in Socrates and that of the latter in Plato. I believe that Westphal's formula for this dynamic synthesis is perceptive. "Criticism," he writes, "without vision is nihilism, while vision without critique is despotism." The outlooks of James, Peirce, and Royce, different as they are, were informed by their concern to do justice to both sides of this equation, and it is for this reason that I believe a recovery of their philosophical spirit is a recovery of philosophy in its own right. Philosophy, they would insist, is not science, nor is it poetry, religion, linguistics, or autobiography. It is, instead, like the "still point of the turning wheel," a vantage point from which to survey the "spokes," or the many expressions of experience and their relations to each other.

My failure to include Dewey in this trio is not due to his lack of emphasis on criticism or vision—on the contrary, he defined philosophy as criticism of criticisms—but because I believe his thought is the final outworking of that instrumental conception of reason which Westphal attributes to the Enlightenment. I agree with Westphal in his indictment of this view which, as he rightly says, reduces reason to effectiveness and efficiency. Dewey's notion of criticism does indeed include what he called "intelligence"—a combination of knowledge and moral insight—but his rejection of Kant's three-fold distinction between the technical, the prudential, and the moral in order to locate value solely in situations with alternatives to be chosen meant not only loss of the moral as a distinct dimension but the eventual triumph of the technical. This outcome stands, moreover, despite Dewey's attempt to reinterpret what corresponds to the prudential so as to equate the desirable with what is approved on reflection and not what is in fact desired.

I hope my excursion into Dewey, which was meant to support Westphal's criticism of calculating reason, is not taken to mean that I do not appreciate his perceptive appeal to Socratic criticism and Platonic vision as resources for confronting the urgent problems of the present—violence, the ambiguities of political power, racism and other forms of intolerance, and maintaining democracy in a pluralistic society. He is certainly right in thinking that a recovery of philosophy, and especially of the moral virtues, is important for grappling with these problems.

At the end of his chapter, Westphal, like some other contributors, takes note of the "at times exasperating diversity" to be found in my writings. As before, I can only plead guilty. However, I am looking forward to the opportunity to reduce this diversity in the years to come, although I would like to call attention to some unifying threads in my philosophical interpretations. In addition to a continuing concern to argue for the importance of what I call "living reason" and a synoptic grasp to counter-balance the analytic mode, I have made the conception of experience a central one. I believe this is evident in my accounts of religion, science, the self, morality, and indeed philosophy itself. The late James Collins once wrote that in the end every philosopher has but one idea that serves as a central focus; in my case, he said that it was the idea of experience. I think he was right, and I was pleased that he went on to point out that he meant experience in the full and rich sense it had for the pragmatists.

## RESPONSE TO ERROL E. HARRIS

I am pleased and grateful that a friend of many years, Errol Harris, took the occasion of this book to write what I regard as a brilliant essay about the much disputed relation between philosophy and religion in Hegel's thought. Harris has an outstanding command of Hegel's philosophy as is shown by his book on the *Logic* in which, among other things, he makes eminent sense of the syllogism of Reason, a topic often neglected by commentator. Harris argues cogently against those who accuse (or applaud, as he says) Hegel for elevating philosophy above religion, convict him of *hubris*, or commend him for a sophisticated atheism.

Harris offers abundant evidence for the view that the whole of Hegel's philosophy is to be regarded as *religionsphilosophie*. I, for one, am convinced that he is right in his contention and, I should add, that anyone who wishes to dispute the conclusion, based as it is on many texts (not drawn at random), faces a formidable task. I am concerned, however, to consider briefly a few points that might help to explain why it is that others have been led to suppose that for Hegel religion is totally engulfed by philosophy. I have in mind two points; the first has to do with Hegel's direct turnabout from the position he took in the early theological writings to the view expressed later in the *Encyclopedia* and the lectures on religion. In the early writings, he claimed that philosophy has to "stop short" of religion because thought breaks up the living unities of love from which religion draws its life, but in Hegel's later view it is clear that philosophy does not "stop short" of anything. I would resolve the problem here, at least within Hegel's own thought, by pointing out that at the earlier time he had not yet come to his idea of reason as the capacity to *unite* and not only to distinguish. One can see this clearly in the later writings when he rebuts charges against reason in religion made by pietists and others with the claim that the critics are talking only about understanding and do not see the force of a reason that overcomes diremptions on a higher level. I would say that Hegel is justified within his own terms in making this reply and, as Harris rightly says, much of the criticism of Hegel made by Kierkegaard is based on the identification of thought with what Hegel called "the understanding."

There is, however, a more serious issue, and it is raised by Hegel's claim that there is an *asymmetry* in the relation between philosophy and religion; while the categories of philosophy are said to be capable of interpreting the religious content, the converse does not hold. Religion, that is to say, not only has no standpoint from which to encompass philosophy, but it is also incapable of articulating its own content in a "rational" way. This leads me to a question I have asked myself many times (I do not find it addressed in the literature) and that is, Did Hegel ever consider theology as an autonomous enterprise, or did he simply annex it, as it were, to philosophy? The question is of vital importance because theology, beginning with the Christian Platonists of Alexandria, was and has been the means whereby the religious content found expression in a conceptual and systematic way from *within* the *household* of faith. What gives critics pause (I am thinking here especially of James Collins and his discussion of "religion within the scope of philosophy,") is the sense that Hegel thought religion had no conceptual articulation of its own until it received it from philosophy, his philosophy. The issue is far too complex to be considered here, but the problem needs to be raised especially in view of the fact that the long-standing body of Christian theology must be taken seriously and *cannot* be put down to "picture thinking" of the sort Hegel attributed to religion in his triad—art, religion, philosophy. If, of course, Hegel was simply assimilating theology to philosophy, that would solve the problem, but it would also obscure the fact that religion had been articulating itself through theology for centuries, even if, as is quite evident, that theology had been made possible by the concepts and categories of philosophical thought.

## RESPONSE TO CARL G. VAUGHT

Vaught's treatment of Augustine's two decisive experiences—theft and conversion—is both profound and original; it shows conclusively that no merely psychological, rhetorical, or Neoplatonic interpretation of his life can take the place of the Christian understanding that sees his odyssey as, first, a turning away from God in self-assertiveness, and, finally, as a return to God in humility. I fully appreciate Vaught's presentation of his theme as a coming together of the factors I have stressed as essential for the recovery of philosophy in the culture as well as in the academy. He cites the importance of the broad and rich understanding of experience associated with the classical American philosophers, the need for plumbing philosophical problems not reducible to those of logic and language alone, the need for reflection to make a difference both practically and theoretically and, finally, the importance of the interplay between philosophy and religion manifested in Augustine's struggle to come to terms with his own waywardness.

This well-wrought chapter speaks eloquently for itself and certainly stands in no need of any commentary I could offer, but there are points I would like to underline as of special importance, and I have a request or two for clarification. I believe that we cannot exaggerate the importance of the need for self-examination in any attempt to understand the meaning of Augustine's experience. That is, we must trace out for ourselves the path he traveled and seek to identify in our own experience the feelings, the anguish, the exultation, the guilt, and the faith he lived through. There is in matters so intimately connected with the self no substitute for acquaintance or direct experience, even if, as I noted previously, there is no need to set such experience in *opposition* to knowledge gained indirectly—what James called "knowledge about."

One of the great merits of Vaught's discussion is the incisive way in which he distinguishes and at the same time relates to each other the aesthetic, political, ethical, and religious dimensions of the pear-stealing episode that first set Augustine on his downward path. Each has its significance, and, while the religious marks out the ultimate, the others are not swallowed up by it in a Hegelian night in which all cows are black.

I would like to raise a question, not about the meaning of the distinction drawn between the kinds of nothingness, but about the terminology used to express it. Vaught calls the absolute abyss from which God brings forth the creatures "metaphysical," and the relative nothingness—evil as the privation of good, or the limit of a corruption that cannot be reached—he calls "ontological" and "epistemological." The distinction is sound enough; the first corresponds to the absolute negation expressed in the Greek "*ouk*" and the second to the conditional negation expressed in the Greek "*mē*." The question, however, is whether anything is gained by using the notoriously ambiguous terms *metaphysical* and *ontological* to designate the difference.

Vaught is quite right to take Oliver Wendell Holmes to task for ridiculing Augustine's continuing concern as a grown man with the childhood prank of stealing the pears. Holmes saw the episode as no more than a scrap of autobiography, and presumably, like Matthew Arnold and Ralph Waldo Emerson, he would have Augustine get rid of or simply not dwell on the sin involved. For Augustine, on the contrary, the event was a profound occasion for engaging the mystery of freedom and its misuse and for seeking to understand the Christian diagnosis of the human predicament and its resolution in the new redemptive community made possible by the sacrificial love of Christ.

Vaught gives us a most perceptive account of the relations between the individual and the community and the changes that occur when Augustine and his friends move from the initial and positive community of friendship to the negative "disjunctive collection of individuals" that results from their gratuitous theft of the pears (229 ff.). He describes the act of plucking the pears as a matter of *individuation* and says that what began as a community of friends ends as a community of individuals. My suggestion is that *individuation* is not the right term here because it implies—and all the more so in the parallel with Adam and Eve—that there is a "fall" into individuality from some prior state in which it did not exist. More appropriate would be the idea of *isolation*; in breaking the bonds that formed their community, Augustine and his companions isolated themselves from their community and from each other and thus became a mere collection of individuals. Community of whatever sort, including communities of evil, can be understood only as a relational affair involving distinct individuals who are unified through their commitment to or faith in a reality that transcends them—God or the ground of existence in the case of the religious community. In genuine community, there is no problem of the individual being "lost" or "swallowed up," since if there were no distinct individuals in the first place there would be no need to unite them. Another way of expressing the point is to say that community does not mean some mystical blending of selves or the negation of individuality, but the existence of spiritual bonds or relations between individuals which overcome their isolation and bring all together in a living unity. The great merit of

Royce's analysis of the nature of community is found in his having discerned the presence of two sets of relations; one concerns the relation of each individual member to the reality that binds the members together—in the Christian community that would mean God as Holy Spirit—and the other concerns the relations in which the members stand to each other in virtue of their all being related to the same unifying reality. The first set expresses the individuals relation to God—the "standing alone" in Vaught's formula—while the second set expresses the "together" which means that, although Augustine and Alypius each experiences the grace of God in his own way, each knows that the other has faith in the same God that he has faith in and belongs to the same religious community.

Vaught's rejection of any attempt to construe the flesh spirit distinction as the same as the body-soul distinction is a matter of major importance. To make this error is to make it impossible to understand not only the experience of Augustine but also the Christian conception of the human creature. Flesh and spirit, as Vaught rightly says, are not two constituents of a person, but two different orientations in relation to God; if there is any further doubt on this point we need only appeal to the words themselves. The Greek word we translate as "flesh" is not the word for body, nor is the word for spirit the word for soul.

As a final point, I agree with Vaught about the transformation of Augustine and the reality of a new creation, but the dynamic character of that creation may be obscured if one insists on total discontinuity between old and new. The new Augustine stands as the living *overcoming* of the bondage that defined the old Augustine, and the one transformed is, after all, the one who did steal the pears.

## RESPONSE TO ROBERT CUMMINGS NEVILLE

Robert Neville's chapter offers not only a brief and incisive statement of the main aims of modernism and postmodernism—terms that have won acceptance in the discussions of recent years—but proposes as well a way beyond both tendencies. He finds this way in the American tradition in philosophy, reaching back to Jonathan Edwards and going forward again through Emerson and the pragmatists to the present. Neville is right to identify the main drift of modernism in philosophy with the task of grounding itself and other disciplines—Kant's certificates of validity—and to see postmodernism in philosophy as the way of subversion—Ricoeur's hermeneutic of suspicion—in exposing the illusions, including the error of logocentrism, in modernist philosophies. Accordingly, Neville locates Husserl and Wittgenstein in the modernist camp, and Derrida and Rorty in that of postmodernism.

Neville's main thesis (I believe it is a signpost for a recovery of philosophy) is that there is an American tradition of thought, distinct from both of the above isms, capable of correcting the errors of modernism, of recognizing the element of truth in postmodern criticism, while offering a constructive alternative to the negativism that characterizes much postmodern thought. The American tradition is clearly delineated by Neville as one rooted in a reconstruction of experience in a number of different ways and, as a result, embraces speculative or systematic philosophy understood in a way quite different from the metaphysics that fell victim to the attacks of Hume and Kant. That this tradition is substantial is seen in the thinkers representing it since the time of Edwards, and, perhaps even more important, in its capacity to survive in what was often a hostile philosophical climate. Consider that while the pragmatists had carried out a major critique of British empiricism, exposing the narrowness and superficiality of its concept of experience, the logical empiricists—both Anglo-American and Continental—and various types of linguistic empiricists proceeded largely unaware of what had happened. As a result, they naively perpetuated the old atomic, sense-datum conception of experience, while seeking to combine it with logics more powerful than the association of ideas, but more abstract and emptier than the transcendental logic of Kant.

Neville's argument in its four phases—the reformation of the conception of experience; the discovery of the presence of this new outlook in Edwards and Emerson; Peirce's breaking away from Kant's version of the "quest for certainty"; the proposal of a way beyond modernism and its deconstructionist critics—is so well conceived and developed that it would be superfluous of me to repeat it. Instead, I shall single out for emphasis points at which I believe the argument is especially compelling and contributes to the recovery of a philosophy focused on the world and our experience rather than on whether there is any world to be experienced that is not constructed by language, habits, social practices, and conventions. The latter question incidentally is the most recently proposed "critical" question which supposedly must be answered before philosophy can proceed.

My first point of emphasis is Neville's perceptive claim that "the legitimate target of postmodern criticism does not include the main themes of the American tradition" (253). The truth of this judgment would have impressed itself more deeply on contemporary thinkers if there were a greater knowledge and appreciation of the originality of the American tradition and the novelty of the path it proposed to follow. Neville, moreover, is right in saying that postmodern critics are mistaken in rejecting systematic philosophy and seeking an escape in some meta region of discourse where it is no longer necessary to confront the world and ourselves directly. Metaphysics of the experiential sort found in Peirce's development of the categories and his evolutionary cosmology and the philosophical grappling with the most urgent problems exhibited by James and Dewey make significant contributions to our understanding of ourselves and the world. By contrast, the skepticism manifest in deconstructionist criticism, even when it is justified against the excesses and omissions of modernism, seems pale and lacking in nourishment.

Neville rightly puts the reconstructed conception of experience at the center of the American philosophical tradition, and I welcome his going back to find this view of experience already present in Edwards and Emerson. As he points out, I have made the theory of experience a focal issue in a number of writings, and my aim in doing so has been to consolidate and extend the critique of British empiricism set forth by Peirce and Dewey especially. James was also engaged in this critique, but, despite his expression "radical empiricism," his assessment of the old empiricism was less radical than that of his colleagues. Unlike Peirce and Dewey who found sense-bound empiricism totally inadequate, James argued that Hume was on the right track but simply did not go far enough and discover relations and transitions within experience itself. I regard this point as valid, but it remains true that James accepted more of the tradition stretching from Hume and Mill than either Dewey or Peirce. I have long believed that the force and revolutionary character of the new conception of experience have gone unheeded by many contemporary philosophers, including even some who claim to have learned from the pragmatists. Participants in the current discussion of realism and antirealism, for example, show little awareness that the pragmatists gave sound reasons for holding that theories of knowledge in general do not provide a logic of inquiry. The point, which is made by all three thinkers, is that the classical view of experience as the domain of sense which extends no further than our own "ideas" generated a number of needless problems, such as how to transcend our ideas and reach the "external" world, and what Dewey called the epistemology industry aimed at resolving the problem of knowledge in *general*. Dewey's claim is that if a theory of experience leads to such problems, it is time to abandon the theory and find another more in accord with what experiencing shows itself to be. The pragmatists had grave reservations about the enormous emphasis placed on the theory of knowledge by philosophers since Locke and Kant first set forth the idea that a prior assessment of the powers of our understanding must be made in order to determine the limits of our knowledge. Hegel described this sort of inquiry as "knowing before you know" and underlined the obvious difference between examining the capabilities of an instrument such as an axe or a pump and determining the limits of understanding. Peirce rarely used the term *epistemology* and thought matters of truth and knowledge, whether in philosophy or in the sciences, must be approached through methodology and the logic of inquiry; James once compared epistemology to a sharpening of the knives in preparation for their use on a great occasion that never comes; Dewey was convinced that the exaggerated concern for the theory of knowledge among philosophers was leading to the postponement of first-order questions.

I am especially indebted to Neville's comments on Dale M. Schlitt's treatment of my conception of experience (See 266 n. 8), because, among other things, he points out that Schlitt omitted my most detailed discussion of the topic in *Purpose and Thought* and confined attention instead to earlier books in which the nature of experience was not the main subject. Moreover, Neville is right to set the record straight by denying that I was motivated by idealist concerns for "totality" and hence made a dichotomy between the mental and the real, and, as Schlitt alleges, that I espoused a mentalist theory of interpretation. In noting my involvement in Peirce's thought from the beginning, Neville states my view correctly when he writes that for me "interpretation is thus not 'mental' in any sense that contrasts with the real world, but is more like the form of the human side of the interaction that constitutes experience" (267). Furthermore, Neville is aware that I follow Peirce in understanding interpretation as an activity taking place within the community of inquiry and not as a thought process that might be seen phenomenalistically. I agree with Neville's point that Peirce had a realistic conception of interpretation, a view that finds extensive support in Carl Hausman's excellent study *Charles S. Peirce's Evolutionary Philosophy*, cited above in my response to Sherburne.

It now occurs to me (although I have no specific passage to recall) that my concern to keep an interpret*er* in the picture may be the reason behind Schlitt's idea that I was putting a subjective or mental cast on the process. The point is that I was opposed to the reduction of the sign-functioning process either to behaviorist or to purely linguistic terms, something readily accomplished by omitting the interpret*er* as one able to read the signs. Peirce generally used the term *interpretant* to mean the idea (also a sign) that interprets the sign at hand, and on occasion he used *interpreter* in the same sense. It might seem as though he had no place for the one who is doing the interpreting. If that were the case, however, we would have to reconcile that with his insistence that inquiry is a human activity with "flesh and blood" inquirers which of course means interpreters as well. The emphasis on the work of an agent, however, need not entail concessions to subjectivity. The interpreter can succeed only by finding the *correct* interpretant for the sign, and in the course of inquiry this interpretant will be under the constraint of what Peirce called the "dynamical object" to which the sign refers. That the attainment of knowledge requires the activities of a community of interpreters by no means implies that interpretation is something mental standing in contrast to a real world. In accordance with Peirce's evolutionary realism, which I find compelling, successful interpreting depends on the interpreter finding the correct interpretation, but that it is correct is not determined by the interpreter, but by the constraint of experience, and the dynamical object plus the normative elements in the logic of inquiry. In any case, as Hausman and others have shown, interpretation for Peirce goes far beyond any process supposed to take place within a self-enclosed, individual mind.

In setting forth what I regard as the distinctive features of the reformed conception of experience, Neville places special emphasis on the evaluative element; while I believe that all features are important, I attach special significance to what I have called the "intensive quality" of experience, which embraces both the aesthetic and the moral. In the case of the former it is the "taste" of the percipient and in the latter the "conscience" which apprehends the quality in the experience of the object or situation. In recent decades thinkers holding quite diverse positions have shown a common tendency to conceive of value as something superadded by the "mind" or the "emotions" to a determinate, factual situation that has nothing in it answering to the experience of value. A corrective to this tendency appears when we come to understand that situations and their constituents are *experienced* as having intensive qualities, so that a particular conversation was experienced as "banal" and a certain photograph was experienced as "shocking." Like James's pure experience, where there is no direct awareness of an object "there" and a self "here," in the experiences of what is worthy, important, vile, sublime, heart-rending, we have no sense of "adding" from our own selves the qualities denoted by the evaluative terms. When one experiences photographs of Nazi concentration camps depicting the terrible plight of their inhabitants, one experiences the situations as *evil* and *horrendous*, which is to say that we experience the *wrongness* of what is happening. The intensive quality belongs to the eperience as a whole and cannot be "located" as being "in" either the situation encountered or the one who experiences.

Neville's analysis of the thought of Edwards and Emerson shows quite conclusively that the distinctive features of the reconstructed conception of experience are to be found in their basic outlooks. The interpretation of Emerson is perceptive and original, and with regard to Edwards, Neville gets to the heart of the matter on an essential point which experience of forty years with Edwards's work tells me is difficult to grasp: the relation between affections and understanding. For Edwards, affections are *responses* made by a person to an other—God, Christ, nature, neighbor—and they depend on the person's having a *true understanding* of the intrinsic nature of the other. Edwards called this understanding "spiritual" and allied himself with the Augustinian tradition of illumination. When we have a spiritual understanding, we grasp and respond to the intrinsic nature and excellence of the reality that "raises" the affection. To introduce a head/heart antithesis here only confuses the matter; the heart cannot but respond appropriately in the face of the proper understanding of its object. Thus, for Edwards, one who does not respond to God with the affection of love has not *understood* what the "love of God," the intrinsic excellence of Divinity, means.

Neville's exposition of what Edwards meant by saying that being consists in "excellence" gives voice to the same point I was making previously about intensive quality. The central idea is in Neville's sentence "Excellence is a function of the objective characteristics of things and is not imposed by the individual mind." He makes the parallel point about the objectivity of experience in connection with Edwards' idea of holy practice. "The connection," Neville writes, "between the inner content of experience and its expression in behavior is not merely an inferential one, but is intrinsic to the nature of the person as such. We are what and how we love, and that is in the actual loving" (257–8).

The phase of Neville's argument entitled "Peirce's Rejection of Kant" is highly important because Peirce expressed his debt to Kant so much that one may overlook the points at which he did not follow Kant's lead. Peirce's basic departure is nicely summed up by Neville in the following sentences (260–261): "there is no way in Peirce's theory to register Kant's problem of how to infer from the subjective order of representations wholly within consciousness to an objective order. . . . There can be no question of how we can know the external world because there is no inner consciousness to which a world might be external. . . . For Peirce there is no *epistemological* question of how we can know, only questions about whether putative knowledge is correct." (italics in original). I would like to see these lines printed on a large billboard for the benefit of those philosophers who are ignorant of the lesson they teach and as a consequence continue to pursue some version of Enlightenment epistemology.

Neville is equally adept at showing how Peirce set aside Kant's transcendental foundationalism and put in its place his own hypothesis about the role of hypotheses in philosophy (forbidden by Kant) and also in the sciences, plus the part that leading principles and habits play in the process of inquiry. In making this shift, Peirce also did away with one of the pillars of foundationalism—the belief that arguments are chains and are only as strong as their weakest link—and proposed instead a rope analogy which says that an argument finds its strength in many strands of reasoning and evidence that come together in its support. I believe Peirce was right in insisting that the outcome of critically controlled inquiry is entitled to the name of knowledge and that it stands until there is good reason to doubt it. I would also take seriously, as Neville suggests, the important place assigned by Peirce to commonsense. Although vague, commonsense is the accumulation of pervasive experience continuing to manifest itself to many people over long periods of time, in contrast to what he called "recondite experience" or scientific results which, though precise, have, in the nature of the case, been attested to by only a small number of people.

When Neville speaks of "going around" modernism (and postmodernism too), he is aiming to show that, while postmodern critics are justified in their attack on foundationalism, they either ignore the speculative tradition in American thought or fail to see that it has its own answer to the liabilities of modernism. Citing Husserl's transcendentalism, Moore's identification of philosophy with the analysis of commonsense expressions, Russell's logicism, and Wittgenstein's picture theory as attempts to achieve self-grounding positions, Neville writes, "Richard Rorty is right to criticize all of them as being fixated upon the problem of finding certainty about knowledge of the external world, and virtually reducing philosophy to epistemology" (262). Neville goes on to make the same point I urged in *America's Philosophical Vision* when he says, "[Rorty] rightly sees that Dewey has abandoned epistemology but believes that this also entails abandonment of the entire speculative tradition in American thought" (268). I cannot see that any such conclusion can be made to follow from Dewey's attack on the theory of knowledge. Moreover, Neville is on sound ground in placing the postmodernists' attack on "logocentrism" and their disavowal of metaphysics in the perspective provided by the American tradition. The fallibilism insisted upon by the pragmatists rules out rigid systems invulnerable to correction by what has been omitted or undervalued, and the sort of metaphysics criticized so forcefully by Hume and Kant is by no means the same as the experience-oriented interpretations of fundamental categories and the general shape of things to be found in Peirce, Whitehead, Hartshorne, Weiss, and others mentioned by Neville (264). The underlying problem is that the majority of the opponents of metaphysics at present are unaware of what Neville calls the "American story." This failure may be due to a persistent hankering after the European story or the consignment of outlooks one finds uncongenial to the history of philosophy.[6] Whatever the reason, the outcome is the same; either the American tradition is ignored, or it is invoked at points where it comes in handy for supporting claims quite alien to it, such as heralding "the end of philosophy."

I believe Neville nicely supports his main argument when he shows how the reconstructed theory of experience serves as a unifying point for a number of American thinkers at present. One may view the diverse outlooks unified in this way both as an attempt to recover philosophy as an important voice in the culture and as the continuation of a philosophy that has been around for some time, but was temporarily obscured first by the pyrotechnics of the linguistic turn and later by the rhetoric of deconstruction.

## NOTES

1. I am very much in accord with Kasulis's insistence that this level of religious discourse is *not* reducible to performatives having no truth value (16).

2. The reader would do well to review James's description of the reflex theory of the mind in "Reflex Action, and Theism," in *The Will to Believe and Other Essays* (New York: Longmans Green, 1897), according to which we possess three "departments": *receptivity*, usually identified as perception; (2) our remodeling of the content of one through histories, arts, sciences, and so on, usually identified as *conception*, (3) the upshot of the cycle, or *action* guided by ends. James's point is that we have no organ or faculty capable of taking in the *entire* given order, and hence we select what interests us and rearrange or remodel this content in ways ranging from physics and mathematics to philosophy. The work of department two, however, is not arbitrary because, in James's view, "the given order lends itself to the remodeling" and shows itself plastic to our scientific, esthetic, and practical purposes. I take him to be saying that department one yields no "copy" of the world, nor does department two, but that the worlds of physics, history, and philosophy emanating from it are under the constraint of what has been received. I believe this is the import of Allan's reference to the interdependence of objective and human factors.

3. Gordon W. Allport, "Dewey's Individual and Social Psychology," in *The Philosophy of John Dewey*, ed. Paul A. Schilpp (New York: Tudor, 1939), 555.

4. Ibid.

5. Nevertheless, that there are problems about his *synechism* can be seen in a recent study, Carl Hausman, *C. S. Peirce's Evolutionary Philosophy* (Cambridge: Cambridge University Press, 1993). There the author is concerned to see whether synechism can be reconciled with the spontaneity on which Peirce insisted in his rejection of necessitarianism.

6. This point was discussed in connection with George Lucas's chapter; see pp. 271–72.

# *Notes on the Contributors*

**GEORGE ALLAN** is Professor of Philosophy and Distinguished Professor of the Liberal Arts at Dickinson College. He was Dickinson's senior academic officer for 21 years before retiring in June of 1995. Allan has published two books exploring the foundations for social value, both published by SUNY Press: *The Importances of the Past: A Meditation on the Authority of Tradition* (1986) and *The Realizations of the Future: An Inquiry into the Authority of Praxis* (1990). He is currently working on a third volume, *The Formations of the Present: An Analysis concerning the Authority of Structure*. Allan is the author of numerous articles in metaphysics and social philosophy. He has also published on a variety of topics in higher education and the philosophy of education, including a book in progress entitled *The Conversation of a College: Philosophical Reflections on Mission, Canon, and Governance.*

**DOUGLAS R. ANDERSON** is Associate Professor of Philosophy at Penn State and is the author of two books on the philosophy of Peirce entitled *Charles Peirce: Creativity and the Philosophy of C.S. Peirce* (Nijhoff, 1987) and *Strands of System* (Purdue University Press, 1995). He is coeditor with Richard Hart of a collection of essays in American philosophy, forthcoming Fordham University Press. His primary interest is the history of American philosophy.

**LEWIS S. FORD** is the Louis I. Jaffe Professor of Humanities (Philosophy) Emeritus, Old Dominion University in Norfolk, VA, and Editor of *Process Studies*. *The Lure of God* (Fortress, 1978) provides a process interpretation of Biblical passages, which in turn are able by their contingent content to enrich the necessary abstractions of process thought. *The Emergence of Whitehead's Metaphysics* (SUNY, 1984) uses composition analysis as a tool for ordering passages in *Process and Reality* in genetic sequence, thus enabling us to ascertain the growth of his theory more precisely. He has edited *Two Process Philosophers: Hartshorne's Encounter with Whitehead* (Scholars Press, 1973) and, with George L. Kline, *Explorations in Whitehead's Metaphysics* (Fordham, 1983). He is the author of many articles including "The Non-Temporality of Whitehead's God," *International Philosophical Quarterly* 13/3 (September, 1973), 347–76; "Whitehead's First Metaphysical Synthesis," *International Philosophical Quarterly* 17/3 (September, 1977), 251–64; and "Contrasting Conceptions of Creation," *Review of Metaphysics* 45/1 (September 1991), 89–109.

**ERROL E. HARRIS** is the John Evans Professor of Philosophy in Northwestern University Emeritus, formerly Professor of Philosophy in the University of the Witwatersrand, visiting Lecturer at Yale University, Roy Roberts Distinguished Professor in the University of Kansas, and subsequently Cowling Professor at Carlton College and Distinguished Visiting Professor of Christian Philosophy at Villanova University. Also: Terry Lecturer at Yale University in 1957, Gilbert Ryle Lecturer at Trent University in 1984; past President of the Metaphysical Society of America and of the Hegel Society of America: Paul Weiss Medalist for Metaphysics for 1989, author of *Nature, Mind, and Modern Science; The Foundations of Metaphysics in Science; Hypothesis and Perception; Salvation from Despair; Spinoza's Philosophy; Cosmos and Anthropos; Cosmos and Theos; The Restitution of Metaphysics*, (and fifteen other books), as well as over 70 articles on the Philosophy of Science, the Philosophy of Religion, Spinoza, and Hegel.

**RICHARD HOCKING**'s doctoral thesis, directed by Professor Wilmon Sheldon, proposed a teleology of space under the title "Space and Intersubjectivity." His first teaching at the University of Minnesota was enriched by learning about Kierkegaard from Professor David Swenson. The present chapter (this volume), "Emergence and Embodiment: A Dialectic within Process," builds on both of these beginnings. Other intervening essays pertinent to this topic include "The Polarity of Dialectical History and Process Cosmology," "The Influence of Mathematics on Royce's Metaphysics," "Event, Act, and Presence," "*Existenz* and Objectivity," and "The Personal Dialectics of the Impersonal." While at UCLA during the Second World War, he began to teach Chinese and Indian thought and encouraged the dialogue between Chinese and Western philosophers. He considers his twenty-one years at Emory University the best of his career, helping Professor Loemker in his building of the Emory philosophy program.

**THOMAS P. KASULIS** studied philosophy under John E. Smith at Yale as both an undergraduate and doctoral student. It was Smith who first encouraged him to study Asian philosophy and to develop the philosophy of religion from a comparative perspective. Kasulis is currently professor and chair of the Division of Comparative Studies at The Ohio State University. In addition, he has been president of the Society for Asian and Comparative Philosophy and a visiting professor at the University of Chicago and Harvard, as well as a research fellow at the East-West Center and Osaka University. His books include *Zen Action/Zen Person* (University of Hawaii Press), the editing and co-translating (with Shigenori Nagatomo) of Yuasa Yasuo's *The Body: Toward an Eastern Mind-Body Theory*, and the co-editing (with Roger T. Ames and Wimal Dissanayake) of a three volume set of books on self in Asian theory and practice (all published by SUNY Press).

**GEORGE R. LUCAS**, Jr. teaches in the Department of Leadership, Ethics, and Law at the United States Naval Academy in Annapolis, MD. He is a Senior Fellow in the Kennedy Institute for Ethics and Professorial Lecturer in Ethics at the School of Business at Georgetown University in Washington, D.C. Professor Lucas received his doctorate from Northwestern University in 1978, and has taught at Emory University, Santa Clara University, Clemson University, and as a Fulbright Professor at the Catholic University of Louvain in Belgium. From 1990 through 1995, he was Assistant Director in the Division of Research Programs at the National Endowment for the Humanities in Washington, D.C. Professor Lucas is Philosophy Series Editor for the State University of New York Press (Albany, New York), and a Senior Consulting Editor in philosophy for *Encyclopedia Americana*. He is the author of three books, and over forty journal articles, translations, and book reviews. He has also edited several book-length collections of articles in philosophy and ethics.

**ROBERT CUMMINGS NEVILLE** began his philosophical career as a typist for John E. Smith, and has taught at Yale, Fordham, SUNY College at Purchase, SUNY at Stony Brook, and Boston University, where he is now a member of the Philosophy and Religion departments and Dean of the School of Theology. He aspires to be an American philosopher in at least some of the senses celebrated here and has published fourteen books, the latest of which are *Normative Cultures* (1995), and *The Truth of Broken Symbols* (1996), both by SUNY Press. Neville has been president of the Metaphysical Society of America, the American Academy of Religion, and the International Society of Chinese Philosophy.

**DONALD W. SHERBURNE** is the author of A *Whiteheadian Aesthetic* and *A Key to Whitehead's Process and Reality*; he is also co-editor (with David Ray Griffin) of the Corrected Edition of Whitehead's *Process and Reality*. A graduate of the Yale Ph.D. program in philosophy, he assisted John Smith in the teaching of a number of courses during his time in New Haven. He taught for 35 years in the Philosophy Department of Vanderbilt University, serving as Chair of the Department for 12 of those years.

**JOHN E. SMITH** retired in 1991 as Clark Professor Emeritus of Philosophy from Yale after thirty-nine years. He served as President of the American Philosophical Association (Eastern Division) and of the American Theological Society, The Metaphysical Society of America, the Hegel Society and the C.S. Peirce Society. His books include *Reason and God, The Spirit of American Philosophy, Experience and God, Purpose and Thought: the Meaning of Pragmatism, The Analogy of Experience, Jonathan Edwards, Quasi-Religions: Humanism, Marxism, and Nationalism*. He served as General Editor, Yale Edition, *The Works of Jonathan Edwards* from 1965 to 1992.

**CARL G. VAUGHT** is Professor of Philosophy at Penn State University and is the author of *The Quest for Wholeness* (SUNY Press, 1982) and *The Sermon on the Mount* (SUNY Press, 1986). His primary philosophical interests are metaphysics, the philosophy of religion, and the history of philosophy.

**MEROLD WESTPHAL** is Professor of Philosophy at Fordham University. After his undergraduate work at Wheaton College,

(Illinois), he wrote his doctoral dissertation under John Smith at Yale University and taught there as his colleague for eight years. He is the author of *History and Truth in Hegel's Phenomenology*; *God, Guilt, and Death: An Existential Phenomenology of Religion*; *Kierkegaard's Critique of Reason and Society*; *Hegel, Freedom, and Modernity*; *Suspicion and Faith: The Religious Uses of Modern Atheism*; and *Becoming a Self: A Reading of Kierkegaard 's Concluding Unscientific Postscript* (forthcoming). He is the co-editor of *Kierkegaard in Post/Modernity* designed to show that Kierkegaard deserves to be as much a contemporary dialogue partner as Nietzsche has become. He has recently been trying to generate a dialogue between Kierkegaard and Levinas and writing about the religious appropriation of the postmodern critique of metaphysics.

**KUANG-MING WU** (B.D., S.T.M., Ph.D. in Philosophy, all from Yale) is Senior Researcher, Quantum Dynamics International; Professor of History, National Chung-cheng University in Taiwan, and John McN. Rosebush University Professor, University of Wisconsin-Oshkosh. He has been Visiting Professor at the University of Texas-El Paso, National Taiwan University, the University of South Africa in Pretoria, and Aarhus University in Denmark. He received a Pacific Cultural Foundation Research Fellowship in 1992. His seven books include *Chang Tzu: World Philosophy at Play* (Crossroad/Scholars Presses, 1982), *The Butterfly as Companion* (SUNY Press, 1990), *History, Thinking, and Literature in Chinese Philosophy* (Academia Sinica, 1991), and *On Chinese Body Thinking* (E.J. Brill, 1997). For the latter, he received a National Science Council Distinguished Award (1995, Taiwan). He has chapters in *Time and Space in Chinese Culture* (Brill, 1995), *Norms and the State in China* (Brill, 1993), *Understanding the Chinese Mind* (Oxford, 1989), and others. Equally at home in the languages of Japanese, English, Chinese, and Taiwanese, he is interested in philosophy of religion, phenomenology, Chinese philosophy, aesthetics, and comparative philosophy.

# Index